CONTROLLING THE PAST

CONTROLLING THE PAST

Documenting Society and Institutions

Essays in Honor of
HELEN WILLA SAMUELS

Terry Cook, Editor

Chicago

Society of American Archivists
www.archivists.org

Printed in the United States of America.

Library of Congress Cataloging-in-Publication Data
Controlling the past : documenting society and institutions : essays in honor of Helen Willa Samuels / Terry Cook, editor.
p. cm.
Includes bibliographical references and index.
ISBN 1-931666-36-9 (alk. paper)
1. Archives—Administration. 2. Archivists. 3. Archives—Philosophy. I. Cook, Terry, 1947- II. Samuels, Helen Willa. III. Society of American Archivists.
CD972.C67 2010
027—dc22

2010049689

About the cover: A montage of images of Helen Willa Samuels' collection of textiles made by artisans in Africa, Asia, and the USA. As Terry Cook notes in the book's opening essay, "[Helen's] passion for collecting textiles from around the world led to her appreciation for nontraditional ways of documenting human experience, even including some textile-based recordkeeping systems."

Helen Willa Samuels and Greg Anderson
dancing at a family wedding, 2005.

Jessica Anderson, photographer.

TABLE OF CONTENTS

Representing Archives / Being Archival

Reflections

DOCUMENTING SOCIETY AND INSTITUTIONS: THE INFLUENCE OF HELEN WILLA SAMUELS

Terry Cook

Documenting Modern Society and Archival Appraisal

As archivists document modern society and its institutions, they control the past. They shape to a major degree what society can know about itself. They choose and preserve (or ignore and destroy) recorded evidence of past precedents and societal ideas that are essential to inform the present and guide the future. Helen Samuels, in her famous 1986 article "Who Controls the Past," was the first archivist (many have followed since) to evoke George Orwell's *Nineteen Eighty-Four.* In that dystopian world, Big Brother through the Ministry of Truth controlled the past by systematically destroying, manufacturing, or revising historical records. Samuels quoted from Orwell as follows: "Who controls the past, controls the future; who controls the present, controls the past. . . . Past events . . . survive only in written records and in human memories. The past is whatever the records and the memories agree upon. And since the Party is in full control of all records, and in equally full control of the minds of its members, it follows that the past is whatever the Party chooses to make it." Against such odious oppression stands the modern archivist and the archival function of appraisal. In rethinking fundamentally how the archivist should undertake appraisal, Helen Samuels made the archivist's control of the past more conscious, more active, and more inclusive. She pushed her profession to consider anew the most central archival function that determines the very nature of the archive that remains. And for her, a collaborative archive formed transparently, and incorporating many voices from all sectors of society, stands as the best defence against Big Brother, or indeed against any other form of monolithic ideology or social tyranny.

Appraisal is the critical archival act by archivists. Helen Samuels and Richard Cox have called it the archivist's "first responsibility," upon which everything else depends. As archivists appraise records, they are determining what the future will know about its past: who will have a continuing voice and who will be silenced. Archivists thereby co-create the archive. Archival appraisal specifies which creators, functions, and activities in society will be represented in archives by defining, identifying, then selecting which documents in which recording media of those creators and activities will become archives in the first place. Appraisal is also the gateway function to all subsequent archival activity. Once records are appraised as having archival value and are acquired or protected by an archival institution, even that privileged state does not ensure equal treatment thereafter. They are continually appraised and reappraised for their "value" when the archivist decides, against the realities of huge backlogs, limited resources, and pressing user, external, and professional demands, which records are to enjoy all, many, or only some limited dimensions of numerous subsequent archival activities, more or less in the following sequence: reordering into more "logical" arrangements and groupings the records that have been appraised and acquired as archival; providing varying levels of technical processing for machine-dependent audio-visual film and sound archives and for computer-generated digital records; analysing series or groupings of records to highlight the salient people, places, ideas, and events (in the mere paragraph or two of a typical archival description) for a series of records that may contain a million pages or thousands of images; creating for some records more detailed finding aids or specialized guides; furnishing conservation services and stabilization of the physical recording media; implementing migration programs (especially for audio-visual and digital records) to new storage media and new viewing/reading/software platforms as old environments deteriorate or become obsolete; copying for preservation by microfilming or digital scanning; and finally—and the function most directly visible to researchers—deciding (through many complex processes, including the archivist's own education and experience) which of these already heavily filtered records (by these previous interventions, or lack thereof) should now be featured in exhibitions, publications, educational outreach programs, and specialized reference services, or selected to be included in online finding aids and as digitized images of documents, and for virtual exhibitions, to be accessible to everyone everywhere. In a very real way, since every archival function requires the archivist to appraise the value, worth, significance, and impact of the proposed action (or inaction) that the archives may take, appraisal is the *only* archival function—never ending, always opening to new possibilities. All other archival activities, as some essays in this book demonstrate, are also a critical part of documenting society and its institutions. A record poorly described so that it is inaccessible, or one poorly preserved so that it becomes unreadable, is, de facto, a record destroyed.

But the archival function of appraisal, more narrowly and traditionally defined, is the initial keep-or-destroy decision of what records the archives actually acquires, of what actually becomes and thus defines the archive. Appraisal not only places some records, and their creators (and the functions and activities in which they were engaged), on the memory pedestal, but also, starkly and with finality, determines which records are to be destroyed, excluded from archives and from all these subsequent archival functions, processes, and enhancements, thus effectually removed from societal memory. By the appraisal process, to come to a harsh reality, about 1 to 5 percent of the total available documentation of major institutions and governments is preserved as archives; an even smaller percentage of records of private citizens, groups, and small organizations in society at large is preserved.

Appraisal as a function challenges most fundamentally both historians' stereotypes and archivists' mythologies about the archivist's role in society. If archivists are no longer commonly depicted as antiquarians stooped over old ledgers in dusty basements, they are not generally acknowledged as people consciously constructing social memory to meet or reflect contemporary needs, values, and assumptions—or as the professionals who control the past by deciding which stories and storytellers (i.e., records creators) of that past will be remembered and be retold in the future. That kind of mediation is commonly perceived as the role of journalists, historians, and other users of the archives. The archivist is still widely seen as a kind of honest broker between the creators of records and the records' later use by researchers, including historians. This view is not surprising, since pioneering archival theorists well into the twentieth century depicted themselves as guardians and passive curators of the documentary past, not as its ongoing interpreters or mediators. Indeed, archivists in Britain until very recently were called "keepers" to reflect this mindset; in Canada, archivists until the 1980s were seen as "handmaidens of historians." Underlying these stereotypes was an earnest quest, by archivists and historians alike, for objectivity, for impartiality, for Truth—all extolled as self-defining professional virtues, but, in reality, all an impossible dream in light of the inescapable subjectivity that any value-creating and value-enforcing activity such as archival appraisal must always entail.

This traditional curatorial mindset of the impartial archivist or the archivist as mere reflector of historiographical trends was fundamentally challenged from 1980 onward. Critical theory or "postmodernism" in many disciplines, the new digital recording media, the sheer scale of human documentation, and an awakened respect for the pluralism and diversities in society all stimulated this questioning. New ideas and new methods were needed. What emerges from this intellectual ferment is a new kind of archivist, an archivist as active agent shaping the archive, a mediator and interpreter of meaning, controlling the past in new and self-conscious and (one hopes) more transparent ways. This book continues this questioning, while honouring the archival thinker who truly revolutionized how the archival work of documenting society and its institutions needed to be reconceptualized: Helen Willa Samuels.

This festschrift honours Helen's ideas and their impact, and some of the authors address in detail the significance of her ideas—how they evolved and how they continue to have resonance. But the book is not a disparate group of unrelated essays on the authors' favourite topics gathered together to honour an esteemed colleague. Rather, the essays were especially commissioned to address a unified theme: how, in documenting modern societies and their institutions, the archivist's control of the past may be transformed in ways more appropriate for our twenty-first-century world.

The Essays: Unfolding the Themes of the Book

In developing the theme of documenting modern society and its institutions, and the archivist's control of the past, this book is divided into two major sections, followed by two special retrospective reflections. As some critics would now warn in reviews of films or novels, here is a "spoiler alert." One peer reviewer of this book in manuscript form thought that this introductory essay was burdensomely lengthy, and suggested that the summaries included herein might better appear as abstracts with each essay. And yet they are not abstracts in the usual sense as written by the authors to describe their own work, but my interpretation, as editor, of how the essays fit together into a unified whole—without, I hope, unduly scooping the authors' own analyses or spoiling their impact. This section paints the big picture of the book and modern documentation issues. But readers may wish to skip over this discussion now and go directly to the next section on Helen Samuels, returning later as they may wish to these summaries as they read the individual essays.

The book's first section, "Documenting Society," contains nine essays that in multiple ways explore the rich contexts in which the appraisal of potential archival sources takes place. How do archivists make the decisions of what people, events, and ideas should be documented, what records should be kept to best document these phenomena, what records to destroy, and thus what records will form the documentary legacy of the past for the future—the archive of the future? How may archivists be seen as "controlling the past"? Yet even as archivists do such controlling, they in turn are often controlled (or restrained) by the contexts in which they work, the organizational cultures they face, the technologies and politics they confront, and the intellectual presuppositions (and blind spots) they themselves carry, all of these changing rapidly over time and in different contexts. The archivist is not, then, a completely free agent, controlling the past against some idealized standard of appraisal value, important as such values are as part of the appraisal mix. The archivist is, in fact, controlled to a significant degree by her or his contexts. That said, the archivist so shaped is the conduit (and spokesperson) for these other contexts (and constraints) as choices are made to discern the tiny percentage of all the documentation created by modern society and in its institutions that shall be preserved as archives. In this way, the appraisal process itself, if well documented, becomes an important lens through which society's values may be seen. If archivists are society's professional remembrancers, to evoke a telling medieval notion, then those acts (and processes) of remembering, of story telling, are themselves a significant barometer of that society.

The first two essays, by Tom Nesmith and Gregory Sanford, introduce the broad sweep of these layers of contextual complexity. Canadian archival educator Tom Nesmith updates and broadens Samuels' research agenda for archivists in the documentation strategy and institutional functional analysis. If Samuels asked many new questions to which archivists must provide answers if they were to do appraisal well (and asking questions is revealed as the abiding central motif of her life in the afterword she penned for this volume), Nesmith extends that questioning in three fundamental ways. First, in controlling the past by deciding through appraisal the recorded human documentation that will survive for future uses, the archivist, as noted above, does not act alone. While the traditional notion has long been discredited that the archivist merely gathers passively some sort of natural residue of records left over when their creators are finished using them, that does not make the appraising archivist the sole creator of the archive that remains in archival institutions. While the archivist through appraisal is certainly the co-creator of that archive, often the principal creator, she or he acts within broad societal values and expectations, within organizational cultures, legislative frameworks, and records management practices. All these profoundly shape what records are created in the first place—or not—for various human activities, and which ones are available to be placed before an archivist for any sort of appraisal. Nesmith raises a long series of questions about these factors, to be answered before the actual archival appraisal *per se* takes place, that are fundamentally important to doing appraisal well and to making the resulting archival records intelligible to researchers. Secondly, to that fragment or trace of human and institutional activity that is recorded and available for appraisal, the archivist brings a whole range of theories and concepts about appraisal values, and employs a variety of strategies and methodologies to attempt to make manifest those values in the records chosen for archival retention, all within the enabling (or constraining) mandates, budgets, history, and practices of the archival institution itself. Nesmith suggests the complexities of this second process as well. Finally, he argues that researchers need access to the archival answers to these two sets of questions if they are to use records with nuance and sensitivity. He suggests codifying the archivist's appraisal questions, research results, and subsequent answers and decisions in a series of interlinked reports or essays, transparently available rather than buried in file cabinets in the archives' inner offices, for purposes of allowing accountability of the archival appraisal process itself and of engaging researchers (and future archivists) in a better understanding of the rich contexts and histories surrounding records. Controlling the past is too important to be done invisibly, behind bureaucratic walls, without collaboration—and without the deep research into the issues Nesmith outlines.

Vermont State Archivist Gregory Sanford shines a bright light on the value of such deeper contextualization and questioning. As a beginning archivist, Sanford worked with Samuels at the Massachusetts Institute of Technology, focusing on oral history projects designed to document more fully various aspects of modern science. He sees the questions asked by the archivist and the research done to prepare to interview a subject for oral histories as a harbinger of the questions and research of the documentation strategy. Both involve—indeed, celebrate!—an activist archivist consciously shaping and improving the record, filling in gaps to flesh out and make more comprehensible the surviving records, and thus the history, of some phenomenon being studied. Both employ careful methodologies and both are fundamentally founded on detailed research and analysis by the archivist into the relevant surrounding contexts. Sanford then weaves a fascinating story of how Samuels' inspiration played out in the Vermont State Archives in two major programs, reflecting her basic assumptions that the archivist actively forges partnerships, studies records and their contexts, and attempts to both collect and make available to society all relevant documentation wherever it is found, in whatever medium, within institutional and resource constraints. In its innovative "continuing issues" program, the Vermont State Archives flags for legislators, journalists, and the public the background information, historical precedents, and summaries of ideas and actions, all with links to scanned images of the actual pertinent archival documents, on a range of public policy issues that flare up in the state. There is strong evidence that these continuing issues are widely used as part of Vermont's governance. By making the State Archives directly and repeatedly relevant to government and the public in this very real way, Sanford and his small staff have been able to undermine the perception of archives as storehouses of old, historical, heritage information far removed from the debates and dialogues of today. And with that perception gone, the second result was a ready reception by government that the State Archives should take a leadership role in records management, including electronic recordkeeping, as the Archives had clearly demonstrated its relevance and usefulness in public policy. Sanford ascribes the fundamental animating power of these programs to functional analysis by the archivist and the deep knowledge so gained about how government actually operates. In order to document society (and its institutions), archivists must understand how society and institutions work (or function) in a fairly profound way, always recognizing that as they do so they are imposing their own filters and values on the documentation and appraisal processes.

The next two essays offer intriguing case studies of aspects of the documentation issues set out by Tom Nesmith. Archival photographic specialist Joan Schwartz and Bentley Historical Library senior archivist Nancy Bartlett remind us that all media are prisms through which the past is constructed and filtered. The traditional archival focus on black text on white pages, black-and-white engravings or maps, or black-and-white photographs, have naturalized certain logocentric assumptions about archives and suppressed the bright palette of colours of the real world in the representations of that world found in archives, at least until very recent decades. Both Schwartz and Bartlett continue the questioning so central to Samuels' thinking by extending Nesmith's contextual questions for photographs and for colour. Both show that documenting society as a process can benefit by taking the macro-level broad questions that Samuels and Nesmith ask and applying these to individual documents or to an overlooked aspect of documents like colour. As with Samuels' studies of broad societal functions such as science or education, so too must individual photographs "be understood as the product of practices, applications, or circumstances which are technologically determined, historically situated, socially and culturally constituted, and gendered." They must also be understood, Schwartz reminds us, "not simply as visual images, but as the visual residue of acts of communication, shaped by the equipment and processes of image-making, and by the assumptions and knowledge, values and beliefs of the society in which they were originally created and subsequently circulated and viewed. . . . It must also be acknowledged that the meaning invested in a document by its author is not necessarily delivered intact to its intended audience, for elements of meaning-making are only made meaningful upon reception and in terms of potential audience frameworks of knowledge and strategies of understanding. In addition, the meaning of a document is multiple and fluid, shaped and reshaped by disciplinary perspectives and institutional discourse." Through close contextualized readings of an individual photographic record—not in the formulaic manner of diplomatics, Schwartz makes clear, but as narrative and construction—light can be shed on how society documents itself, on what documents *do* (and *did*) rather than what they are about, and on how archivists themselves document that process of documentation.

Part of understanding what documents do, and how archivists respond, and thus what researchers can see, involves exploring the colourless representation (in large part) of a colourful world. Taking the University of Michigan as her case study, Bartlett pushes issues of archival societal documentation into the complicated and ambiguous area of perception—that is, the psychological meanings and readings of documents, especially visual ones. She shows that colour in many contexts "figures prominently as an illustrative tool, informational property, authenticating device, and essential indicator of the visual identity of the university." While archivists themselves happily use colour in exhibition and website design, they paradoxically adhere to monochromatic narrowness when considering the vitality of colour in their descriptions of documentation, or when appraising for documenting the past. Together Bartlett and Schwartz move issues of documentation forward from the traditional archival comfort zone of fact-based content and textual hegemony to exciting spaces of interrogation, ambiguity, and imagination, all with richer contextuality as Nesmith advocates and Samuels initially encouraged.

The next three essays, by Richard Cox, Bruce Bruemmer, and Robert Horton (respectively, an archival educator, a private-sector corporate archivist, and a public-sector state archivist), switch the focus to modern institutions and their documentary problems, thereby picking up some of the themes from Gregory Sanford. Recordkeeping in modern institutions faces significant problems. The first documentary problem, Richard Cox notes, is the incredible volume of modern records, which shattered the illusion that archivists could (or should) keep everything if technology and costs allowed them to do so. Cox notes that the sheer bulk of modern records was one of the motivating factors behind Samuels' pioneering work in appraisal; previous archival writers had not stepped back to look at the big picture as she did, beyond the taxonomic labelling of values. Such appraisal values are well and good, but how can one find manifestations of them among billions and billions of records? To emphasize this point, Cox looks at the impact of record-making technologies in the organizational workplace, especially the photocopier. The advertising hype surrounding the widespread advent of these machines around 1960 and afterward, with significant gender connotations, demonstrates a persistent refrain in modern recordkeeping: that technology is the great panacea to solve the problems of office efficiency and economy. Of course, photocopying did the opposite: while it allowed information to be much more easily shared, it clogged records management systems with multiple copies and thereby diluted the overall record available for archives. In this, Cox notes a striking similarity to the hyperbole surrounding the introduction of personal desktop computers, which allegedly were to herald the paperless office. And now we hear the siren call of technology once again as electronic/digital records—where everything can be kept because of ever-shrinking digital storage costs, and increasingly intelligent search engines can find what is of value—are proposed as the new panacea. Cox calls instead for a return to Helen Samuels' essential insight that very active appraisal to make hard decisions at a macro-functional level, rather than technological determinism or archivist passivity, will support a better documentary and archival reality.

Bruce Bruemmer looks differently at archival responses to documenting complex institutions, one of which is the modern business corporation. Most archives are funded by taxpayers, at least in part, or by some benevolent foundation, whether at the federal, state, regional, municipal, or university level. The conceptual and operating assumptions of archivists from such institutions underpin most of the Western canon of archival theory, strategy, and practice. As a result, business archivists (this they share with religious archivists) often find themselves at significant variance with their archival colleagues, and feeling very much like second-class citizens within archival associations. The Sun Maid/Sun Mad Raisin incident on the cover of the *American Archivist* a few years ago is only the symbolic tip of a large iceberg of misunderstanding. Bruemmer urges a speedy return to the "big tent" approach to archives best illustrated by Helen Samuels' all-encompassing approach of the documentation strategy—aiming to document the entire records of the nation, a virtual national archives, which no one would argue should not include business records, given the huge impact of such corporations on modern society. The alternative, he warns, may see further fragmentation of the archival endeavour, just when it needs more cohesion: business archivists may follow the precedent first of the records managers in the 1950s and then of many government archivists in the 1980s of leaving the big tent of the Society of American Archivists.

Bob Horton offers a thoroughly fascinating case study from Minnesota showing the real-world pressures that have a large impact, often a negative one, on archivists as they try to document governments, especially in a digital environment. Despite the good laws and regulations that are in place, the hard reality of alliances and friendships (or otherwise) among politicians, tax and budget freezes, privacy, and obsessive focus on costs can derail even very good recordkeeping strategies. Horton demonstrates that with rare exceptions—he would think them miraculous were they to occur—the ideal of enterprise-wide solutions are not likely to happen, no matter how well archivists, records managers, auditors, and their allies articulated their need and what they might look like. That ideal all can readily support; the reality of its implementation, much less so. Archivists need to transform their thinking, planning, and action from vague notions of the public good, history, and heritage, to delineating tangible, concrete benefits within public policy and the realities of public administration, and Horton suggests how that might be done. Taken together, Cox, Bruemmer, and Horton offer appropriately cautionary notes that reinforce Samuels' call for strategic thinking and planning, and learning from (and including) all the stakeholders, in the same spirit as Gregory Sanford outlined earlier as happening in Vermont.

The final two essays in the first section, by Rick Barry and by Richard Katz and Paul Gandel, look to the future in a very complementary way. Both essays posit that documenting institutions and documenting society will be radically transformed in the digital age. Both place their arguments in historical context, and trace the long evolution of organizational behaviour and culture and the changing archival responses to society's need for memory. Both essays evince a very nuanced understanding that the use of digital technology to create, manage, communicate, understand, and archive records, changes everything in a fundamental way. Long-time records management consultant Rick Barry at first continues Bob Horton's cautionary analysis of the failure of archives and records management to cope with the challenges of managing organizational change. Archivists and records managers too often remain locked in mental frameworks that are no longer relevant, especially as information technology changes the way organizations work, manage, communicate, and thrive (or not). Records professionals have generally failed to appreciate the critical need to influence changing organizational behaviours by understanding the key points of decision making and then inserting value-added perspectives there. Such perspectives come from business-process-based functional analysis that offers the archivist and records manager opportunities to influence organizational behaviour, to say nothing of allowing the critical archival task of appraisal to be performed with greater acumen. Barry ends with a useful checklist whereby records managers and archivists may achieve greater success, and close the gap between professional leaders who have articulated credible solutions and practitioners who have had difficulty getting them implemented.

Richard Katz and Paul Gandel, information technology specialists with special interest in using technology to improve business processes and education, look beyond the organization, which is Rick Barry's primary focus, to the pervasive and still barely understood societal changes resulting from digital technology, which will increase exponentially. The very standards by which people judge what information can be known, trusted, valued, appraised, accessed—all fundamental issues to the archival endeavour—are being transformed beyond recognition, with profound implications. The power of organizations and institutions as structures (the "tower" in their phrasing) is being replaced by the virtual world of network computing and social interaction (the "cloud" as they have it). The relationship between the tower (archives themselves as institutions, *and* the organizations from which archives obtain records) and the cloud is far from clear, and yet failure to transform archiving to this new societal reality dooms archival activity to irrelevance. Accepting this essential change is made easier by Katz and Gandel's comparisons of four major eras of archiving (which they whimsically label Archivy 1.0, 2.0, 3.0, and

4.0) for, respectively, oral cultures and storytelling; written records in eras of document scarcity and restricted access; modern bureaucracies based on mountains of paper-based records; and the digital era into which we are now well launched. The archival profession must transform itself to embrace Archivy 4.0, as it has adapted to the three earlier changes, but to do so will require, as Helen Samuels always urged, archivists' continual questioning of what we do and why, of what is essential as principle or theory and what reflects a particular era or technology or circumstance, and is no longer useful. Both sets of authors, Rick Barry, and Richard Katz and Paul Gandel, coming from different perspectives, see the power of context as central to thriving in the digital era—context as the traditional strength of archivists, but context rethought and reapplied if documenting institutions and society in the digital era is to flourish.

The second section of this book changes the focus about documentation. If the first section addresses issues related to understanding, managing, and then appraising all documentation to choose the tiny percentage that will survive as archives, the second looks at documenting that surviving documentation itself and at who is doing the documenting. Put another way, the small percentage of human documentation that becomes archives still amounts to hundreds of billions of pages and images, millions of hours of sound and film, and far greater equivalents in bytes of digital information. How can such a mass be effectively described so that the needed relevant records can be retrieved, with understandable and authenticating context, from this sea of data and information? This wrapping of data or information with value-added contextual meaning transforms it into reliable evidence and thus the basis of knowledge. When this should happen during the life of the record, by which individuals, using what human and technical processes, are questions now requiring much different responses than developed for traditional archival practice. In eras of document scarcity, lasting well into the twentieth century in terms of archival holdings, prominent archives still calendared documents one by one, letter by letter, writing short summaries of each; or later on, still produced detailed listings or catalogue cards at least at the folder, file, or album level. But the huge volume of recent records arriving in archives, especially those in digital formats, renders such item-level detail, when done by human intervention, no longer possible, except for rare "treasures" and some very limited special media, like art works or rare maps.

David Bearman and Elizabeth Yakel suggest exciting alternatives to traditional archivy, and in doing so pick up some of the themes raised by Katz and Gandel at the end of the first section, as they looked to the future.

The second theme of this section is exploring the nature of the archivist, and her or his role both in appraising records, documenting society and its institutions, and in describing records—researching that value-added context. What mental and rhetorical models do archivists develop to frame their world and work? What remains of the traditional ties of the archivist with the academic historian and the discipline of history? What special perspective, if any, does the archivist bring to the work? What ethical concerns shape these processes of appraisal and description, in short, of documenting societies and their institutions? What power does the archivist wield and thus what responsibilities? To these concerns, Brien Brothman, Fran Blouin, James O'Toole, Verne Harris, and Randall Jimerson bring their considerable talents. Taken together, a much clearer image emerges of what controlling the past through archival activities signifies for history, memory, and identity. These essays make clear that documenting society and its institutions extends beyond appraisal *per se*, at least as narrowly defined as selecting archives for acquisition.

On documenting documentation, or the contextual description of archival records, David Bearman, long-time archival theorist and consultant, offers fascinating insights into the possibility of using computers to decode vast numbers of born-digital or made-digital documents (books and records) based on the structure, layout, format, and functionality of various genres of document. Inspired, he notes, by early discussions with Helen Samuels on the role of function and transaction in understanding records, Bearman turns around the usual macro-level perception of functionality (understand the functions and their top-down decomposition and one will understand the context, nature, and often content of related records) to a micro-level perspective: understand the forms of documents (or impose more consistent formats of documents prior to creation so that they are understandable) and one can discern the function, the context. As importantly, a computer can be programmed to find and link matching functions within disparate documents. A name appearing in a title page, footnote, index, or text of a book, for example, signifies different meanings from its placement in a particular format. Linking these in context across million of books, into a kind of supra-index, all quoted references in footnotes to the original source text in its context, or all record metadata relating to some field on a form (a geographical location, a product, a person, a time period) across hundreds of databases, opens incredible new vistas for knowledge formation and raises the base platform of knowledge that all future research can build on. This is not the machine replacing the human, but discerning what machines can do if provided with intelligently formatted and structured documentation, leaving the archivist free to focus on researching deeper value-added contextual information.

And archival educator Beth Yakel demonstrates that in documenting documentation, the archivist is not, and should not be, alone. Too often, like the monks in their medieval scriptoriums carefully hand-copying manuscripts to preserve them across the centuries, archivists have done their description in isolation within the professional cloisters. With Web 2.0 social networking changing most users' expectations of how they access information and interact with institutions that hold it, Yakel argues convincingly that the walls should come down. Inspired by Samuels' model of a collaborative team of stakeholders working on a documentation strategy, Yakel extends this insight to archival description or, as she rightly prefers, the representation of archives, and to a much broader community of stakeholders. Mirroring Samuels' fundamental question, Yakel asks who re-presents the past, as archives. She outlines a new paradigm for thinking about archives, reconfigured from a one-way conversation of expert professional to suppliant users, to a two-way (or multiple-way) conversation among many stakeholders, in which the archivist is an important partner, but no longer the controller. The result will be descriptions of archives reflecting greater richness, and new communities finding meaning in archives where authority is shared, not hoarded.

Evidently Bearman and Yakel are presenting new models for the archivist in terms of describing and representing records. Archival theorist and electronic records archivist Brien Brothman explores models somewhat differently. He looks directly at the visual models that archivists design to represent their concepts, strategies, and ideas. These models appear (and are presented) as rational frameworks to bring order and clarity to complex ideas and related actions, but Brothman demonstrates that they (and their designers) have implicit and rarely articulated assumptions that cry out for interrogation. Brothman supplies that interrogation in his analysis, arguing that if a picture (in these visual models) is worth a thousand words, sometimes a picture hides (simplifies, overlooks) a thousand issues. He probes three case studies in making his argument: the international InterPARES project based on using diplomatics to address issues with electronic records, and then, by way of contrast and comparison, the records continuum from Australia and the documentation strategy from the United States. Ranging across many disciplines, Brothman interrogates deeply the systemic naturalized processes embedded in the rhetoric, design, and non-acknowledged historicism of models. Despite claims to holding no ideological position, for example, InterPARES stands exposed for its socially and historically conditioned ideas and practices. Models in that case deflect criticism, mask contentious issues, and bury important contextual, historical, and contrarian factors behind a patina of essentialist scientific objectivity. Models are presented as mere means for clarity of communication, rather than understood as interpretative instruments reflecting cultural and historical contexts. This Brothman demonstrates by offering the first sustained critique of the juridical assumptions and diplomatics underpinnings of InterPARES and comparing its rigidities to the much more inclusive scope of the records continuum and documentation strategy. Documenting how archivists document their own ideas, functions, and activities, including in visual presentations and modelling, is critically important, Brothman shows, to understanding the documentation itself, for the models (and ideas and technologies behind them) do much to define and shape the documentary record in very fundamental ways.

The next two essays take up this point directly, nicely complementing each other in looking at the evolution of the character of the modern archivist. Without diminishing the role of records creators and record administrators during the active life of records, nor the potentially large influence on the record by technological heuristics or social-networking researchers, the archivist is still the critical person who shapes the archive that remains. Archivists not only design the models that Brothman deconstructs, but they conceive and articulate the theories, concepts, strategies, and methodologies that underpin them. To understand documentation, therefore, one must understand the documenters. Fran Blouin, longtime director of the Bentley Historical Library, situates modern appraisal against the background of a gradual breakdown over the last century of the close relationship between the archivist and academic history, a rupture he calls "the history-archival divide." As modern history and archives had their origins in the positivist, scientific, and curatorial assumptions of the nineteenth century, they at first shared ideas about the importance of the major institutions of the nation state as both the focus for most historical research and the origins of the most important archival records. From them, truth about the past could be discerned. By the mid-twentieth century, as the volume of records escalated, archivists still attempted to mirror the main (if by then broadening) trends in historiography as the key arbiter of archival value. But as academic history expanded its interests, from the 1960s onward, to social and cultural history from the "bottom up," so that virtually every record had potential research value; as the volume of records in paper and then digital formats exploded; and as many more researchers came to value and use archives for reasons well beyond those of academic history, basing the selection of modern documentation on the ever-changing trends of historiography was no longer defendable. To this dilemma caused by the archives-history divide, Blouin asserts, Helen Samuels provides a very influential response. The archivist would establish values in appraisal from the context of the records themselves, the degree to which they participated in the most important functioning of their creating institutions, and how the records were created and shared across institutions, jurisdictions, societal sectors, and with citizens. The archivist became a student, then, not of historical themes and trends, but of organizational activity (through institutional functional analysis) and its collaborative processes (through documentation strategy). The ability of a record to best reveal the intensity of these functions and collaborations, determined by archivists' research into records and their contexts, now became the focus of value-setting in appraisal.

If the archivist is no longer the historian-archivist of the mid-twentieth century, what is his or her unique perspective? Archival educator Jim O'Toole answers with a fascinating journey through the profession's search for a sense of identity, a search that has been going on over the past half century. If archivists were no longer historians with a bit of on-the-job archival training, for reasons Blouin makes clear, alternative models of the archivist as librarian or as records manager were similarly rejected as unworkable. There was thus considerable ennui in the profession in the 1970s and 1980s—almost an identity crisis of knowing what archivists were not, but with difficulty in articulating what they actually were. O'Toole assesses various attempts at identity-formation around discussions of graduate-level archival education, certification of individual archivists, and accreditation of archival institutions, as well as explicit attempts to define an archival perspective. His own exposition of that perspective, based on an evolving shared knowledge, values, and practice, argues for asking and answering fundamental *why* questions, and not just methodological *how* ones, and praises the recent flourishing of archival history and the history of records by those inside and outside the profession. In all this, he lauds the pioneering work of Helen Samuels who insisted that conceptualization must precede collecting, thinking before acting, so that the key elements of the archival perspective may thrive.

If Blouin and O'Toole's essays view the archivist in historical perspective, the last two authors in this section of the book look at society's documenters through a philosophical lens. South African archival administrator Verne Harris considers the ethics of the archivist as decision maker, and American archival educator Rand Jimerson explores the power of the archivist in controlling the past. They give us, respectively, the poetry and politics of archives at the beginning of the twenty-first century. The two essays are nicely complementary, for the exercise of power always has ethical dimensions and obligations, and ethics often speaks (and should speak) truth to power. Harris himself notes that "there can be no purely ethical question, nor for that matter a purely political one. The ethical and the political are always implicated in one another." He shows, with real-world examples, that professional codes of ethics that archivists have devised are almost worthless. Ethics rather is an ongoing engagement with continually shifting contexts, which in turn requires incessant attention by archivists to recontextualize their principles, politics, and practice; to recognize that their inclusions also marginalize the non-included; their decisions in all archival functions to act exclude others not acted upon. To this abyss of impossible choices, we need to bring a welcoming hospitality to strangers, strangeness, the other. How this may work—never perfectly, but as an unceasing and committed quest—Harris shows with a powerful reading of the prison records of Nelson Mandela. In this vision of the ethical archivist, Harris (like Hugh Taylor and Jacques Derrida before him) sees archives as a quasi-religious, spiritual quest. He also credits the openness of perspective developed by Helen Samuels as a fundamental turning point in marking this challenging but necessary new direction for the profession.

Similarly, Rand Jimerson revisits Samuels' now-famous evocation of George Orwell's analysis of who controls the past, and what it means for archivists when they are increasingly seen, and self-acknowledged, as having a very powerful role in shaping the past that the present and future will know. Jimerson looks afresh at Orwell's career, and all his principal writings. Orwell's attitudes toward records and documentation, and their role in supporting tyranny or keeping it at bay, culminated in his final and famous dystopia, the novel *Nineteen Eighty-Four*. There records were routinely altered, forgeries created, and embarrassing records destroyed so that Big Brother and the omniscient state could act with impunity, escape accountability, destroy democracy, and imprison not only citizens' freedoms, but their very souls. In the politics of archives, archivists in their appraisal decisions especially stand as a bulwark against modern tyranny and various hegemonies where, as Jimerson nicely puts it, absolute power is wielded not with a gun, but with a pen. Following Samuels' pioneering example and her ongoing inspiration, archivists can counter power by gathering more diverse and inclusive collections that show greater attentiveness to multiple voices and to the documentary needs of a compassionate common humanity. Here Jimerson and Harris arrive at almost the same spot, alike invigorated by Samuels' archival inclusiveness.

The last section of the book appropriately comes full circle and full focus back to our honorée, Helen Willa Samuels. While the entire book demonstrates the powerful and continuing influence of her ideas, as editor, I wanted two special reflections beyond those in the individual articles, or my own introductory remarks. Rather than producing a list of titles of works published, papers presented, and talks given, as may be usual in festschrifts, I asked Beth Kaplan to reflect on Samuels' principal published works, in the order in which she wrote them, to trace the nature and changes in Samuels' ideas over a quarter century. Kaplan shows with considerable nuance the interconnections, evolution, and meanings of Samuels' work. Across the book's chapters, the authors come to similar conclusions about one or another of Samuels' publications, or one or another of her ideas, but Kaplan weaves these together into a coherent and attractive clothe—and did so without having access to any of the other essays.

And speaking of weavings, Helen Samuels closes the volume with a reflective, often witty, yet serious afterword drawing together the various strands of her life and archival ideas. It may be unusual for the honorée of a festschrift to be asked to contribute to her own volume, but I wanted Helen's voice here. My intent was not to give her the last word in the sense of commenting on the essays (indeed, she was not allowed to see them before completing the afterword) or in writing a final piece in her long career (in fact, I hope that she will write more as she continues to explore issues of documentation around new educational technologies). Instead, I wanted Helen to tell her own story, from the inside, from her personal experiences, not anticipating or disputing the authors' assertions in this book, but reflecting on the most important influences in her life and the formation of her ideas. I hoped that this would be another entrée to understanding her work, and I was not disappointed. I posed a long series of questions to Helen; in answering those questions, and by drawing on her memories and her archives, she tells her story. All archivists who appraise, acquire, describe, and diffuse modern documentation—who control the past—both tell stories and have their own stories. For what else is archives but documenting society and its institutions so that enduring stories may be told and retold and re-retold for generations to come? *History* has its etymological roots in English not only in *story,* but in words signifying wit, wisdom, vision, and idea—not coincidentally all features of Helen's own story as told here.

Too few archivists have written autobiographical books or essays, and that is a shame, for it perpetuates a stereotype of the archivist as an invisible, quiet, studious curator, deep in the stacks, applying straight-forward procedures and standards, not an active agent mediating and interpreting, let alone co-creating, the archive in a real world of both powerful stakeholders and marginalized actors. It is important that we hear the autobiographical voices of archivists, so that they (and by extension, all archivists) are seen to have faces, and names, and ideas, and lives, and influences, so we may celebrate their agency and perceive how they develop ideas that have influence. Archivists have a personal and professional context as much as do archival records. Helen's essay demonstrates this agency of the archivist for the record, in both senses of that word.

To anyone influenced by her ideas and seeking their genesis and context, Helen's story will resonate strongly. Her autobiographical reflection will also appeal more generally to all archivists, those starting out and those well into their careers: both will be inspired by her vision (and experience) as a "learning archivist" and by what that signifies for the archivist who today confronts immense problems in learning how to document society and its institutions in the digital era. Helen outlines for the archivist a fundamentally important process as much as its result. Finally, the generosity with which she tells her story, her collaborative spirit, and her readiness ever to share credit, underlines another powerful reason why this book exists.

The Influence of Helen Samuels: Personal and Professional

I first met Helen Samuels on Monday afternoon, March 20, 1989, when she came to Ottawa and spoke to the assembled staff of what was then the National Archives of Canada. Her topic was *documentation strategies*. The publicity poster issued by the Archives for the occasion invited staff to come and find out about what lay behind "the newest buzz word in the archival profession." More intriguing was the question on the poster: "How might documentation strategies be used to improve our ability to document modern society?" What intrigued me was that the question posed was not about how to do appraisal better. Nor what records should we acquire. Nor what historical research trends should we be more attuned to documenting. Nor what categories or typologies of records—minutes, certificates, memoranda, executive correspondence, photographic negatives, case files, etc.—should be included (or excluded) in our acquisition schema. Rather, the question was beyond all that: *how to document modern society!* The expansiveness of Helen's vision, her daring not to ask the usual questions about appraisal and acquisition, immediately caught my attention. Little did Helen know that, twenty years later, her invitation then to archivists to "document modern society" would form part of the title of a festschrift prepared both to honour her signal contributions in answering that question, and to continue with the twenty authors in this volume the exploration that she started.

My personal notes taken at the 1989 session are extensive. Clearly I was inspired, for the National Archives of Canada at that moment was searching for a new paradigm for its appraisal function. The Schellenbergian consensus had broken down for us, in theory, in strategy, and in practice. To me, what became manifestly clear in listening to Helen was the bigger significance of the *process* of the documentation strategy. One might quibble about defining which documentary problem or subject or theme ought to be covered, and why the one chosen for such efforts—say, documenting modern science—was inherently more important than, say, documenting gender or transportation or immigration or a hundred other possible themes. One might point as well to the logistical problems of bringing all the involved stakeholders together in one place to collaborate on the strategy. But the important message I took from Helen was that appraisal was a *societal* activity and had a *societal* focus, much more than it was about reflecting or anticipating research trends in history or documenting the key activities of one's parent or sponsoring institution. If this expansive perspective were the goal, then the archivist indeed needed "new tools," as Helen then put it. And the tool was a process, rather than chasing a predefined result. Responding to surveys or inventories of vast amounts of records produced from time to time by records managers, or to ad hoc requests from agencies for authority to destroy records, at which time the archivist discerned what records among those proposed for destruction might have research value—these were old tools, old methods, old thinking, perhaps valid in a simpler era of relative document scarcity and before the digital revolution.

Helen told us to step back. She counselled that appraisal was impossible in the old ad hoc or reactive modes. Instead, a *strategy* required a sequencing of steps, and an active engagement by the archivist in research and analysis to discern the context of document creation, followed by action to implement the research results with acquiring the best records for long-term archival preservation. Helen told us to understand the phenomenon to be documented, by conducting research into the functions, and subfunctions, and sub-subfunctions, and related programs and activities involved, before looking at individual institutions, interconnections between institutions, structural hierarchies, or actual records. She told us to be inclusive, to remember that many "records" were actually published, many processes well documented in print in books, journals, and reports safely preserved in libraries. Other "records" were well managed by other means in such curatorial institutions as galleries and museums. Where, then, after such expansive consideration based on research, were there to be found gaps in the documentary universe? Where were the missing voices? What needed to be documented—perhaps not by acquiring conventional recording media, but by actively undertaking oral history interviews and actually creating new records for archives? The "thought process" she outlined in her talk in Ottawa was intellectual, conceptual, research-based, and holistic, as well as strategic, planned, and sequential, moving from generalities to whatever levels of smaller or local granularity that time and resources allowed. For me, Helen's words were a revelation—and a revolutionary message.

Helen and I became fast friends and frequent correspondents after that. Her inspiration from that lecture led me later that year to articulate the theory, strategy, and methodology of macroappraisal, and to implement it in subsequent years at the National Archives of Canada. I drew inspiration from other sources, to be sure, some of whom were Helen's own mentors as well, but I searched for that additional knowledge and for those other useful precedents and thinkers because Helen set me on the loose, as it were, on that March day back in 1989, unshackling me from traditional approaches and professional orthodoxy.

About that time, sensing my attempts to do something different with appraisal, Helen sent me what she described as one of her favourite books, with the injunction to "read this and think about the archival implications." David Macaulay's *Motel of the Mysteries* is what we would now call a graphic novel, featuring pen-and-ink drawings, about a team of scientists in the year 4022 conducting archaeological excavations to find evidence of some long-lost country called Usa, now buried many feet under the detritus from a catastrophe that occurred some two thousand years before. As they dig, someone hits an air pocket and plunges down a shaft. The team follows. Discovering a "Do Not Disturb" sign, deciphered from some ancient writing, the scientists find what they assume is a quiet place of contemplation and worship, with a curious altar. They conclude that they must be in the inner burial chamber of one of the great gods or kings. A second sign found nearby—"Toot 'n' C'mon' in"—must indicate some mystical cult with links going back to yet earlier times and the Egyptian king, Tutankhamen. And on the book goes, artifact by artifact, gradually piecing together "the whole fabric of that extraordinary civilization"—all done without context, without knowing anything other than the object/fact in front of them—and so the results are hilariously erroneous: the sacred porcelain altar is, in reality, a toilet in a washroom in a suburban motel, not some high temple of ancient veneration. The archival implications that Helen alluded to were clear: unless archivists want their institutions to be filled with metaphorical collections of toilets they believe to be altars, they had better step back, research the functional contextuality of records, understand the documentary issues across the entire universe of information, and then actively document how society functions, rather than collect more toilets. As Helen often stated as her central mantra, conceptualization must precede collection.

Helen would be the first to say that she did not come up with the documentation strategy alone—and she repeats that disclaimer in her afterword in this book. She responded to calls from Gerald Ham especially to rethink appraisal, and she shared ideas in the early evolution of the documentation strategy with Joan Warnow-Bluett, Larry Hackman, Richard Cox, Jim O'Toole, and Tim Ericson. She was influenced too by research projects and committees of which she was a member at MIT and SAA. Yet Helen's signature statement on the documentation strategy in "Who Controls the Past" had the clarity, brevity, and acuity to make the concept her own. And the passion with which she shared these ideas in other writings, in lectures and workshops, and in myriad conversations, all over North America, was exciting and contagious—including, as but one example, that March day for me in Ottawa. The institutional functional analysis that underpinned her *Varsity Letters*—leading to a documentation strategy or documentation plan for one institution rather than across multiple institutions for society—was also matched by parallel (or earlier) developments: macroappraisal in Canada and its various spin-offs in other countries and jurisdictions; the PIVOT project in the Netherlands; Hans Boom's appraisal formulations in Germany; and, in the United States, Bruce Bruemmer's work on computer companies, and David Bearman and Rick Barry's analyses of international organizations. These developments indicate that the disruption to old ways of thinking about appraisal on all levels that Helen advocated was catching fire. The documentation strategy itself, sometimes under the guise of documentation planning, has been implemented for the records of Congress and music companies, for health-care institutions and for documenting geographical localities, for American physics and state-wide business entities. Every monograph on appraisal published in the past decade pays tribute to the influence of Helen's ideas. Both issues of the 2008 *American*

Archivist contain articles on the documentation strategy, thus showing that it still has significant resonance with a new generation. And then there are the essays and authors in this present volume, not just paying tribute to a colleague and friend, but in many cases also to an idea, and an effort toward extending that idea to renewed relevance for archiving.

While this book's authors refer to the twin contributions for which Helen is best known—the documentation strategy and the institutional functional analysis—and explain their subtleties and expand their possibilities, a brief introductory distinction should be made here for readers from other archival traditions. In terms of their surface practical application, these concepts have quite different foci. In terms of their deeper significance and meaning, Helen asserts that they share important characteristics. Documentation strategy was designed to coordinate the appraisal and acquisition activities of multiple archival institutions dealing with many records-creating organizations and individuals, to ensure the better overall archival documentation of some particular issue, activity, geographic area, or function. Institutional functional analysis, as its name implies, was concentrated on the internal structures and activities of a single institution, like a large modern university, business corporation, or national or state government, and developing a documentary plan to appraise its records so as to document most effectively its key functions once these were identified. Yet both share more deeply the need to conceptualize the big picture before collecting those individual "toilets," to do sustained research to understand the context in which records are created, to identify communication patterns within and between institutions where records follow functions and activities, and then apply the results to identify the best records as archives. In her afterword in this book, as well as in *Varsity Letters*, Samuels makes clear this symbiotic relationship between the institutional functional analysis and the documentation strategy.

Yet Helen's influence is deeper than the documentation strategy or institutional functional analysis *per se*, and their various manifestations in practice, and their various theoretical or strategic reworkings. As several authors assert in the essays that follow, Helen fundamentally challenged the way archivists think. If the archivist controls the past, how we understand that control has changed radically since Helen penned her landmark article in 1986. She crossed a series of boundaries that archivists to that point had rarely traversed and, in doing so, demonstrated the fundamental unity in her work, whether on documentation strategies or functional analysis: That archivists in the first instance were not appraising records, but appraising and documenting society. That archivists should not attempt in appraisal to mirror or follow research trends in any particular discipline or researchers' immediate subject content needs. That archivists accordingly must research and understand the documentary problems of society being addressed, and the entire contextual universe of relevant records creators of recorded information relating to that problem, whether documenting some theme across the jurisdiction of many institutions or the multiple functions of the single sponsoring institution. That archivists should work closely with librarians, and that published records be integrated conceptually with unpublished ones. That private-sector archives and personal papers, on the one hand, and institutional or organizational records, on the other, were not two solitudes, but complementary aspects of the total archival record. That the archivist should work collaboratively rather than competitively with other archivists. That major documentation strategy decisions should involve all stakeholders, including creators and field specialists, as well as the archivists and librarians and curators of all relevant recording media in numerous archives, libraries, museums, galleries, and other curatorial institutions relevant to the documentary issue at hand. That archivists as a result, following these ideals, would over the generations build a virtual archive nationwide—a rich, fuller, coordinated documentary collection for the entire nation—with duplication and trivia squeezed out and more voices included, no matter where the actual documents may be housed in individual curatorial institutions. That archivists should, where necessary, fill gaps in the total record by creating new records with oral- and video-history interviews and recordings. That archivists should listen and learn, hearing stories other than those of their own disciplines, backgrounds, and institutions, and documenting these "others" as fully as possible. That ultimately archivists must ask not what records should be kept, but what societal phenomena should be documented. That archivists intent on answering that question seriously must therefore work in a planned, active, and strategic manner. Helen was asserting very strongly that archivists are not just curators of the documentary traces of the past; they control and shape that past in fundamental ways.

As Verne Harris rightly notes in his essay, these ideas taken together are electrifying, even revolutionary, for they evoke a new epistemology, a new politics, and a new ethics for the archival profession: "The archivist is not a passive assembler, a custodian, a keeper. Rather, she is an active shaper of social memory, and should embrace the role of memory activist." As Rand Jimerson well asserts, the postmodern archive was made possible as the traditional boundaries around archival orthodoxy crumbled. For that crumbling, for all these electrifying insights into archives, Helen Samuels easily stands with Schellenberg and Norton of earlier generations as one of the greatest landmark pioneers of twentieth-century American archival practice.

How did this astonishing re-imagining of our profession take place? Without intending to scoop Helen's afterword, nor some of the authors' analysis of her ideas and their contemporary role in evolving American archivy, I propose that several factors were at play. Helen's Jewish upbringing in New York City, where telling stories and hearing stories was so fundamentally important to her family and culture, gave her an appreciation for listening to stories and a desire to document them. Her first loves, music and dance, showed her important areas of human creative activity that traditionally are poorly documented in most archives, and led her to wonder why that was so. Her passion for collecting textiles from around the world led to her appreciation for nontraditional ways of documenting human experience, even including some textile-based recordkeeping systems. Her exposure early on to oral history made natural to her the filling of memory gaps so that undocumented stories could be told. Her education in library science and early library experience before entering an archival world then comprised almost exclusively of colleagues educated in history made her think differently; academic librarians in various fields very naturally talked to each other in different institutions and, by interlibrary loans, shared sources as a normal and expected part of their daily work. Why didn't archivists? And arriving at the Massachusetts Institute of Technology as institute archivist where she had a blank slate, for that venerable institution then had no archival holdings in its archives, Helen was forced to think strategically about how she would document her institution, and beyond that the fields of science, technology, and engineering in which MIT and its illustrious staff were world leaders. What did a music librarian know about science and technology? In setting out to learn, Helen Samuels reinvented her profession.

Helen cites in her afterword passages from Helen Elaine Lee's novel *The Serpent's Gift*, about the power of storytelling in response to a continual questioning of life by its central character. To that she connects the great rewards in many phases of her own life that came from continually questioning what was before her. If I may offer an epigram back to Helen, from Anne Michaels' recent exquisite novel *The Winter Vault*—which is all about the power of memory, story, and listening—a character reflects that "Every object is also a concept. If you place two or three or ten things next to each other that have never been next to each other before, this will produce a new question. And nothing proves the existence of the future like a question. . . ."

Helen in like manner placed two, or three, or ten archival "things" (or concepts) together, for us, in new juxtapositions, forcing us to ask new questions, and thereby gave archivists a very different future. By opening so many doors, so many possibilities, crossing so many boundaries, questioning so many orthodoxies, the diminutive librarian became an archival giant. Documenting societies and their institutions proceeds now in richer, fuller, deeper ways because of her work. The resulting archive that is our collective entrée to the past is more open, more collaborative, and, ironically, less controlled.

For that, Helen, your profession, your colleagues, and your friends honour you with this volume. For your continual mentoring, your seeding of ideas, and your encouraging us to dream and to dare, we thank you.

Documenting Society

DOCUMENTING APPRAISAL AS A SOCIETAL-ARCHIVAL PROCESS: THEORY, PRACTICE, AND ETHICS IN THE WAKE OF HELEN WILLA SAMUELS

Tom Nesmith

Helen Samuels opens her seminal 1986 article on archival appraisal with a passage from George Orwell's *Nineteen Eighty-Four* that warns that those who control the making and keeping of records thereby control understanding of the past.[1] Her use of Orwell reflects an entirely new perspective in the English-speaking archival world on appraisal, one that she launched in this work. Before she wrote this article, archivists had rarely, if ever, said that knowledge of the past was profoundly affected by appraisal, rather than simply mirrored through the selection process. Samuels also tried to widen archival perspectives on appraisal by arguing that archivists ought to conceive appraisal as a cooperative multi-institutional activity, rather than something to be done by their own archives in isolation from others, and only with records under its particular mandate. She thought that teams of archivists from various archives should collaborate on interinstitutional projects to document key aspects of past and present societal life. Moreover, such cooperative approaches would only succeed if based on significant research into the wider contexts of records creation, transmission, and use. And, widening the scope of this work even more, she said that records creators, records managers, librarians, museum curators, and researchers should collaborate as part of these documentary teams. Samuels' conception of this "documentation strategy" underscores an important but often overlooked point about appraisal—that for our modern complex societies and their larger institutions, appraisal perforce is a broadly based societal-archival process of making, locating, managing, retaining, and then researching and selecting the records to be archived, whether or not a documentation strategy is implemented in exactly the way she proposed.

Most archivists have tended to see appraisal as an activity carried out primarily *by archivists* in a single decision-making process to keep or reject records, or at least they perceived that appraisal should be so. The roles of other players in the appraisal process, however, and their influence on archivists, have received much less attention. Since Samuels wrote in the 1980s, the powerful (and sometimes Orwellian) impact of these others on the records that archivists may get to appraise has become more obvious in the wake of major recordkeeping scandals in many countries. Institutional and personal records have been destroyed, manipulated, forged, dispersed, hidden away, lost, stolen, neglected, or allowed to deteriorate.[2] Even when such sad, undesirable fates do not interfere, records are much shaped by the political, economic, legal, and technical environment, personal attitudes, and work processes of those who create records and others who subsequently manage them. A kind of archival "appraisal" is thereby going on in society long before most archivists can intervene in the process. These forces determine which personal and organizational activities will be documented at all and which ignored, and which will be documented well, adequately, or poorly, using one, several, or many recording media. And when archivists do get directly involved, the societal-archival appraisal processes, reflecting the wishes of sponsors, community supporters, and users of archives, also determine—often in unrecognized and unacknowledged ways—the outlooks of archivists themselves, and thus what records are actually appraised to be acquired as archives. Within this broader perspective, appraisal can be considered a highly varied societal process in which archivists play a key, but not the only, or sometimes even the primary, role.

Samuels' invitation to archivists to rethink their role in appraisal might also be extended to the familiar idea that archivists select records that are already created by others. Samuels suggested in her 1986 article that archivists should work with others to see that records are created where needed to document important activities. In light of postmodern insights into the interactions of observers and the phenomena they observe and represent, one can suggest that archivists also help create records in appraisal in other ways that were not anticipated by Samuels or others in the 1980s. In the societal appraisal process, archivists help create documents to be kept by contextualizing them, which gives them meaning (or existence) as documents of this or that phenomenon. This contextualization is necessary if certain documents are to be selected over others with seemingly less or no meaning (or value). Archivists help create documents in order to (and as they) appraise them.

These new views of the archivist's active role in shaping records and knowledge have begun to be acknowledged in archival literature on appraisal.[3] They have resulted in calls for greater archival accountability for the influence archivists have over appraisal decisions. But they have not resulted in much discussion as yet of just how archivists might fulfill that ethical obligation. How can archivists respond to this concern today? This essay will suggest they can do so through greater understanding of the societal-archival appraisal process, of their own role in creating records through appraisal, and of their responsibility to the public and to posterity through archival appraisal accountability mechanisms to document their appraisal research and decision-making processes. One of those mechanisms could be the kind of publicly available report on the history and current methods of appraisal at an archives that will be discussed here. Thus, documenting appraisal as a societal-archival process involves recasting the theory of appraisal, seeking out practices reflecting that, and addressing the ethical issues arising from it

This idea of such a report arises from my related work on a project intended to reconceptualize archival theory and practice in light of wider currents of thought now influential in the academy and society. (A number of colleagues in Canada and elsewhere have also been active in this effort.) I have tried to contribute with restatements or redefinitions of some key archival concepts, such as the terms *archives, record, provenance,* and *reliability and authenticity of records.* The statements attempt to reflect a vital insight from those intellectual currents: that means of communication shape the reality they document, rather than merely convey it. And thus archiving, as a communication process, shapes the reality that emerges from that process in the archival reading room, and works its way from there into society through books, exhibits, and now, more and more, television, movies, and the Internet. I have also woven these basic restatements further into archival practice to try to show how each of the major functions archivists perform can be viewed as records-creating activities.[4] Much of that work has focused on the function of archival description. My suggestion for practical descriptive work is premised on the idea that the knowledge of records and archiving actions that a wide variety of archivists and others have thought necessary in metadata and descriptive systems and standards has become so voluminous that no formal practical systems could convey it all. Sue McKemmish states this problem well:

> ... it should be stated that the richness, complexity, diversity, and idiosyncracies of the contexts in which records are created, managed, and used cannot be fully represented in models, systems, standards, and schema, but this does not detract from their significance and strategic importance to practice. . . . By attempting to define, to categorise, pin down, and represent records and their contexts of creation, management, and use, descriptive standards and metadata schema can only ever represent *a partial view* of the dynamic, complex, and multi-dimensional nature of records, and their rich webs of contextual and documentary relationships.[5]

If existing practices need improvement, but no method could fully represent all that might be knowable and relevant about records and the archiving actions taken with them, then descriptive practice might be better enhanced by adding a new feature to it. What might be added? There could be, as a general overlay to any descriptive system, a series of essays or reports on the approach taken to description by that archives and the nature of the contextual information found in it. A researcher entering the descriptive system of a particular archives would have automatic access to these reports, and through hyperlinks could reach the level of complexity needed for a particular project or topic. A researcher could go directly to the records descriptions themselves or consult with an archivist. In this way, a researcher could choose the degree of contextual information that seems relevant, but at the same time be alerted to (and have available) a wider and deeper range of contextual information and guidance, should that emerge as more important than initially expected for any particular research project.

These reports or essays would serve as a guide to thinking about and using the wide range of contextual information about records that could be useful to researchers. They would act as a map to what is valuable to know about records. In the area of description, one such essay could provide an introductory overview of the various types of contextual information about the records in the system that a researcher might find useful. Other reports could be available on societal contexts that shape records creation, or on creators and their functions, recordkeeping systems and processes, organizational cultures, information technologies and other material features of records ("material literacy," as Ala Rekrut calls it), custodial history, types of individual documents encountered in various media, how to assess them with diplomatics, or to understand what their ideal form might be, and their anomalies and particularities.[6] These reports would not only prepare researchers for using the contextual access points the formal system may have, such as creator name and functions; they would also, in effect, help researchers to "read" an archives—or get behind the documents and the limitations of formal descriptive systems and standards to the less visible and complex histories that actually produce and shape the evidence the records may bear.

Taken as a whole, these kinds of essays could offer as full a *conception* of the history or contextualities of the records as can be provided, even if all the specific information about that context for the particular records held is not actually known—and, of course, it will never all be known. This would give a researcher an idea of what is important to know about the history of the records to take into the search for information in the actual descriptions of particular records. That narrative will help locate information, if many of the types of possible links between key features of contextual knowledge are provided.

This approach could be taken for other archival functions as well. For example, there could be overview reports on the preservation work of a particular archives and how it can shape the characteristics and interpretation of the records. There could be reports on the variety, rationale, and selection and development process for public programming activities. The entire set of essays on the various archival functions amounts to a key aspect of public programming itself. These reports could also be prefaced by one on the history of the particular archives. And, of course, there should be one or more overview reports on appraisal, the heartland of Helen Samuels' archival focus. The reports, including those on appraisal, would not be the type that are produced day-to-day in the course of performing a specific appraisal or other archival activity. They would be overview statements of what a researcher might need to know about how a function has been conceived and performed over time at an archives. Their aim would be to provide researchers with insight into what they might want to know about records in order to help them locate and understand the records. Like the reports on description, those for other functions would not contain information on everything a researcher or archivist may want to know. Knowledge would be offered, but the primary aim would be guidance on what *to think about* as one approaches the archives, and where to look for further information or insight. The reports would be works in progress, as they would be continually revised as firmer knowledge is acquired and new lines of inquiry open up. They would serve as a set of interconnected reports covering the various functions of a given archives. They might also be connected to a broader set of such reports for a regional or even national archival system. As Magia Ghetu Krause, Elizabeth Yakel, and others are suggesting in the Web 2.0 social-networking environment, it is entirely possible that users, donors, and other interested parties may also interactively contribute their knowledge and comments to these contextual reports or essays.[7]

What type of information might be made available in an overview report on the appraisal function of an archives? What does the user of the archives need to know about appraisal? How do archivists explain the appraisal process best? The challenge of appraisal practice is not just in deciding what records to keep and setting up a procedure for doing so, but also in reflecting critically on and explaining why certain records were kept, and why a usually much larger related body of records, on authority of the archivist, was destroyed and thus irrevocably removed from our collective memory. Such critical reflection on both keeping and destroying records is an often overlooked aspect of appraisal practice. I am aware that, under macroappraisal, and some manifestations of the documentation strategy, very detailed research is conducted and extensive written appraisal reports are produced. This is a fundamental improvement over past practices and serves both as an enriched and cumulative research base of knowledge for archivists doing their work in all archival functions (not just appraisal) and as an accountability instrument documenting and explaining the keep-destroy decisions. These macroappraisal reports, however, relate to individual appraisal projects, usually the records of one function or major activity in a large department within a large organization or, for the documentation strategy, to aspects of a subject or activity such as documenting American physics. What I am advocating here is a broad, generalized, overview statement of the ideas (appraisal theory, if you like), strategies, methodologies, and environmental factors, over and above these specific projects and their reports, that would place them, and all appraisal activity, in context.[8]

The overview report should explain what appraisal is, following the reconceptualization suggested above, as an important part of the societal-archival process of record creation within which many players and factors influence the outcome. Accounting for what archivists know of that process is thus essential to understanding *the creation of the record*, or the provenance of the record, and the evidence the record now bears, as well as gaps and silences in the record series or fonds. If archivists are to be more sensitive to the action or *process* of appraisal, and the role of the archivist in that, they need also to be as aware of, and to share, their understanding of the other influences that shape the overall appraisal process from which records emerge. Inscribers and pre-archival custodians of records document some things and not others (that is an appraisal decision of sorts) and they choose to destroy certain records, disperse them, offer only certain records to archives, while holding back others for other times. At the same time, sponsors of archives impose acquisition mandates that constrain appraisal work in various ways; conversely, the sponsors or important users of an archives may intervene to prompt and even impose particular acquisition decisions and, alas, destruction decisions (the "Heiner Affair" in Australia is a sensational example of the latter).[9]

The appraisal report, then, could explain that appraisal is a process that may unfold over many years. And there may even be various phases in the archivist's particular part of this overall process. More than one archivist may be involved in making appraisal decisions with a given body of records, over a sometimes lengthy period of time. The archivist's appraisal is usually done with records that have been through the initial stages of the societal appraisal.[10] These initial stages have a powerful influence on what archivists *get* to appraise. There are signs that archivists are focusing more on the "appraisal" done prior to the archivist's appraisal, as demonstrated in several case studies in Richard Cox and David Wallace's *Archives and the Public Good: Accountability and Records in Modern Society*. It contains chapters on document destruction in the 1980s prior to archival intervention in apartheid-era South Africa, during the Iran-Contra Affair, and by the United States Internal Revenue Service. Other researchers have also begun to pay attention to this issue of societal appraisal.[11] These new insights are vital, but they still (through no fault of their authors) remain on the margins of archival knowledge and practice. The essays, scattered chapters, or even internal archives reports will not be found by researchers who search the websites of archives looking for information in archives. If they are not found, how will researchers be alerted to the issues that they highlight—issues of records lost or missing or destroyed or dispersed or merged with others, and when, where, by whom, and why? Archivists could use the overview appraisal report to refer to the kinds of issues this literature raises, point to similar examples in the history of their own archives, and refer researchers to these works for further insight.

The overview appraisal essay could begin with a section that notes that an understanding of the appraisal process begins with awareness of the basic societal circumstances underlying the archivist's appraisal process. The report should note that appraisal is deeply affected by the key functions a society has felt it important to perform over time and how it has performed them, including oral and documentary means of communication. In an introductory overview report, this broader point can only be illustrated, not fully described. For example, the health-care function has always been an important societal function, but it has been carried out in different ways at different times, with different methods of communicating and recording. Across Canadian history, varying emphasis has been placed on care at home, care by charitable and private services, and public care, shared by different levels of government, in different ways, at different times, in different and ever-changing institutions. Archivists will not only want to convey a sense of how such societal functions work at given times, but also that those who perform the function value certain activities more than others, how they have communicated this, and sought to have it remembered. The overview appraisal report should point out that this complex pattern affects the creation and location of records for researchers to use, what archivists might get to appraise, and how they might make appraisal decisions. The report could also note that there are functions that a society does not seem to value as highly (or at all) at a given time. Who performs them and how? That obviously says something important about a society at a given time, but it also provides clues to the location of records for researchers to use and that archivists might get to appraise. This is important because what a society did not value highly might well provide information valuable to people today—there is a need to know that some records no longer exist and are not in archives because society collectively through its archivists thought the activities and people the records once reflected were not worth preserving in memory. The overview appraisal report would provide a general introduction to these themes and their complexities. Related linked essays could be written over time to explore in greater depth specific aspects of the societal context, where this seems relevant to the work of a particular archives, fonds, series, or even, in rare special cases, items or at least genres of documents.[12]

The archivist's intervention in this appraisal process begins with some understanding of these general aspects of the societal appraisal process that occur largely before archivists encounter the records they produce. The introductory appraisal report could show how a sponsoring institution or mandated area of archival action is positioned within this broader societal context. The report could outline how these questions might be answered for a given setting: What functions have been considered important? What has been less valued? How have these been communicated and what has been recorded of that? What do the players in the mandated area want to remember through records? And here, of course, is where the archivist encounters the mix of forces that create some of the chief tensions in appraisal practice (with all their ethical implications). As archivists engage society's and their own institution's appraisal process, they note that the latter two value certain things more than others, and want to see certain things remembered more than others. Archivists have to approach this tension in appraisal practice with a critical perspective informed by the best societal and institutional analysis they can make.

The overview report could then have a section on the history of the given archives in relation to the evolution of its appraisal process. This is relevant because archivists and researchers inherit the work of their predecessors. This work is ever present; it is there every time archivists and researchers look at records acquired by earlier appraisal values, strategies, and methods. The report might outline why the archives was established; that rationale is essentially a societal appraisal decision. An archives is usually created to acquire certain records and not others. What socio-political factors shaped its creation and initial acquisition mandate? The appraisal report could outline those and other factors which have since affected appraisal decisions across time, such as laws (archival and otherwise) that may dictate what is created and kept, archival mandates and policies, and how they have affected appraisal decisions. Copies of such laws and policies from various times could be made available through hyperlinks. What actual authority in law and policy was granted to the archives to do appraisal at various times? Was this authority sufficient? Why or why not? What is the history of the implementation of these laws and policies? Were they implemented effectively? What creators of records and what records or media did the laws and policies leave out, if any, and why? How did the archives respond to that, and to changes in recording technologies? Among other things, this would allow opportunity to explain why, despite their pervasive societal presence and influence, so few born-digital or film and sound records are to be found in archives. Which creators cooperated well with the archives and why? Which ones did not and why? How did the archives respond to any lack of cooperation? What auditors' reports on the appraisal (or broader recordkeeping) process might exist for various periods? What other special or formal inquiries (such as royal commissions in Canada) might have evaluated the appraisal process or even held it to formal account? Are there internal program review reports by the archives itself on its appraisal program? These could be accessed through links in the overview report.

The report might try to provide insight into the orientation these factors and conditions have given appraisal. If, for example, the archives is a Canadian provincial government archives, perhaps it was established long after the province was created. Thus there may have been no formal archiving or appraising done with government records until the archives was established. What happened to such records prior to the archives' creation? Did other archives acquire them? If so, which archives and which records? Researchers will want to know where they can find them. Did certain other agencies in the provincial jurisdiction play an appraisal and archival role before the archives was created? Did libraries, museums, galleries, collectors, or private institutions play a role? What government records might still be in their hands and in the personal custody of former officials? If precise information about this is not known, then the essay could at least alert researchers to the possibility that records may have been removed by former officials, be in their possession, or be among their private manuscript materials in the archives in question, or perhaps in other archives.

Did the archives' mandate include private records or government records? When did it acquire these responsibilities and why? What role, if any, did jurisdictional evolution play in the fate of records appraisal? What impact did the personality and interests of the chief archivists have—perhaps emphasizing "collecting" private sources over "managing" government ones, or vice versa—on the resource allocations within the archives and thus its possible appraisal focus and its actual acquisitions? Have records been lost to flood, fire, or other disasters, and what was the effect on surviving records? What role may have been played in acquisition by mechanisms such as oral interviews by archivists or their designates; motion pictures or photographic documents made by archivists or designates; transcription, photocopying, microfilming, and other duplication methods; by the tax credit process, purchase of records, access to information, freedom of information, or privacy laws; and by deaccessioning for transfer elsewhere or for destruction?

The overview appraisal report might then discuss the schools of thought that have been used over the years. Was the Jenkinsonian hands-off approach used? Schellenberg's approach, reflecting major research trends? Samuels' collaborative documentation strategy? Cook's societal-based macroappraisal? Or a combination of such approaches, as in the Minnesota Method? Were there other less well-known or localized approaches, or idiosyncratic variations of these broader appraisal theories and strategies? If there was evolution in thinking about these approaches to appraisal, when and why did that occur? And what were the strengths and weaknesses in actual experience with these various schools or approaches? What approach is currently in use for institutional records? Which is in place for private manuscripts? Which for each of the non-textual recording media? When were these approaches adopted? What is their rationale? How are they implemented? What is the administrative process of appraisal? Who makes the appraisal decisions? What criteria are used and why? What paper trail is created? Where are these documents? What is the function of the various documents along that trail? What are the terms of access to them? As mentioned above, some of this information is beginning to appear in archival reporting, notably at the

Library and Archives Canada website statement on macroappraisal. But more information could be added there and much more could be done by archives generally to introduce and highlight these issues for the public and for researchers.[13]

Assuming that there is access to at least some of this information, it should be available, linked to the overview appraisal report, in policy statements and documents, and linked to the specific reports on the appraisal process and rationale for particular bodies of records in the archives. The overview report could describe very generally the basic contents and characteristics of these specific appraisal reports and point to the particular files in the archives' own current records management system or in similar older files in its custody where the function is documented. An archives would then have a three-dimensional accountability system for the appraisal function. It could be entered through the introductory overview report, which would then lead to reports on the appraisal of specific bodies of records, to other contemporary files on the appraisal function in the current records management system, and to older files in the archives' own archives.

After providing general information on appraisal procedures and documents, the overview report could then turn to the archivists who were involved in appraisal. It could explain that the names of archivists who made appraisal decisions are available in the particular appraisal reports for specific bodies of records, and could identify the key managers and perhaps the chief archivist who had a significant hand in the keep-destroy decision making. The overview report could also state that a biographical sketch and curriculum vitae accompany (or are linked to) the specific reports each archivist prepared, and that there are links in the reports to other reports each archivist prepared and to copies of their principal writings on archives, including, especially, any writing on appraisal.

The overview appraisal report could then be integrated into a wider set of such reports on the various other archival functions, archival concepts, selected types or genres of records, recordkeeping and classification systems, the history of the host archives, and aspects of context such as societal environments, organizational culture, and administrative requirements. The key terms in the overview appraisal report could be linked to related information across the other overview reports and in all other documentation connected to them, such as the actual descriptions of records, appraisal decision-making reports for particular records, and preservation intervention reports for specific records. To take a hypothetical example, the overview appraisal report at an archives could include a section on the impact of the Second World War on records creation, management, and archiving because the war had a profound effect on the societal-archival appraisal process for the sponsoring institution's records. The desire to ensure memory of the institution's contributions to victory prompted significant changes in attitudes toward archiving, and the archives in question was given a wider role than before in appraisal of records. The overview report could explain the exact nature of the new role in appraisal.

The overview might then highlight and explain why, as a result of these changes in appraisal policy, new archival value was attributed to case files. To illustrate this, for a state archives, the overview might mention a few examples—such as extensive files for military and public service personnel, and smaller series, such as one that documented a joint military and penitentiary services program that during the war used male prison inmates, conscientious objectors, prisoners of war, and those with certain psychiatric "medical" deferments (such as declared male homosexuals) to construct internment camps for Japanese Canadians, prisoner of war camps, and roads and military buildings in remote areas.[14] The penitentiary service, as the primary administrator of the program, had custody of the case files; since most of the two hundred participants in it were inmates, the service was pleased to archive the series as evidence of its otherwise little known contribution to the war effort. The overview appraisal report need not say much more than that for this example. Its aim is to illustrate major changes in appraisal policy, and tie them generally to important overall themes, such as the evolving societal context in which records appraisal has been done. It could include a link to a separate overview report on the societal context affecting records creation and the given archives; this report could elaborate further on the impact of the war on the archives and provide additional insight into the societal-archival appraisal process.

Most researchers, of course, would find out about the existence of most records in the actual descriptive system of an archives, not from the overview appraisal report. For the hypothetical wartime case files, researchers might have discovered them in the descriptive system and been able to follow a link from there to the overview appraisal and societal context reports to learn more about the wider appraisal context for these records. Researchers could follow links to additional reports from any report that mentions this series. For example, in the descriptive system, researchers find that only a poor-quality microfilm of the series exists. They could then follow a link to the particular appraisal report done on these records to learn more about when, why, and by whom the originals were destroyed and details about the making of the film copy. This report should also link to reports on the appraisal of any related series wherein the keep-destroy decisions of the archives are documented and explained.[15] The appraisal report for the wartime case-file series should mention any leads that were followed in pursuit of the originals, such as the discovery that certain original files in the series were removed from it, recoded, and made the basis of a new record-keeping system. (This, of course, would have—or should have—also been flagged in the descriptive system.) This pointer to the recordkeeping dimension of the story could then be a link to an overview report on the main types, structures, strengths, limitations, and evolution of recordkeeping systems in the given jurisdiction or agency. Case-file recordkeeping systems will deserve mention in this overview as a key type of such systems. A further link might then be provided to a distinct report on their particular characteristics and histories in that jurisdiction.

Reports on recordkeeping systems will inevitably mention specific types of individual records, such as those used to create a case-file series like our hypothetical example. Researchers might well be aided by both an overview report on the roles and key features of individual documents and media, and specific reports on significant ones worth highlighting further, such as those in certain types of key case-file series. These reports could provide insight into the role of individual records in carrying out functions, categories of information they convey, the circumstances that may have caused deviations from their stated roles and information conveyed, and how they are preceded and succeeded by other individual records. These reports are illustrative and do not provide comprehensive descriptions of all types of individual records and media. They serve as part of the general map for researchers through the complexities of archival records provided by the entire set of reports.

Since the case-file example being used here to illustrate this system deals with microfilm of poor quality, the specific appraisal report for these records and the descriptive system entry for them could provide a link to the specific preservation report done on the microfilm by the archives' preservation services. This report would outline the type of film used, its condition, what may have been done at the archives to protect it, and comments on what effect microfilming with the film and techniques used might have had on the information these records convey. It might report that the film was digitized in order to enhance its legibility and availability and then discuss how digitization in turn also affects what we can know from these records.

Given that these case files were digitized, it may well be that research interest in them is such that they merit a specific reference report. A reference report would outline the uses that have been made of these records—and what further uses might be made of them. It may be that in the immediate postwar period, the penitentiary service consulted them to consider progressive penal programs, as many of the inmates in this program went on to have productive lives after serving their sentences. This hope faded, however, when problems with the original program became evident as time passed. Participants who had been asked to be subjects of medical experiments complained later in life of related illnesses and thus mistreatment in the program. Some obtained monetary compensation for this after a government inquiry. For some Aboriginal participants, it turned out that the only record of their attendance as children at a residential school was in these files. After a government inquiry into abuses of children at these schools, monetary compensation for these men was based on these records. Lawyers for the wrongfully convicted helped build a pivotal case on one of these files. Families of participants sought access to them for medical and genealogical purposes. Links might be provided to published materials that are based on these uses. And archivists should suggest potential additional uses for these records—perhaps in further reviews of such programs by the military, penal system, or scholars, or in documentaries, planning of historic sites, movies, novels, and plays. This reference report with these particular suggestions would be linked to an overview reference report that outlines more generally the evolution, varieties, and especially the possible uses of records in this archives and, where relevant, other ones too.

This overall system of deeper contextualization of archives is only sketched here in part to suggest how the overview appraisal report could be seen as part of a broader archival accountability and descriptive system. And such an overall system could only be undertaken as a long-term, ongoing, institutional project. Furthermore, the system suggested here does not contain anything truly new, as much of this type of information can be found in archival and other published literature, websites, blogs, listserv communications, as well as in the reference letter files, informal notes, and unrecorded memories of archivists—much of which is often already shared orally with researchers or in written responses to their inquiries. But this scattered and fragmented information about records needs to be researched and explored further and brought into archival work much more directly and programmatically as a major focus of archival accountability and descriptive systems.

The discussion of appraisal reporting in this partial outline of such a system is based on a theory of appraisal that views it as a societal-archival process in which records are co-created—not just selected—by archivists. In this, archivists share the creation and appraisal processes with others, as noted, all acting within the societal milieu of the time. Archival practice within this process should ultimately be driven by societal objectives. The archivist's appraisal practice should attempt to move the profession and his or her own institution toward the goal of a broadly based societal archives—the ideal animating Samuels' documentation strategy—by intervening in the broader appraisal process to protect what contributes best to that goal. That involves a skillful navigation through and against interests that would shape it only toward their preferred valued actions and their narrower memories. The archivist's appraisal work should be characterized by accountability for the conception of that societal objective and for the archivist's role in the creation of records, which thus brings an obligation to explain how the creation of the records has been pursued. One mechanism to achieve greater accountability is the reporting method outlined here. Archival practice would occupy a sounder ethical position if archivists acknowledge the roles of the various players (including the archivist) in the making of records through the appraisal process. Archivists would also be in a sounder ethical position if they view (and openly acknowledge) societal well-being as the heart of their professional purpose in appraisal and all else that they do.

Attempting to be ethical within this theory and practice of appraisal involves formulating and responding to complex considerations. How much of the appraisal process as described here *is* actually relevant for others to know in order to fulfill archival obligations to them? How much should be shared in public? Much may be under formal legal access restriction. With personal records, issues of privacy of the donors, and of those with whom they interacted, cannot be ignored. Should archivists in their workplaces and through their professional bodies resist access and privacy restrictions, and to what degree? Should they try to get creators and donors to be much more open than they usually are about why they are archiving what they do archive? Motivations on either side of this relationship may not be the best. Even if archivists do not reveal specifics publicly, should they alert researchers and users to the less-than-noble motivations that may be behind an archiving decision, without being specific?

The accountability agenda that archivists have rightly espoused—for governments and other institutions to be held accountable for their actions through good records management and archiving, and now for archivists to be accountable for their conduct as well—prompts profound questions. How much can really be revealed about archiving—at least before a significant passage of time? If much cannot be revealed for various understandable reasons, what is the impact of that on archiving itself or on using archival records? Does that compromise the integrity of records in serious ways? But are not archivists, particularly since Jenkinson, the self-proclaimed champions of protecting that integrity? How do archivists function with integrity and transparency in this complex environment? How much truth about record creation and archiving can a society or profession even grasp? How much does it need to comprehend the almost infinite complex contexts of records? How much truth about them can a society or profession stand? And yet without such questions at least being probed as deeply as possible, who indeed is left to "control the past"?

Notes

1 Helen Willa Samuels, "Who Controls the Past," *American Archivist* 49 (Spring 1986).

2 For a few of many possible examples, see Verne Harris, "'They Should Have Destroyed More': Destruction of Public Records by the South African State in the Final Years of Apartheid, 1990-1994"; Chris Hurley, "Records and the Public Interest: The 'Heiner' Affair in Queensland, Australia"; Victoria L. Lemieux, "The Jamaican Financial Crisis: Accounting for the Collapse of Jamaica's Indigenous Commercial Banks"; and David A. Wallace, "Implausible Deniability: The Politics of Documents in the Iran-Contra Affair and Its Investigations," all in *Archives and the Public Good: Accountability and Records in Modern Society*, ed. Richard J. Cox and David A. Wallace (Westport, CT: Quorum Books, 2002).

3 Terry Cook, "Macroappraisal in Theory and Practice: Origins, Characteristics, and Implementation in Canada, 1950-2000," *Archival Science* 5, nos. 2–4 (2005); Richard J. Cox, *No Innocent Deposits: Forming Archives by Rethinking Appraisal* (Lanham, MD: Scarecrow Press, 2004); and Barbara Craig, *Archival Appraisal: Theory and Practice* (Munich: K. G. Saur Verlag, 2004).

4 See Tom Nesmith, "Reopening Archives: Bringing New Contextualities into Archival Theory and Practice," *Archivaria* 60 (Fall 2005). For my earlier conceptual work, see "Still Fuzzy, But More Accurate: Some Thoughts on the 'Ghosts' of Archival Theory," *Archivaria* 47 (Spring 1999); and "Seeing Archives: Postmodernism and the Changing Intellectual Place of Archives," *American Archivist* 65 (Spring/Summer, 2002). For further elaboration of this approach to the concept of provenance and to the public programming function, see my "The Concept of Societal Provenance and Records of Nineteenth-Century Aboriginal-European Relations in Western Canada: Implications for Archival Theory and Practice," *Archival Science* 6, nos. 3–4 (2006); and Tom Nesmith, "Archivists and Public Affairs: Towards a New Archival Public Programming," in Cheryl Avery and Mona Holmlund, eds., *Better Off Forgetting? Essays on Archives, Public Policy, and Collective Memory* (Toronto: University of Toronto Press, 2010). A growing number of archivists have been involved in similarly rethinking the archives and the archive in light of modern conditions and contemporary critical theory. The names of the most prominent among them, rather than a list of their great many publications, are provided here: Nancy Bartlett, Brien Brothman, Rick Brown, Terry Cook, Richard J. Cox, Barbara Craig, Adrian Cunningham, Bernadine Dodge, Wendy Duff, Mark Greene, Verne Harris, Caroline Heald, Margaret Hedstrom, Chris Hurley, Rand Jimerson, Elisabeth Kaplan, Eric Ketelaar, Lilly Koltun, Candace Loewen, Heather MacNeil, Sue McKemmish, Laura Millar, Joan M. Schwartz, James O'Toole, Ciaran Trace, David A. Wallace, and Evelyn Wareham.

5 Sue McKemmish, "Placing Records Continuum Theory and Practice," *Archival Science* 1, no. 4 (2001): 354 (emphasis added).

6 Ala Rekrut, "Material Literacy: Reading Records as Material Culture," *Archivaria* 60 (Fall 2005).

7 For a brief introduction to this system of reports or essays, see Nesmith, "Reopening Archives." For work by others who are exploring similar approaches, see Chris Hurley, "Parallel Provenance: (1) What If Anything is Archival Description?" *Archives and Manuscripts* 33, no. 1 (May 2005); and "Parallel Provenance: (2) When Something is Not Related to Everything Else," *Archives and Manuscripts* 33, no. 2 (November 2005); Heather MacNeil, "'Picking Our Text': Archival Description, Authenticity, and the Archivist as Editor," *American Archivist* 68 (Fall/Winter 2005); and the special issue of *Journal of Archival Organization* 5, nos. 1–2 (2008), edited by Jean Dryden. For an example of the possibilities of using Web 2.0 social networking approaches in archival settings, see Magia Ghetu Krause and Elizabeth Yakel, "Interaction in Virtual Archives: The Polar Bear Expedition Digital Collections Next Generation Finding Aid," *American Archivist* 70 (Fall/Winter 2007).

8 Under macroappraisal at the then-National Archives of Canada (now Library and Archives Canada), two such generalized overview reports were produced (originally in 1991, and revised and put online in 2000) outlining in considerable detail the appraisal theory, strategies, and methodologies that underpin the macroappraisal process for Canadian federal government records. This is a promising start, which other institutions are beginning to follow as well, but I am

suggesting here that considerably more detail about the record-making and social environment, organizational cultures, and appraisal processes be included in such overview essays. Library and Archives Canada (LAC) has a much briefer and more limited overview of its private-sector records appraisal program at its website. A number of other leading archives are also making information about their appraisal programs more widely available at their websites, although the primary audience for this seems to be their own staffs, records and information managers, and government officials. This information is designed to help them to implement appraisal programs, and not primarily to help them or the public and researchers understand how appraisal policies and processes have actually evolved and why, or how they have shaped the records and the information records convey. The information that is available is highly relevant to this purpose and includes links to legislation that authorizes appraisal mandates, current appraisal policy statements, appraisal objectives and basic criteria, definitions of terms, and examples of general records schedules and forms used in appraisal. But it is not prominently displayed at the home pages of such archives so as to direct the public and researchers to it as central to their concerns. Indeed, this positioning, in effect, tells the public and researchers that this information is not important to them. The information now provided also lacks other relevant information such as links to the actual appraisal decision reports themselves, and the kind of overview introduction and guidance to the various elements of it that I am proposing here. For Library and Archives Canada, see "Government Records Appraisal and Disposition Program" at http://www.collectionscanada.gc.ca/government/disposition/007007-1034-e.html. As noted there, LAC does intend to place "summary descriptions" of its appraisal reports at its website. For LAC's statement on its private sector records appraisal program, see http://www.collectionscanada.gc.ca/collection/framework/003024-200-e.html. The National Archives and Records Administration of the United States (http://www.archives.gov/records-mgmt/initiatives/appraisal.html) and the National Archives of Australia (http://www.naa.gov.au/) provide information on their appraisal work in the sections of their websites devoted to "Records Management." The National Archives of the United Kingdom places this information in the "Services to Professionals" section of its website, but does provide a link to that section at the "About Us" feature aimed at a more general audience on the homepage. See http://www.nationalarchives.gov.uk/default.htm. (All sites accessed July 13, 2009.)

9 Hurley, "Records and the Public Interest: The 'Heiner Affair' in Queensland, Australia."

10 Eric Ketelaar notes that Jacques Derrida calls this all-encompassing societal archiving process *archivization*. On a variant of this, Ketelaar coined the term *archivalisation* to denote the process of "the conscious or unconscious choice to consider something worth archiving." See his "Archivalisation and Archiving," *Archives and Manuscripts* 26, no. 1 (May 1999): 57.

11 For a very small sample of this interdisciplinary literature, see Adam Hochschild, *King Leopold's Ghost: A Story of Greed, Terror, and Heroism in Colonial Africa* (New York: Houghton Mifflin Harcourt, 1998); Ian Hamilton, *Keepers of the Flame: Literary Estates and the Rise of Biography from Shakespeare to Plath* (London: Hutchinson, 1992); and Michael Millgate, *Testamentary Acts: Browning, Tennyson, James, Hardy* (New York: Oxford University Press, 1992). Although not specifically about archiving, Gary Taylor's book, *Cultural Selection: Why Some Achievements Stand the Test of Time and Others Don't* (New York: Basic Books, 1996), is highly relevant to an understanding of the processes of selecting all cultural phenomena for preservation, including archives.

12 The essay by Joan M. Schwartz that follows in this volume is a fine example of the richness of such contextualizing analysis recommended here at the item level.

13 See note 8 above.

14 This hypothetical example draws inspiration from a wide variety of studies in the history of records, such as Robert McIntosh, "The Great War, Archives, and Modern Memory," *Archivaria* 46 (Fall 1998); "Supplement: The Archival Legacy of the Department of the Interior," *Archivaria* 25 (Winter 1987–88), which contains articles on aspects of the history of the department's records by Terry Cook, Gabrielle Blais, Doug Whyte, and Doug Bocking; Judith Roberts-Moore, "Establishing Recognition of Past Injustices: Uses of Archival Records in Documenting the Experience of Japanese Canadians During the Second World War," *Archivaria* 53 (Spring 2002); Tywanna Whorley, "The Tuskegee Syphilis Study and the Politics of Memory," in Cox and Wallace, eds., *Archives and the Public Good*; Rekrut, "Material Literacy"; Guy St. Denis, "Passing the Means Test: The Old Age Pension Applications of Norfolk County, Ontario, 1929-

1948," *Archivaria* 37 (Spring 1994); David Hume, "Life's Embarrassing Moments—Right Treaty, Wrong Adhesion: John Semmens and the Split Lake Indians," *Archivaria* 17 (Winter 1983–84); Lorne F. Hammond, "Historians, Archival Technology, and Business Ledgers," *Archivaria* 28 (Summer 1989); Joanna Sassoon, "Photographic Materiality in the Age of Digital Reproduction," in *Photographs, Objects, Histories: On the Materiality of Images*, ed. Elizabeth Edwards and Janice Hart (New York: Routledge, 2004); Carolyn Strange, "Stories of Their Lives: The Historian and the Capital Case File," and Steven Maynard, "On the Case of the Case: The Emergence of the Homosexual as a Case History in Early Twentieth Century Ontario," both in *On the Case: Explorations in Social History*, ed. Franca Iacovetta and Wendy Mitchinson (Toronto: University of Toronto Press, 1998); and National Archives of Canada and National Library of Canada, Aboriginal Healing Foundation, and Legacy of Hope Foundation, *Where are the Children? Healing the Legacy of the Residential Schools* (Ottawa, 2003).

15 Jean-Stéphen Piché provides an early statement of the potential of such web-style information technologies to enable extensive linking for public access of various heretofore internal records that document archival functions. See his "Doing What's Possible with What We've Got: Using the World Wide Web to Integrate Archival Functions," *American Archivist* 61 (Spring 1998). And Terry Cook makes an early call for government and institutional archives to account for the institutional records they choose not to acquire by adding "negative" entries in their public descriptive systems that would describe such records alongside the descriptions of related ones they did acquire. He also argues that private-sector acquisition programs should similarly account for their appraisal decisions by listing private individuals and institutions whose records were not acquired (and why) alongside a list of those that were acquired (and why). See his "Fashionable Nonsense or Professional Rebirth: Postmodernism and the Practice of Archives," *Archivaria* 51 (Spring 2001): 34–35.

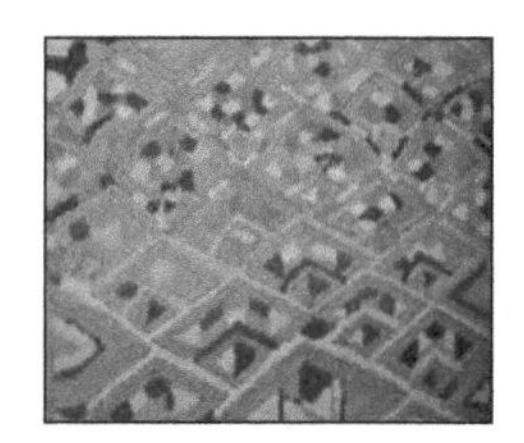

TRAVELING IN A HELLENIC WORLD: AN ODYSSEY FROM ORAL HISTORY AND DOCUMENTATION STRATEGY TO CONTINUING ISSUES AND INTEGRATED RECORDKEEPING

Gregory Sanford

The ancient Hellenic world was a place of constant transformation. Gods transformed themselves to mingle with humans, and, in turn, physically transformed humans to reward, protect, or punish. Heroic journeys brought transformation to the voyagers and those they visited. The transformation stories, from Leda's swan song to Odysseus's travels, helped give meaning to the natural world and the stars above.

My own Hellenic transformation began on a less heroic note. One hot and humid summer day, I found myself wheezing along in the wake of a diminutive woman with the apparent metabolism of a hummingbird. It was 1977 and my guide, Helen Samuels, was mapping my new world as a member of the oral history program at the Massachusetts Institute of Technology. That world was delimitated by the offices of the oral history program and my own office within the Institute Archives. It too was a world of transformations, a place for making sense of things through stories and for understanding not only what was, but what could be. As for her influence on my subsequent career, she may be the Helen who launched a thousand slips on my part, but I remain indebted to her for giving me the courage to risk failure in order to create something better.

One of the great transformations of the ancient Hellenic world was from oral to written communications.[1] Plato, and through him Socrates, discussed this transformation through the story of Theuth and Thamus, as found in *Phaedrus*. Thamus, a god and ruler of Egypt, expressed misgivings about Theuth's invention of writing:

> . . . this discovery of yours will create forgetfulness in the learners' souls, because they will not use their memories; they will trust to external written characters and not remember of themselves. The specific which you have discovered is an aid not to memory, but to reminiscence, and you give your disciples not truth, but only the semblance of truth. . . .[2]

The dichotomy between oral and written discourse, between preliterate and literate cultures, has long occupied our thoughts.[3] Walter Ong, for example, described written language as a technology that turned us from "oral situational thinking to increasingly abstract thinking, which moves in interlocked, sequential, linear patterns."[4] Neil Postman, among others, commented upon how new information technologies blur the lines between written and oral communication.[5] Hugh Taylor explored how these new technologies also break down the older compartmentalized, sequential, linear world of writing and what that means for archivists.[6]

Within the narrower context of my own Hellenic odyssey, the reintegration of oral and written communication is tied to the inauguration of an oral history program at the Massachusetts Institute of Technology in 1975 under the direction of Dr. Charles Weiner and the modernization of MIT's archival program under Helen Samuels, starting in 1977. The oral history and archival management programs were closely linked. Dr. Weiner was on the search committee that hired Helen, and the Institute Archives was not only the repository for MIT's oral history tapes and transcripts, but also a partner in some oral history projects. This was evidenced, in part, by my being hired by the oral history program, but placed under Helen's supervision within the Institute Archives. MIT was not the only institution to link oral history programs with archives, and it is possible to see in such partnerships an origin of documentation strategies.[7]

The 1970s was a period of great enthusiasm for oral history. Much of this enthusiasm stemmed from the promise of capturing the memories and experiences of the un- or underdocumented. Oral histories were also used by archives to augment existing paper records. This often took the form of addressing the limitations of the paper records by providing context based on the oral recollections of those who either created or were subjects within the collections. In such projects, oral historians did extensive research within the paper records in order to frame questions to the creators or subjects.[8]

My own cross-training between oral history and archival management began in 1975 when, upon his retirement, U.S. Senator George D. Aiken deposited 750 cubic feet of his records with the University of Vermont. Though this was, at the time, the largest collection accepted by UVM, the university quickly created an oral history program to complement the paper records.[9]

Since the give-and-take of politics is largely conducted orally, the oral histories captured Aiken's recollections of the personalities and political exchanges that were not apparent from the written documentation of various initiatives and positions. Aiken, for example, first gained prominence in 1931 through his defeat of a flood-control bill promoted by the Vermont speaker of the house. In the oral histories, Aiken recounted how he came to be on the committee that reported the bill adversely and how he waited to call the committee vote until the chair, a bill supporter, was absent. The committee's records confirmed that the chair was absent the day of the vote. Alone, however, the written record only provides evidence of who was there that day and how they voted. Oral histories were also used to identify time-obscured figures among Aiken's frequent correspondents from the 1930s and 1940s. Aiken's recollections of these individuals were then incorporated into finding aids so researchers could better understand his relationships with the correspondents.

Other archives-based oral history projects sought to develop larger thematic contexts, unanchored to specific collections of documents. One MIT oral history project, for example, focused on the experiences of women in physics. The cultural environment these women confronted in what had been a male-dominated branch of science was not evident from either their individual or collective records. The oral histories gave a greater sense of the interactions these women had with their not always welcoming male colleagues or students.

One of the more interesting MIT projects used videotape to document the opposing viewpoints concerning the Seabrook nuclear power plant. Videotape provided additional documentation, conveying visual messages along with the oral testimony. It provided a striking contrast in images of the corporate boardroom setting in which utility company employees were interviewed, and the kitchen, complete with a woodstove, in which one member of the opposition Clamshell Alliance was recorded. This project not only captured, in part, Walter Ong's preliterate "oral situational thinking," but also built, as much as relied on, MIT's documentation of the Seabrook controversy.

The primary focus of the MIT oral history program in the late 1970s was documenting the interplay between science and technology as exposed by the unfolding controversy surrounding emerging recombinant DNA technologies. This joint archival/oral history effort actively sought to capture the evolving perspectives of scientists, politicians and governmental bodies, science writers and reporters, and others. Capture included paper records, audiotapes, film, and other media.

MIT's recombinant DNA oral history project foreshadowed documentation strategy by defining a research topic; selecting advisors and establishing a site for the strategy; structuring the inquiry and examining the forms and substance of documentation; and selecting and placing the documentation. The broad subject was the interplay of science and society, while the defined topic was the political, scientific, and social responses to recombinant DNA research. Advisors were drawn from the oral history and archival communities as well as from participants in the unfolding debate. Traditional sources of documentation were identified and, because of the ongoing nature of the issue, were augmented by creating documentation through oral histories with participants or through recording public hearings. The Institute Archives was identified as the repository for the documentation. Equally important for the context of this essay, there was constant interaction with the communities involved in the public and scientific dialogues over recombinant DNA, including presentations and articles through those communities' organizations and journals.

Though the framework and evolution of the recombinant DNA program may have been more inchoate than the above implies, it is possible to see elements within it that would reemerge in documentation strategies. The interplay between multipartner, subject-based, oral history projects that were so popular in the 1960s and 1970s and the development, within the archival profession, of documentation strategies in the 1980s, deserves further study.[10]

My tenure at MIT ended before Helen formally articulated her documentation strategy concepts and methodologies, but I followed her work and those who built upon it.[11] Given my background as an oral historian, I was more confused by, than oblivious to, subsequent professional controversies among some archivists that questioned the "social engineer" role envisioned for archivists by Helen in the documentation strategy, and later in her institutional functional analysis. My professional training and experience was of active partnerships with records creators; the creation of new records (oral recordings) to augment existing collections; and understanding that the way interviews were researched and conducted very much shaped the records that became part of the archives. From my then-limited experience in archival management, I understood as well that mission statements, collection policies, processing decisions, and outreach choices—all determined or articulated by the archivist as a social and cultural mediator—affected how, or even if, records were preserved or researched, and how those records gained value in an ever-changing memory over time. That archives were somehow fixed and locked in time, inviolable after crossing the archival threshold, as traditional archival theorists asserted, seemed to fly in the face of the reality I knew. Archives were not passive receptacles filled by default or process, but active agents forming and shaping society's memory. From that collective experience, therefore, I had assumed that a degree of "social engineering" was inherent to most archival programs. I retained and refined that mindset when, four years after leaving MIT, I became the Vermont state archivist.[12]

In 1982, the Vermont State Archives, a division of the office of the secretary of state, was less an example of a passive repository than a moribund one. Virtually all record acquisitions were the result of statute or other legal mandates rather than appraisal either by the Archives or the administratively distinct record management program. Processing was spotty and idiosyncratic and, since the 1920s, the main focus had been on the annotation and publication of eighteenth-century government records. In the 1970s, a rudimentary conservation lab had been added for work on eighteenth- and early nineteenth-century records that had been taped into bound volumes. Twentieth-century records were largely left to their own devices by the Archives, except for gubernatorial records which were sent to be microfilmed and stored at the record management program. To illustrate how misunderstood the archival function had become in government, the state's human resources department responded to a request for an additional archivist by sending me a former prison guard. The rationale was that the guard, just like archivists, kept things under lock and key. That experience reflected the common perception that the Archives simply held old stuff that might be of interest to historians, but was not germane to ongoing public dialogues.[13]

To effect change required developing an understanding of the function of the Archives within state government. In Vermont, that was a difficult challenge. Statutes, which are one indicator of institutional function, primarily focused on the Archives publishing records deemed to be of "general historical interest." Records management services, by statute, were performed by a different division within a different department. While the evidentiary role of the Archives had long been understood, as illustrated by periodic legislative mandates to preserve laws, town charters, state deeds, gubernatorial records, and legislative committee testimony, that role was undermined as new technologies, bureaucratic structures, and changing work processes affected how those various records were created and managed. Neither legal mandates nor archival practice kept pace with these changes.[14]

Within that reality, what was the Archives' institutional role? Here Helen's vision of the activist archivist was important. "Is the archivist's responsibility to manage existing records or to play a role in assuring adequate documentation of an institution? . . . To meet the challenges posed by modern documentation, archivists and their colleagues must become active participants in the creation, analysis, and selection of the documentary records. This places archivists . . . in the role of documenters of their institutions, rather than simply keepers of their records."[15]

To achieve that level of participation, archivists need to generate a more complete understanding of their institutional role than offered by popular perceptions of archives as "dark and dusty" preserves for historians. In turn, that requires leaving the confines of the archives to interact with key players within the institution to understand their business processes and, ultimately, how they create and use records. That can be easier said than done. Couple a strong association of archives with history to the political sensitivities of state government and elected officials tend to get nervous when an archivist turns up, uninvited, to talk about records. One can almost see them wondering whether they should check the polls since archivists usually only show up at the end of a political career.[16]

The one place open to all was the statehouse (as it is termed in Vermont) where legislators, government officials, citizens, and reporters freely mingled. Statehouse observations made it clear that most legislators, officials, and reporters did not have the time, training, or inclination to come to the Archives and read through finding aids or sift through boxes of records. Legislative committee minutes provide a useful example. The committee minutes kept by the legislator serving as clerk were generally disparaged as without value; indeed, the fact that the Archives preserved them contributed to a negative image of archival practice ("why do you keep those records?" was a frequent question, rarely linked to awareness that the legislature mandated their retention). Equally few legislators took the time to listen to hours of recorded testimony, which had effectively replaced minute-taking, in preparing to report or vote upon bills.

It was also clear that officials already had numerous existing information sources, drawn from lobbyists and the expert testimony of agency heads and their own staff. This information was carefully crafted and aggressively marketed in order to influence decision making in support of administrative initiatives or the agenda of special interests.[17] Long-term contextual information was often absent, given the motivation to provide a favorable response to the immediate legislative interests of those pushing the various information sources. The information itself was often presented in brief, bulleted summaries supported by oral testimony.

Interaction with key creators and consumers of public records provides insights into how to reframe understandings of the archival function. One important insight is the need for archivists to understand how, and why, government officials use records and information. The truth of the matter is that, with some exceptions, most legislators did not use records, but rather quick summaries of record-based information. The same is true of most senior-level bureaucrats who testified before legislative committees, thus making the records at least twice removed through various filters. It is interesting to note that over the last several years the executive and legislative branches have moved to eliminate mandated agency reports, primarily to save costs but also in recognition that few officials actually read the reports.

Another observation is that the perceived value of records/information grew when that information was directly linked to a need to act. Public dialogues, within a legislative setting, are linked to the need to act, that is, the need to draft, amend, and vote upon bills. Providing records/information not associated with this need to act was not very useful; conversely, providing contextual information that can inform a decision enhances the value of the archives to those decision-makers.

Others have commented, often in discussing the "information age" or the perceived "information glut," on the need to tie records/information to the need to act. Neil Postman, for example, wrote that, "the tie between information and action has been severed. . . . [O]ur defenses against information glut have broken down; our information immune system is inoperable. We don't know how to filter it out; we don't know how to reduce it; we don't know how to use it."[18] More simply put, a respondent to Rick Barry's 2003 survey on archives and society suggested that, "Maybe one reason we are perceived badly, if at all, is because we aren't connecting to people's actual needs."[19]

These insights suggested the need for a strategy for redefining perceptions of the archival function within a public institution by not only linking records to action, but also by linking the profession's identification of archival records as having continuing value to the parallel or complementary idea that government itself confronts continuing issues. Each generation, within its social expectations and fiscal realities, must grapple with issues such as education, public safety, taxation, public health, economic development, crime and punishment, and the environment. They must do so through government processes that are set by constitutional, statutory, and other legal mandates and shaped by practice and precedent. The Archives holds records of many of these deliberations and precedents, which in turn can provide very useful context for decision makers. If the information could be synthesized into forms legislators were familiar with (overviews and summaries, for example) while retaining their link to the source records, then archival records could become a new and relatively trusted information source that could inform political and public decision making.

It is essential to make a clear distinction here that this did not entail reshaping our appraisal and arrangement and descriptions decisions simply to reflect anticipated use. Rather, this "continuing issues" approach required an understanding of the business processes of (in this case) the legislature in order to understand the broader contexts of legislative records and then to find ways, in addition to the traditional intellectual controls centered around archival description, to present the information that recognized decision-making patterns. The records themselves continued to be organized and described to reflect their original order and context of creation, and they continue to be appraised to document as fully as possible all key functions of the state government, not just "hot button" or trendy issues.

The initial efforts of the Vermont State Archives at presenting continuing issues were thus linked to processes rather than to topical issues. These processes or subfunctions were identified in the Vermont Constitution. As with all constitutional language the description of the processes was broad and open to interpretation. There were no readily available sources for tracing how these interpretations evolved over time. To confront the weakness of existing archival records, the Archives gathered information from published sources, such as legislative journals, and yes, even oral (unrecorded) interviews with past and present legislators. Identification of initial continuing issues was aided by two Vermont Supreme Court decisions that raised a series of questions within the public and the government on how to respond to those decisions.

The first case was *Brigham v. the State of Vermont* (1997), which found Vermont's method of funding education inequitable and thus unconstitutional. The legislature responded by passing a statewide property tax (Act 60 of 1997) that met the court's equity requirements. The second was *Baker v. the State of Vermont* (1999), which found that gays and lesbians did not have equal enjoyment of the constitutional "common benefits" clause because their decisions to enter into personal partnerships did not have the same legal protections accorded heterosexuals joining in marriage. The legislature responded by enacting a civil union law (Act 91 of 2000) that extended marriage-like benefits to gays and lesbians.[20]

Both decisions, and the subsequent legislative deliberations, closely divided the state. Among the "process" issues that became embedded in these sharp public dialogues were the following: What is the role of judicial review? Could the justices be impeached for overstepping judicial boundaries? Should not the public, through referenda, have the right to decide these crucial issues, rather than simply leaving it to the legislature?

Could the governor veto the measures? Could the court decisions be rendered inoperative by amending the constitution? Eventually another core issue emerged when the electorate fragmented and party allegiances, already weak in Vermont, were challenged by a growing number of multicandidate races. Vermont's constitution required a majority winner for certain statewide races; absent a majority winner, an election would be decided by the vote of a joint assembly of the legislature.

Since judicial review, impeachment, vetoes, and so on were long-established, constitutionally-based processes within government, they provided opportunities for applying the concept of continuing issues. This did not entail reshaping appraisal and processing decisions to meet current topical interests of the property-tax advocates or of the gay-and-lesbian-rights activists. Indeed, the decision was made early on to avoid presenting information on such highly emotive issues as the history of marriage.[21] In each case, the Archives provided a brief summary of the history of a particular process for a quick read by legislators, reporters, and the public. A slightly longer overview of how each process evolved was then provided and, for those who wished to delve further, there were links to copies of the actual records. In order to reach the intended audiences, the continuing issues were presented on the Archives website. Since each legislative committee room, government office, and news service had Internet access, we were able to reach our audiences without requiring them to visit the Archives; equally important, we were able to reach these audiences, notably the legislature, in the rooms where they had to act in response to the court decisions and public expectations.[22]

To give one example, the continuing issue on impeachment had a very brief section linking the issue to House Resolution 35 of 2000, which called for the impeachment of the supreme court justices in the wake of the *Baker* decision. Separate sections gave a quick overview of the history of impeachment in Vermont and a discussion of the impeachment clauses of the Vermont Constitution. Finally, there was a section on the actual impeachment cases that had been addressed by the general assembly over the years.

Since continuing issues addressed core processes of government, they frequently referenced the Vermont Constitution, which set out the basic functions of government as well as the rights of citizens. Therefore, a section on amending the constitution was added to the suite of continuing issues.[23] The "Amending the Constitution" presentation followed the same pattern of brief summaries of different aspects of the process, followed by a history of amendments. One presentation, summarizing the most frequent types of proposals of amendments, clearly became part of the legislative dialogue as supporters or opponents of particular proposals referenced the number of times a proposal had come up and what its fate had been.

The nice thing about continuing issues is that they continue. For example, since we first posted the "Amending the Constitution" presentation, there have been numerous attempts to amend the constitution in order to lengthen terms of office (Vermont is one of only two states with two-year terms for state offices). Outside of adding the new proposals and adjusting the section enumerating the number of times certain proposals have been made, the time needed to update the section is limited. This is a benefit, given the labor-intensive work of putting the original presentations together.

The continuing issue outlining the history of elections where the joint assembly acted in the absence of a majority winner is another telling example.[24] The weak party allegiances within Vermont, coupled with an emerging Progressive Party and the presence of viable independent or third-party candidates, keeps the issue of election by joint assembly almost continually current.[25] This also illustrates the interrelationships among the continuing issues themselves, for discomfort with the majority requirements resulted in turn in proposals to amend the constitution to allow plurality elections, to adopt instant run-off voting, and so on. These proposals were added to the continuing issue section on "Amending the Constitution."

Perhaps the greatest value of the continuing issues initiative, however, lies in translating our own professional shibboleths, such as archival records having a continuing value, into contexts that are understandable—and useful—to our parent institution, and in tying archival records, and the information they contain, into the ongoing decision making of government. In Vermont, where there are few information resources available to the legislature, becoming a source of useful information demonstrated the continuing value of the archival record itself. Linking the archival function to the institutional need to act thus raises awareness of the archives and opens additional opportunities for integrating archival management perspectives into broader institutional activities of the government.

Two examples deserve brief mention. By becoming associated with the ability to know, through the contextual research underpinning continuing issues, the Archives became associated with Vermont's laws governing access to public records (generally referred to as *the right to know*). Secondly, since the continuing issues initiative required understanding government (primarily legislative) business processes and the records they produced, the Archives was increasingly seen as a resource for managing records.[26]

Statutes governing public records grew in an ad hoc fashion over the decades, often leaving government and citizen alike uncertain over which public records were open and which were restricted. This confusion was leavened by growing concerns over the potential threats within public records to privacy and security. To anchor the growing awareness that the archival function touched on government accountability and a rather ill-defined right of privacy, the Archives created an online database to all laws governing access to records that became a resource to government officials, reporters, and citizens.[27]

The second example was the growing understanding within government that the Archives was a resource for helping manage active records rather than only a repository for storing old records. The regular interactions with government officials necessitated by the continuing issues initiative also generated a loose understanding that archival management was an active, rather than passive, function. Identification of the Archives as a resource for understanding statutory mandates governing access to public records further bolstered awareness of the concept of an activist archives.[28]

Government agencies first began to consult with the Archives on how to manage records in compliance with the public records laws; eventually, the Archives received broader inquiries on managing records. While a greater sense of the processes of government helped the Archives respond to such inquiries, better analytical tools were needed to enable it to become truly responsive.

Here again, the work of Helen Samuels in developing institutional functional analysis was important to shaping our odyssey. As with the link between oral history and documentation strategies, there were antecedents to the development of institutional functional analysis. Within Vermont, these antecedents were frequently associated with the application of information technologies to state government.

In 1957 Vermont joined the movement for creating commissions to study the operations of state governments in search of better organizational accountability and efficiency. Known as Little Hoover Commissions, these bodies examined the structures of state governments to see how they could be streamlined. Vermont's Little Hoover Commission used IBM executives (IBM had recently established a plant in Essex Junction, Vermont) to see how centralized data processing could improve government services. Their report recommended that government business processes could best be supported by data processing if government was viewed and restructured along functional lines. Thus all personnel processes should be grouped within a personnel department, all activities related to revenue (tax, fees, etc.) should be grouped within a revenue department, and so on. This early attempt at integrating functions and structures of government had only limited success.[29]

In 1991 Governor Richard Snelling launched the Vermont Information Strategy Plan (VISP), which was a top-down functional approach designed to break down "silos of information" within agencies and departments and allow the cross-boundary sharing of records and information. The Vermont State Archives, through a 1994 grant from the National Historical Publications and Records Commission, became an active participant in VISP planning.[30] VISP proved very labor intensive for the participating agencies and was in place for only a few years beyond Governor Snelling's death in 1991.

Functional analysis reappeared as a government initiative in 2003 under the administration of Governor James H. Douglas. The immediate context, using the same language about information silos and the opportunities presented by information technology, was a strategic enterprise approach. As originally established, the enterprise approach was limited to hardware and software, primarily for the purpose of creating a single state web portal and centralized email and document management systems. Again, an activist mindset was important to initiating contacts with the Department of Information and Innovation (DII) to raise recordkeeping issues that are integral to an enterprise-wide approach.

Like DII, the Archives is a logical vehicle for enterprise-wide initiatives; our responsibilities also cross each branch and agency of government. We already knew that VISP's top-down approach of functional analysis had failed, in part because it is hard to define the enterprise without first defining its parts. By the time the new wave of enterprise-wide initiatives started, the Archives had already decided to build toward a functional view of government by defining records through the business processes they support. This effort was bolstered by the development of a uniform classification scheme, the Vermont Functional Classification System (VCLAS), which addresses not only business processes and records, but also agency histories and legal requirements. VCLAS, in its design, is a documentation strategy that facilitates information gathering and analyses from multiple angles—all of which are critical to archival appraisal.[31]

Another lesson learned from VISP was to identify business processes and records within the scope of defined projects, rather than trying to broadly apply functional analysis across government without real context. The Archives' Targeted Assistance Program (TAP), through which an agency seeking records management assistance can partner with the State Archives, provided the perfect opportunity to do this. Under TAP, the requesting agency must establish a project team where business, information technology (IT), records, and legal perspectives are equally represented and valued before the Archives will agree to a partnership. TAP partnerships have become the epitome of a successful enterprise approach. The insight of each project member is built into our documentation strategy and offers validity checks for ongoing process improvement.

Lacking the resources to fully sustain these efforts by itself, the Archives began collaborating with the Enterprise Project Management Office (EPMO), a relatively new office within DII. The EPMO was already providing project managers for agency IT projects. In addition, EPMO business analysts had started working with agencies to identify business processes and workflows with an eye toward improving these processes through the use of information technologies. From EPMO's point of view, its collaboration with the Archives was equally valuable. All large information technology requests had to be approved by DII, and EPMO knew that state information technology efforts would fall short if the systems they approved could not meet recordkeeping requirements.

Since records management responsibilities were still held by another department, DII, the Archives, and the Department of Buildings and General Services (BGS), which oversaw the records management program, started a voluntary collaborative effort known as Information Strategies: Taskforce on Archives, Records and Technology (iSTART) in 2007. The goal of iSTART is to provide consistent advice on records and information management, including electronic records and electronic recordkeeping systems.[32] In 2008, iSTART's membership was expanded to include the Attorney General's office. With this addition, iSTART's membership now had business, records, IT, and legal representation.

The iSTART program filled a long-standing need within the state of Vermont for consistent guidance and advice on managing records and information. As a result, DII began to rely on iSTART to identify and create standards that agencies and vendors would need to meet before receiving approvals to implement information technology projects. Likewise, the Archives began to rely on iSTART to provide opportunities for working with agencies as part of TAP and other programs. As more interdependencies between the Archives and DII surfaced, Buildings and General Services began to rethink its role in the area of records management. By July 2008, actions taken by the Archives, BGS, and the legislature resulted in the state's records management program being moved to the Vermont State Archives.

With the consolidation of records and archival management under the Archives and the iSTART collaboration, the benefits of our documentation strategy were quickly materializing—bringing us closer to the vision espoused twenty years earlier by Helen Samuels. First, the state Department of Human Resources approved a new job classification—records analyst—and supported the hiring of not one but three analysts to serve a dual purpose within state government: records manager and appraising archivist. Second, state agencies partnering with the State Archives started to see the benefits of functional analysis and how it supports both business processes and records management, particularly in relation to their IT projects.[33] Third, there was no longer an artificial separation between business processes and records management, records management and archives, and business processes and archives: all are documented through VCLAS and all are considered integral partners to our appraisal efforts.[34]

This work is still unfolding as this essay is being written; the odyssey continues. That odyssey began with a sweating oral historian desperately trying to keep up with Helen Samuels as she strode across the MIT campus on my tour now over thirty years ago. I have continued over the years to race to keep up with Helen as she has set out her ideas, stories, and strategies for transforming the archival world and the techniques applied by archivists. I have embraced her call as well for activist archivists—researching, conceptualizing, and strategizing before collecting. Throughout those years, she has freely shared her thoughts and offered her encouragement, to me, and to many other colleagues, in person and in her writing. For that, and for her friendship, she has my gratitude—and her profession's gratitude—for her "continuing" inspiration.

Notes

1 Written communication systems obviously predated the Hellenic Greeks. During the Mycenaean period, the Greeks adopted, and then abandoned, a writing system based on the Babylonian alphabet.

2 Plato, *Phaedrus, The Dialogues of Plato*, trans. B. Jowett (New York: Random House, 1937), vol. 1, 278.

3 There is, however, no clean break between oral and written cultures. Greeks read written text out loud. Well into the nineteenth century, reading was a collective experience within families and public spaces. See, for example, David M. Levy, *Scrolling Forward: Making Sense of Documents in the Digital Age* (New York: Arcade Publishing, 2001), 188; and William J. Gilmore, *Reading Becomes a Necessity of Life: Material and Cultural Life in Rural New England, 1780–1835* (Knoxville: University of Tennessee Press, 1989), 132.

4 Walter J. Ong, "Writing is a Humanizing Technology," *ADE Bulletin* 74 (Spring 1983), http://www.ade.org/ade/bulletin/N074/074013.htm (accessed December 2006).

5 See, for example, Neil Postman, *Conscientious Objections: Stirring up Trouble About Languages, Technology and Education* (New York: Vintage Books, 1988). It was through Postman that I was reintroduced to *Phaedrus.*

6 See, for example, Hugh A. Taylor, "My Very Act and Deed: Some Reflections on the Role of Textual Records in the Conduct of Affairs," *American Archivist* 51 (Fall 1988): 456–69.

7 The American Institute of Physics, where Joan Warnow-Blewett was a pioneering practitioner of the documentation strategy, witnessed a similar partnership. Helen Samuels does not recall any conscious linking of oral history to the subsequent development of her thinking on documentation strategies, but saw the oral history program's cross-discipline/cross-institution approach to documenting a defined issue as "logical and important." Email to author, September 9, 2006.

8 Dr. Saul Benison of the University of Cincinnati strongly anchored his oral history work on written collections; he was also one of those who encouraged Helen Samuels to accept the position at MIT.

9 Charles Morrissey was director of the Aiken Oral History Program and Dr. Samuel Hand was program director. Prior and subsequent to my employment at MIT, I was assistant director of the program.

10 It is interesting to note that several of my colleagues whom I met through professional oral history meetings also went on to careers in state archives. Among these were Jerry Handfield, the

Washington state archivist, and the late Lila Goff, who was the assistant director of the library and archives at the Minnesota Historical Society.

11 Noteworthy among these was fellow Institute Archives' alumna Joan Krizack, who published in 1994 *Documentation Planning for the U.S. Health Care System*, utilizing the documentation strategy approach.

12 Actually, I became editor of state papers, and the Archives was then known as the State Papers Division. This reflected the program's focus on annotating and publishing early state records.

13 For further information on the environment within which the Archives operated, see Gregory Sanford and Tanya Marshall, "Managing Change at the Vermont State Archives," in *Leading and Managing Archives and Records Programs: Strategies for Success*, ed. Bruce W. Dearstyne (New York: Neal-Schuman, 2008).

14 The preservation of the "official correspondence" of governors, mandated in 1864, initially focused on appointments, proclamations, and pardons. Use of the letter-press book led to the preservation of outgoing correspondence. By the 1890s, the advent of filing cabinets and carbon paper led to the capture of incoming and internal correspondence, which then began to include communications with agencies. The first statutory change to the 1864 language was in 1953 to allow the microfilming of gubernatorial records. JoAnne Yates, *Control Through Communication: The Rise of System in American Management* (Baltimore: Johns Hopkins University Press, 1989) is an excellent source on technological influences on recordkeeping.

15 Helen W. Samuels, *Varsity Letters: Documenting Modern Colleges and Universities* (Metuchen, NJ: Scarecrow Press and Society of American Archivists, 1992), 12.

16 I say this only somewhat tongue in cheek. I was often asked, "Why are you interested in my records?" or told to come back when the official had announced impending retirement. An awareness of the need to manage records actively rather than retrospectively was largely absent.

17 On one memorable occasion, I listened to the then-state chief information officer testify against our proposal to adopt professional standards for managing records, since it might entail using international standards written in foreign languages. She did not want a standards-based environment that might undermine expectations that she should rapidly produce off-the-shelf information technology "solutions." To committee members, who were largely unfamiliar with standards, this appeared to be an issue the experts could not resolve among themselves, so they defeated the bill.

18 Neil Postman, "Informing Ourselves to Death," an address to the German Informatics Society, October 11, 1990, http://www.mat.upm.es/~jcm/postman-informing.html (accessed June 2008).

19 Report on the Society and Archives Survey, page 49, available at http://mybestdocs.com (accessed June 2008).

20 The continuing issues initiative predated these decisions, but they did encourage us to shape further and expand our efforts in this initiative.

21 Such a history would have been extremely complex, limited by the paucity of archival records, and unavoidably interpreted through the biases of the opponents and supporters of civil unions, to the detriment of public perceptions of the Archives.

22 Even by providing online access to continuing issues, we could not completely meet the needs of each audience. Here again the interplay of oral and written communications, particularly in a political environment, plays a role. Legislators often want oral testimony further summarizing the online material. By contrast, reporters want quotes from individuals, not documents, for their stories.

23 This also had ties to the public response to *Brigham* and *Baker*, since both inspired efforts to amend the constitution.

24 This issue shows the range of sources that can be drawn from. The last time the joint assembly did not choose the plurality winner was in the 1976 lieutenant-governor's race. Oral interviews revealed that several key legislators were aware that the plurality winner was about to be charged with grand larceny and did not want the office tied up by a criminal investigation and trial.

25 Examples include U.S. Senator Bernie Sanders of Vermont, who runs as an independent, and the Progressives, who have established a sustained legislative presence. During the 2008 gubernatorial election season, newspapers were filled with speculations about there being no majority

winner and the Democrats, who control the legislature, using the joint assembly to elect their candidate over the popular Republican incumbent. This, in turn, has led to increased use of the continuing issues section on majority election found on the Vermont State Archives website.

26 For reasons beyond the scope of this essay, the existing records management program had fallen into some disarray, primarily directing its advice to municipalities rather than the state.

27 One example of the Archives' growing role in accountability issues is provided by the 2005 report of the Legislative Council on Public Records, Privacy, and Electronic Access in Vermont, available at http://vermont-archives.org/publications/legislative/pdf/Public_records_study_report.pdf. The online database is available at http://vermont-archives.org/records/access/index.htm.

28 It is important to note that in an age of "gotcha" journalism and political opposition research, the archives' association with records as evidence can be risky. This is not to underplay accountability as an important role for public archives, but merely serves as a caution that many public officials have had negative experiences with public records in archives being pulled out of context by their opponents or journalists. In Vermont, the use of former Governor Howard Dean's records by opposition researchers to derail his 2004 campaign for the Democratic presidential nomination created as many problems as opportunities for the Archives. Doubtless, too, such negative publicity based on archival records may influence other or future politicians to be somewhat wary of having their records in archives at all.

29 A brief overview of IBM's recommendations is in Gregory Sanford, "Centralized Data Processing: The View From 1957," http://vermont-archives.org/publications/voice/pdf/CentralizedDataProcessing.pdf. That this early attempt at functional analysis did not fully translate into better records management decisions is evidenced by the appraisal decision to preserve the punch cards used by the data processing technology of the time. The record center contains boxes of the cards with no way to retrieve the information they contain.

30 NHPRC grant 94-037. Under the grant, Helen Samuels, Terry Cook, and other experts served as advisors to the project.

31 VCLAS is described at http://vermont-archives.org/records/vclas/index.htm.

32 Information on iSTART is available at http://vermont-archives.org/records/iSTART/index.htm.

33 The records analysts work in tandem with EPMO's project managers and business analysts.

34 The new framework for managing records and the partnerships with DII and EPMO are largely the work of the assistant state archivist, Tanya Marshall, who, under the new combined program, has also become senior records analyst.

THE ARCHIVAL GARDEN: PHOTOGRAPHIC PLANTINGS, INTERPRETIVE CHOICES, AND ALTERNATIVE NARRATIVES

Joan M. Schwartz

> *Was the planting of the garden a kind of map? But the more I explore of the garden and its associations, the more the line is blurred between what is the gardener's story and what is mine. Planting a garden is about making a series of choices, and then the interpretation of those choices also becomes a series of choices. I need to know more about the person who made the garden or I won't be able to decipher any more from the choices that were made there.*[1]

In Helen Humphreys' novel *The Lost Garden*, set on an estate in the Devon countryside of wartime Britain, Gwen Davis, a young horticulturalist, leaves London to volunteer in the Women's Land Army, established to grow crops for the homefront. In the course of clearing the estate for agricultural production, she discovers a trilogy of "lost" gardens, overgrown, but bearing evidence of the original plantings. Amid the nettles, branches, dead plants, and a mass of Sweet Briar Rose, she finds three markers, each bearing a single word: Longing, Loss, and Faith. It is a garden that has been purposefully planted, and Gwen works methodically to interpret the message embedded in it. "To the eye," she notes, "it is not a pleasing array," and it is this very placement of plants that "would never have been arranged together" that leads her to conclude that the garden "has not been planted for the eye. It has been planted for the heart." Gwen concludes that the garden carries a message, told through the original order of the plantings, their relationship to each other at a given time, and the order in which they bloomed. In her efforts to decipher the meaning of the plantings, she also realizes: "There are many ways to tell a story. In opposition to. In sympathy with. What to leave out. What to put in."[2]

The Archival Garden: Form and Function, Technology and Practice

Archives, like gardens, are "about making a series of choices"—choices governing what is preserved and how it is organized and made accessible. History is an interpretation of those choices, involving yet another series of choices. This essay draws attention to the archival photograph as one of the "many ways to tell a story"; to the photographic plantings photographers sow in their decisions of what to record, why, how, and when; to the choices archivists make in arranging these photographic plantings in the archival garden; and to the choices which visitors to the archival garden subsequently make in their interpretation and use of photographic cuttings taken from the archival garden.

Archives, like history, has traditionally been a "discipline of words."[3] Equally, questions asked by archivists, like those posed by historians, "have usually not been phrased in ways that photographic data can answer directly."[4] This logocentrism of archives persists, even as avenues of communication and modes of documentation move from paper-based to electronic forms, and even as archivists educated as historians are replaced by "heritage professionals" trained in archival or information "science." Despite archival angst over relatively recent shifts—from paper to digital, from custodial to postcustodial realms of records creation and archival preservation—little attention has been paid by archivists and archival educators to the changing relationships between human observers and image-based technologies of communication. But as Lisa Gitelman and Geoffrey Pingree astutely point out, all media were once new media.[5] In this simple observation is a caveat for archivists: society is documented in many ways and documentation comes in many forms: words—whether written, printed, or spoken—communicate what we can describe; numbers convey what we can count or measure; images record what we can see. We choose one form over another, or employ more than one form in concert, to achieve the degree of truthfulness or completeness which is possible, desired, or required. In documenting society in archives, just as in seeking to understand society through its archival documents, we employ forms of documentation according to our abilities, both intellectual and technological: to master the written word or the word processor; to collect or analyze numerical data; to generate or decipher statistical information; to draw or read maps; to produce or comprehend sketches or diagrams; to take or interpret photographs.

The form of a document is shaped by technologies and practices which vary across space and time; that is to say, by the tools—for communicating, for recording, for preserving—which society has at its disposal and by the ways in which individuals or groups, corporations or governments, choose to employ them. Photography is one such tool, and photographs must be understood as the product of practices, applications, or circumstances which are technologically determined, historically situated, socially and culturally constituted, and gendered. They must also be understood, not simply as visual images, but as the visual residue of acts of communication, shaped by the equipment and processes of image-making, and by the assumptions and knowledge, values and beliefs, of the society in which they were originally created and subsequently circulated and viewed.

The function of a document—what it was created to do—and the authority with which it is vested are embedded in its informational content and in its presentational form. In appraising and describing some documents, visual documents in particular, presentational form is overlooked or marginalized as an element of meaning-making, and, all too often, function is conflated with informational content. Without resorting to the rigidly deterministic analysis of diplomatics, interrogation of a document requires an understanding of all elements of meaning-making and their transformations over space and time. It must also be acknowledged that the meaning invested in a document by its author is not necessarily delivered intact to its intended audience, for elements of meaning-making are only made meaningful upon reception and in terms of potential audience frameworks of knowledge and strategies of understanding.

Writing about the relationship between photography and autobiography, Linda Haverty Rugg proceeds from the observation that the invention of photography transformed the way we picture ourselves.[6] Photography also transformed the way society pictures itself and the way we document society. This essay addresses that transformation. It examines the ways in which photographs document society, and asks what it is that archives preserve when they acquire photographs. It assumes that documentation, preservation, and interpretation are all acts which involve choices: choices of, choices by, and choices for. Through a series of close contextual readings of a single photograph, this essay investigates those choices and the alternative narratives which emerge from them. Drawing a critical distinction between archival matters of fact and historical matters of meaning, this foray into the metaphorical archival garden will offer insights which have far-ranging consequences for the ways in which archivists—as well as historians, curators, and other heritage professionals—appraise, acquire, arrange, process, describe, or use visual materials. It will also serve to dismantle further the notion that archivists operate only as Jenkinsonian stewards of fact and do not impose meaning on the records in their care.

In this essay, I adapt, not adopt, Helen Samuels' key thinking about documentation strategy and institutional functional analysis; in doing so, I suggest not only the ways in which her key ideas have spawned new applications, but also, and perhaps more importantly, why archivists must be open to considering, testing, and tweaking new approaches to archival materials, from within and also from without the world of archives. In documentation strategy, Samuels unravelled the contexts of inter-institutional records creation, and thus the need for collaboration among archivists responsible for those institutions' records and related private and personal records, as well as the need to work within broader intellectual spheres of meaning-making—libraries, literature, museums. In her institutional functional analysis, she examined the functional context of hundreds of record systems and scores of activities within a single, large institution, such as a modern university.

I have drawn inspiration from these two models, by extrapolating beyond the multi-institutional universe of documentation strategy, beyond the multidimensional universe of institutional functional analysis, to focus on a single photograph. I also look to scholars, across a range of disciplines—perhaps most notably anthropology—who have explored the importance of context to understanding a single artifact in terms of its creation, purpose, and use.[7] However, from Helen, despite her focus on multi-institutional strategy or multifunctional analysis, and mine on a single photograph, I draw five lessons: (1) that context in archives extends beyond the principles of simple provenance and original order; (2) that photographs "function"; (3) that it is critically important to understand the functional context of creation and the documentary universe of circulation of photographs, and indeed all archival materials, as deeply as possible before intelligent action can be taken by the archivist; (4) that central to such action is a commitment to research by the archivist into such context, not as a luxury, but as a necessity, to gain the knowledge crucial to the success of the archival mission; and (5) that greater emphasis on "function" and "functionality" of the sponsorship, creation, technological origins, multiple uses, receptions, and distributions of photographs can shed great light on their nature and role as records, rather than focusing primarily on their subject content or the fame of their creator/photographer. In these ways, Helen Samuels' contributions to archival thinking can be seen to have interpretive clout beyond the explicit strategies that she developed.

I take as my central premise that, if archivists wish to document society in all its richness and complexity—as Helen Samuels has so wisely urged and, indeed, taught us to do—we must first understand how a society creates tools to document itself and why, what the choice of tools signifies, and what elements of meaning-making different tools generate. This matter, and more specifically the way in which archivists engage with photographs, has long concerned me. Here, I proceed from these lessons learned from Helen to explore ideas which swirl in and through William England's 1859 view of the suspension bridge at Niagara (see figure 1).[8] Unlike unique, camera-made positives, such as mid-nineteenth-century daguerreotypes or late-twentieth-century Polaroids, William England's photograph of the Niagara Suspension Bridge was produced in multiple prints, circulated in diverse contexts, and is now preserved in different institutions. Its meaning is not fixed, nor wholly contained within the image, but rather is dynamic, formed and reformed by the contexts in which it was created and subsequently viewed, shaped and reshaped by disciplinary perspectives and institutional discourse.

FIGURE 1: *William England, "The Niagara Suspension Bridge," 1859. Albumen print, 236 x 280 mm, on plain cardboard mount 465 x 582 mm. Library and Archives Canada: Edward McCann Collection, 1988-286, PA-165997.*

What follows is a demonstration of how a single photograph can be tracked and unpacked across multiple sites of meaning-making in an effort to situate and understand the documentary power of the image within the contexts of its creation, circulation and viewing, and subsequent preservation and use. In so doing, I peel back the layers and relationships which gave it, and continue to give it, meaning, using the photograph as a research tool, a conduit to choices made at the point of records creation in order to reveal how society documented itself visually, and why. Ultimately, I argue that in "documenting society" this photograph furnishes evidence which goes well beyond the visual facts contained in the image, and that in probing the choices it manifests, alternative narratives—with lessons for both visual literacy and archival practice—clearly emerge.

Photographic Plantings and Initial Choices

In 1859, William England, chief photographer for the London Stereoscopic Company (LSC), was dispatched to North America to fill a gap in the company's inventory. England spent six months in the United States and Canada taking photographs, both single and stereoscopic, as part of a project by the company to produce its first series of New World views.[9] He produced more than two hundred stereoscopic and fewer than a dozen 10-by-12-inch wet-collodion glass negatives; his large-plate views include images of the Natural Bridge, Virginia; Falls on the Passaic River, New Jersey; the Genesee River, New York; the St. Lawrence at Quebec; and the St. Lawrence and Victoria Bridge at Montreal. However, most of his single landscape views were taken at Niagara; there is one of the Spiral Staircase and Table Rock; two views of the American Falls; one of the GWR locomotive "Essex" at Clifton Depot; and three views of the suspension bridge. England's views of the Falls themselves were praised as "wonderful examples of the vividness with which, in skillful hands, photographs may be made to reproduce even the most fleeting grandeur of these tremendous cataracts."[10]

"The Niagara Suspension Bridge" was taken in 1859 by William England for the London Stereoscopic Company. This simple statement linking subject, date, photographer, and publisher is important, not because England's name necessarily belongs to the pantheon of prominent nineteenth-century photographers, but because it connects the material evidence to a historically-situated observer, and raises issues of authorship, authority, and audience. In it, we confront the "choices by" both photographer and publisher, as well as the "choices of" the general occasion in history and specific moment of exposure, and the "choices for" particular audiences. It also suggests links between photographer, technology, and society. Exploring these relationships establishes the original commercial, intellectual, and political contexts of creation, circulation, and viewing.

William England was in his forties when he photographed the recently completed suspension bridge at Niagara. He was an experienced photographer whose intellectual baggage, visual imagination, and photographic practice were shaped by being a British commercial photographer in the mid-Victorian era. He went to North America on assignment, charged with the task of producing commercially viable views. He arrived at a time when civil strife was brewing in the United States as tensions mounted between the North and the South over the slavery question, and as British interest in North America ran high with the first royal visit to take place the following year for the official opening of the Victoria Bridge.[11] It was also a time when railroads and bridges held enormous fascination.

England's work was framed by the marketing requirements of the London Stereoscopic Company. In composing the scene, in recording the train in the middle of the bridge, in arranging the family in the foreground, England exercised judgment in portraying the material reality which confronted him. Yet, however creative or artistic England may have wished to be, his landscape photography was ultimately circumscribed by his relationship to a commercial operation seeking lucrative images. "The Niagara Suspension Bridge" was not created for the purpose of promoting North America as a tourist destination, or encouraging immigration to Canada. What England photographed must, therefore, be seen as a reflection of anticipated audience interests. His views, intended for mass distribution, had to have wide appeal among the middle- and upper-class buying public. This distinction, between England as the photographer and the London Stereoscopic Company as the publisher of "The Niagara Suspension Bridge," recognizes the power relations that existed between the company and its chief photographer, and acknowledges that England's North American views were produced within a corporate agenda. Of course, authorial intention does not always translate into audience impact. The existence of the image bears witness to the former; assessment of the latter is far more problematical. As will be seen, a review of the LSC series in *The Art-Journal* sheds light on contemporary reception, albeit in the usual journalistic rhetoric. Personal responses to England's views, penned in diaries or letters, have not been located.

William England's photograph of the suspension bridge at Niagara warrants "unpacking"; to do so, I adopt an approach of layered looking. I shall proceed in stages which mirror its contexts of creation, circulation, viewing, preservation, and use. Beginning with his single albumen print "The Niagara Suspension Bridge," I explore its elements of meaning-making, first in the individual image, then in its relationship to its stereoscopic counterpart and the series of which it was a part, then through a comparison of that series with the series which William Notman, the preeminent Canadian photographer based in Montreal, published at the very same time. Having come to some conclusions about the meaning of this one image in these various contexts, I then look briefly at the way in which the elements of its meaning-making are subsequently privileged or marginalized—indeed shaped, obscured, or subverted—by disciplinary perspectives and institutional practices which frame the ways in which we see and understand this image today. My aim is to show, if not explicitly then through examples, that our use of historical photographs (or other visual sources, for that matter) must begin with an awareness of the questions we ask and what the viewer—be it the creator of the image, the nineteenth-century viewer, or the twenty-first century user of archives—brings to the looking. What emerges is a sense of the competing—and perhaps complementary—visions of place and ways of documenting society reflected and constructed within the image, within the series, across series, across disciplines, and across institutions.

William England, "The Niagara Suspension Bridge," 1859: Visual Image, Physical Object

William England's photograph, "The Niagara Suspension Bridge," shows the famous wire-hung bridge built by the great Prussian-born American civil engineer, John Augustus Roebling (1806–1869), nineteenth-century North America's answer to Britain's Isambard Kingdom Brunel. The bridge spanned the Niagara Gorge about a mile and a half below the Falls. This photograph provided viewers with visual information about the construction and proportions of the bridge, details about the towers, the trusswork, and the train. It also records the local topography of the Niagara Gorge—the height of the gorge, the geological stratification—as well as the dock for the *Maid of the Mist* tour boat and mid-nineteenth-century costume. In so doing, it stands as a document about the society which both produced and consumed it, a society enthralled with signs of progress, fascinated with feats of engineering, and struggling with the findings of both Charles Lyell and Charles Darwin.

"The Niagara Suspension Bridge" is an albumen print from a wet-collodion negative, and cannot be understood apart from the historicity and specificity of the photographic processes and practices which brought it into being and made it look the way it does. The state of photographic technology available to England required that he transport camera, chemicals, and dark tent down the escarpment to the river's edge. The long exposure transformed the churning waters of the Niagara River, making their way from the cauldron at the base of the Falls to the mouth of the Gorge, into a flat surface of soft swirls. The scene is all the more remarkable for the fact that it was not a chance shot, a moment snatched from the passage of time, an instantaneous or even spontaneous composition. It was premeditated, meticulously planned, and carefully composed in order to take full advantage of the fact that trains stopped regularly on the bridge to give passengers a view of the Falls and the Gorge. Such a scheduled stop would have required England to plan his actions well in advance: to set up his dark tent, to arrange the family in the foreground, and, at the last minute, to coat his glass plate just prior to exposure in the camera, and then develop it immediately after. The fact that he recorded the scene in both single and stereoscopic format at the same time attests to his assessment of the market appeal of the scene as well as to his careful timing of the whole operation.

This view would have generated meaning for viewers at the time in several ways, and can be interrogated accordingly: as a pictorial composition in the context of other visual images, whether painted, printed, or photographed; as one image in the LSC series of views of America; as a material object produced in different physical formats; and as a cultural text, the meaning of which was embedded in prevailing ideas about suspension bridges, Niagara Falls, and North America. These all bear examination; however, the degree to which it sold, and entered the Victorian imagination, was a function of its market appeal. As John Szarkowski, curator of photography at the Museum of Modern Art, New York, has suggested, this photograph "reflects almost perfectly the chief interests of mid-nineteenth-century photography . . . everything of the most favored subject matter of the period except an ancient architectural monument—generally unavailable to photographers working this country."[12] It clearly included something for everyone—scenery, human interest, an engineering marvel. Here was a sublime place inspiring awe, a wonder of Nature, the Gorge and its geological strata; here too was a site of Man's mastery over Nature, the *Maid of the Mist* dock in the foreground and the family—tourists, perhaps?—posed along the shore revealing Nature tamed. The bridge demonstrated the way in which human ingenuity was able to overcome natural obstacles. The train was a symbol of progress. The only element missing from the scene was a Tuskaroara basketweaver or beadwork seller to satisfy the prevailing interest in the aboriginal peoples of far-off places, a subject documented by England in his stereoscopic view "Group of Indian Women at Bead Work, Goat Island, Niagara."

The way in which this image generated meaning derived, in part, from its materiality as a physical object. "The Niagara Suspension Bridge" was one of the few views produced in whole-plate, as well as in stereoscopic format. Its presentation as a single mounted print communicated meaning within a hierarchy of economic and cultural factors. Its production as a card-mounted stereoscopic view with letterpress title, logo, and text within a series devoted to American scenery followed a very different social trajectory, bearing less prestige but carrying greater impact. That William England chose to record this scene in both formats may be taken as indicative of the anticipated market appeal of their respective circulation trajectories.

Of particular interest was the bridge itself. William England would have been well aware of the prevailing fascination with bridges which had flourished in Britain since the opening of Thomas Telford's great Menai and Conway suspension bridges in 1826 began a period of bridge building which saw the opening of Isambard Kingdom Brunel's Chepstow Bridge over the Wye in 1852 and his Royal Albert Bridge at Saltash seven years later. Work on Brunel's Clifton Suspension Bridge over the Avon Gorge at Bristol—even longer than Roebling's, although not intended for railway use—had been suspended since 1854, and would not be completed until after his death.

In his book *American Technological Sublime*, David Nye distinguishes between dynamic forms of the technological sublime in which space and time were conquered by the telegraph, the steamboat, and the railroad, and static forms of the technological sublime in which obstacles and forces of Nature were conquered by bridges and skyscrapers. He also suggests that natural wonders such as Niagara Falls "became emblems of divinity comparable to the wonders of the ancient world and the greatest architectural achievements of modern times."[13] Thus England's view of the bridge, the train, and the gorge would have commanded considerable public attention. Here, in "The Niagara Suspension Bridge," the "dynamic sublime" of the railroad, the "static sublime" of the bridge, and the "natural sublime" of the gorge converged. The photograph offered a view of this "utilitarian monument" which combined "beauty, science, and service," and which "symbolized technology, progress, and patriotism in the national consciousness."[14] A favourite subject of painters, photographers, and lithographers,[15] the suspension bridge at Niagara became "almost as great an attraction as the Falls themselves."[16] Upon completion of the bridge, Roebling wrote to his family, "The passage of trains is a great sight, worth seeing."[17] But for others, the experience of crossing by carriage was terrifying. After crossing the suspension bridge in 1869, Mark Twain wrote:

> You drive over to Suspension Bridge and divide your misery between the chances of smashing down two hundred feet into the river below, and the chances of having a railway train overhead smashing down onto you. Either possibility is discomforting taken by itself, but, mixed together, they amount in the aggregate to positive unhappiness.[18]

Part of what Patrick McGreevy has called the "complex intertextuality" of the cultural landscape of Niagara Falls,[19] "The Niagara Suspension Bridge" is representative of contemporary portrayals of both Niagara Falls and feats of civil engineering, and may be viewed as an expression of the geographical engagement with Niagara Falls as well as a manifestation of nineteenth-century curiosity about place and the role of photography in satisfying the armchair traveller. The elements of the composition symbolize many of the interests of the mid-Victorian era. In emphasizing the wonder of Nature, feats of engineering, and symbols of progress, this single image would have held enormous fascination for the nineteenth-century viewer back in London. As an image mass-produced for public consumption, it was also a site where notions of place and identity were confirmed and constructed, although one is left to ponder the differences in the meanings generated, and the popularity acquired, by this image between European and North American audiences. England's choice and portrayal of subject matter configured meaning. Regardless of the optical precision and commercial intent with which "The Niagara Suspension Bridge" was produced, the placement of the frame, by determining what was included and what was excluded, was far from innocent; the facts depicted were not without meaning or effect.

Having suggested what the photograph is *of,* and what the photograph is *about,* let me consider what "The Niagara Suspension Bridge" might have been created *to do.* At a basic level, it was created to extend the powers of human observation across space, becoming both a surrogate and a pre-text for travel. In the production of geographical knowledge, it served as a way of bringing to detached and distant observers what was visible, and giving them a basis for visualizing what, otherwise, was not immediately within view. Statistics and dimensions took on textures and proportions, and allowed viewers to get some sense of this remarkable bridge: two roadways with a semi-enclosed carriageway on the lower level and a railroad track on the upper deck; the open timber trusswork; the single span supported by four cables draped over plain masonry towers; all designed by Roebling to accommodate the problem of heavy moving trainloads and high winds in the gorge. However, there are also important aspects of the landscape in this photograph which cannot be seen but, when imagined, are powerful elements of meaning-making: the international boundary bisecting the bridge, the gorge, and the train, as well as the track, laid with mixed gauge to accommodate both the broad gauge of the Great Western Railway of Canada and the standard gauge of the New York Central.

While discussion of this photograph has invariably focused on the bridge and the train, with parenthetical reference to the dock in the foreground, the stratigraphy of the gorge in the distance has eluded art-historical comment. However, to contemporary viewers of England's image, the layers of rock, seen clearly in the detail which the wet-collodion negative was able to produce on albumen paper, would have been freighted with religious and historical significance. At the time, advances in geology called into question prevailing ideas about the age of the Earth. In the seventeenth century, the Anglican bishop and theologian James Ussher had established the first day of Creation to be Sunday, October 23, 4004 BC. His computation, based on biblical sources, historical accounts, and astronomical tables, became the accepted chronology for Christendom when it was incorporated into an authorized version of the Bible printed in 1701. But Charles Lyell's *Principles of Geology: Being an Attempt to Explain the Former Changes of the Earth's Surface by Reference to Causes now in Operation* (1830–1833), suggested otherwise and changed the way Victorian viewers would have interpreted the sedimentary layers exposed in the Niagara Gorge.[20] The book, which had gone through no fewer than nine editions by the time the London Stereoscopic Company dispatched William England to the New World, presented the view that the Earth was far older than Bishop Ussher had established, and the Niagara Gorge was singled out for attention in Lyell's subsequent *Travels in North America, Canada, and Nova Scotia with Geological Observations.* In chapter 2 he noted:

> . . . some Daguerreotype representations of the Falls have been executed with no small success. They not only record the form of the rocks and islands, but even the leading features of the cataract, and the shape of the clouds of spray. I often wished that Father Hennepin could have taken one of these portraits, and bequeathed it to the geologists of our times. It would have afforded no slight aid in our speculations respecting the comparative state of the ravine in the 19th and 17th centuries.[21]

It was not only Lyell's work in geology which would have focused attention on the layers of sedimentary rock in the Niagara Gorge. The year which saw William England tour Canada and the United States for the London Stereoscopic Company also witnessed the publication of Charles Darwin's *On the Origin of Species.* Darwin had read Lyell's *Principles of Geology* during his voyage on HMS *Beagle,* and his theory of evolution only further undermined Ussher's biblical chronology. Just as Darwin was influenced by Lyell, so Lyell became a proponent of evolution, publishing *Geological Evidences of the Antiquity of Man*[22] at the very time that England's view was circulating in both the Old and the New World. In the context of the circulation of these ideas about geological time and species evolution, the stratigraphy of the Niagara Gorge would have appealed to the popular imagination and imparted particular meaning to England's photograph. Indeed, as David Nye has pointed out, looking down the stratigraphic layers became an exercise in looking back in time.[23]

In the mid-nineteenth century, there was great distrust of suspension bridges for the simple reason that so many of them—in Britain, France, and the United States—had collapsed over the years, frequently with tragic loss of life. In 1831, for example, the suspension bridge near Manchester, England, failed when the rhythmic tread of a company of troops marching in step set up such a violent harmonic motion that a pin in one of the suspension chains broke, and the bridge collapsed at one end. Hence the army rule, often ridiculed as superstition, that troops should break step when crossing a bridge. Little wonder that, in 1845, when it was proposed to span the Niagara Gorge with a suspension bridge to carry not just foot traffic but also carriage and railway traffic, the experts declared the scheme impossible. Vibrations from such a heavy load, they insisted, would destroy a wire-hung bridge.[24] In May 1854, the summer before Roebling's suspension bridge at Niagara was completed, the Wheeling suspension bridge over the Ohio River collapsed when a high wind produced a series of undulations; the bridge was destroyed as the momentum of its own weight acquired a force stronger than the cables supporting it. No lives were lost in the Wheeling catastrophe, but it aroused all the old fears about suspension bridges. In the context of such concerns about safety, the visual information presented by "The Niagara Suspension Bridge" offered a form of evidence, furnishing nineteenth-century viewers with proof that the experts were wrong, and offering assurance to a nervous public that a delicate wire-hung suspension bridge could, indeed, withstand the stress of a moving train.[25]

The London Stereoscopic Company, "The Niagara Suspension Bridge," Stereoscopic View, 1860

At the same time that William England took his large-plate view of the suspension bridge at Niagara, he also produced a stereoscopic view using a twin-lens camera (see figures 2a and 2b). His two images, though similar in visual content, are very different physical objects which circulated and generated meaning in very different ways. The stereoscopic view, when seen through a special viewing device, gave the realistic illusion of three-dimensional space. Although the principles of stereoscopic vision had long been known, it was only in 1851 that Sir David Brewster's lenticular stereoscope, first described in 1844, was exhibited to great acclaim at the Great Exhibition in London. Having attracted the attention of Queen Victoria and the Prince Consort, it became enormously popular as an instrument of both entertainment and education. That same year, the advent of Frederick Scott Archer's wet-collodion process for producing negatives on glass permitted industrialization of stereo photography and the mass-production of card-mounted albumen print stereoscopic views for the commercial market. By the time William England set off for the New World, the London Stereoscopic Company boasted an inventory of one hundred thousand different views.

"The Niagara Suspension Bridge" was produced and marketed as part of the London Stereoscopic Company's series, *America in the Stereoscope*.[26]

FIGURES 2A AND 2B: *William England #18 –"The Niagara Suspension Bridge," 1859. Card-mounted stereoscopic albumen print from the series* America in the Stereoscope, *published ca. 1860. Recto, purple mount with gold lettering; verso, light blue with American eagle logo. Library and Archives Canada: Phillips Collection, 1987-022, PA-200389 (recto), PA-200390 (verso).*

The cards sold for $5 per dozen for coloured views, $4 per dozen for plain; the series was also available for purchase as a complete set in a handsome gold-lettered case. The difference of size and format between the single print and the stereoscopic view was not simply a matter of cost and prestige. In stereo format, the image circulated more widely, but it was also viewed under different circumstances, and understood in different ways. While the subject matter was readily discernible at a glance on the card, the excitement of viewing the scene in glorious three-dimensions was a deliberate, haptic experience—a performance of sorts—which required the card to be selected from a box and placed in a viewer which was then brought to the eyes. The subject matter was also to be appreciated in a specific context provided by printed information on the verso of the card. Each stereoscopic view in the LSC series was accompanied by "a brief but carefully written description . . . , giving such particulars as are requisite for a complete comprehension of the theme, in its grandeur, or its beauty, or its combination of both."[27]

The descriptive text affixed to the verso of the card-mounted stereoscopic view of the bridge read:

> This Bridge, as it now stands (occupying the site of a bridge by a Mr. Charles Elliott [Ellet]), was constructed under the direction of Mr. John A. Roebling, at a cost of 500,000 dollars, and crosses the Niagara River at a point about two miles below the Falls. Its total length, from centre to centre of the towers, is 800 feet; its height above the water, 258 feet; and its width, 24 feet. Like Goldsmith's bed, it contrives 'a double debt to pay,' being used for both railway and ordinary traffic, the carriage and footway being 28 feet below the floor of the railway tracks. It was first crossed by a locomotive, March 8th, 1855.[28]

This brief paragraph framed the way in which the scene pictured on the recto of the card was to be viewed and understood—through reference to the great engineer who designed it, its considerable cost, its geographical location, its physical dimensions, its two-fold utilitarian service, and the relative recency of its inaugural use. Situated within, and constructed by, the larger context of the company's promotional catalogue and the other images and verso texts, the stereoscopic view belongs to a series which combines both visual and verbal representations and offers a substantial narrative in its own right. That narrative can then be examined for the ways in which it complements or supplements, confirms or contests, perceptions of place constructed by other authors, by other series, and through other evidentiary sources.

While we may claim that words framed the act of viewing, it is instructive to note how the caption printed on the front of a card sometimes differed from or was amplified by the title of the extended text printed on the back of the card mount. For example, England's view captioned "Rustic Bridge at Sleepy Hollow, Tarrytown, New York" on the recto shows not just another "rustic bridge"; the title, "Rustic Bridge, Sleepy Hollow. Scene of Washington Irving's 'Headless man,'" on the verso frames the viewing more specifically. The accompanying text further amplifies the literary connection:

> Sleepy Hollow, which is situated about two miles above Tarry Town, a village on the Hudson River, is well known, by name at least, to most lovers of legendary lore as being the spot where the Headless Horseman in Washington Irving's "Legend of Sleepy Hollow" indulged in his equestrian feats. The bridge over which Ichabod Crane was pursued by the same horseman, and the old Dutch church to which the luckless pedagogue fled for sanctuary, are still there, and form objects of interest to the tourist.

Here, then, is the spot of literary legend and a destination "of interest to the tourist"; the view puts a "face" to a place "well known, by name at least."

In July 1860, *The Art-Journal* credited England's North American photographs with bringing people into "closer and safer acquaintance with the New World than all the books that have been written on the subject."[29] This statement positions us squarely at the intersection of discourses of photography, travel, and geography; highlights the role of photographs in the vicarious experience of place; and acknowledges their function in the construction of ideas about North American reality.

The response to England's North American views in *The Times* (London) articulated prevailing ideas about photographic seeing:

> It is hardly too much praise to say that a good set of stereoscopic views is equal in interest to a good book of travels, with all those additional advantages which the former must derive from giving us their quick, life-like glimpses into costumes, manners, and modes of life of all kinds, and reproducing with minute fidelity the scenery which is always so characteristic of a people. Stereoscopes, in fact, anticipate travel. The peculiar genius of the Egyptians, as manifested in their rock-hewn temples and colossal monuments, can be appreciated and understood in beautiful little stereoscopes without quitting an arm-chair. The great pictorial features of British India are familiar to millions who have never been within the tropics. We can study and admire the sacred shrines of the Holy Land, and look with something like dismay on those arid plains which spread in a sea of hot sand round Mounts Horeb and Sinai. Robertson has made the mosques of Constantinople and the ruined temples of the Aegean as familiar as Tintern or Melrose.[30]

Here was an expression of faith in the ability of the photograph to allow the viewer to "travel . . . with all the vividness of reality." Here is evidence of the function of the photograph to serve as a vehicle of vicarious experience. Here is the basis for claiming that William England's images framed perceptions of the New World transmitted through *America in the Stereoscope*. But where were armchair travellers led on William England's stereoscopic grand tour of the New World?

Canadian cards included views of Montmorenci [sic] River and Falls, Montreal streets, the Chaudiere Falls, Quebec and the Citadel, the Rideau Falls, the Victoria Bridge, and views around the new capital of Ottawa. British North America was thus limited to the central United Province of Canada, which at the time consisted of the southern portions of what is now Quebec and Ontario (then called Canada East and Canada West). Most of *America in the Stereoscope* focused on picturesque river, mountain, and sylvan scenes. City views and historic sites were far outnumbered by views of "gaps" and "gorges"; "natural" and "rustic" bridges; and above all "cascades" and "falls"—with Niagara Falls being singled out for particular attention. Intended primarily for a European market, views of sublime nature and pastoral landscapes offered mental, if not physical, respite from the noise and bustle of the city, and allowed viewers to escape vicariously to the peaks and cascades of the Catskills, scenic spots along the Hudson and Passaic Rivers, geological formations in the White Mountains of New Hampshire, the glens of Upper New York State, or the brink of Niagara Falls to appreciate landscape and, through contemplation of the handiwork of Nature, commune with God. Ultimately, *America in the Stereoscope* delivered a safe, culturally sanitized, and physically insulated introduction of the New World to the armchair traveller. The "checkered beauties of cataract and river, lake and mountain"[31] presented a narrative about fresh air, clean water, and open spaces to the city dweller, especially in London, whose inhabitants were living in increasingly industrialized surroundings and unsanitary conditions during this age of coal fires, soot fogs, air-borne "miasmas," and the "Great Stink of 1858." These images confirmed for them that an Arcadian existence still existed somewhere. The London Stereoscopic Company's photographic "Grand Tour" of North America perpetuated the preconceived ideas and preexisting itineraries of various travellers' published accounts and literary tours, reinforcing an imaginative geography of North America which portrayed the United States and Canada as sufficiently urbanized to affirm the presence of western civilization, yet largely Edenic to offer respite from European urbanization and industrialization. Ultimately, authorial intention does not always translate into audience impact. The existence of the image bears witness to the former; assessment of the latter is far more problematical.

There is a narrative implicit within a series of stereoscopic views. England's images were not only individual records of facts, in glorious three-dimensional detail, about a given location, but they also worked through selection and sequencing to form a geographical tour with an embedded social narrative. That narrative lies not simply in the accuracy of representation, but more importantly in the choice, order, and description of subjects. Physical presentation not only shaped the viewing process, but underlined seriality through card-mount colour, imprint, logo, labels, and descriptive text. *America in the Stereoscope* was issued initially on cream-coloured mounts; subsequent series appeared with the New York City imprint on red mounts, and with the London imprint on purple mounts. The verso of each card also bore an emblem with patriotic resonance: the United States views carried the American eagle; Canadian scenes displayed the British coat of arms. Textual descriptions—sometimes prose, sometimes poetry, sometimes both—on the verso of each card were an integral part of a process in which verbal and visual representations joined forces to provide both entertainment and education. The labels of booksellers and printsellers, in places as diverse as London and Weston-super-Mare on one side of the Atlantic, to Boston and Philadelphia on the other, attest to both the company's methods of distribution and its considerable geographical reach.

Competing Images and Complementary Imaginings: William England and William Notman

The LSC's *America in the Stereoscope* was not the only major series of stereoscopic views published in 1860. That same year, Montreal photographer William Notman issued a series of over five hundred views for the stereoscope. The two series are strikingly different in their portrayals of the United States and Canada, one offering an escape from Old World industrialization, the other highlighting evidence of New World progress. Notman's views attracted attention in the *Illustrated London News* when they formed part of a gift presented to the Prince of Wales on the occasion of his visit to open the Victoria Bridge. The gift took the form of a bird's-eye maple box with leather-bound portfolios of single and stereoscopic views: 54 sheets of stout bristol board, 10 with "the largest sized plates yet taken in Canada," 13 with two views of "ordinary dimensions," and 31 with nine stereopairs on each. It is these stereoviews, subsequently printed and offered for sale to the public, which form what has come to be known as the *Maple Box* series.[32]

The views produced for inclusion in the *Maple Box* were subsequently marketed to the public as card-mounted stereos. They were also offered for sale as half-stereos for inclusion in albums. Titles were listed in Notman's twenty-six-page catalogue of more than five hundred items, complete with a testimonial from the *Illustrated London News*, and notices for his photographs of the Victoria Bridge "in all its stages of construction" mounted on "Demy Bristol Board" at $2 each, and a few large, 22-by-18-inch views from various points of the completed bridge for $5 each. Only one copy of the original catalogue has been located, in tattered condition, in the Toronto Reference Library. The text, advertising, and list of titles offer insights into the nature of the series as well as Notman's marketing savvy. In the catalogue, Notman also advertised revolving stereoscopic viewers for sale, no doubt as a way to boost sales.[33]

Notman promoted his series as "Comprising the leading Cities, River & Lake Scenery, the Victoria Bridge and Niagara Falls," with "new views being continually added." Cards sold for $4.50 per dozen, a price which compared favourably with the LSC charge of $4.00 per dozen. In November 1860, *The Art-Journal* judged Notman's series to be "of great merit"—skillfully manipulated, artistically arranged, and judiciously selected. "They give us, indeed, almost a perfect idea of the interesting country which is just now attracting special attention in England—the ties that bind us to our valuable colony have been drawn closer and closer by recent events."[34] Foremost of the "recent events" was the visit of the Prince of Wales to open the Victoria Bridge in Montreal and lay the cornerstone of the Parliament Buildings in Ottawa earlier that year.

Just as it is important to link William England to his role as chief photographer for the London Stereoscopic Company, so it is important to situate William Notman in time and place in order to understand what each man brought to the act of looking and to the practice of photography. Notman had arrived in Canada in 1856 having left his native Scotland to escape the legal repercussions of "some creative accounting."[35] He was a shrewd and ambitious businessman. Quick to recognize an opportunity and keen to establish a professional reputation, Notman took the initiative, not only to document the construction of the Victoria Bridge, but also to prepare the gift for the Prince of Wales.[36] As his work in the 1860s would later show, he was politically astute, and his portraits, views, and photographically illustrated books were aimed at Montreal's elite, whose fortunes were tied to nation-building and economic development. Notman's vision was not that of the imperial centre or the peripatetic photographer; rather, his was tied to the future of the place he now chose to call home. His work celebrated achievements and possibilities, took advantage of market opportunities, and benefitted from the individual dreams and collective aspirations of his clientele.

These two series can be studied as products of, and participants in, the processes by which the landscape myths and metaphors of North America were established. Embedded in the imaginative space defined by selection and ordering, image and text, there reside carefully crafted narratives about place. Both series shared a focus on Niagara Falls. Both series have certain subjects in common, especially natural and man-made attractions. For example, the Tuskaroara curiosity sellers, popular around the Falls as a tourist attraction in their own right, were photographed by both England and Notman.[37] However, there is also a fundamental difference in the format of the LSC and Notman stereoviews: whereas the LSC card mounts present the viewer with an extensive text on the verso, Notman's offer only the series number and title. Might this reveal Notman's assumption that his audience was primarily local and, therefore, knowledgeable about the geography of British North America? Where the LSC series paid perfunctory attention to North American cities and emphasized Arcadian scenes, Notman's extensive series was a tribute to technological progress and urban development; it included some forty of the Victoria Bridge, sixty of Montreal and vicinity, and forty of Quebec and vicinity. Aside from the shared interest in Niagara Falls, one is left to ponder the degree to which the stereoscopic views in *America in the Stereoscope* reflected Old World ideas, market taste, and landscape preferences, in contrast to New World notions of place, identity, and pride in urban development expressed in Notman's *Maple Box* series.

Disciplinary Perspectives

Having looked at the work of William England and William Notman as representative, respectively, of views from the metropolitan centre and the imperial periphery, let me suggest that there are other competing visions to explore, and turn to the ways in which disciplinary perspectives and institutional practices can also frame photographic meaning, influence the nature, locus, and efficacy of scholarly inquiry and primary research, and skew our understanding of how England chose to document the physical and social world in which he lived and worked.

Increasingly over the last thirty years, art historians have expanded the purview of their discipline, inventing such terms as "vernacular photography" and "archive style" to legitimize serious aesthetic consideration of photographs that previously had been largely confined to the realm of archives. William England's images of the suspension bridge at Niagara offer a case in point. Until relatively recently, England received little attention from art historians of photography. In her book, *A World History of Photography*, Naomi Rosenblum described William England as "a highly competent" photographer whose work lacked the "inspired tension" of some of his contemporaries, "perhaps because its aim was simply to provide the kinds of information the public wanted."[38] Rosenblum refers to England's photograph of the Niagara suspension bridge as "well-composed and satisfying as a document," leaving no doubt that what England produced was information, not art. Similarly, in *Seizing the Light*, Robert Hirsch asserts that "the majority of stereo cards are direct, straight-forward tracings of the world that reflect the viewer's expectation for an informational map, rather than artistic expression."[39]

In his 1981 survey text, *Photography: A Concise History*, British art historian Ian Jeffrey noted that England was one of several European landscape photographers who tended to "mediate distant views by means of foreground detailing, seated figures and the like."[40] This mediation not only gave viewers visual access to the scene but also tended to heighten the stereoscopic effect through careful attention to the elements of spatial depth. England's view of Lake Orta in northern Italy bears close compositional resemblance to his "The Niagara Suspension Bridge" in the arrangement of foreground figures and distant subject.[41] However, I am less concerned with the compositional arrangement or aesthetic quality than with the meaning of the figures in the landscape, and in relation to ideas about the landscape. Indeed, we may ask, what did the landscape mean to the photographer, to the figures in the photograph, and to the viewers of the photograph?

Writing about vision and modernity in the nineteenth century, Jonathan Crary has claimed that "the most significant form of visual imagery in the nineteenth century, with the exception of photographs, was the stereoscope," adding that "there are few serious studies of the stereoscope."[42] Perhaps this is partly Jeffrey's own fault. In his 1981 survey, Jeffrey devotes less than two full pages in a 235-page text to stereoscopic photography.[43] He calls the stereoscope "a new and infallible aid to immediacy" which "revealed that illusion itself was sufficient to make a picture interesting, and saleable,"[44] adding that "the process relieved photographers of the need to think hard about synthesis." Jeffrey also cites contemporary critical references to "stereoscopic trash" and points out that "stereographic pictures found an enormous, and not very discriminating, market."[45] His observation that "stereographic space was sufficiently intricate and rewarding in its own right" attributes the popularity of stereo photography to the privileging of format over form. Jeffrey does not reproduce even a single stereoscopic view, either in conjunction with his discussion of stereoscopic photography or for that matter elsewhere in the book, a further tacit marginalization of the stereoscopic format. In other words, the wonder of three-dimensional effect took precedence over the quality of pictorial composition.

Clearly Jeffrey had an art historical epiphany between his 1981 survey and his 1999 study of William England's North American images, *An American Journey: The Photography of William England.* In it, Jeffrey seeks to elevate William England to the pantheon of art historical photographers, having decided somewhere along the way that it was not merely illusion that made England's work "interesting and saleable."[46] The dust jacket rhetoric calls *An American Journey* a "tribute to the technical brilliance of an underrated photographer, as well as to the men and women who created the realities of the new world."[47] Jeffrey puts a masterful spin on an essentially formalist study. While he claims to be paying respect to the stereoscopic format, only one image, "Terrapin Tower and the pier from Goat Island, Niagara," is reproduced in stereo. In publishing England's work as single images and in focusing his research on the original glass negatives, Jeffrey pays no attention to the colour of the preprinted cardboard mounts, the titles and accompanying verso texts, the overall catalogue of views, or the marketing and the reviews, thereby separating England's images from the larger LSC project—in effect, separating the content from its context.

Ironically, whereas William England worked in stereo and is best remembered for his various series of stereoscopic views, Jeffrey seeks to validate the underlying artistic potential of the stereoscopic medium by denying the very nature of the format. He claims that stereo photography "has received relatively little attention in the principal accounts of the medium . . . in part . . . because stereo cards are no more than a means to an end and not to be thought of as artworks in themselves."[48] He acknowledges stereo was a business; it did "tremendous educational work"; it belonged to a history of entertainment.[49] Yet he claims, despite the mundane medium, England succeeded in producing "art"—a claim proved by releasing England's images from the fetters of the stereoscopic format and reproducing them as they were, in fact, never seen.

Conflating photographic history with art connoisseurship, Jeffrey has done William England a disservice. His effort to elevate England to the pantheon of great nineteenth-century photographers—a position he well deserves—and to validate the aesthetic capacities of the stereoscopic format effectively isolates England's images from their original photographic format and dislodges them from the contextualized documentary universe in which they were circulated and viewed. Jeffrey, I think, has succeeded in his aim of revealing the "technical brilliance of an underrated photographer." But he does so with scholarly sleight of hand, at the expense of the commercial nature, physical format, and textual framing of England's images. In reproducing England's views half-stereo, he seeks to convince his audience that England was a consummate photographic artist who produced aesthetically pleasing, carefully composed, and technically superb images through the little appreciated format of the stereoscopic view. Putting a social spin on his analysis, Jeffrey also suggests England's work is about imagining Arcadia and, by extension, constructing America.

From a disciplinary perspective, it is not as art that stereoviews demand the attention of historians—and of archivists. Rather, it is as documents which can be examined for the ways in which they both reflected and constituted notions of landscape and identity, for the ways in which they articulated relationships between people and place, for the ways in which they fostered imperial dreams and colonial realities. It is for these reasons that the London Stereoscopic Company's series of North American views deserves closer scholarly scrutiny than Ian Jeffrey's *An American Journey* allows. Is the only way to appreciate England's artistry to marginalize the very medium in which he worked so effectively? Or is it through understanding the very format in which he worked that his mastery of the medium emerges and his powerful influence on the Victorian imagination resides?

Institutional Discourse

Institutional discourse is naturalized and transparent from within, foreign and opaque from without. This is nowhere more apparent than in the design of institutional websites and web browsers which are, evidently, presumed by their creators to be straightforward, and easily and universally understood. It is, therefore, critical to reflect upon the ways in which different heritage institutions describe and make accessible the means with which society has been documented. Database construction, search strategies, and specialized vocabularies define and confine the user community willing and able to extract information from these websites. William England's photographs offer a point of departure for such reflection. The inclusion of his large single print of the suspension bridge at Niagara as well as his stereoscopic views in the holdings of both the National Gallery of Canada and Library and Archives Canada presents an opportunity to examine the ways in which institutional discourse frames photographic meaning.

William England's view of the suspension bridge at Niagara appears as a plate in Ralph Greenhill's *Engineer's Witness*, a collection of photographic "memorials to the unremitting energy and enterprise that transformed America in a brief fifty-year span from an agrarian and pastoral utopia to a bustling, commercial, and urban behemoth."[50] There, it performs the usual function assigned to historical photographs; presumed to be both realistic and truthful, it serves as a "window on the past"—a form of time machine. Transporting viewers to the camera position on the bank of the Niagara River just below the Falls, it allows Greenhill's audience to take in this scene with nineteenth-century eyes. While Greenhill's introduction explains the difficulties of using the wet-collodion process in the field, neither the photograph nor the technology that produced it is the subject of his discussion. Rather, the text accompanying the photograph focuses steadfastly on the bridge, offering those details and a history of construction and use necessary to appreciate this engineering triumph and view it as evidence of "the imagination, industry, and sheer exuberance of nineteenth-century America." In writing about this image, Greenhill was not looking *at*, but rather looking *through*, the photograph.

England's print, originally in Greenhill's private collection, was purchased by the National Gallery of Canada in 1985 (the same year *Engineer's Witness* was published), in the process moving it from a source of historical information to an object of artistic contemplation. Three years later, the National Archives of Canada acquired the only other known print from another private collector, Edward McCann. The afterlife of these two prints reflects the institutional discourses into which they were inserted. It also presents an opportunity to examine the way in which institutional discourse—specifically acquisition mandates, descriptive standards, and online access—can frame photographic meaning. If historians and other users of archives are "naturally" drawn to text and have persistently failed to appreciate the role of visual materials in the making and the writing of history, then archivists, curators, and other heritage professionals—through their ideas and standards, practices and actions, whether consciously or unconsciously, intentionally or unintentionally, overtly or systemically—are, in large measure, responsible.[51]

Both the National Gallery of Canada and the National Archives of Canada (now Library and Archives Canada) have highlighted England's "The Niagara Suspension Bridge" as an institutional "treasure." In 1989, the National Archives chose it for a commemorative poster, *More Than Meets the Eye*, issued to celebrate the sesquicentennial of photography.[52] A few years later, the National Gallery included it in the exhibition and publication *Magicians of Light: Photographs from the Collection of the National Gallery of Canada*, to mark a quarter of a century of collecting photographs by the Gallery.[53] As a consequence, "The Niagara Suspension Bridge" circulated in two different and largely separate discourses, one documentary, the other aesthetic. Each imposed an institutional framework for understanding the image, more or less conforming to the general rule that the indexing of, and therefore access to, a photograph is by creator's name in galleries, by subject content in libraries, and by provenance in archives. Photographic meaning is reconfigured accordingly.

Institutional discourse also involves professional judgments and choices—in this instance by a curator and an archivist—governing acquisition and use; some decisions are more transparent than others. Both the National Gallery of Canada and the National Archives of Canada purchased England's "The Niagara Suspension Bridge" from prominent collectors in the late 1980s, a time of growing interest in the history of photography. Neither institution explicitly states the rationale for acquisition, leaving viewers to assume that the image conforms to the acquisition criteria and selection policy of each institution's collecting mandate.

The text in *Magicians of Light* has an author, James Borcoman, curator of the National Gallery's Photographs Collection. The text accompanying the Archives' poster is authorless, and while one may not expect a poster text to carry a credit line, archives tend toward an institutional facelessness which perpetuates the invisibility and presumed neutrality of the archivist. This stands in direct contrast to museum or gallery practice which values the public profiles of their curators, often both establishing and promoting the reputation of art (or other) historians on staff through institutionally funded publishing programmes.

More specific clues to the value placed on the image are contained in the texts written for the catalogue and poster. In the "tombstone" data that heads the entry in *Magicians of Light*, the photographer's name is privileged, followed by his nationality and life dates, an assigned title, date, process, dimensions, and method and date of acquisition.[54] In the four paragraphs that follow, Borcoman's text emphasizes the career of the creator as well as the compositional elements of the image. However, his statement that "the toylike character of the train suspended over the Niagara gorge on a bridge that has all the appearance of being nothing more than a fragile web of lines adds a dreamlike fantasy element to the solidity of the structure in the foreground" is a personal response offering ahistorical speculation. Even the explanation of the glassy surface of the waters of the river as it rushes downstream from the base of the Falls is described as "an incongruity that adds to the picture's charm." For Borcoman, England's photograph is an object of aesthetic contemplation. It is about intriguing contrasts, pictorial antecedents, and how "the intractable and hostile character of the landscape has prevented the photographer from creating the conventional, picturesque composition that was fashionable at the time." The curatorial eye sees the image as "original, informative, and captivating," pointing to it as a "fragile balance" between natural forces and human control. Ultimately, the conclusion, that "the trailing rope in the foreground, leading to who knows where, reminds us of unfinished business," is not about the image or about England, but about Borcoman, his perception of the image, and his authority to speak on its behalf. While such aesthetic critique is assumed of (and even expected from) gallery curators, archivists are seldom credited with such interpretive authority over the document, or the broader documentation of society.

The text on the Archives' sesquicentennial poster presented photography as a medium of record. This emphasis on historical evidence rather than aesthetic contemplation suggests that how archives make their holdings accessible is, itself, an interpretation of how society was documented. It involves choices: some are made by archivists, who may or may not possess requisite expertise in specific media of record; others are dictated by professionally accepted "standards" which, as I have argued elsewhere,[55] masquerade as value-free, but which are decidedly humanly-created and value-laden; and yet other choices are decided by in-house photographers, exhibition designers, editors, web masters, and others in public outreach or media relations, with their own standards, priorities, and practices, which can confuse or even contravene archival principles.

Description is a means of documenting the documentation of society that has been acquired by cultural institutions, and nowhere is this made more obvious to the public than in online access to institutional holdings. Cybermuse, the online "Art Education Research Site" of the National Gallery of Canada, lists six works for William England in the Artist's Index; the Artist's Page for William England gives his birth and death dates and places, but offers no supplementary online biography, audio, and media information. It does include a link to a gallery of images, where each of England's images is presented by title under a stylized Cybermuse thumbnail indicating "image n/a." An Artwork Page for each image indicates title, place, and date; photographic process and physical dimensions; acquisition method and date; and a National Gallery of Canada number in brackets, the significance of which is not specified. Of the six works listed on the Artist's Page for William England, four were taken at Niagara on his 1859 North American travels; of these four, two are of the suspension bridge. Another two were taken in Switzerland ca. 1863–1870. Close attention to the descriptive details for the two bridge images is instructive.

One print, "The Niagara Suspension Bridge, U.S.A., View from the Canadian Side" bears the dimensions 7.7 by 14.7 cm; the other, "The Railway Suspension Bridge from the *Maid of the Mist* Dock, Niagara," measures 23.7 by 28.2 cm.[56] The two works differ considerably in size. Without an accompanying thumbnail and an intimate knowledge of photographic formats and England's career, would it be obvious to a viewer that one is a stereoscopic view? The National Gallery, like Ian Jeffrey, presents England as an artist while veiling the fact that he worked primarily in the popular stereoscopic format. Indeed, format is subsumed under dimensions and wholly inaccessible by keyword search. Furthermore, there is no indication that the stereoscopic views once formed part of a larger series, nor is there an explanation that the views themselves do not bear England's name, but rather the imprint of the London Stereoscopic Company. Label information privileges England as the artist, and inclusion in the Gallery's holdings implicitly confirms that his images are considered artworks. As such they seem to require no contextual information beyond the name and life dates of the individual who created them.

By contrast, search results are not that simple or straightforward on the Library and Archives Canada website, where many of the field names, codes, terms, and links on results pages, intelligible perhaps to those working in the institution, are not at all useful or clear to the researcher. Yet the information on the Archives' site, even if difficult to access or shrouded in unfamiliar terminology, contributes to our understanding of the image in its original context of creation and subsequent social trajectory in a departmental fonds or a private album. Curiously, on both the National Gallery and Library and Archives Canada sites, web-savvy users are confounded by institutional search engines which selectively and inconsistently recognize the conventional search strategy of placing a compound search term—for example, a proper name such as "William England"—in quotation marks. In short, how documents are described, catalogued, and entered into databases, and the search protocols of those databases, all *de facto* shape and reshape the document, our access to it, and even our ability to understand it.[57] And there are other differences. On the Archives' web page, provenance is clearly indicated and subject matter is privileged. The National Gallery lists artists; Library and Archives Canada lists creators. The lesson: descriptive standards are neither value-free nor universal. Nor are they as consistent as the term "standard" may imply to outside researchers.

A series of published stereoscopic views is capable of producing at least two narratives: one is produced by the photographer in the entirety of the series; the other is created by the purchaser who selects scenes to form a new, personal narrative. However, the original narrative of the photographer/publisher and the subsequent narrative of the purchaser/collector are easily lost when stereoviews survive as individual cards attributed to a recognized photographer or when they are separated and catalogued by subject within collecting institutions. The order of the LSC and Notman series can be reconstituted because promotional catalogues have survived or finding aids have been published. For other series, lists affixed to the verso of card mounts preserve the contents and sequence of the series as originally issued. Such inventories permit a richer analysis of individual cards within the larger intellectual context of the series. Furthermore, consultation of the verso as well as the recto of stereoviews is essential for an understanding of the image, not only as part of a series in the original order, but also as a physical object. This relationship—between image and inscription, between recto and verso—must be respected by archives in order to preserve the original physical and intellectual documentary contexts of viewing and meaning-making.

The meaning of England's photograph of the suspension bridge at Niagara, and the way it is understood, is also affected by institutional practices for scanning and presenting stereoscopic views which destroy the presentational form, materiality, and meaning of the image. As already noted, on LSC views, for example, the colour of the card mount is indicative of its place and date of publication, sale, and circulation: purple on the recto and light blue on the verso indicate publication in London, while red on the recto signals the series issued in New York. Such details are easily lost when photographs are put online cropped; when card mounts are eliminated; when only one side of a stereo pair is shown; when the rich tones which allow identification and dating of original albumen prints are uploaded as black-and-white thumbnails (sometimes from scans of contact prints or microforms). Such images are more often muddy shades of grey when the thumbnail has actually been converted to black-and-white from a digital file originally created in colour in order to conserve server space. Extended descriptions, literary extracts, even poetry on the verso of stereoscopic views offer insight into the meaning of the images in the original contexts of circulation, but card-mount backs are seldom accessible online, and even more rarely are recto and verso shown together.[58] Choices of format and process and choices by photographer and publisher are marginalized, if not lost entirely.

In these and other ways, institutional practices have serious implications for the way in which historical research is carried out. On the one hand, online access expands the possibilities for research from holdings in archives and libraries to collections in museums and galleries; on the other, institutional collections which treat photographs as works of art throw up systemic obstacles to access by subject or format, and to the recovery of functional context. Unbridled enthusiasm for digitization has largely ignored the challenges to scholarly research generated by, rather than solved by, computerized access to holdings. More attention needs to be paid to the ways in which online databases and virtual exhibitions are themselves powerful forms for presenting and privileging information, for in and of themselves, such databases and exhibitions constitute the way in which our heritage institutions now document the documentation of society.

Documentation strategy in its literal application, with its emphasis on collaboration and its evaluation of all forms of evidence, can help, conceptually, to break down disciplinary and institutional silos and overcome the obstacles they pose to contextual understanding. Equally, my analysis here suggests that the management of photographs in archives can more effectively be pursued through greater collaboration—across media, disciplines, and institutions; in research, acquisition, description, and web access—if photographs are, themselves, understood in functional terms. Such collaboration, now more than ever enabled by digital tools and Wiki applications, needs to be freed from the crippling and divisive effects of the territoriality of mandates, notions of authority over the record, and possessiveness of the "original." This is not to abdicate responsibility for mandate, authority, or possession, but to encourage a more holistic and collaborative understanding of archival records in all media within the larger documentary and institutional arena. Documentation strategy, in effect, recasts England's photograph, like archives, as a participant in a much larger project of records preservation and meaning-making.

Repurposing: The Photograph between Reality and Design

Several years ago I was rushing to meet a friend in Ottawa's Byward Market and took a shortcut through a large downtown bookstore. As I hurried past a display table of novels by Canadian authors, a photograph on a bookcover caught my eye. Certain I recognized the image, I stopped to investigate. There, on the front cover of the 1997 trade paperback edition of Jane Urquhart's novel *The Whirlpool* was a photograph of a man, sitting on a ledge, with what appeared to be the Horsehoe Falls at Niagara in the background. The caption indicated that the cover design and colour tinting were by Sari Ginsberg, and the cover photograph was "Niagara Falls, Ont., 1859, by William England / PA-143218 / National Archives of Canada." Beyond the fact that "Ontario" did not exist as such in 1859, something else was not quite right.

The photograph, I felt sure, was one half of a stereoscopic view by William England, but I was convinced that the image had been laterally reversed. I bought the book and a few days later compared the reproduction on the cover to the original stereoscopic view in the Archives' holdings. There I found that England had, in fact, taken at least two stereoviews of the scene: in one, the man seems to be holding one hand to his chin in contemplation; in the other, he holds a walking stick. Both were printed and mounted on cards bearing the American eagle logo and title "Horse-shoe Fall, Canada Side"; the verso of each carried the same excerpt from N. P. Willis's *Canadian Scenery*:

> This photograph exhibits a portion of the Horse-shoe Fall as viewed from the Canada side. "The awe-inspiring grandeur—the tremendous power of the Fall, and the immeasurable depth to which the mighty waters descend, is beyond the power of imagination to realize. The waters, for which this great Cataract is the outlet, cover an area of 150,000 square miles—floods so grand and inexhaustible as to be utterly unconscious of the loss of the ninety millions of tons which they pour every hour through succeeding centuries over these stupendous precipices."

Table Rock is a very real, very distinctive place. Oriented as it is reproduced on the Urquhart book cover, the "portion of the Horse-shoe Fall" in the background could not physically be "from the Canada side." The photograph had been flipped horizontally, no doubt to satisfy the publisher's concern that the seated figure in the image conform to the dynamic direction of looking from left to right. What are we to make of this flagrant distortion of physical (and documentary) reality? What is it about photographs that allows book designers and magazine editors to take a photograph of a real person sitting in a real place and, with a key stroke, turn physical and evidentiary fact into visual fiction? Does this use constitute a new narrative, cut loose from its photographic moorings in nineteenth-century reality and attached to an alternative reality? Or is the photograph now a non-narrative, a design element devoid of meaning, employed to launch a work of fiction set three decades after the man in the photograph sat for William England's camera?[59] This exercise in "repurposing" is, perhaps, an extreme form of recontextualization. However, England is still credited with the original photograph, even if there is no acknowledgment that the image is a half-stereo, cropped and reversed laterally. An even more glaring example of Roland Barthes's "death of the author" would be the many instances where photographs by known photographers are used as cover images credited only to CORBIS or GettyImages, thus ignoring the creator and eliminating the original context of creation entirely.

In *The Fine Line: Making Distinctions in Everyday Life*, Eviatur Zerabavel declares: "Framing is the act of surrounding situations, acts, or objects with mental brackets that basically transform their meaning by defining them."[60] Whether framed and exhibited on the proverbial white walls of the gallery, cropped and reproduced on the pages of a book, or matted individually and stored by artist or by location, visual materials undergo profound changes in meaning when the photograph is removed from the album, the watercolour from the sketchbook, the map from the atlas—just as textual materials are diminished when the letter is separated from the government file, the page from the ledger, the certificate from the personal papers—in effect, when the record is isolated from its documentary context. What is archival in one physical form is art in another; what is factual information in one viewing context is aesthetic composition or technological product in another. Ultimately, then, archival documents, art works, museum artifacts, and library resources are not necessarily different objects, easily distinguished by collecting mandate, but rather the same objects which can fit comfortably in different institutions because they are capable of exhibiting alternative narratives.[61] From an archival perspective, the primary concern should be the preservation of the enduring elements and contexts of meaning-making which ensure that the ways in which the facts of the image were invested with and generated meaning survive intact across all archival functions, from physical arrangement to intellectual description to online access. What happens to that narrative when the image leaves the building is another matter altogether.

Archival Lessons in Garden Maintenance: Recognizing Choices and Preserving Meaning

In the "lost garden" of the Devon countryside, the Sweet Briar Rose, lavender, and saffron crocus in the Garden of Longing; the peonies, irises, and potentillas in the Garden of Loss; and the mass of white 'Madame Hardy' roses in the Garden of Faith each convey a message, but what message? Gwen Davis struggles to read it:

> I have lost the thread of this garden. I have not found it in its original language. I have discovered it in a foreign script and I have tried to translate it so that it makes sense to me, in this world, but it won't come down to me. . . . The past is a language I don't know how to read or answer.[62]

The notion of the past as a "foreign country" is a familiar one, popularized in the opening lines of the 1953 novel *The Go-Between* by British writer Lesley Poles Hartley and used by David Lowenthal as the title of his 1985 exploration of the role of the past in shaping everyday human affairs.[63] The mid-nineteenth century is a foreign country; they did do things differently there. They excitedly embraced photography in ways now taken for granted, on the one hand, or presumed completely obsolete, on the other. They responded to photography as a new and miraculous technology of information transfer with naïve fascination and unbridled faith in its accurate portrayal of reality. But Humphreys deviates slightly from this notion, instead offering the metaphor that the past is written in a foreign script, that it is a language that we must learn to read. In the archival garden, then, if photographic plantings are a foreign script, they can only be deciphered with an understanding of their visual vocabulary, physical structure, and other elements of meaning-making—in effect, by learning a new language of contextualized visual literacy.[64]

Photographs are not simply facts in visual form; like a quote from a speech, visual fragments snatched from a larger reality and the actions in which they have participated cannot be fully understood when content is taken out of context. The same may be said of archives. Archives do not preserve facts *per se*; they preserve facts in context. They do so in order to preserve the meanings attached to, and communicated through, those facts. *Respect des fonds* and original order are fundamental archival concepts and practices aimed at the preservation of meaning through context. This investigation of the narratives embedded in, and generated by, a single photograph, suggests how the creators, keepers, and users of archives construct, confirm, confuse, or efface meaning. Initially embraced as a surrogate for first-hand observation, "The Niagara Suspension Bridge" has subsequently been recast as a work of art, its meaning variously shaped by historical circumstances, geographical imaginings, disciplinary perspectives, institutional practices, and market forces. Interrogation of this image within the contexts of its creation, circulation, viewing, interpretation, preservation, and repurposing has highlighted the frameworks which gave, and continue to give, it meaning. From alternative narratives of materiality, authorial intention, market taste, audience reception, and institutional discourse, archival lessons emerge.

Archivists are sensitive to the contexts needed to understand textual materials; they must also become familiar with the contexts and elements of meaning-making of photographs which so easily masquerade as objective fragments of past visual reality. In them, materiality and presentational form communicate meaning. "The Niagara Suspension Bridge" is not just a visual image; it is a physical object: an albumen print from a wet-collodion negative. It matters that it exists as a single print on a card mount *and* as a stereoscopic view. When digitized for online access, card-mounted prints, especially those with letterpress text, must not be cropped to the edge of the image. Card-mounted stereoscopic views must be digitized whole, both recto and verso, and in colour. Metadata should include information about the series as a whole, and the place, numbering, and sequencing of each image therein. And, recalling the distinction between author and scribe, we need to ask whether authorial intention necessarily resides completely in the photographer as creator of the image.[65] While we now credit William England with his views of the suspension bridge at Niagara and the series of American and Canadian views of which it was a part, England was in the employ of the London

Stereoscopic Company, which commissioned the series and marketed it under its own imprint and without attribution to England. Does such a realization help us to ascertain whether the "look" of the image reflects artistic genius or commercial appeal? Need they be mutually exclusive? Can one contribute to the other? Likewise, must *artistic* and *documentary* necessarily be seen as diametrically opposed and mutually exclusive, the sole and separate purview of galleries and archives, respectively?

Nothing in the content of William England's "The Niagara Suspension Bridge" reveals what the photograph is *about*—why it was taken, or what it was meant to convey. It is a record *of* visible appearance at a given point in time; an iconographical analysis yields few secrets. Its content offers visual facts; however, the meanings invested in, and generated by, those facts are constructed, negotiated, contingent—inextricably tied to the technological, historical, functional, and documentary circumstances and to the social, cultural, political, and economic contexts in which it was originally created, circulated, and viewed, and subsequently re-created, circulated, and viewed. We can look *at* it, we can see *through* it, or we can think *with* it. No effort to recover and carefully consider its functional origins—the technological constraints which shaped its look; the authorial intentions which determined its audience and directed its trajectory; the documentary universe in which it circulated; or the political and economic circumstances brought to its viewing—can lead to absolute meaning. We need to recognize that, ultimately, it is ambiguity and imagination which govern how meaning shifts as photographs circulate and operate across institutional, discursive, and disciplinary boundaries, as well as across time and space, society and culture, and acknowledge willingly and openly our contribution to those shifts.

Looking at a photograph is not a search for "truth" at one or another point in its social biography; rather, it is, in itself, a mode of inquiry. Let us stop thinking of photographs as nouns, and start treating them as verbs, transitive verbs. They *do* things. We need to ask not only what they are *of*, and what they are *about*, but also what they were created to *do*. And when they are preserved or digitized, published, or in other ways repurposed and recirculated, we must ask how their material nature has been altered, and in the process, how the relationships embedded in them have changed, why, and to what end. Archival lessons from these alternative narratives teach that we must not only reformulate our questions in ways that photographic data can answer, but we must also expand the range of questions we ask, so that we may better understand and account for the movement of photographs and the changes in their meaning across temporal and spatial, discursive and institutional boundaries—so that we may better document the way society itself has been documented.

In this essay, I have examined some of the choices that infuse "The Niagara Suspension Bridge" with meaning, and have shown that, in documenting society, photographs participate in narratives which they help to reflect and construct. Those narratives are the product of choices. That they are discussed in detail here has been my choice. There are yet other choices to explore, choices involving the medium of record and its presumed truth value, choices embedded in the relationship of photographic evidence to other forms of documentary evidence—whether watercolours or prints, maps or travel accounts, literature or poetry. Closer scrutiny of the choice of recto titles and verso texts, geographical distribution, and series order may yield yet more narratives.

> In the end I will have to make a choice about how to tell my story. And I will have to make a choice about how to tell the story of the person who made this garden, and the garden itself. There has to be a moment of going forward, when all possibilities are left behind.[66]

In the systems we choose, the standards we create, the descriptive terms we select, the original order we discern, the appraisal decisions we make, the fonds or collections or items we acquire, we confront "moments of going forward," moments when one narrative is privileged and another is marginalized. It is our job to be aware of those moments and to understand the power of the choices we make, and to recognize that in making those choices, we leave possibilities behind. As Helen Samuels has demonstrated in both word and deed, we need conceptualization before collection, thinking before doing, but then, as Helen Humphreys has suggested, we must make choices and move forward.[67]

Notes

The title of this essay has its origins in Helen Humphreys' *The Lost Garden* (Toronto: HarperCollins, 2002). The metaphor of the archive-as-garden is not only a "fertile" idea, but also a fitting acknowledgment of two of Helen Samuels' passions: archives and gardening.

1 Humphreys, *The Lost Garden*, 134.

2 Ibid., 100, 139.

3 Carol E. Hoffecker, "The Emergence of a Genre: The Urban Pictorial History," *Public Historian* 5, no. 4 (Autumn 1983): 37.

4 Thomas J. Schlereth, "Mirrors of the Past: Historical Photography and American History," in his *Artifacts and the American Past* (Nashville: AASLH, 1980), 15.

5 Lisa Gitelman and Geoffrey B. Pingree, eds., *New Media, 1740-1915* (Cambridge, MA: MIT Press, 2003), XV–XVI. These essays examine a variety of media in their historical contexts, and move beyond the story of technological innovation to view emergent media as sites of ongoing cultural exchange. They consider how habits and structures of communication can frame a collective sense of public and private, how they inform our apprehension of the "real," and how they produce meaning and power.

6 Linda Haverty Rugg, *Picturing Ourselves: Photography and Autobiography* (Chicago: University of Chicago Press, 1997).

7 See, for example, a useful articulation of "deep context" in Clifford Geertz, "Thick Description: Toward an Interpretive Theory of Culture," in *The Interpretation of Cultures* (New York: Basic Books, 1973), 3–30. This theory is productively engaged in the work of Elizabeth Edwards on photographs; see her *Raw Histories: Photographs, Anthropology and Museums* (Oxford: Berg, 2001). For an archival perspective, see Elisabeth Kaplan, "'Many Paths to Partial Truths': Archives, Anthropology, and the Power of Representation," *Archival Science* 2, nos. 3-4 (2002): 209–20.

8 The bridge, in local parlance and on prints, was variously known as Suspension Bridge, the Niagara Suspension Bridge, the Railway Suspension Bridge, the Niagara Railway Suspension Bridge, and the International Suspension Bridge. On the cardboard mounts of both the series of single prints and the stereoscopic cards in the series *America in the Stereoscope*, published by the London Stereoscopic and Photographic Company, England's photographs of the bridge are labeled "The Niagara Suspension Bridge."

9 For many years, the negatives that William England produced for the LSC formed part of the Hulton Picture Collection, now under the umbrella of GettyImages; several of these are online at http://www.gettyimagesgallery.com/collections/Archive/william-england.aspx (accessed June 15, 2009).

10 *The Times* (London), May 3, 1860, quoted in *Catalogue of Stereoscopic Views and Instruments, Imported and Manufactured by the London Stereoscopic Company* (New York, 1860), reproduced in T. K. Treadwell, *The London Stereoscopic Company's "North American Series" of Stereoviews* (Institute for Photographic Research, Monograph Series, no. 1, 8th ed., July 2000, n.p.).

11 Queen Victoria's son, Albert Edward, the Prince of Wales (later King Edward VII), made the first royal tour of British North America in 1860, when he spent two months touring Newfoundland, the Maritimes, and Canada. He opened the Victoria Bridge across the St. Lawrence at Montreal on Saturday, August 25, 1860, and laid the cornerstone of the Parliament Buildings at Ottawa a week later on September 1, 1860. He subsequently toured the United States, visiting Detroit, Chicago, St. Louis, Cincinnati, Pittsburgh, Washington, Richmond, Baltimore, Philadelphia, New York, West Point, Albany, Boston, and Portland before heading home on October 20, 1860.

12 John Szarkowski, *Looking at Photographs: 100 Pictures from the Collection of The Museum of Modern Art* (New York: Bullfinch Press, 1999), 18.

13 David E. Nye, *American Technological Sublime* (Cambridge, MA: MIT Press, 1994), 23.

14 William R. Irwin, *The New Niagara: Tourism, Technology, and the Landscape of Niagara Falls, 1776–1917* (University Park, PA: Penn State University Press, 1996), 46.

15 As Elizabeth McKinsey has pointed out, most images were made from "a position below the bridge looking upriver, placing the bridge squarely in the center of the picture left to right." Indeed, William England, too, produced several such views, but here the bridge is depicted in the opposite direction. Elizabeth McKinsey, *Niagara Falls: Icon of the American Sublime* (New York: Cambridge University Press, 1985), 254.

16 This notion has been explored by many authors writing about the bridge, including Ralph Greenhill, *Early Photography in Canada* (Toronto: Oxford, 1965), plate 11; David McCullough, *The Great Bridge* (New York: Touchstone, 1982), 71–84; Nye, *American Technological Sublime*, 78; and Irwin, *The New Niagara*, 44.

17 McCullough, *The Great Bridge*, 82.

18 Quoted in McCullough, 71.

19 Patrick McGreevy, "Reading the Texts of Niagara Falls: The Metaphor of Death," in *Writing Worlds: Discourse, Text and Metaphor in the Representation of Landscape*, ed. Trevor J. Barnes and James S. Duncan (London and New York: Routledge, 1992), 50–72.

20 Lyell and others built on the earlier work of William Smith, the "father of English geology," whose survey work in the early decades of the nineteenth century established the relative dating of rocks through the study of fossils in sedimentary layers.

21 Charles Lyell, *Travels in North America, Canada, and Nova Scotia with Geological Observations*, two volumes, 2nd edition (London: John Murray, 1855), 1:92.

22 Charles Lyell, *Geological Evidences of the Antiquity of Man* (London: John Murray, 1863). Lyell's book was so popular that it went through three editions within the first year of publication.

23 See David E. Nye, "Visualizing Eternity: Photographic Constructions of the Grand Canyon," in *Picturing Place: Photography and the Geographical Imagination*, ed. Joan M. Schwartz and James R. Ryan (London: I. B. Tauris, 2003), 74–95.

24 McCullough, *The Great Bridge*, 75.

25 The suspension bridge at Niagara was, in fact, the world's first successful railroad suspension bridge and the only noteworthy railroad bridge of its type ever built; it lasted until 1897.

26 The series of stereoscopic views is given various titles—*America in the Stereoscope, Views of America, Views of American Scenery*, and *American Views*—on card mounts, catalogue listings, and newspaper accounts. In this essay I use *America in the Stereoscope* for the LSC series of North American views.

27 "America in the Stereoscope," *The Art-Journal* (London), July 1, 1860, 221.

28 Text on verso of stereoscopic view no. 18 – "The Niagara Suspension Bridge" published by the London Stereoscopic and Photographic Co., ca. 1860. Library and Archives Canada, Phillips Collection / 1987-022, no. 3 / PA-200390. Ellet abandoned the project in 1849; Roebling started work on his bridge in 1851.

29 "America in the Stereoscope," *The Art-Journal*, July 1, 1860, 221.

30 *The Times* (London), May 3, 1860, quoted in *Catalogue of Stereoscopic Views and Instruments* (1860), n.p. British photographer James Robertson was chief engraver at the Imperial Mint in Constantinople. Robertson photographed the Crimean War in 1855, and, in 1857, was appointed official photographer to the British Army in India where, with his brother-in-law, Felice Beato, he photographed the aftermath of the Indian "Mutiny."

31 Ibid.

32 See Colleen Skidmore, "'All that is interesting in the Canadas': William Notman's Maple Box Portfolio of Stereographic Views, 1860," *Journal of Canadian Studies* 32, no. 4 (Winter 1998): 69–90.

33 Two models were offered: one capable of holding 25 views cost $12; "the same Instrument on handsome Pedestal to contain 100 views" sold for $25.

34 "Stereoscopic Views of Canada," *The Art-Journal*, November 1, 1860, 351.

35 *Notman's Canada: Photographer to the Queen*, a documentary film, Andrea Nemtin, producer, Murray Battle, co-producer and director (PTV Productions, 2004).

36 The gift, to be from the Canadian government, was Notman's idea; however, a dispute over the cost delayed presentation. Although there is no evidence that the title was bestowed upon Notman as a result of the gift, Notman subsequently took on the title of "Photographer to the Queen."

37 "Group of Indian Women at Bead Work, Goat Island, Niagara" is one of the titles in the LSC series *America in the Stereoscope*; William Notman's stereoscopic view is entitled, "Tuskyroara Squaws Selling Curiosities."

38 Naomi Rosenblum, *A World History of Photography* (New York: Abbeville Press, 1984), 158.

39 Robert Hirsch, *Seizing the Light: A History of Photography* (Boston: McGraw Hill, 2000), 93.

40 Ian Jeffrey, *Photography: A Concise History* (London: Thames & Hudson, 1981), 60.

41 "Lake Orta" by William England, reproduced in Helmut Gernsheim, *The Rise of Photography, 1850-1880: The Age of Collodion* (London: Thames and Hudson, 1988), 182.

42 Jonathan Crary, *Techniques of the Observer: On Vision and Modernity in the Nineteenth Century* (Cambridge, MA: MIT Press, 1992), 116.

43 Jeffrey, *Photography: A Concise History*, 36–38.

44 Ibid., 37.

45 Ibid., 38.

46 Ibid., 37.

47 Ian Jeffrey, *An American Journey: The Photography of William England* (Munich and New York: Prestel, 1999), inside front flap.

48 Ibid., 8.

49 Ibid., 10.

50 Ralph Greenhill, *Engineer's Witness* (Toronto: Coach House Press, and Boston: David R. Godine, 1985). "The Niagara Suspension Bridge" (plate 19) is discussed on pages 58 and 60.

51 For a fuller discussion of this challenge to the paradigm of the "visually illiterate historian," see Joan M. Schwartz "Coming to Terms with Photographs: Descriptive Standards, Linguistic 'Othering,' and the Margins of Archivy," *Archivaria* 54 (Fall 2002): 142–71; on the failure of historians to use visual records, see Jim Burant, "Visual Archives and the Writing of Canadian History: A Personal Review," *Archivaria* 54 (Fall 2002): 92–117.

52 *More Than Meets the Eye* (poster), (Ottawa: National Archives of Canada, 1989).

53 James Borcoman, *Magicians of Light: Photographs from the Collection of the National Gallery of Canada* (Ottawa: National Gallery of Canada, 1993).

54 The tombstone data reads:

WILLIAM ENGLAND
British (1816-London, 1896)
The Railway Suspension Bridge from the "Maid of the Mist" Dock, Niagara, 1859
Albumen silver print, 23.7 x 28.2 cm
Purchased 1985

55 See Joan M. Schwartz, "'We make our tools and our tools make us': Lessons from Photographs for the Practice, Politics, and Poetics of Diplomatics," *Archivaria* 40 (Fall 1995): 40–74; and again "Coming to Terms with Photographs."

56 Careful observation reveals that five of the six works in the National Gallery are between 7.2 by 14.7 cm and 7.4 by 15.3 cm.

57 Whether using Archivianet, the former National Archives of Canada online research tool, which is slowly being phased out, or the new Archives Search developed by Library and Archives Canada to supercede it, an online search for work by William England requires creativity and persistence. "Search Tips" in Archivianet advises: "Enter in the appropriate field whatever terms you feel best describe the document. It can be a work's title, a general description, the artist's name, copyist, a place name, etc."; however, using quotation marks around the name "William England" in the keyword field yields the message, "No records match your request," with suggestions for reasons for the lack of results. A keyword search using the standard bibliographic search strategy—England [comma] William—yields 225 hits, the vast majority of which relate to former Prime Minister William Lyon Mackenzie King when he was travelling in England. Adding quotations marks—"England [comma] William"—reduces the results to thirteen item-level descriptions, two with linked images. The new Archives Search, while capable of making far more material accessible, is awkward and tedious to use, especially for researchers unfamiliar with the way in which archival databases are structured, and often yields an overload of information in a form unintelligible to the public. Item-level descriptions are less precise, and inscriptions on originals are not consistently transcribed. The Archives Search, like Archivianet before it, also suffers from lack of quality control in linking description to the scanned image. As a result, more images are available online, but, for example, William England's "View up Notre Dame Street from building in foreground with series of arches at street level" (accessible on Archives Search but not on Archivianet) shows, instead, the recto of the stereoview "The Chaudière Falls – Ottawa River, Canada." Archivianet can be searched at

http://www.collectionscanada.gc.ca/archivianet/index-e.html. Library and Archives Canada's new Archives Search is accessed at http://www.collectionscanada.gc.ca/search/index-e.html. (Both accessed September 21, 2009.)

58 The New York Public Library Digital Gallery offers a model for online access. Forty of William England's stereoscopic views can be found online, in full colour, recto and verso, by searching the Name field for "England, William" at http://digitalgallery.nypl.org/nypldigital/index.cfm (accessed July 14, 2009).

59 Jane Urquhart's *The Whirlpool* was previously and subsequently reissued by McClelland and Stewart with different cover images. The 1997 trade paperback used a detail from John Trumbull's oil painting *Niagara Falls from Below the Great Cascade on the British Side*, c. 1808; the *New Canadian Library* series paperback published in 2002 carried the watercolour *View of Niagara Falls*, 1804, by Canadian painter William Green. Beyond the larger issue of repurposing visual materials and the motives behind their use by the publisher or their approval by the author, is the question of whether England's photograph of a contemplative figure on the brink of the Falls contributes historical authenticity to Urquhart's fictional account or provides a visual jumping-off point for imagining the story. While a detail from Trumbull's painting was used as a cover illustration, publishers seem far less audacious in making the kind of aesthetic interventions which England's view has sustained.

60 Eviatur Zerabavel, *The Fine Line: Making Distinctions in Everyday Life* (New York: Free Press, 1991), 11.

61 For a recent stimulating analysis of these porous and problematic borders around which archivists especially have erected walls far too rigid, see Geoffrey Yeo, "Concepts of Record (2): Prototypes and Boundary Objects," *American Archivist* 71 (Spring/Summer 2008): 118–43.

62 Humphreys, *The Lost Garden*, 180.

63 L. P. Hartley's famous opening line, "The past is a foreign country; they do things differently there," was adopted by David Lowenthal for the title of his well-known book, *The Past is a Foreign Country* (Cambridge: Cambridge University Press, 1985). For an essay which closely complements the themes presented here, using Lowenthal's central premise, and which is directed primarily to users of the newly perceived archives as constructed and mediated by archivists, see Terry Cook "The Archive(s) is a Foreign Country: Historians, Archivists, and the Changing Archival Landscape," *Canadian Historical Review* 90, no. 3 (September 2009): 497–534.

64 This linguistic twist resonates with Estelle Jussim's claim that "words and images each have their own unique characteristics and their own ambiguities." See her "The Research Uses of Visual Information," *Library Trends* 25, no. 4 (April 1977): 773.

65 I discuss this distinction in "'We make our tools and our tools make us,'" cited above.

66 Humphreys, *The Lost Garden*, 202.

67 This essay is a revised, expanded version of "Arcadia and Progress: Competing Visions of Canada, 1860," the Shannon Lecture for the Department of History, Carleton University, October 20, 2006, and "Archival Lessons from Alternative Narratives: Interrogating William England's *The Niagara Suspension Bridge*, 1859," the keynote address to *Through the Image*, a conference organized by the Nordic Network for Visual Social Science, Stockholm, October 25, 2007. Over the years, I have benefitted from the advice and assistance of many people, in particular: Brian Osborne, Queen's University, Kingston; Jim Opp, Carleton University, Ottawa; Colleen Skidmore, University of Alberta, Edmonton; Eric Boudreau and Pierre Pugin, Library and Archives Canada; Nora Hague, Notman Photographic Archives, Montreal; Christopher Coutlee and Alan Walker, Toronto Reference Library; Leon Meyer, Hulton Getty Picture Collection, London. I acknowledge the support of Library and Archives Canada, Queen's University, and the Social Sciences and Humanities Research Council of Canada. My greatest debts are to Helen Samuels and Terry Cook, who are a constant source of encouragement and inspiration.

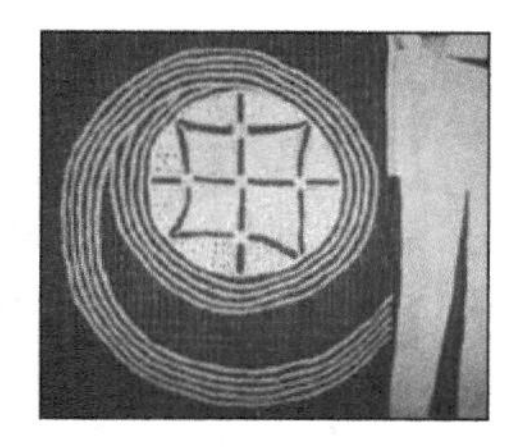

THE COMPLICATION OF COLOR IN AN ACADEMIC ARCHIVE

Nancy Bartlett

Excuse these
Brown Suggestions—
Wisdom is
seldom dressed
in Pink—

Emily Dickinson[1]

Color and archives do not readily mix.[2] Any consideration of the two together risks dismissal as an ambitious exercise in the esoteric marginalia of archival studies, best left in the hands of conservators with expertise in ephemera and its materiality. Yet even this modest exploration of the value of color, and its situation in an academic archive as a case study, reveals useful paradoxes and inherent dilemmas for further considerations of the visual culture of archives. Archival conceptualizations and practice slip in and out of the equation of color over time, as Helen Samuels herself may enjoy, in this essay in her honor on the presence, the absence, the benefit, and the inevitable problems of color in an academic archive.

This exploration seeks to highlight the unquestioned conditions upon which archives have generally been imagined, built, communicated, and sustained in their privileging of monochromism, or what passes for black and white.[3] It also exposes the bleeding of color into and out of the repository and aims to look beyond the exceptional concentrations of color at the conservator's workbench, in the exhibit case, and on the archives' website. The effort is made against the backdrop of much current academic research, teaching, learning, administration, socialization, and communication in which color in its original context figures prominently as an illustrative tool, informational property, authenticating device, and essential indicator of the visual identity of the university.[4]

The pursuit of color is furthered in the example of the University of Michigan archives. This is not only a convenience for the author in terms of the location of primary sources or institutional support to pursue questions concerning the very nature of archives.[5] It is also an appropriate case in that the parent institution has several important variations of color as essence and indicator in its collective cultural and academic ambitions and contributions over time.

Three variations may be used to introduce and signify the mixed use of color on Ann Arbor's campus of the University of Michigan and the enigmas this variety encapsulates. The first involves the university's celebration of its institutional memory of 150 years. In 1967, the University of Michigan staged its sesquicentennial with an outdoor display of hundreds of new photographs of campus, produced by professor of art, author, and prominent photographer Phil Davis; the images on display and in the accompanying printed volume were all black and white. Collective memory was commemorated monochromatically.[6] At the same time and without any conscious contradiction, the university introduced a "more colorful and individualized" flag, with a "sidebar" of new colors of fabric for each of the university's sixteen schools and colleges. (Description of these new colors was not entirely inspiring: the color for the School of Business Administration was described, officially, as "drab" or "cracker.")[7]

The second variation was also a University of Michigan event, although this time academic rather than a celebration of self. Michigan hosted an exhibition on "fugitive color" in 1981, featuring color photography "to broaden our color sensitivity" not long after the Museum of Modern Art held its first exhibition of color photography in 1976.[8] What survives in the archives of Michigan's event is the exhibition's catalog, printed in black and white.

The third variation is the University of Michigan's most explicit and enduring color association. It began as a student initiative in an era of new interest in chromatic allegiances on campuses across the country. In 1867, a committee of students in the Literary Department selected maize and azure blue as "the emblematic colors of the University of Michigan." They declared their decision and elaborated in the *University Chronicle* that, "the list of colors now is: Harvard, red; Yale, blue; Brown, brown; Dartmouth, green; Bowdoin, white; Hamilton, orange; Williams, purple; New York, lavender; Union, magenta; Columbia, blue and white; Michigan University, azure-blue and maize."[9] Commitment to the *idea* of Michigan colors has never deviated from the original choice as expressed in the words *maize* and *azure-blue.* But the optical versions of the choice have altered continually. The university's twin colors had originated as imagined elements of the air—"colors that float in the light," according to the school's song of 1870, "The Yellow and Blue." But they have darkened over time in iterations from the palest shade of cornflower on dance cards and letterheads of the nineteenth century, to the medium blue on the 1967 flag, to the blackened blue of the contemporary football program.

In 1912, the University of Michigan Senate made a first attempt to anchor the chosen school colors in consistent standards. Samples were surveyed and efforts were made to render the decision permanent through physical evidence. Ribbons of the "correct" colors were located and entered into the records of the Senate.[10] Over time the ribbons faded and the university proceeded through much of the twentieth century to express itself in a great range of variations in color without consulting the ribbons or even acknowledging their existence in the archives.

The new flag of 1967 signaled another effort at solidification of color, "in view of existing confusion as to what the precise University and academic colors should be, and the wide range of their interpretation in actual practice." The aim was again to achieve "a definitive color chart of the academic colors" while defining in words "ripening maize" as "slightly orange yellow" and blue as "the deep azure blue of a summer sky."[11] Yet color consistency continued to slip. As identity came more and more to mean assets both realized and envisioned, the university's Office of Vice President for Communications became concerned about consistency and control of every version of the institution's image, including its colors. In 1996, a commercial firm was hired to return to the question of the truest maize and blue.[12] A spectrophotometer was used on site in the archives to create a "spectral fingerprint" of the 1912 ribbons. Numeric specifications from the images were exported via ColorMail to a lab where Textile

Master software enabled the original data to be studied for the loss of original information through fading, then adjusted, and translated into a modern dye formula.[13]

Despite all the effort at definition, the combination of time, technology, and campus culture conspires to allow still for variation in the use of the official colors. A particularly deep blue and dark yellow are now associated with Michigan's Athletic Department while the Business School prefers "gold" instead of maize, with no reference whatsoever to "drab" or "cracker."[14] The inherent variables of online communications and interactive media inevitably corrupt any effort at absolute consistency in either creation or viewing, let alone describing, even though digital specifications for color are offered by the Office of Vice President for Communications alongside those for print.

Wordplay and color both solidify and satirize the notion of a campus chromatic code. On the one hand, the university lays legal claim to its identity with the wordmark "M GO BLUE." Yet the university's Plant Operations playfully inverts the order of "Go Blue" to "We Make Blue Go" for the slogan on its vehicles, and the now-decommissioned nuclear reactor's "swimming pool" used the macabre mimicry of "M Glow Blue."[15] Long-term fans of Michigan athletics refer to themselves as the "Old Blues."[16]

Chromatic and aquatic associations continue in Michigan's name for its new institutional repository, Deep Blue, and its digital asset management system, BlueStream. In architecture too, color becomes caricature. Architect Gunnar Birkerts' athletic building for Michigan, from 1990, sports a blue façade and an obvious salute to the football helmet in the curved profile of its roof, equally evident in his schematic sketches in the archives and in the first glimpse fans catch of the building as they proceed along State Street toward Michigan Stadium for game time.[17]

By contrast to this pattern of successful whimsy, the outer limits of play were reached unwittingly by architects Robert Venturi and Denise Scott Brown. Their 1998 adornment of the stadium itself, featuring enormous blue lettering and oversized school icons across a yellow parapet that was pitched as a "halo," met with a hailstorm of protest. Voluminous correspondence to the university president lambasted the Philadelphia-based designers for the perceived carnivalesque desecration of the stadium known affectionately as "The Big House." The addition did not survive beyond a second season. The playful fonts are now in limbo, offsite in an undisclosed location under the charge of the university's History and Traditions Committee, while serious letters of protest fill folders in the archives.[18]

The Question of Colorless Content

While prominent on the playing field and defended from misuse above the bleachers, campus colors have been marginalized in both the material and the attitude of the archives in Ann Arbor and beyond. There is an easy archival allowance for shift and slippage, in and out, of colors at large. The vast majority of archives are a seemingly uniform darkness and light, of text upon the page in the classic "system of contrasts" within which "typography is the art of using black to expose whiteness."[19] Content rendered in shades of black and white, by hand or machine, out measures any intentionally polychromatic content other than that within the not inconsequential outliers of maps and atlases, albums and loose ephemera, film and photography, or the most recent digital deposits and their pixilated displays. Long before American academic archives had come into being in the early twentieth century, modern mechanizations of organizational communication had diminished the role of medieval and renaissance flourishes on records. Consistencies and efficiencies in the era of mechanical reproduction favored the two tones of great contrast over polychromatic flair. No longer was there the privilege of the colorful document, which as a mode of a more limited communication had ensured employment for colorists who specialized in completing an illuminated manuscript with visual design for theological, indexical, as well as artistic purposes.[20] Even the use of color for measured drawings of nineteenth-century architecture and engineering ceased as India ink came into favor in the newer printing processes.[21] Color went missing from bureaucratic, academic administration while it instead emerged in the private realm of nineteenth- and early twentieth-century student friendship albums, scrapbooks, programs, and posters.[22] Black and white were the intended predominant, perceptual properties upon the materiality of the modern office document and the modern administrative image or graphic illustration.[23]

Of course black and white have never been absolute contrasts, or consistent in and of themselves. Shades of gray and yellow are close cousins of black and white, and their paler derivatives gain prominence over time in the aging process of some organic inks and papers. Subtle color variation sneaks in, as the 1981 catalog for the fugitive color exhibition at Michigan points out: "Anyone who has looked at early photographs knows the startling range of hues present in albumen, carbon, salted paper, platinum, and cyanotype 'black and white' prints."[24] The stereotypical descriptors "faded" and "dusty" seem to go hand in hand in any characterization of archives, seen or only imagined, so that white and black shift in their slippage toward anemic shadows of monochromatic contrast. Carolyn Steedman, in her volume *Dust: The Archive and Cultural History*, wrote with poetic license of both the content, and its chromatic atrophies, and the mood, the odd nightmare, illness, and even "delirium" associated with "the great, brown, slow-moving strandless river of Everything, . . . its tiny flotsam that has ended in the record office you are at work in," as in "a grey exhausted day in the record office."[25] Color was evoked by her for its weakest shades as an atmospheric characterization of the mood as well as the material of archives; even the color red is referenced as feeble decay in its appearance as "red rot . . . from the spine of the ledger."[26] Containers and tools themselves embellish this notion, at least for those who fancy deliberate intent, allowing for such facile stereotypes, with the only competition for gray being beige or tan, white or black, on and in boxes, folders, sleeves, slips, index cards, and the very pencils at use in the reading room.[27]

Brown leather and gold lettering are the surviving, muted contrasts from the earliest era of the University of Michigan's history, as the fine-tooled bindings of the private libraries from the cofounders of the school in its infancy in the early nineteenth century. (Tocqueville himself had marveled that men in Michigan had such collections.) These remain on view, in the reading room of the archives, as a visual anchor from the founding years. They are only very rarely read, but they are often viewed as an adornment and an anecdote for tours, as an antiquarian contrast to the black carts and beige boxes in daily transit close by. Such tours of the archives typically end at the director's office, where two oil paintings by Jasper Cropsey of the University of Michigan campus in 1855 provide unique, full-color views of the observatory and of "campus" (a few buildings in fields with livestock in the foreground).[28] The colors of these paintings exist in isolation from most any other nineteenth-century illustration of the campus or its content, either printed or produced by hand. Their place of privilege in the director's office is as art rather than archives; as such they do not share close quarters with Cropsey's other works. The artist's penciled sketches of the campus—in black and white, of course—are instead locked in the archives vault well within the stacks.[29] Much further away lie the earliest known color renderings of a campus imagined, but never built. The prominent architect Alexander Jackson Davis had been commissioned by the University of Michigan Board of Regents to create a campus plan and design campus structures. He obliged, in 1838–39, with nine beautiful watercolors whose status as art rather than archives is affirmed by their location in the Metropolitan Museum of Art in New York.[30]

The Cringe against Color

The disinclination of archivists to validate color as an important and distinctive archival attribute figures innocently as part of a larger cultural context.[31] Theoretical writings on color and culture make note of the resistance to color for centuries and even a fear of color at work as far back as Aristotle's era.[32] Black and white have historically trumped other combinations of hues, saturations, and brightness in their appearance of truthfulness, precision, and integrity. All other colors have been suspect, considered fugitive, foolish, deceitful, and "unnatural." Color is not impartial, it seems, and it even hints at being alive in its deceptions in the world. It inspires caution among a wide variety of academics and artists alike.[33] Artist David Batchelor's book, *Chromophobia*, includes the etymological explanation that, "Figuratively, colour has always meant the less-than-true and the not-quite-real. The Latin *colorem* is related to *celare*, to hide or conceal; in Middle English 'to colour' is to embellish or adorn, to disguise, to render specious or plausible, to misrepresent."[34] Artist and color theorist Josef Albers acknowledged, "Color is fooling us, cheating us, deceiving us—you can call it if you want—all the time." Gestalt psychologist Rudolf Arnheim observed, "Color is the most capricious dimension of visual imagery." László Moholy-Nagy, newly reconsidered for his experimental work in color photography, wrote, "It starts to dawn on me that there is no such thing as natural color in photography because the chemical reactions and the mixture of artificial light sources will always distort reality."[35] "Deepening hues to signal dubious content" is the aim of current research at University of California–Santa Cruz in an effort to register diminishing degrees of credibility of suspect entries in Wikipedia. University of Michigan alumna and essayist Janet Malcolm even went so far, in her dismissal of that first color photography exhibition at the Museum of Modern Art, to claim that, "it is black-and-white photography that demands of the photographer close attention to the world in color, while color photography permits him to forget it."[36]

Discomfort and distrust of color have long been legitimized as a "mature" and therefore reasonable reaction to the embrace of color by infants and adolescents, and it seems now also to become a badge of disgrace for the inept on the Internet, at least in the world of Wikipedia. Kierkegaard expressed the aging process as a loss of carefree comfort in color: "The hues that life once had gradually become too strong, too harsh, for our dim eyes."[37] There is the popular metaphor of living, or dreaming, in Technicolor, implying youthful vitality and imaginative energy as contrasted with more somber tones of maturity.[38]

A third dimension of unease about color, beyond its perceived deceit and its appeal to the immature or unrestrained, has at least been open to the honesty of the dilemma: "philosophers from Wittgenstein to Derrida revel in the question of what is impossible and use color problems to articulate it."[39]

Monochromatic Archivistique

Archivists have tacitly exhibited their own reservations, either by inadvertently overlooking color and other visual qualities and devices or by echoing this notion of impossibility. One need not look far for evidence, among even the most insightful authors, to discover the absence of color, or more generally any visuality in the archival discourse. Eric Ketelaar's essay on "the archival image," to take one example with a suggestive title, makes no mention of color and its illustrations are black and white. Image equals identity, not optical essence. In his 1990 volume *Understanding Archives and Manuscripts*, James M. O'Toole also bypassed color and other visual attributes in a claim that "what makes the records 'archives' is neither age nor appearance, but rather content, meaning, and usefulness" as though appearance and meaning were at odds.[40] Frank Boles wrote about appearance and "images" in his volume on appraisal, and aligned these with text as best he could: "once visual images are thought of as documents rather than pretty pictures, the selection framework created in this volume can be applied to them as well."[41] None of these are explicit dismissals of color, but their emphasis is on evidence embedded within an alphabetic vocabulary, grammar, and syntax. The genealogy of this framework has connections to Ann Arbor: Michigan's Robert Warner and Ruth Bordin emphasized in their modern manuscripts manual, from 1966, the two tools for vast amounts of modern, monochromatic records, namely "the great bulk of typewritten and mimeographed materials of the last generation . . . which really merit preservation."[42]

While most archivists make little or no mention of color in writing, there are those who confess discomfort and even dread over color as it challenges the archival systems and standards of duplication, preservation, and description. Who can blame them? As Rudolf Arnheim asked about color, "How can one build a system on elements that are so shifty?"[43] As for duplication, "only toners containing carbon black should be used" according to NARA's instructions for "Archival Copies of Thermofax, Verifax, and Other Unstable Records."[44] Widely used in archives for the past several decades for preservation and access, microfilm has also privileged black and white to the point of significant losses of information from colorful originals including maps, drawings, photographs, color-coded forms, etc. The disregard of color in both microfilming and subsequent digital scanning of the Sanborn Fire Insurance Maps is a particularly regrettable case of information loss, since the depicted buildings' construction materials were coded with five colors on the original maps.[45]

Nicholson Baker, the *bête noire* of cultural collections' critics, forced the issue of color upon both librarians and archivists in his high-profile essays on the limitations of preservation of newspapers through microfilming. His book *Double Fold*, published in 2001, achieved tremendous popular attention and put institutions of heritage immediately on the defense. Color was characterized as the "victim" of monochromatic preservation programs in Baker's *cause célèbre*. The question of conservation and color was nothing new in 2001. Baker had simply and effectively (for sales) dramatized any number of issues associated with preservation.

Where color was victim for Baker, it was culprit just a few years earlier in Ted Turner's efforts to colorize classic black-and-white films and television programs. Television critic Eric Mink viewed colorization as "bastardization," and the Writers Guild of America West deplored it as "cultural vandalism."[46] The intensity of debate lasted less than a decade and the issue quietly dissipated with Turner's decision to stop colorizing movies, a decision based more on disinterest in the market than principle. Even preservationists who express an earnest interest and healthy respect for color's complications admit that color intimidates. "Color photographs created by chemical processes . . . are inherently unstable," according to *Photographs: Archival Care and Management*.[47] Anne R. Kenney and Oya Y. Rieger emphasized that, "capturing and conveying color appearance is arguably the most difficult aspect of digital imaging."[48] The Northeast Document Conservation Center echoed this warning: "currently, color prints made from digital files are not considered preservation quality."[49] Henry Wilhelm devoted over seven hundred pages to *The Permanence and Care of Color Photographs* even while he acknowledged that, "materials that have not been refrigerated will progressively fade until they become useless."[50] And in another essay he noted that, "Not a single print from the first decade of Kodacolor is known to have survived in good condition."[51] (Wilhelm was otherwise involved in Michigan's exhibition on fugitive color.) "Fading begins the moment a print is produced," according to Kayley Vernallis in "The Loss of Meaning in Faded Color Photographs."[52]

Academics are perhaps more sanguine and likely less informed about color degradation, with one proposing that, "image decay from 1997 to 2003 is precisely what should be preserved."[53] (One wonders if the cult of ruins in cultural studies obliquely prejudices some to favor distressed or discolored documents. Susan Sontag wrote suspiciously, along these lines, that, "the cold intimacy of color seems to seal off the photograph from patina.")[54]

The disconnect between archival description and color is a different alienation than the active reaction color engenders in preservation and duplication. For centuries there have been efforts to establish universal systems of representation and reference for colors by authors *other than* archivists. Philosophers, botanists, artists, advertisers, capitalists in industries as varied as automobiles and cosmetics, archeologists, architects, soil scientists, linguists, and most recently "color engineers" working with "color management systems" have all, in their own disciplinary fashions, made efforts to systematize an articulation of color in words, as a description, a tool, and an epistemiologic orientation to visuality. Scholars have even specialized in the history of such efforts. One determined that Modern English emphasizes hue over brightness, in contrast to the color lexicon of the Old English existing prior to the twelfth century.[55] Furthermore, in what would dismay Michigan's most avid alumni and delight its rivals, there is the discovery that blue and yellow were considered at odds in the Middle Ages and therefore unsuitable for dyers to mix or to imagine in combination within their recipes for color production.[56]

But definitions of colors do not necessarily align with the intentions of archival access systems.[57] The *Art and Architecture Thesaurus* warns that "hue, saturation, and brightness are no natural classification."[58] Color terms are indeed primarily used as adjectives, as philosopher Edward Averill observes.[59] Color, it seems, is heavily dependent upon context to inspire any search for its rediscovery through textual tools in the archives. "Do you have any color?" is a not uncommon query. But it almost always serves as a supplement to a subject or an object in an image on which to assign the attribute of color, such as the colors *of* costumes, *colorful* wallpapers, or color *in* scenes of campus. In an obvious example, "blue" becomes meaningful in association with "book" in the academic parlance referring to commercially printed examination booklets. (Architect William Le Baron Jenney placed an exceptional emphasis upon color in his conditions for teaching at Michigan, in 1876, by requiring his students to use notebooks of a very precise material, "very securely bound in half cow-hide, deep red with dark colored cloth sides."[60] For Jenney, the materiality and its color figured into the deliberate profile of the new architecture program he would lead.)

It almost goes without stating that color often carries much greater meaning than a thesaurus alone can signify or a catalog can catch, and its significance can slip away from even the most compelling collections. The rediscovery of color can more than compensate for its initial inaccessibility. Sally Stein crafted her dissertation, *The Rhetoric of the Colorful and the Colorless: American Photography and Material Culture between the Wars*, around her realization that the Library of Congress collection of famous

Farm Security Administration (FSA) photographs included a wealth of unknown color images interfiled with the iconic black and white. Her research led to a new consideration of color as documentary device in the Depression. The Library of Congress validated that interest in its exhibition and publication entitled *Bound for Glory: America in Color, 1939-1943* and most recently in its establishment of a Flickr Commons pilot project, launched on January 16, 2008. The project team for Flickr Commons chose the color FSA images as one of the first two collections from the Library of Congress because "approximately 1,600 color photographs in the Farm Security Administration/Office of War Information (FSA/OWI) collection have proven popular with diverse communities, both national and international. In addition to representing excellent photographic work from the 1930s-40s, the FSA/OWI photos consistently surprise and delight viewers unaware of the existence of high quality color images from that period."[61]

Visual "Language" and Literacy in Archives

The few recent and noteworthy articles on "visual literacy" by archivists include an occasional passing mention of color, but none dwell upon it for long.[62] One must infer color further into the exceptionally astute essays of Elisabeth Kaplan, James O'Toole, Ala Rekrut, Joanna Sassoon, Joan M. Schwartz, and Hugh Taylor. The search is otherwise in vain for an explicit mention of color in most any book or article intended for archivists on the value of archives and what is to be discovered within them, either in volumes on understanding archives generally or on actually constructing archives through appraisal. Professional literature for archivists remains mostly void of color, other than its inclusion on the recent front covers of the *American Archivist* and occasional pages within volumes on photographic and architectural archives.[63]

Instead, the most analytical observations about the informative values of color seem to be beyond the texts of archivists as authors. Among the most instructive is Edward R. Tufte's volume *Envisioning Information.* In a chapter on "Color and Information," he described (and emphasized in italics) "the fundamental uses of color in information design: to *label* (color as noun), to *measure* (color as quantity), to *represent or imitate reality* (color as representation), and to *enliven or decorate* (color as beauty)."[64] In Tufte's functional attributions to colors, we find ready matches of color with significant scientific advances achieved by Michigan academics. For example, biochemist Minor Coon used column chromatography to distinguish and measure elements of an enzyme system. Engineer Emmett Leith gained international acclaim for his breakthroughs in holography, including his visionary experiments in color imaging. Color contributed to a new discourse of visual "reality" and its representations in his laser demonstrations and those of his followers, whose photographs of Leith's delight at holographic rays of red and blue provide a uniquely "mixed medium" in his archival records.[65] Physicist Jack van der Velde and his colleagues used color to track and record the pathway of proton decay in their nearly miraculous capture of a supernova event. From a subterranean pool, to a computer screen, to a 35 mm camera viewfinder, and onto film, color carried the story. In this case, van der Velde would no doubt credit color with serving admirably the multiple roles of *labeling, measuring, representing, enlivening,* and indeed *preserving* the event. The diversity of academic disciplines in which color functions both validates Tufte and demonstrates the disconnect between function and verbal accessibility, since the color in these three cases from biochemistry, engineering, and physics at Michigan is in the content, yet not in the catalog.

Color communicates even more than the tabular data of science. It is also elsewhere at work on campus at the University of Michigan in the offices of other faculty whose fame can be traced both verbally and visually in the archives. It is *imagined, mixed,* and *managed* in the work of colorist and architect William Muschenheim, whose palette of yellow, gray, white, orange, and blue in paints and pencil sketches on drawings and in buildings was his most significant contribution to modernism in Michigan and his original home in Manhattan. Color *enacted* debate in the Socratic notes of law professor Yale Kamisar, whose greens and reds, yellows and blues, do battle across the pages as his rehearsals lead to lectures.[66] Color was even *distorted,* intentionally and artistically, in the medical illustration boards of Professor Gerald Hodge.

Around the time he was leaving Harvard for the University of Michigan, Arnheim asked and answered the question of utility and purpose of color in his essay "Colors—Irrational and Rational," providing us with a meaning that bridges tabulation and expression, information and inspiration. "What are colors for?" he asked. "The question becomes genuinely interesting only if one is not satisfied by the answer that colors help identify objects, as indeed they do, and that otherwise they are given to us by the gods and the artists in order to increase our *joie de vivre*, generated by stimulation and harmony. If instead one is convinced that visual patterns, whether works of art or not, are made to convey certain cognitive statements about basic facts of human experience, the question of what it is that colors tell us poses itself forcefully."[67] Imagined, enacted, deliberately distorted, counted, measured, mentioned or not, they offer up questions worthy of consideration and a framework for visualizing and verbalizing the world through time. Arnheim and Schwartz ought to inspire archivists to reframe many of the questions to which they might seek answers, in order to illuminate the productions and perceptions of visual media including the various attributes of color.

There is a certain irony in the ambivalent regard and disregard of color and the archives. Art historian Ernst Gombrich, who addressed some of the same questions of visual perception as Arnheim, helps frame the irony in his observations about color. Color lends itself, he noted, more to the irreversible *making* process than it does to *matching*.[68] Therein lies the rub for archives. If colors imagined and anticipated are, as Barthes would claim, "the promise of a pleasure," then their value is found as much in the forward movement of action as in reaction, creation as in restoration, discovery as in description.[69] Here archivists share the inclination to "make" color rather than "match" it: in their energies to create colorful websites, to "correct" color scans, and to otherwise embellish the image of archives through additive colors and contrasts of PowerPoint, Photoshop, and desktop publishing. Cropsey's view of the University of Michigan campus becomes the banner above the business of the archives' website, cropped and contained within the decorative border. Colorful and convenient, Cropsey becomes an image outside as much as within the archival tour. So, too, does the archives' printed bookmark, a miniaturized reproduction of the pale palette of colors originally intended for an ornamental detail in the Michigan Union of 1917. An oversized sketch becomes a more convenient carrier of color as calling card for the archives. An imbalance of making over matching seems the case. And yet, is it really so?

The ultimate paradox and the endless riddle may very well concern whether color in fact leads us further along in our archival sensibilities and understanding, despite our facile and fickle relationship with it.

Archives have become verbs as much as nouns, adjectives and adverbs; processes as much as places; perceptions and questions as much as final answers or definitive truths. They offer predicaments as well as proof; they house spirit as much as substance. Joanna Sassoon has written eloquently of the phantoms of the archives, discovering the disappearance, of "the odd echo . . . something [that] had been there once, but was no longer there."[70] Terry Cook, too, references the trouble with assumptions of simple translucence in archives. He embellishes upon Jacques Derrida in his advocacy of a deeper penetration of shifting visibility: "To make the invisible visible once more, to make the inarticulate articulate," is Cook's aim and his allegiance with Derrida's invitation to "speak to the ghost," otherwise referenced by Hugh Taylor as the "spiritual reality" available to the open mind in the archives.[71] Judith Mottram could assure those who answer Cook's call that color in archives, as in art, involves "the audience in the construction of meaning . . . in a more distributed coalition" over time.[72] By more fully considering color, and by respecting its vitality, its autonomies and dependencies, its appearance, evolution, and ability to dissolve into the past or distinguish itself anew for the future, archivists may perceive with greater clarity both the contradictions and the content in our keep.[73] If, as Mary Tivy asserts, "the past is the most popular tourist destination on earth," then this intense journey with its paths through the archives must surely be enriched by the pursuit of a polychromatic vision and a palette of richer imagination.[74]

Notes

1 These ten words, described as a manuscript and a letter, were authored by Emily Dickinson and were produced by graphite pencil on cream-colored paper. The item is within box 22 of the J. Franklin Jameson Papers in the Manuscript Division of the Library of Congress. See Morey Rothberg and Vivian Pollak, "An Emily Dickinson Manuscript (Re)Identified at the Library of Congress," *The Emily Dickinson Journal* 10, no. 2 (2001): 43–51.

2 This essay honors the many fine contributions of Helen Samuels to the work of academic archivists. The inspiration comes from my close friend Rudolf Arnheim (1904–2007), who challenged me to search beyond the text to the visual essence of archives, perception, and memory. I am very grateful to Francis X. Blouin, Teresa Brinati, Terry Cook, Tom Nesmith, Ala Rekrut, Joan M. Schwartz, Anna and Per Svenson, and Brian Williams for their interest and encouragement in this essay.

3 Françoise Meltzer, "Color as Condition in Symbolist Verse," *Critical Inquiry* 5, no. 2 (Winter 1978): 253–73.

4 Helen Samuels' *Varsity Letters: Documenting Modern Colleges and Universities* remains the essential functional analysis of academia and its archival evidence. Her *Varsity Letters* is a key resource for my efforts to explore "varsity colors."

5 For over twenty-five years, the author has had the privilege of observing and participating in several academic and professional programs organized and hosted by the Bentley Historical Library in the pursuit of research on archival administration and scholarly use of modern documentation. (The Bentley Historical Library serves as the archives of the University of Michigan.) Key among these have been the Mellon/National Endowment for the Humanities Fellowships for the Study of Modern Archives, hosted annually from 1983 to 1997, and the Sawyer Seminar on Archives and Social Memory, a yearlong series of weekly seminars leading to the publication *Archives, Documentation, and Institutions of Social Memory: Essays from the Sawyer Seminar*, edited by Francis X. Blouin Jr. and William G. Rosenberg (Ann Arbor: University of Michigan Press, 2006). Through the Mellon program, the author first met Helen Samuels. Helen provided equal measures of wit and wisdom through her many contributions in the program's meetings both formal and informal, often while multitasking with knitting needles in hand.

6 Other famous photographers had used black and white as well to document Michigan and its environs, including Margaret Bourke-White, Henri Cartier-Bresson, Alfred Eisenstaedt, and Robert Frank.

7 Erich A. Walter, ed., *Our Michigan: An Anthology Celebrating the University of Michigan's Sesquicentennial* (Ann Arbor: University of Michigan, 1966), 167.

8 David Litschel, ed., *Fugitive Color: A National Invitational Show of Color Photography* (Ann Arbor: University of Michigan, 1981). Litschel noted in his introduction that, "Photography is in the throes of a great transformation. The explosion of interest in color is as influential for photography's future now as was Alfred Stieglitz's serious use of the hand-held camera around the turn of the century. Increasingly, young photographers have chosen to work with color, schools are teaching it, critical writings explore its special achievements, and museums and galleries are receptive to exhibitions of it."

9 "College Colors," *University Chronicle*, March 16, 1867. The March 9, 1867 issue reported that "it has become a custom among colleges for the students to select for themselves a particular color or combination of colors, by which they may be distinguished from other men, and particularly from students attending other institutions. . . . The practice was first introduced in Harvard and Yale, a little more than a year ago."

10 Ribbons are a part of the University of Michigan anthem, with its "Hail to the ribbons that nature has spun, Hurrah for the Yellow and Blue!"

11 Walter, *Our Michigan*, 167.

12 Liene Karels, "Which Maize? Which Blue?" *Michigan Today*, Fall 1996.

13 "The University of Michigan Reveals Its True Colors," http://www.techexchange.com/thelibrary/UofM_TrueColors.html. The December 19, 1997 obituary in *The Ann Arbor News* for the Michigan alumnus who headed the firm was entitled "'Maize and blue' color maker dies."

14 The University of Michigan Identity Guidelines include PMS color specifications at http://www.logos.umich.edu/print.html.

15 Jane R. Elgass, "Plant Operations Launches CARE Recognition Program," *University Record*, May 24, 1999.

16 The "Old Blues" were not pleased with the change in attire on the basketball court, when the "Fab Five" freshmen players switched to black shoes and black socks. The color choice also motivated another university's president to telephone Michigan's president in protest. See Ian Robinson, "An Unwanted Legacy," *Michigan Daily*, www.michigandaily.com, posted April 1, 2008.

17 Archivist Greg Kinney presents the origins of Michigan's colorful helmet, within the suite of web pages consulted much more than any others of the archives: "Michigan's famed winged football helmet dates back to 1938, when Fritz Crisler arrived from Princeton University with his penchant for detail and style. 'Michigan had a plain black helmet and we wanted to dress it up a little,' Crisler recalled. 'We added some color (maize and blue) and used the same basic helmet I had designed at Princeton.' There was one other consideration. Fritz thought this unique helmet could be helpful to his passers as they tried to spot their receivers downfield. 'There was

a tendency to use different-colored helmets just for receivers in those days, but I always thought that would be as helpful for the defense as for the offense,' offered the former Wolverine football coach and athletic director." See "Michigan's Winged Helmet" at http://www.bentley.umich.edu/athdept/football/helmet/mhelmet.htm.

18 Rebecca A. Doyle, "'Halo' design to get a second look, with public comments," *University Record*, September 13, 1999.

19 Paul Kahn and Krzysztof Lenk, "Design: Principles of Typography for User Interface Design," *Interactions* 5, no. 6 (November–December 1998): 15–29. The quotation is identified by Kahn and Lenk as "an old German saying."

20 Christopher De Hamel, *A History of Illuminated Manuscripts* (London: Phaidon, 2005), 105.

21 According to Henry Petroski, "Color continued to be used in the early years of the twentieth century, but with decreasing frequency as copying methods that could not produce color became more widespread." See Henry Petroski, *The Pencil: A History of Design and Circumstance* (New York: Alfred A. Knopf, 1989), 234.

22 In their essay on the history of scrapbooks, Katherine Ott, Susan Tucker, and Patricia P. Buckler point out that, "the success of color-printing technologies in the late eighteenth and nineteenth centuries meant that the general public now had cheap and plentiful color images at their disposal. . . . Small color scraps—the leftover pieces from larger printing jobs—seemed too precious to be discarded and too valuable to be given away. . . . The fad of collecting them fueled the printing industry, and the fad of collecting them in a scrapbook or scrap album inspired another product." See Katherine Ott, Susan Tucker, and Patricia P. Buckler, "An Introduction to the History of Scrapbooks," in *The Scrapbook in American Life* (Philadelphia: Temple University Press, 2006), 7.

23 China offers quite another historical trajectory: "Originally, in China the difference between calligraphy and painting was barely perceptible for the word for 'writing' also meant 'drawing' and 'decoration.' In the fifth century BC a technique evolved that was considered to be more expressive than polychrome painting. This made use of monochrome ink, usually black, but also, occasionally, gold and silver." See Barbara Rose, *Monochromes from Malevich to the Present* (Berkeley: University of California Press, 2004), 12.

24 Diane Kirkpatrick, "Color and Photography," in Litschel, ed., *Fugitive Color*.

25 Carolyn Steedman, *Dust: The Archive and Cultural History* (New Brunswick: Rutgers University Press, 2002), 18–19. The author questioned Steedman's view in a brief essay entitled "The Healthy Distrust of the Archives' Inhabitant," in *Archives News* 43, no. 4 (June 2001): 162–67.

26 Steedman, *Dust: The Archive and Cultural History*, 28.

27 Ala Rekrut recognizes a significance in the color coding of standard archival supplies. She has written that, "the colours of 'archival' supplies are light and neutral, the forms uniform and utilitarian—clinical, orderly, dispassionate and unbiased." See Ala Rekrut, "Material Literacy: Reading Records as Material Culture," *Archivaria* 60 (Fall 2005): 25. Yet Amy Lowell's poem about the Library of Congress is instead a vision of contrasts of white, yellow, red, "an old world remaking, whirling into the no-world of all-colored light," as a "vast, confused beauty." New commercial catalogs for archival materials feature what are promoted as new color options for containers. Metal Edge, Inc., for example, advertises "SafeColor® Drop Front Boxes," "SafeColor® Photo Boxes," and "SafeColor® Document Cases." The description for the photo boxes states, "Photo Boxes just got better. SafeColor® photo boxes not only look good but also have an extra layer of protection. We cover our existing photo boxes with an acid/lignin-free embossed paper with your choice of 3 popular colors (Green, Red, or Black). The colorful paper adds to the beauty and durability of the photo box." See Metal Edge, Inc., *Archival Storage Materials* XVI, 99.

28 Rather somber and static images, they seem to forecast poet Anne Stevenson's characterization of Ann Arbor a good century later as "a hopeless candidate for the picturesque." In his poem "Kicking the Leaves," Donald Hall wrote of Ann Arbor in October as "a day the color of soot" yet with "leaves of maples, reds of seventy different shades, yellow like old paper." See both in Laurence Goldstein, ed., *Writing Ann Arbor: A Literary Anthology* (Ann Arbor: University of Michigan Press, 2005).

29 Jasper Cropsey was an American landscape artist and member of the Hudson River School of painters. Color was an important element for him. According to the Newington-Cropsey Foundation, "the English were most impressed with Cropsey's views of American autumn. . . . The English could not believe the brilliant reds and oranges of the autumn scenes, so Cropsey sent for and received [in England] New England leaves pressed onto postcards to demonstrate that his colors were true." See http://www.newingtoncropsey.com/jasper3.htm.

30 Outside of the director's office are two large-format, studio portrait color photographs of Alvin and Arvella Bentley. Arvella Bentley honored her late husband by donating significant funds to the archives and thereby enabling the construction of the Bentley Historical Library, in which the University of Michigan archives and Michigan Historical Collections are located. These photographs, too, are on the tour, as artwork on display in the archives.

31 There are exceptions, of course, in the archival discourse. The advent of digital objects and systems introduces a new urgency and openness to issues of color and its potential as a "significant property." See, for example, Margaret Hedstrom and Christopher A. Lee, "Significant Properties of Digital Objects: Definitions, Applications, Implications," DLM-Forum 2002, http://www.ils.unc.edu/callee/sigprops_dlm2002.pdf.

32 David Batchelor, *Chromophobia* (London: Reaktion Books, 2000).

33 Jasper Johns makes intensive use of gray for the very purpose of a highly intellectualized exploration of color. See, for example, the catalog *Jasper Johns: Gray* (Chicago: Art Institute of Chicago, 2007).

34 Batchelor, *Chromophobia*, 52.

35 Lázló Moholy-Nagy, *Color in Transparency: Photographic Experiments in Color, 1934-1946* (Göttingen: Steidl, 2006), 21.

36 Janet Malcolm, "Photography: Color," *The New Yorker*, October 10, 1977.

37 As quoted in Charles A. Riley II, *Color Codes: Modern Theories of Color in Philosophy, Painting and Architecture, Literature, Music, and Psychology* (Hanover, NH: University Press of New England, 1995), 17.

38 The idea to present food in Technicolor was apparently seen by Hollywood in the 1930s as a potent stimulus. "Ever the perverse little devil, it could deliver an overwhelming sensuous charge" to the extent that Buster Keaton vowed never to appear with Technicolor food "because I'm not going to have a scene stolen from me by a turkey wing." See Scott Higgins, "Technicolor Confections," *Journal of Visual Culture* 6, no. 2 (2007): 275.

39 Riley, *Color Codes*, 17.

40 James O'Toole, *Understanding Archives and Manuscripts* (Chicago: Society of American Archivists, 1990), 3. In all fairness, even though color is not explicitly mentioned, O'Toole does focus on the symbolic value of records and in doing so his writings reflect an empathetic analogy with the arguments in the present essay. He attends to meaning beyond text as such by detailing the emotive, visceral value of documents with their attendant ribbons, seals, and special bindings.

41 Frank Boles, *Selecting and Appraising Archives and Manuscripts* (Chicago: Society of American Archivists, 2005), 133.

42 Ruth B. Bordin and Robert M. Warner, *Modern Manuscript Library* (New York: Scarecrow Press, 1966), 6.

43 Rudolf Arnheim, "Colors—Irrational and Rational," *Journal of Aesthetics and Art Criticism* 33, no. 2 (Winter 1974), 153.

44 Norvell M. M. Jones, "Archival Copies of Thermofax, Verifax, and Other Unstable Records," Technical Information Paper Number 5 (1990), U.S. National Archives and Records Administration, 1.

45 The University of Utah decided to create its own digital collection of 1,300 Sanborn maps in color in order to overcome the limitations of the black and white surrogates produced by Chadwyck-Healey from holdings at the Library of Congress. See Kenning Arlitsch, "Digitizing Sanborn Fire Insurance Maps™ for a Full Color, Publicly Accessible Collection," *D-Lib Magazine*, July/August 2002.

46 "Colorization," The Museum of Broadcast Communications, http://www.museum.tv/archives/etv/C/htmlC/colorization/colorization.htm.

47 Mary Lynn Ritzenthaler and Diane Vogt O'Connor, *Photographs: Archival Care and Management* (Chicago: Society of American Archivists, 2006), 254.

48 Anne R. Kenney and Oya Y. Rieger, *Moving Theory Into Practice: Digital Imaging Tutorial*, 29, http://www.library.cornell.edu/preservation/tutorial/tutorial_English.pdf.

49 Monique Fischer, "Photographs: Creating Long-Lasting Inkjet Prints," Northeast Document Conservation Center Preservation Leaflet, http://www.nedcc.org/resources/leaflets/5Photographs/04InkjetPrints.php.

50 Henry Wilhelm, *The Permanence and Care of Color Photographs: Traditional and Digital Color Prints, Color Negatives, Slides, and Motion Pictures* (Grinnell, Iowa: Preservation Publishing Company, 1993), 724.

51 Henry Wilhelm, "Color Photographs and Color Motion Pictures in the Library: For Preservation or Destruction?" https://www.ideals.uiuc.edu/bitstream/2142/591/2/Wilhelm_Color.pdf.

52 Kayley Vernallis, "The Loss of Meaning in Faded Color Photographs," *Journal of the American Institute for Conservation* 38, no. 3 (Autumn–Winter 1999): 459.

53 Nathan Carroll, "Unwrapping Archives: DVD Restoration Demonstrations and the Marketing of Authenticity," http://muse.jhu.edu/journals/the_velvet_light_trap/v056/56.1carroll.pdf.

54 As cited in Paul Grainge, "TIME's Past in the Present: Nostalgia and the Black and White Image," *Journal of American Studies* 33 (1999): 383–92.

55 Ronald W. Casson and Peter M. Gardner, "On Brightness and Color Categories: Additional Data," *Current Anthropology* 3, no. 4 (August–October 1992): 395–99.

56 Michel Pastoureau, *Blue: The History of a Color* (Princeton: Princeton University Press, 2001), 72.

57 New color indexing software, however, is quite another matter and lends itself beautifully to the notion of visual access to content, even while the RAW format preferred by professional photographers for its color capabilities promises a greater, not lesser, challenge to digital discovery and delivery of color in archives over time.

58 B. A. C. Saunders and J. van Brakel, "The Trajectory of Color," *Perspectives on Science* 10, no. 3 (Fall 2002): 317.

59 Edward Averill, "Why Are Colour Terms Primarily Used as Adjectives?" *Philosophical Quarterly* 30, no. 118 (January 1980): 19–33.

60 William Le Baron Jenney to James B. Angell, August 16, 1876, James B. Angell Collection, Bentley Historical Library, University of Michigan.

61 See the online exhibition "Bound for Glory: America in Color, 1939–1943," http://www.loc.gov/exhibits/boundforglory/; "American Memory: Color Photographs from the Great Depression" feature within the announcement of Flickr Commons pilot project, http://blog.flickr.net/en/2008/01/16/many-hands-make-light-work/; and "For the Common Good: The Library of Congress Flickr Pilot Project," http://www.loc.gov/rr/print/flickr_report_final.pdf.

62 Elisabeth Kaplan and Jeffrey Mifflin, "'Mind and Sight': Visual Literacy and the Archivist," *Archival Issues* 21, no. 2: 107–27.

63 The first full-color cover of the *American Archivist* appeared in 1992 for a "special issue" featuring "European Archives in an Era of Change." Teresa Brinati, director of publications at the Society of American Archivists, noted in an email communication to the author, January 30, 2008, that "with regard to the *American Archivist*, 'color' on the cover has played a role throughout its production and even serves to identify different eras: dark blue ink on blue paper from 1938–1960; dark blue ink on slate 1961–1967; wintergreen ink on light green stock 1968–1972; milk chocolate brown on goldenrod 1973–1975; royal blue background with reversed out typography 1975–1978; four alternating colors for the covers (per volume) with b/w photos introduced 1979–1987; white covers with duotone artwork beginning Fall 1987; first full-color cover . . . Fall 1992." Unfortunately, the Winter 1982 issue of the *American Archivist* also deprived a Sanborn Fire Insurance map of its original color since it was reproduced in black and white.

64 Edward R. Tufte, *Envisioning Information* (Cheshire, CT: Graphics Press, 1990), 81.

65 "Emmett Leith, Inventor of Practical Holography," http://www.eecs.umich.edu/eecs/about/EECSNews/EECSNewsSS06.pdf.

66 University of Michigan President James J. Duderstadt, too, used color extensively as an indicator of emphasis and an organizational tool in his digital notes and drafts.

67 Arnheim, "Colors—Irrational and Rational," 151.

68 See Ernst Gombrich, *Art and Illusion: A Study in the Psychology of Pictorial Representation* (Washington: Pantheon, 1961) and further references to Gombrich's making and matching in Riley, *Color Codes*, passim.

69 For Roland Barthes, the promise was embedded within the very name of colors, a pleasure he experienced as he purchased "Indian yellow," "Persian red," "celadon green." It was an anticipation of interaction, of making something with color, "because of the notion that I am going to do something with it." See Michael Taussig, "What Color is the Sacred?" *Critical Inquiry* 33 (Autumn 2006): 49.

70 Joanna Sassoon, "Chasing Phantoms in the Archives: The Australia House Photograph Collection," *Archivaria* 50 (Fall 2000): 120.

71 Terry Cook, "Remembering the Future: Appraisal of Records and the Role of Archives in Constructing Social Memory," in *Archives, Documentation, and Institutions of Social Memory: Essays from the Sawyer Seminar*, ed. by Francis X. Blouin Jr. and William G. Rosenberg (Ann Arbor: University of Michigan Press, 2006), 170; and Hugh Taylor, "'Heritage' Revisited: Documents as Artifacts in the Context of Museums and Material Culture," *Archivaria* 40 (Fall 1995): 18.

72 Judith Mottram, "Contemporary Artists and Colour: Meaning, Organisation and Understanding," *Optics and Laser Technology* 38 (2006): 406.

73 Contradictions should not necessarily engender conflict, or confusion. Rilke expressed with eloquence his alert awareness, and acceptance, of contradiction: "I fear in myself only those contradictions with a tendency toward reconciliation. It must be a very narrow spot in my life if the idea should occur to them to shake hands, from one side to the other. My contradictions shall hear of each other only rarely and in rumors." See Rainer Maria Rilke, *The Book of Images* (New York: Farrar, Strauss and Giroux, 1991), xv.

74 As quoted in Hugh Taylor, "'Heritage' Revisited," 14.

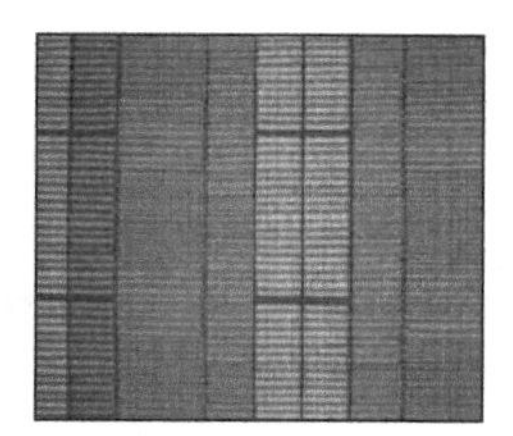

TECHNOLOGY'S PROMISE, THE COPYING OF RECORDS, AND THE ARCHIVIST'S CHALLENGE: A CASE STUDY IN DOCUMENTATION RHETORIC

Richard J. Cox

Prior to 1980, writing about archival appraisal was relatively modest in quantity and scope. Most archivists had stopped thinking about appraisal once Schellenberg had enunciated his codification of appraisal practice being used at the National Archives of the United States.[1] The notions of evidential and informational, primary and secondary, values were widely accepted, representing a kind of mantra that archivists recited when queried about how they identified records as being archival. Even today, the terms are bandied about freely, even when they cannot be precisely defined or effectively applied in archival appraisal and acquisition policies and practices. Archivists *say* they keep records for a variety of values, but their rationale is often subjective—or worse, vague—and, when in a few instances in this era, they have been challenged in courtrooms to explain their approaches, archivists had found the process a difficult one.[2]

After 1980, the function of archival appraisal was transformed, if not practically, at least in a conceptual manner. Before that time, archivists lumped together appraisal and acquisition (or collecting), generally operating as if their repositories could acquire documents in a limitless fashion and, as well, effectively document the universe (however they might be defining the universe). Archivists have always worried about the increasing volume of records that they need to contend with, but this reality did little to transform their attitudes or practices when it came to appraisal.

They nibbled at the edges of the challenge, stressing the development of acquisitions policies, experimenting with sampling approaches, and conceiving of ideas like that of intrinsic value that would enable them to identify original documents that, once reformatted to another recording medium like microfilm, could be destroyed. That old world of archival appraisal underwent a seismic shift in the 1980s with a growing concern about the effectiveness of appraisal approaches and an assessment of their end results, a shift in which Helen Samuels was a key player.

Several critical factors emerged in the new vision of archival appraisal. Some archivists began to discuss the implications of societal changes, such as the growing sense of a global society, multinational corporations, increasing interrelated government activities, and international research. All of these developments challenged traditional archival appraisal practices that tended to focus on records surveys and the records within a single organization, sometimes even a single office. Many archivists recognized the difficulty of documenting a single event, product, geographic region, business activity, or institution without somehow taking into account the larger documentary universe. Some archivists, records managers, and manuscript curators began to experiment with moving their focus from specific documents to business functions, from developing repository-specific acquisition policies to planning cooperative documentation strategies, and from intensive surveys of existing records to analyses of trends and events and the kinds of documentation that should exist and should be gathered.[3]

A few basic questions or issues influenced the shift in archival appraisal. Archivists have always been concerned about the growing volume in records; archivists were the ones, after all, who gave birth to records management and its focus on the economy and efficiency of records work.[4] By the 1980s, it was obvious that the growing dependence of the modern office on personal computers, soon to be joined by laptops and portable data assistants, and refinements in older technologies from the telephone to the fax machine, all were contributing to an unprecedented growth in records volume. Before the emergence of the personal computer, for example, there were frequent reports about the continuing paperwork growth in government and corporations. In 1977, a pharmaceutical company reported that it had to fill out twenty-seven thousand government forms annually and an oil company stated that it was spending $21 million a year on government paperwork. Even a major university could report that it was employing twenty-six people a year to track and complete forms on government grants and contracts.[5] Study after study stressed the need to streamline federal paperwork regulations because of the costs of compliance and the burdens of administering the records and information.[6] Around this time, records managers latched on to the notion of "copy management" as a new component of their field, seeking to control "copying practices, procedures, and devices to ensure the effective and economical creation of necessary copies."[7] One estimate reports that office copies increased from about 20 million a year in 1955, before the advent of xerography, to an amazing 9.5 billion a decade later, and to an astounding 2 trillion copies a year in 2004. As this commentator suggests, "add another trillion or two for the output of laser printers and you end up with something like five hundred xerographically produced pages *this year* [2004] for every human on earth."[8] These and other technologies also influenced new ways that organizations were working, especially in the creation of the modern networked organization. Technology, despite everyone's best intention to not become determinists about such matters, did seem to be driving changes that heralded, if not the end of archival work, then at least fundamental changes in its principles and practices.

Archival appraisal seemed to be on the cutting edge of such concerns and dilemmas. Samuels, and her colleagues and allies, argued that the documentary universe was expanding so rapidly that new approaches not requiring the examination of every record (or even every record file or series) needed to be developed. There were simply too many records for personal inspection, a point that many commentators made even if they did not adopt new appraisal strategies.[9] These new appraisal advocates contended that methodologies allowing a broader perspective on the documentary universe, one that took into account the interrelatedness of records created and maintained by numerous organizations and individuals, needed to be formed and refined as needed. Critics of such practices and ideas developed quickly, stressing either that the documentation strategy or, later, the macro-appraisal approach, was too unwieldy and impractical or claiming that the traditional approaches worked just fine.[10] And, indeed, the evidence still suggests that, for most archivists, appraisal work was little changed since Schellenberg, although the rhetoric about appraisal, its principles and more theoretical dimensions, has been fundamentally transformed. Concerns about the technological dimensions of records have been at the heart of many of the claims made about weaknesses in both old and new appraisal approaches, with some worrying that the resulting quantity of records is now so great as to compromise all appraisal processes, and others claiming (more likely, hoping) that the massively increasing storage capacity for digital memory at ever-lower cost will eliminate the need for an archival function such as appraisal.[11] Of course, some of the new appraisal approaches were also criticized for requiring larger staff and greater resources, although the advocates of these approaches would argue (and still do) that shifts in priorities and the reallocation of resources were just as important (perhaps more important) in the changes in appraisal theory.

Helen Samuels' early writings and some of her subsequent work was derived from working in circumstances where technology played a critical role. She was involved with the Joint Committee on the Archives of Science and Technology (JCAST), a group issuing what is still one of the best research and planning documents in the profession's history, even though it is now more than two decades old.[12] Her work with JCAST led her to collaboratively author a methodology for appraising the records of science and technology and, simultaneously, fed her imagination to articulate the early ideas about the documentation strategy.[13] Out of this came her later work, more closely reflecting the macroappraisal concepts, on documenting higher education.[14] In all of this work, the challenges of modern information technology, primarily the volume of records and the increasingly networked nature of modern organizations, were present and prominent.

Records, from the ancient to the postmodern world, have always been intimately connected to technology. And, of course, their administration and preservation have been heavily influenced by their technical foundations. A clay tablet must be handled very differently than a digital document, even though commentators about the preservation of electronic records often resort to discussing the maintenance advantages of the clay tablet.[15] Yet there has always been hype associated with and influencing how records are managed, including how they have been appraised. Thomas Misa, in his interesting discourse on the nature of technology and culture in the past five centuries, argues that we must take a "middle-ground stance towards technology, resisting the undue pessimism of some writers and rejecting the unwarranted optimism of others." Adopting "extreme positions," Misa warns, can "lead us away from a serious engagement with the problems and potentials of technology."[16] This essay, partly drawing on an informal study of claims made in advertisements about the miracle of electrostatic photocopying, considers the contrasts between the promises of technology and its reality. The essay also considers how this earlier hype was echoed at the advent of the personal computer and its subsequent variations. A consideration of the exaggerated claims for office and personal technology suggests the need not only for innovative archival appraisal approaches, such as those influenced by Samuels during the past twenty years, but also the need for new ones for today. What continues to be needed is the development of new appraisal concepts, strategies, and methodologies—not a quest for a technological panacea—for the challenge of the continuing growth of records' quantity and technical complexity. A change in resources for doing such appraisal would require staff with enhanced technical knowledge, but the new strategies also require sharper ability by archival managers to refine priorities and redistribute resources for these new priorities.

Since the dawn of writing, humanity has searched for and experimented with ways of speeding up the copying of documents. Polygraphs, involving the use of multiple pens, date back at least to the early seventeenth century. By the late eighteenth century, letterpress copying, a messy and awkward reproduction system with uneven results—considered revolutionary in its time—was well established in business offices and government agencies; letterpress copies were created by the use of oiled and tissue papers pressed onto the original inked document by a hand-operated mechanical device. Not long after, the earliest forms of carbon paper were created, although this method of copying would not become common or reliable until the widespread use of the typewriter in offices by the end of the nineteenth century.[17] Copying was especially propelled forward with the invention of photography in 1839, and by the end of that century the first organized and entrepreneurial efforts to develop systematic and reliable photocopying were evident. In 1905, George C. Beidler marketed the first commercial photocopier and within a short time libraries, archives, and corporate offices were utilizing one or more of these copiers (Photostat, Rectigraph, Cameragraph, or Dexigraph), although all of these were clumsy and expensive machines to use, often producing blurred or smudged images.

This changed by the middle of the twentieth century, when Chester Carlson patented his electronic photocopier; it was marketed by the late 1940s and became commonplace by the end of the next decade.[18] David Owen argues that the "invention of the Xerox machine was an epochal event in the history of communication and, therefore, in the history of civilization. It gave ordinary people an extraordinary means of preserving and sharing information, and it placed the rapid exchange of complicated ideas within the reach of almost anyone—a potent and, indeed, subversive capability, whose reach and ease of use have been exceeded only relatively recently, by the World Wide Web and email."[19] These, and other forms of office equipment related to the creation of documents (such as the stapler, address machine, check writer, typewriter, and so forth), all contributed to the steady standardization of office work spaces and the uniformity of record forms.[20] And, in particular, the office copier contributed to the rise of what some have termed office copier folklore, where, instead of oral transmission, myths and other folk notions are transmitted by copying technologies.[21]

Haloid Xerox produced the first commercially successful photocopier, the 914, in 1960. Writing two decades ago, one commentator suggested that "today we are addicted to copiers. We keep them in our offices, stores, schools, and libraries, and even in our homes." In the late 1980s, copiers were generating nearly 500 billion copies annually, leading this assessment to suggest, "after the telephone, the copier is probably the most important modern communications tool in use."[22] Prior to the creation of the personal computer, the photocopier was certainly the most profound and powerful office technology, a device that made many office workers forget what work was like before its invention, practical development, and commercialization.

Fascinated as a child with printing, Carlson developed an early interest in copying techniques, registering patents for his concepts in the late 1930s and early 1940s when he was just in his thirties. He searched relevant research literature, worked with engineers on building a prototype, and experimented with multiple versions of the technology in search of a model that could be replicated and sold for office applications. Noting that "technology doesn't evolve steadily and continuously," Owen describes how, in the early 1950s, a number of different copying options employing varying technologies arrived in the marketplace.[23] An interesting aspect of the origin of the photocopier is that many companies saw it as too risky a venture. It was only in the production of the early machines, as highly flawed as they were, and their placement in real offices, that they were able to prove themselves. As Owen concludes, the "914 was so easy and pleasant to work with that people began using it to satisfy needs they hadn't known they had,"[24] an observation reflected in the immense and rapid growth in the volume of copying.

The case of Xerox and its copier demonstrates a pattern of characteristics attributed to the significance of information technology in the organization. Haloid, the company that eventually became Xerox, took a risk in supporting the development of the copying technology. It invested a considerable sum in development, far more than it thought it might recover, and gained an edge in a technology that was far more successful than anyone thought possible. In 1959 Haloid Xerox was just a small, indistinguishable company, but in seven years the Xerox Corporation was the "fifteenth largest publicly owned corporation in America as ranked by market capitalization."[25] In fact, Xerox's problems have mostly stemmed from its efforts to diversify away from copying technology, as it has always maintained its edge in the copier industry.

Nicholas Carr has advanced an approach to Information Technology (IT) that has implications for the day-to-day work of records professionals. Carr argues that it is time for a "more conservative approach to IT management. As the infrastructure matures, the companies that succeed will not be those that reflexively pursue innovation, that seek to push the proverbial envelope, but rather those that are pragmatic in planning and competent in execution."[26] For a long time, archivists and records managers have seen information technologies as their great nemesis, changing so quickly and effortlessly as to always outrace solutions for administering the records these systems produce. By contrast, Carr perceives a settling down, one perhaps that ought to encourage records professionals to consider the long-term possibilities of controlling all records, digital or otherwise. There is, perhaps, a limit to innovation that we have reached in creating new digital technologies—at least a level of innovation that corporations will accept in their investments in their technological infrastructures. Archivists and records managers ought to be able to consider steadier solutions to administering such records, rather than looking over their shoulders in fear that a new technology will eradicate all their best efforts.

What we do know about the impact of office copying is how it, with other technologies, contributed to an immense change in the nature of corporations and other organizations. Abigail J. Sellen and Richard H. R. Harper, in their study on the myth of the paperless office, demonstrate that the demise of paper as a business communication and recording mechanism is another form of folklore, mustering statistics on the growing uses of paper in the typical office. Paper continues to play a role because it effectively supports many crucial tasks such as authoring, reviewing, planning, collaboration, communicating, annotating, and cross-referencing.[27] These roles are an integral dimension of what an office is and what it does:

> An office is not simply an interface to information but . . . an interactive amalgam of information, people, and artifacts working harmoniously together. As such, an effective office consists of a much broader array of tools than a collection of PDAs and laptops could ever provide. It encompasses an information environment that spreads out around the desk and office walls. It consists of artifacts that support not only an individual's immediate needs, but also the needs of teams of people (such as the use of wall charts and whiteboards). It also consists of combinations of tools and artifacts used in conjunction with one another in artful ways.[28]

Examining the office this way also suggests something about how office photocopying was part of an array of technologies enabling organizations to network and function according to their priorities, if sometimes in ways that made their records more complicated for archivists and records managers needing to control or appraise them. The complexity of organizational records is not merely the result of digital technologies (a conclusion reached because of our more recent focus on the challenges posed by such technologies), but rather the result of the mix of records technologies and their generation of ever-increasing quantities of records. The archivist's response should be to focus more on strategic appraisal, as Helen Samuels suggested, a process running counter to what many others seem inclined to think: that the new technologies will enable us to save everything.

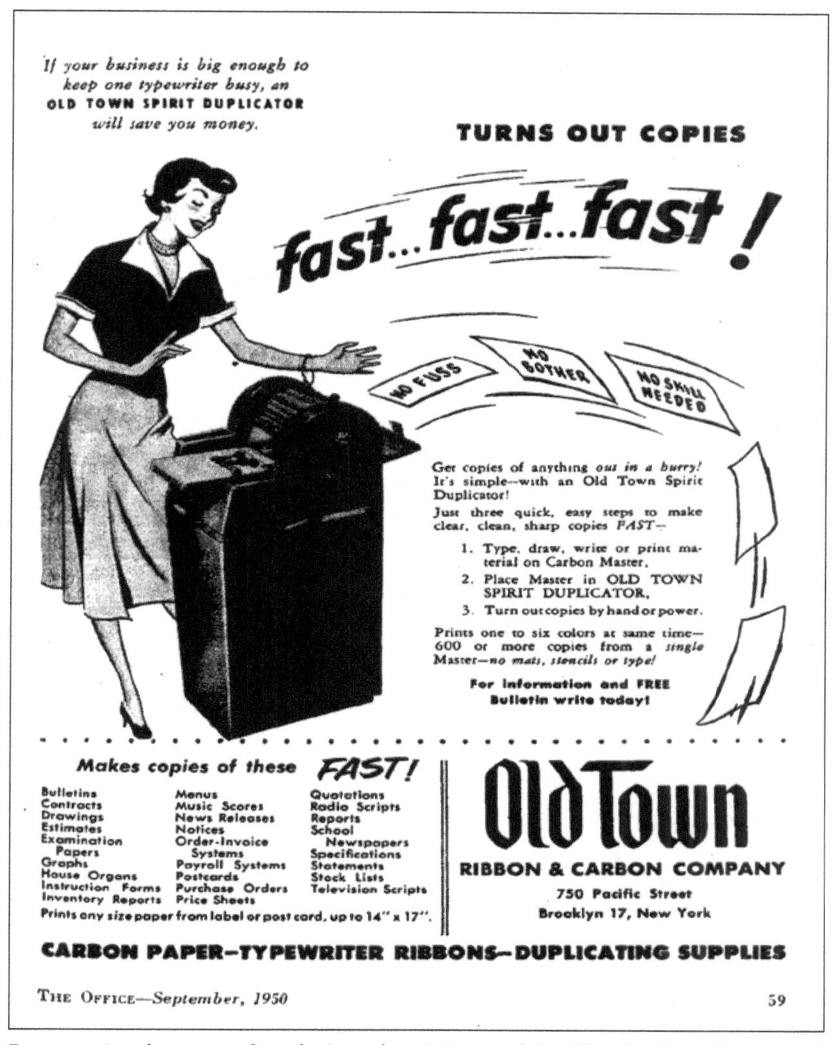

FIGURE 1: *An advertisement from the September 1950 issue of the* Office *for the "Old Town Spirit Duplicator" featuring a women operating the gray, boxy copier with the promise of turning out copies "fast... fast... fast!" The copying could also be done with "no fuss, no bother, no skill needed."*

We can comprehend the nature and consequences of the older office technologies, enabling us to put them, and the later technologies, into a more useful perspective. Examining advertisements for office copying equipment is akin to studying the artifacts of ancient societies. The illustrations are quaint, the promises simple, and the equipment, bulky and ugly, almost as if it were from another universe. Yet, it is all too familiar as well. This is especially the case with copier advertisements prior to the advent of the Xerox era. A September 1950 *Office* advertisement for the "Old Town Spirit Duplicator" (see figure 1) features a primitive looking sketch of a women operating the gray, boxy copier with the promise of turning out copies "fast . . . fast . . . fast!" and with "no fuss, no bother, no skill needed." This less efficient stencil copier, which produced six hundred copies from a single master, utilized a copying process far different from what the Xerox machines would make possible just a decade later.[29]

These early advertisements are also raw material for scholars interested in studying the changing roles of gender in the modern office, a topic that has been considered by some scholars for both the modern office and its antecedents.[30] Indeed, paging through one advertisement after another, one begins to believe that in the 1950s and after, office technology was primarily designed to make women happy. An advertisement from 1955 depicts a cartoon of a troubled woman, crying "I'm no chemist! I'm no mechanic!" and pleading for her boss to buy her a "Stenafax."[31] A 1958 advertisement spreads over two pages and features a woman standing behind large stacks of documents, beaming, and proclaiming, "Look what I turn out in one hour."[32] The parade of advertisements reflects an interesting array of product names for the various copiers—Copy-rite, Copyflex, Copyease, Rapid Printer, Thermo-Fax, Stenafax, Speed-O-Print, Verifax—all designed to deny the obvious clumsy mechanical features that they brought to the office.[33]

Duplicating, even as primitive as it now seems in comparison to the later development of copiers and the analogous voluminous printing from personal and laptop computers, seemed to have become the focus of office recordkeeping at the midpoint of the last century. The August 1952 issue of the *Office* is a good case in point. Full of advertisements about duplicating, this issue also features a number of essays. The issue opens with a case study of one municipal government's duplicating program, reporting that the "city's offset duplicator turns out faithful reproductions of printed and typed forms, drawings, instructions, receipt books and form letters," all at savings in money and time.[34] This issue then includes straightforward, how-to descriptions of office duplicating.[35]

Figure 2: *Advertisement for the Xerox 914 from the July 1960 issue of the* Office, *featuring all the extraordinary promises for a new era of office work.*

The introduction and widespread adoption of the Xerox 914 revolutionized the copying process (see figure 2). It used "ordinary paper," bringing an end to messy chemicals and complicated loading and adjusting, and enabled everything to be copied whether "written, typed, printed, stamped or drawn" in whatever color.[36] It jump-started

FIGURE 3: *A typical advertisement of the photocopier as the vanguard of an office technology revolution promising the solution to every work efficiency problem, from the January 1978 issue of the* Office.

the growth of copying in an unprecedented fashion. The various models introduced by Xerox in subsequent years reflected many of the earlier advertisements. A 1969 advertisement declared, "The Xerox 2400 is for when she has better things to do than hang around making copies," furthering the stereotype of women's work as secretarial (no one had to tell us who the "she" was).[37] Of course, advertisements for devices employing the earlier copying technologies continued for many years, even as the success of the Xerox machines transformed the process; those of us who are old enough can remember using the earlier technologies.[38] (I retired a Thermofax machine when I changed positions in 1978, replacing it with a modern photocopier, and I remember being amazed that such older machines were still being used.) Increasingly, as time passed, the advertisements declared war on Xerox, promoting their products in comparison to what Xerox had to offer. A 1977 advertisement by Toshiba declared, "O.K. Xerox, Try and Copy This," with a clever drawing of Toshiba's own copier.[39] Xerox had achieved what every company wishes for—a semantic merger of its brand name and the business function or process it enables or produces.

The advertisements for the new generation of photocopiers generally focused on features and improvements certain to appeal to professional records managers, urging economy and efficiency in the administration of documents. One 1967 advertisement declared, "How 14 Dennison Copiers save Raytheon $75,000 a year on copying costs," with a jubilant woman (of course) holding up a sign with the company's contact information.[40] An advertisement for the Xerox 3600 announced, "How to increase your department's productivity without increasing your department," with a photograph of the photocopier in the background.[41] These appeals to economy and efficiency (such as in figure 3) were standard for the records management field in this era as well as now, and they reflected essentially what divides records managers and archivists.

Such advertisements provide a historical window whereby one can look into the changing nature of the office and the characteristics of modern work. Twenty years ago, two scholars examined ten thousand computer advertisements from the years 1950 through 1980, determining that the advertisements accurately reflected changing trends in information technology and applied use of the technology. Their research identified many of the issues I have addressed here—advertisements making promises for revolutionizing work and reflecting or mimicking social and cultural aspects of the office (such as the gender issues). Their study suggests that the "ads show quite clearly the computing industry as a microcosm of America, revealing several general themes about U.S. culture." For example, in the 1950s and early 1960s, the ads "appeal directly to the American Dream of Success—power, profit, prestige, prosperity, and unlimited growth. They tout efficiency, speed, and economy as the salient features of the new technology to be employed in making business grow bigger and larger."[42]

Photocopiers have had a profound impact on the modern office, in both office culture and the nature of work itself. In speeding up copying, they have contributed to new forms of office folklore and, as well, have provided diversions to office workers.[43] Erik Pell, in his history of xerography, asserts that the Xerox 914 "would become known as the most profitable item ever manufactured in the U.S.," and that the copier "would revolutionize the American office."[44] Moreover, copiers provide a kind of metaphor for the means by which society handles information: one journalist seeking to characterize the Internet in a discourse on rights in cyberspace, referred to it as a "global collection of copying machines."[45]

For some archivists and records managers, there may be a sense of nostalgia about the older office, even before the days of efficient mechanical copying. There is always a sense of longing for older technologies, effectively captured by Charles D'Ambrosio's fictional account of a typewriter repair shop:

> There were pockets of people who warily refused the future, or the promise or whatever it was computers were offering, and stuck by their typewriters. Some of them were secretaries who filled out forms, and others were writers, a sudden surge of them from all over Seattle. There were professors and poets and young women with colored hair who wrote for the local weeklies. There were aging lefties who made carbons of their correspondence or owned mimeographs and hand-cranked the ink drums and dittoed urgent newsletters that smelled of freshly laundered cotton for their dwindling coteries. Now and then, too, customers walked in off the street, a stream of curious shoppers who simply wanted to touch the machines, tapping the keys and slapping back the carriage when the bell rang out, leaving a couple of sentences behind.[46]

And archivists and archives were not always quick to embrace photocopying, as can been seen in the case of one of America's oldest historical societies. There was a long resistance to acquiring and using a photostatic copier because of concerns about lessening the market value of the holdings of the Historical Society of Pennsylvania (HSP) by copying. As Sally Griffith notes, "Although the Society had been notably generous in granting access to its collections and had even sponsored the publication of many of its prized possessions, there seems to have been a distinct difference in perception between allowing a document to be copied by hand or in print and having a photographic facsimile made."[47] In the 1930s, microfilming was introduced at the HSP as a means of providing access to the collections. Thirty years later, the first photocopy machine was acquired. A consideration of these seemingly minor details suggests that the HSP lacked the resources it needed for its most basic or routine work.

What looms before us now is the matter of whether the growth of paper records—partly propelled by the photocopying technology—will end, and a greater reliance on electronic records will terminate the dominance of paper. Some have been arguing that this has already occurred. David Stephens, analyzing trends in records management a decade ago, pulled data from various sources to argue that while paper was still growing in modern organizations, from 5 to 20 percent a year, electronic records were growing from 20 to 60 percent a year. Stephens contended that what used to be the focus of records management—paper documents—had now shifted to digital information, fundamentally transforming the field.[48] Yet this is a contested notion, one that continues to engage records professionals as legacy paper systems linger alongside the development of new digital systems.

Ian Batterham, in his practical book about preserving document copies, provides a more realistic assessment, asserting that "the legacy of this 250 years of office copying, with all its invention and variation, with its overlapping and eclipsing, is the millions upon millions of copies that remain. These languish in historical collections of many types: archives, libraries, personal document holdings and even art galleries. Some copies are as pristine as the day they were created, others are showing signs of degradation such as embrittlement of the support, yellowing of the background and fading of the image."[49]

What all this suggests is that appraisal will become more and more important, given its aims of both identifying the records of critical value to the organization and reducing the bulk of data that future researchers, organizational workers, and citizens will have to go through for the information they require. The present and still evolving electronic networked society in which we live harkens back to the documentation challenges Helen Samuels began to write about as she reflected on the complexities of modern government, business, and educational documentation.

Whatever the responses, both positive and negative, have been to her various appraisal ideas, the reality is that the records and information regime that we now face requires rigorous, planned, and constantly evaluated appraisal approaches such as those she and her colleagues or followers (I admit that I followed in her carefully placed footsteps) began to construct a quarter of a century ago. The continuing presence of the photocopier, now accompanied by the rattles and hums of the printer networks linked to personal computers and laptops, suggests that we will continue to face a complicated office environment for administering records. The glut of paper records resulted from the office revolution of half a century ago, as represented by the photocopier. The glut of information, now well represented by the torrent of electronic mail and the constant surfing on an expanding web universe, caused by several generations of a computer revolution, provides the other half of the picture.

Archivists, as they continue developing appraisal methods and theories, also need to become more conversant with the implications of information technologies. They need to be more sensitive, following along from the very sexist photocopier advertisements of the mid-century, to the gender connotations of records and of their own work. Is computer technology, at least in some of its manifestations, more likely to attract male than female users? Are men or women more attracted to record-keeping positions in government and business and how is this reflected in the systems designed to capture and control digital records? Why do archivists accept in their own work the need for such traditional patriarchal concepts as hierarchy, order, and control? While we can all smile at the blatantly sexist portrayals of the mid-century advertisements, maybe archivists need to appraise themselves for their own biases, and the biases inherent in records and systems, as much as they appraise records. The sensitivity being shown to such matters by those studying the history of documentary forms, such as correspondence, demonstrates the value of such perspectives.[50]

The biggest hype of all, greater than the many promises made in advertisements marketing the earlier photocopier, may be the chimera that every bit and byte of digital information can (and so should) be saved. Archival appraisal, as concept, strategy, and methodology, beckons as a more convincing alternative, but one still needing the work of a new generation of thinkers following in the footsteps of Helen Samuels.

Notes

1 Frank Boles' introduction to his 1991 research study on archival appraisal, written with Julia Marks Young, reflects the influence of Schellenberg on archival appraisal in the United States; see his *Archival Appraisal* (New York: Neal-Schuman, 1991).

2 The best example of this was the legal challenge to the appraisal of records of the Federal Bureau of Investigation in 1979, leading to a court-ordered reappraisal in 1981–82, demonstrating that the language of Schellenberg often failed in practice; see Kimberly A. Tryka, "Reappraisal of the Records of the Federal Bureau of Investigation: A Case Study," *Records and Information Management Report* 20 (September 2004): 1–14. See also the essays by Verne Harris, "'They Should Have Destroyed More': The Destruction of Public Records by the South African State in the Final Years of Apartheid, 1990–1994"; and Terry Cook, "'A Monumental Blunder': The Destruction of Records on Nazi War Criminals in Canada," both in *Archives and the Public Good: Accountability and Records in Modern Society*, ed. Richard J. Cox and David A. Wallace (Westport, CT: Quorum Books, 2002).

3 Some sense of the debates, experimentation, and new concepts can be seen in Barbara Craig, *Archival Appraisal: Theory and Practice* (Munchen: K. G. Saur, 2004); Frank Boles, *Selecting and Appraising Archives and Manuscripts* (Chicago: Society of American Archivists, 2005); and my own *No Innocent Deposits: Forming Archives by Rethinking Appraisal* (Metuchen, NJ: Scarecrow Press, 2004), all with very different perspectives about what was good, what worked, and where the profession was moving. All cite Helen Samuels' writings.

4 This was one of the characteristics I identified in my "The Documentation Strategy and Archival Appraisal Principles: A Different Perspective," *Archivaria* 38 (Fall 1994): 11–36.

5 "The Drive to Cut Paper Work: One Step Forward, Two Steps Back," *U.S. News and World Report* (April 18, 1977), 51.

6 Rogene Buchholz, "Reducing the Cost of Paperwork," *Business Horizons* 23 (February 1980): 82–89.

7 See B. Thomas Marking, "Copy Management: An Emerging Program," *Records Management Quarterly* 14 (January 1980): 20–22, 38 (quotation on page 21).

8 David Owen, *Copies in Seconds: How a Lone Inventor and an Unknown Company Created the Biggest Communication Breakthrough Since Gutenberg—Chester Carlson and the Birth of the Xerox Machine* (New York: Simon and Schuster, 2004), 282.

9 David Bearman, "Archival Methods," *Archives and Museum Informatics Technical Report* 3, no. 1 (Spring 1989), provided a very clear statement about this challenge, although he remained skeptical about some of the new appraisal approaches adopted in response. Bearman did have hope for the kinds of ideas and concepts suggested by the documentation strategy approach, noting that "The intellectual attraction of the documentation strategies approach should be that it focuses on appraisal of activities and functions rather than of records" (see chapter 1).

10 See, for example, Terry Abraham, "Collection Policy or Documentation Strategy: Theory and Practice," *American Archivist* 54 (Winter 1991): 44–52; and "Documentation Strategies: A Decade (or More) Later," paper presented at the annual meeting of the Society of American Archivists, Washington, DC, August 31, 1995, available at http://www.uidaho.edu/special-collections/papers/docstr10.htm. For an explanation of the idea of macroappraisal, see Terry Cook, "Macroappraisal in Theory and Practice: Origins, Characteristics, and Implementation in Canada, 1950–2000," *Archival Science* 5 (2005): 101–61.

11 For a recent example of the tension between the concern of losing the digital documentary heritage and the belief that perhaps everything can now be saved, see Daniel J. Cohen and Roy Rosenzweig, *Digital History: A Guide to Gathering, Preserving, and Presenting the Past on the Web* (Philadelphia: University of Pennsylvania Press, 2005), 9–10, 227–28.

12 Clark A. Elliott, ed., *Understanding Progress as Process: Documentation of the History of Post-War Science and Technology in the United States; Final Report of the Joint Committee on Archives of Science and Technology* (Chicago: Society of American Archivists, 1983).

13 Joan K. Haas, Helen W. Samuels, and Barbara T. Simmons, *Appraising the Records of Modern Science and Technology: A Guide* (Cambridge: Massachusetts Institute of Technology, 1985).

14 Helen W. Samuels, *Varsity Letters: Documenting Modern Colleges and Universities* (Metuchen, NJ: Scarecrow Press and Society of American Archivists, 1992).

15 See, for example, James Fallows, "File Not Found: Why a Stone Tablet Is Still Better Than a Hard Drive," *Atlantic Monthly* 298 (September 2006): 142, 144–45.

16 Thomas J. Misa, *Leonardo to the Internet: Technology and Culture from the Renaissance to the Present* (Baltimore: Johns Hopkins University Press, 2004), 260.

17 For an account of early copying devices, see Barbara Rhodes and William Wells Streeter, *Before Photocopying: The Art and History of Mechanical Copying 1780-1938* (New Castle, DE: Oak Knoll Press, 1999).

18 Michael E. Sawyer, "The Photocopying Machine: How Did It Begin," *Law Library Journal* 71 (Winter 1979): 91–98.

19 Owen, *Copies in Seconds*, 13.

20 See Phil Patton, "The Evolution of Your Office," *American Heritage* 52 (June 2001): 37–42, for a popular discussion of this phenomenon.

21 See, for example, Alan Dundes and Carl R. Pagter, *Urban Folklore from the Paperwork Empire* (Austin, TX: American Folklore Society, 1975); and *Never Try to Teach a Pig to Sing: Still More Urban Folklore from the Paperwork Empire* (Detroit: Wayne State University Press, 1991).

22 Dean J. Golembeski, "Struggling to Become an Inventor," *Invention and Technology* 4 (Winter 1989): 8–15 (quotation on page 8).

23 Owen, *Copies in Seconds*, 179.

24 Ibid., 240.

25 Ibid., 253.

26 Nicholas Carr, *Does IT Matter? Information Technology and the Corrosion of Competitive Advantage* (Boston: Harvard Business School Publishing, 2004), 112.

27 Abigail J. Sellen and Richard H. R. Harper, *The Myth of the Paperless Office* (Cambridge, MA: MIT Press, 2002), 53, 76.

28 Ibid., 191–92.

29 *Office*, September 1950, 59.

30 Such as Margery W. Davies, *Woman's Place Is at the Typewriter: Office Work and Office Workers 1870–1920* (Philadelphia: Temple University Press, 1982); and Sharon Hartman Strom, *Beyond the Typewriter: Gender, Class, and the Origins of Modern American Office Work, 1900–1930* (Urbana: University of Illinois Press, 1992).

31 *Office*, May 1955, 107.

32 *Office*, January 1958, 174–75.

33 *Office*, August 1955, 110, 115; December 1955, 38; May 1956, 104, 109, 142; January 1958, 101.

34 Herbert Winston Jr., "How Duplicating Stretches the Taxpayer's Dollar," *Office*, August 1952, 7–12 (quotation on page 7).

35 Irvin A. Herrmann, "How to Prepare Masters for Office Duplicating," *Office*, August 1952, 47–75; George G. Hart, "Operation and Control of an Office Duplicating Department," *Office*, August 1952, 77–85, 134–36.

36 *Office*, July 1960.

37 *Office*, July 1969.

38 An advertisement was run for a stencil copier in December 1963, promising that it provided the "simplest, fastest and most economical method of making numerous copies of printed, typed, written, diagrammed or drawn originals." *Office*, December 1963, 23.

39 *Office*, July 1977, 145.

40 *Office*, January 1967, 21.

41 *Office*, July 1971, 14–15.

42 William Aspray and Donald deB. Beaver, "Marketing the Monster: Advertising Computer Technology," *Annals of the History of Computing* 8 (April 1986): 127–43 (quotations on pages 138–39).

43 Jean Loic Le Quellic, "From Celestial Letters to 'Copylore' and 'Screenlore,'" *Reseaux: The French Journal of Communication* 5, no. 1 (1997): 113–44.

44 Erik M. Pell, *From Dream to Riches: The Story of Xerography* (Rochester, NY: n. p., 1998), 84.

45 Mike Godwin, *Cyber Rights: Defending Free Speech in the Digital Age*, rev. ed. (Cambridge, MA: MIT Press, 2003), 190.

46 Charles D'Ambrosio, "Drummond & Son," *New Yorker* (October 7, 2002), 85.

47 Sally F. Griffith, *Serving History in a Changing World: The Historical Society of Pennsylvania in the Twentieth Century* (Philadelphia: Historical Society of Pennsylvania, distributed by the University of Pennsylvania Press, 2001), 89.

48 David O. Stephens, "Megatrends in Records Management," *Records Management Quarterly* 32 (January 1998): 3.

49 Ian Batterham, *The Office Copying Revolution: History, Identification, and Preservation: A Manual for Conservators, Archivists, Librarians and Forensic Document Examiners* (Canberra: National Archives of Australia, 2008), 16.

50 Three recent studies of letter writing consider gender issues in the production of records; see Dena Goodman, *Becoming a Woman in the Age of Letters* (Ithaca: Cornell University Press, 2009); Konstantin Dierks, *In My Power: Letter Writing and Communications in Early America* (Philadelphia: University of Pennsylvania Press, 2009); and Catherine J. Golden, *Posting It: The Victorian Revolution in Letter Writing* (Gainesville: University Press of Florida, 2009).

BROWN SHOES IN A WORLD OF TUXEDOS: CORPORATE ARCHIVES AND THE ARCHIVAL PROFESSION

Bruce H. Bruemmer

To work with Helen Samuels was to practice archives under a big tent: a lot of space for many ideas and different perspectives. And like a tent, the space created was functional, not ornamental, and could be moved down the road if the terrain was not adequate. One of my first experiences with the big tent included computer scientists, records managers, archivists (including Helen), and historians in debate over how best to document mainframe computers. The language barriers hijacked the discussion between the four groups at nearly every turn, but the lesson for the archivists was that the documentation of very complex ideas and issues could not take place in the vacuum of archivists talking only to archivists. After all, this collaborative approach was the model of the Joint Committee on the Archives of Science and Technology (JCAST), as well as the MIT appraisal guide to the records of modern science and technology, in which Helen Samuels first cut her archival teeth and showed her imaginative approaches to meeting modern archival challenges.[1]

The experience affected my own work in trying to approach the documentation of business records. While the *High-Technology Company: A Historical and Archival Guide* was written from the perspective of a manuscripts curator and historian looking inward from the outside of a live business, the work took place within a corporation and engaged its employees. The guide attempted to functionally map a company to provide a starting place to preserve those records that best documented its strategy, products, marketing, finances, facilities, and personalities. Given the complexity of a large business, the guide was painfully simplistic.

Any attempt to drill down in any one function uncovered a host of complicated issues. Just the rapidity of changes in personnel, organization, and product lines made archival documentation a moving target. In spite of this, the experience was exhilarating. Rather than examining evidence only at the end of the records cycle, the writers had the opportunity to move upstream and ask questions about documentation as it was being created—an insight and strategy that has now become fairly commonplace, but was then unorthodox and even rejected by some as unarchival.[2]

After a few years' perspective, our efforts began to look even more naïve. Technological change had accelerated within the structure of the business and its documentation. Little did we realize in the late 1980s that we were in the middle of a major transformation of the computer industry that would leave only one major company, IBM, barely intact where seven others had once flourished. More important, electronic records were already in the mainstream of business records, making the capture of historical documentation even more elusive.

That was the view of a business from the outside. At the change of the millennium I decided to join the private sector as the corporate archivist for a global company of 82,000 employees. Instantly I identified with the George Gobel line: "Did you ever get the feeling that the world was a tuxedo and you were a pair of brown shoes?" I found myself turning my back on years of academic archival techniques like a balloonist might dump ballast to keep desperately aloft. As I became more familiar with the work of other archivists in different companies, I realized that this angst was not mine alone. Those that were successful in a corporate setting had a gift for developing social networks within the company and adapting quickly to changing environments.

This salesmanship was identified by Gord Rabchuk as the one critical skill to ensure the survival of a corporate archives. "There is no universal path to stardom for corporate archives," he wrote in the 1990s. "Our best bet for survival will be the ability to demonstrate our information management skills and a familiarity with internal information networks." Want to celebrate? We can produce a book or an anniversary. Interested in digital asset management? We know more about metadata than IT folks can imagine. Is the CEO retiring? Just look at the resources that we can add to the party. Need compliance? We understand authenticity in electronic records. Even those archivists who have mastered the question of how the archives "adds value" to the bottom line constantly look to keep themselves relevant while protecting a core collection of records that document the past organization. As Philip Mooney of the Coca-Cola Company wrote, we "must be aggressive self-promoters, seeking every opportunity to sell the use of the archival record for business enhancement."[3]

These may not be the only qualities that distinguish business archivists from the rest of the profession. Since the formation of the Society of American Archivists' Business Archives Section in 1979, corporate archivists have underscored the differences between the corporate and public sectors. Their expressions have ranged from mild annoyance that corporate needs have not been addressed to calls for a divorce from the SAA. While many dismiss the idea of separation from the national professional group, there is the example of the 1974 formation of the National Association of State Archives and Records Administrators by government archivists over some of the same issues. Although business archivists generally speak the same language as their colleagues, there is unease with the application of nearly every function of archives. As one successful corporate archivist offered in frustration, "We process differently, we interact with clients differently, we budget differently, we have uniquely different resources to draw on, our governance laws are different, our hiring practices and promotion policies are different, our user base is different, our organization structures are different, . . . our access policies are different, our museums are different, and the skills we look for in an archivist are different."[4]

How fundamental are these differences? Are there true intellectual gulfs between archives in different sectors, or is the difference one of emphasis? Once I entered the private sector, the dissimilarities between academic and business approaches became painfully clear. The issues that put corporate archives at sixes or sevens with their colleagues can be found in at least these areas:

- processing and description
- appraisal
- relationship to history
- the mission of the archives

- contribution to the greater good of society
- survival in a hostile environment

An organization is not an organization is not an organization in terms of its documentation nor its archival focus. These six areas are a good proving ground to illustrate the extent of difference between business archives and archives in other sectors.

Processing and Description

Given the small size of most corporate archives and the perpetual need to keep the "head count" low, the corporate archivist is under pressure to keep the task of records processing to a minimum. Records are not processed for public consumption as in the public sector; rare is the corporate archives that serves up data instead of information. Corporate executives do not come to the archives to look through boxes; they expect answers from the archives. Processing is quite different in the corporate archives when the main end user is the archives staff.

The archival profession can claim none of the general productivity gains reported during the last decade by American business. Business describes productivity in terms of labor, capital, and knowledge. One either increases the value of knowledge through new applications, products, or services, or one improves operational efficiency by doing more with less. The best work to date on increasing the productivity of processing paper records is the popular study by Mark Greene and Dennis Meissner, which challenges many dearly held assumptions about some of the tasks involved in processing (refoldering, removing paper clips, detailed file and item listing, etc.).[5] However, corporate archives did not need much prodding from the article to abandon the niceties of preservation; it was an economic necessity. Some in the profession might view this as just the implementation of sloppy archival procedures, but if corporate archives followed the procedures recommended in the Guidelines for College and University Archives, they would not last long. The computer, which is the engine of productivity gains in business, is of little help in slogging through a box of records. Likewise, increased processing time adds marginal value in terms of new products or services (except, perhaps, in the case of archival images, which may require item processing to be used in self-service catalogs).

Conversely, the role of the computer in archival description has resulted in the production of some of those new products and services. Once in machine-readable form and with a reasonable amount of structure, data in the archives can be retrieved as never before. But again, the end product is fundamentally different in the private sector. Most corporate archives are not open to the public, so corporate archivists have little need for the wide dissemination of information outside the computer firewall. Corporate archives have no use for bibliographic-oriented communication schemes (beginning with SPINDEX through MARC-AMC), or the adoption of Encoded Archival Description, RAD, or content standards that are aimed at sharing descriptive information outside the organization. Even within corporate intranets, the use of content standards has little return on investment. Most clients of the archives want synthesis—not fonds, record groups, series, or folder headings. This is not to say that the development of descriptive tools in the public sector has no application in the private, but it is true that the needs and expectations of the client of corporate archives are fundamentally different.

Appraisal

Starting with F. Gerald Ham's "Archival Edge," moving through Helen Samuels' documentation strategies, and continuing with functional analysis, archival appraisal has tended to be drawn in larger and larger parameters, looking at—as with documentation strategies—the entire documentary universe. A major weakness with documentation strategies is that there simply are not enough archival resources to share adequately the burden of documenting a specific area.[6] Timothy Ericson suggested that "prospective participants should ask themselves, given all of the demands on their time and resources, [whether] the adequate documentation of a particular topic is really the first priority." Even outside the private sector, cost analysis is an important factor, if not the most important one, in appraisal. There has been interesting recent work using the Internet to mitigate some of the resource issues inherent in a documentation strategy. Unfortunately, the world of business archives is bounded securely by corporate firewalls, and collaboration tools—like those used in the LGBTRAN project associated with the Chicago Theological Seminary to produce "virtual archives"—are unlikely to work in the business environment, although the possibilities with corporate retirees are intriguing.[7]

A scenario of limited resources against a vast organization may seem like a unifying feature of the archival profession, but corporate archives are surprisingly low-staffed, even compared to their colleagues in the public sector.[8] A common complaint in the minutes of the Corporate Archives Forum is the quantity of records, electronic and paper, requiring the archivist's attention. Yet, the consideration of appraisal in the corporate setting has received only modest attention since then. A 1993 primer on corporate archives and history contained not one chapter dedicated to appraisal. Four years later, a major component of *The Records of American Business* was devoted to appraisal, including an excellent analysis by Christopher Baer relating to railroad records at the Hagley Library, an essay by Mark Greene and Todd Daniels-Howell relating to corporate records acquisition at the Minnesota Historical Society, and my article on functional analysis.[9]

Of all of these three works, Baer presents the strongest argument in favor of the notion that the appraisal of the records of the modern corporation is a process apart from most others. He developed a triangular appraisal model using strategy, structure, and function, all of which can be further refined by detail. Borrowing a line of criticism from Hilary Jenkinson, he observes that to "attempt to fit the records of modern business into the world of theory as derived from traditional European archivists is rather like being asked to shoehorn an automobile assembly line or particle accelerator into the Orangerie at Versailles."[10] Equally important, Baer draws a distinction between the creation of records in the public sector with those in a business setting, where "perpetual memory" is not seen as a universal good. If one accepts an archival theory of records created on the basis of "perpetual memory," then business records can easily fall outside the bounds of that theory. As an example, Baer notes that "Conrail, the successor to the [Pennsylvania Railroad], could not succeed without destroying the PRR's ossified corporate culture, and that included destroying or disposing of its memory and records."[11] This distinction is important because it can undermine at the outset the macroappraisal strategies offered by the other authors.

Elizabeth Adkins, former archivist of the Ford Motor Company, while acknowledging the dearth of appraisal work by corporate archivists, suggested yet another fundamental difference in archival appraisal inside the corporation. She noted that in her experience at Ford and Kraft, "executives and employees tend to request bits and pieces of information from our records, not records that provide evidence of how business has been conducted over the years." This primacy of informational over evidential value "might mean that we should develop our own approaches to appraisal."[12]

Of course, the idea that appraisal may in some way be fundamentally different in the private sector may simply be a reflection of the flux that appraisal theory has enjoyed during the last twenty-five years. Even Baer, borrowing from the black box appraisal scheme of Frank Boles and Julia Marks Young, suggests that appraisal "is essentially an exercise in cost-benefit analysis," and as such would be shaped by the types of products and services offered by the corporate archives. Yet one can argue that appraisal in corporate archives is a bit different. Paul Lasewicz takes a poke at using both structural and functional appraisal strategies in a corporation. He notes that a strategy based on structure "is seriously undermined by the extreme fluidity that characterizes the organizations of today." Nowhere is this better illustrated than by my own employer, Cargill, which announced a major restructuring in 1999 and the naming of one hundred business units. Eight years later that number had altered through mergers, acquisitions, divestitures, and realignment to about eighty business units. Because of a major branding change, only two business units had kept their exact name throughout that period—not a circumstance that would enhance the use of record groups. With functional analysis, Lasewicz criticizes the goal of documenting a company "at a level far beyond what the company will ever need for its own purposes." This is true based on my own work with the Control Data Corporation. While the lack of resources means that it is unlikely that a corporate archives could even attempt a broad-based functional analysis on a multidivisional, multifunctional, global business, it is the end product—the "added value" that appraisal brings to the archives—that really determines the level of granularity in documentation. Back to Baer's point, the difference between complex businesses and complex public institutions may be the perceived value of perpetual memory.[13]

Of necessity, many corporate archives become extremely strategic in their selection based on anticipated use. This is somewhat ironic since "anticipated use" goes back to Schellenberg's model of informational value noted by Adkins above—precisely the model rejected by Helen Samuels and others—which led to functional analysis. At best, the essence of "modern corporate dynamics" and the informational use of archives promote a tug of war between these two camps of appraisal. For example, Cargill sold its resins business in the 1990s as it tied its strategic intent to the food industry. At that point, documentation in the archives relating to the resins business was no longer very useful as that product brand had been sold to a competitor. From a documentation standpoint, however, the business was still an important aspect of Cargill's culture and heritage. Overnight, their records became low-grade historical ore rather than a high-value corporate resource. While governments may end departments and academia may end programs, their archives are unlikely to question the basic value of records documenting such departments and projects, the functions of which often continue in new structures. Corporate archives do question the continuing value of records when the function, process, or product ends.

Relation to History

During the past twenty-five years, American archivists have increasingly pulled away from academic history. In the late 1970s, the prevailing discussion about the education of archivists concerned a choice between a history or library science degree. By the 1990s, a history degree as an entry to an archival career was off the map. Furthermore, archivists frequently took aim at the relationship, calling attention to the limits of growth of the profession if it continued to define its main clients as historians. Archivists took note of the need to advocate broad use, rather than relying on a traditional core of academic historical use that did little to support archival programs.

In the corporate archives, the primacy of history is only invoked when it is safe to do so. For a few companies, such as IBM and the pre-divestiture AT&T, there was a day when historians were on the payroll cranking out many useful publications, but even those two programs could not sustain the changing corporate environment of the 1990s. Paul Lasewicz, corporate archivist at IBM, poignantly asked in 1997 the modern archival question, "is there life after history?" His solution was to bind the resources of the archives and the skills of the archivist to knowledge management.[14]

This expression of support of "knowledge management" is less important than what it says about history. The holy grail for the survival of the corporate archives is not one magic device, but a changeable combination of tools depending on each corporation's circumstance. A review of the minutes of the Corporate Archives Forum, a group of a dozen archivists involved in global corporations, reveals a diverse toolkit containing familiar elements such as anniversaries and books, as well as less traditional programs involving media asset management systems, artwork, and corporate compliance.

The rejection of historical primacy might seem to imply that corporate archivists do not work with the past. Often the term "history" is avoided in a corporate setting because the word is painfully associated with low usefulness, superficial value, and irrelevance. However, "heritage" plays an important role in many corporations, and it is the job of the archivist to supply the connection. As described before, few corporate employees come to the archives to view records. They expect the archivist to synthesize and interpret data, and deliver information. In other words, the archivist *is* the historian. Not surprisingly, most clients in a corporate environment view these two roles synonymously. They call the archivist for historical interpretation, and they believe what archivists tell them. Unless you have an audience of knowledgeable retirees, the role of archivist as company historian is unchecked. It is a heady position—imposing in scope—and a little frightening.

The archivist as interpreter is a role that archivists from Hilary Jenkinson to William Maher have defined as overstepping the bounds of good practice (although not in the eyes of Helen Samuels). To Jenkinson, the archivist "exists in order to make other people's work possible." Maher, in attacking the effect of the entertainment industry on history, warns "our mission is not to interpret the documentary record or limit it to one set of meanings . . . our goal is to manage the documentary record for use by others who will form their own opinion and picture of the past." The postmodernists warn of the malevolent role of the "archon," who alone has "the power to interpret the archives," even as postmodern archivists firmly reject this traditional noninterventionist view. To this traditionalist Jenkinsonian mantra, corporate archivists simply shrug their shoulders. "If we are true strategic thinkers," writes Rabchuk, "we should be comfortable with the redefinition of the archivist's conventional mandate." In a corporate setting, if an archivist does not assume this role, no one will, and corporate history will lie fallow, like a surplus commodity.[15]

The Mission

While no archives is likely to survive by ignoring the mission of its parent organization, in the public sector these organizational objectives are sufficiently broad to support a wide range of activities including scholarly research, general public interest, and broad societal access to government information. Ultimately, these archives are responsible to the public, the university community, and/or taxpayers.

To paraphrase Calvin Coolidge, the business of corporate archives is business. Writing after writing by successful corporate archivists underscores this adage. Ultimately, corporate archives are responsible to the shareholders, and the primary interest of shareholders is to increase their investment. While shareholders certainly value other aspects of a corporation, such as community involvement, environmental responsibility, and charitable giving, their first priority is financial. A corporate archives can justify its existence from a number of perspectives, but its survivability is much more assured if it can contribute to the bottom line. More and more corporate archives are expected to fulfill these expectations. In the 1990s, the AT&T archives existed completely through revenues generated by "charge backs" for services. The Coca-Cola Company archives claims a major role in a multimillion dollar legacy trademark business. Many corporate archives, such as Cargill's, participate in annual service level agreements where business units are asked to pay an annual sum based on their prior year's use of services and products.

All of these examples reveal efforts by archives to demonstrate their value to a business in the language of business. Indeed, corporate archivists have criticized the inability of archivists in general to effectively communicate the value of archives in terms that would be more meaningful to those who fund archival programs. Philip Mooney notes that the archival community "taken as a whole, has adopted a myopic view of their roles and responsibilities within their parent organizations that had detrimentally affected administrators' views of the value of archival functions and the respective resources required to support them." Gord Rabchuk is even more strident, noting "the typical understanding of archives in business has carried too many negative connotations, largely because we have sold an obsolete product that has demonstrated little, if any connection with the dynamics of modern business."[16] Perhaps in a perfect world, some business executives really do look at the past to learn from it, in spite of the quarter-to-quarter time frame of most American businesses. In any case, a presentation about the strategic past does not happen without an incredibly entrepreneurial and savvy archivist who is used to taking some risks.

Perhaps most public archivists are simply uncomfortable with the mission of corporate archives. In his analysis of why religious archives seem to march to a different drummer than the rest of the profession, James O'Toole comments on the tension in America between religion and state, and how that tension plays out in the archival profession. He writes, "Given the understanding of religion as a private matter, restricted to a limited sphere of personal activity, the association of an archives with a particular religious group is at best somewhat anomalous and at worst suspicious." While corporate archives do not encompass quite the same cultural issues, they raise the same questions of loyalties and allegiances. Are there moments when archival professionalism is at cross purposes with a capitalist business? And how does the rest of the profession regard this tension? In his analysis of professionalism and archivists, Richard Cox points to institutionalized altruism. While at one point Cox defines this attribute in terms of service orientation and the protection of clients, he later describes it as archivists' "long standing desire to make historical records accessible to the public." This places corporate archivists, religious archivists, and any other archivists who maintain records inaccessible to the public in a type of professional limbo. I recall my own perplexity at an oral history conference when I met an oral historian for a government security agency. I asked him about the scope of his interviews. He couldn't discuss that. What sort of outreach did he do? He couldn't discuss that either. As an archivist then working at a university, I was outraged. Now, as an archivist working for one of the largest privately-held businesses in the world, I understand.[17]

Greater Good

Perhaps the most prominent issue separating corporate archives from the rest of the profession is the perception that the corporate archivist does not work for the greater good of society. This was illustrated with the debate over the *American Archivist* Sun "Mad" Raisin cover. The graphic was a parody of the Sun Maid Raisin brand, and was taken from a political collection highlighted in one of the issue's articles, with the "maid" transformed into a grotesque skeleton grinning madly. A number of corporate archivists (the author included) wrote a letter objecting to the overt anti-business tone of the cover. The corporate archivists felt that they had enough trouble advocating archives within a capitalist organization without the *American Archivist* fueling the fire by looking like *Mother Jones.* This was for corporate archivists a case of salesmanship, not censorship. Most of the readers, including the editor, felt that the cover was proper in the context of the content of that issue, and that corporate archivists were, at best, thin skinned, or at worst, tampering with the editorial freedom of the journal.

Richard Cox ramped up the discussion in a surprising direction when he directly questioned the professional ethics of all corporate archivists. "What intrigues me," he wrote in a letter to the editor, "is how the individual functioning as an archivist or records manager can work in the corporate environment in any realistic way, adhering to any sense of professional ethics or mission."[18]

The reality is that "Raisingate" (a term coined by former SAA president Tim Ericson) was symptomatic of the differing perceptions of private- and public-sector archivists toward each other. Most archivists probably sided with Philip Ashdown, who wrote a letter to the editor referring to the corporate archivists critical of the cover not as colleagues, but a "phalanx of corporate spokespeople." He praised the use of controversial art for covers, urging the archival profession toward "the impartial preservation of our documentary heritage." For me, with five years of archival employment in the private sector and twenty years in the public, Raisingate confirmed that there was an unresolved issue within the profession about the mission of the corporate archives and their contribution to the greater good of society.

While the SAA code of ethics contains a statement on "respecting each institution and its mission," there is no professional ethical statement that outlines one's societal responsibilities. Wayne Grover's original code, on which many parts of the SAA code is based, did contain a section that states, "the archivist has a moral obligation to society to preserve evidence on how things actually happened and to take measures for the physical preservation of valuable records." Even if one is not a postmodernist, most archivists would have a difficult time adopting this subjective ethic, which is perhaps why Grover's original statement did not make it into subsequent SAA codes. The Canadian code states that the work of archivists is for "the benefit of present users and future generations." Few corporate archivists would quibble with that sentiment if the present users are defined as the employees, customers, and communities of the business.[19]

The notion of greater good provided by archives is not limited to public accessibility, but includes public protection. Cox asks, "What is the archivist to do . . . when he or she discovers illegal or questionable activity on the part of their employers?"[20] The implication of this question sets up intractable conflicts for corporate archivists. First, there is the obvious question that Cox wants to raise: Is the loyalty of the archivist to the public or to the archivist's employer? Secondly, there is the conflict between the archivist as neutral guardian of authentic data and interpreter of information—the Jenkinson/Maher versus "postmodernist" debate discussed before. Lastly, there is simply the issue of having the knowledge and ability to identify what constitutes illegal activities. There are few archivists who are also accountants and lawyers, or philosophical ethicists for that matter. How then are corporate archivists to insert themselves as whistleblowers, and is this role critical to being a professional archivist? SAA's code of ethics is of little help, noting that "archivists must uphold all federal, state, and local laws."[21] There is no professional context to this point, making it useless. Could an archivist have saved the world from the harm of Enron? It is unlikely. The court took four months to turn a complex financial case into a guilty verdict, and knowledgeable experts were still debating whether Jeffrey Skilling actually masterminded the unraveling of the company. If public protection is the quality that makes a corporate archivist unethical, then even academic archivists might do well to shift uncomfortably in their seats.

Hostile Environment

History has shown that employment as a corporate archivist is a short-term affair compared to employment in other sectors. Nearly all of the earliest corporate archival programs have disappeared or are administered by a person unwilling to be called an archivist. Some were victims of the financial performance of their firms; others were lost in mergers and acquisitions. Often it is the double punch of both that knocks a program out of existence. The Burroughs Corporation had a fine archival program in the 1980s until its merger with Sperry in 1986. At that point, the archives could not release any material with the Burroughs name on it without permission from the brand managers who were in charge of developing the company name, Unisys. This is typical when a new brand is being launched, but quite a liability to an archives whose documentation relates only to the old brand. Shortly afterward, the stock price of Unisys plunged and the archival collection was donated to a university. This scenario is virtually unknown in the academic and government world, but uncomfortably common in the private sector.[22]

Corporate archives can find their fortunes dramatically altered with a change in the executive suite. "That change will occur is an accepted fact of life in most corporations," writes James Fogerty. "Uncertainty—whatever its side effects—is present in corporate life in ways unknown to government bureaucrats and their functionaries, with the result that decision making is driven by considerations that are peculiar to business." Unless a corporate archives builds a diverse network of support, it is at risk. One of the best archival programs in 1990 in the Twin Cities was maintained by the H. B. Fuller Company. With a change in one board member related to the company's founding family, the corporate archives was forced to rebuild itself as a records management operation where the term *archives* could not be uttered. The archivist had done everything right to establish the original program, but she could not survive this change without a drastic change in direction.[23]

As there are threats within the organization, there are threats without. In a sector that is always striving for productivity, the opportunity to outsource a program to reduce head count is always attractive. Archival consultants do not always have a vibrant, in-house archival program as their first priority. While many anniversary celebrations provide a lever to build a program (my own, for example), often the potential is left unfulfilled by consultants who, at best, do not know any better, or at worst, are dilettantes. Some former corporate archivists have charged these history factories with purposefully undermining programs, and others have cast suspicion on academic programs only too willing to accept a high profile collection from a large company. In the business world, all of this is fair game. It is a Darwinian world that places survivability in the hands of the archivist; if an archivist cannot communicate the business need for the program against all competitors, it may deserve to die.

Again, I note this as an element that distinguishes the private sector from the public. The notion of competition in archives is abhorrent to most archivists, as noted in the American ethical code. You will never see South Dakota offering to run Minnesota's state archives for a fraction of Minnesota's cost. But the equivalent exists in the private sector, and in numerous forms from various quarters. So if corporate archivists act as if something is always chasing them, it is because something always is.

A House Divided

The six areas explored above are near the core of what archivists do, and in each case corporate archivists are slightly askew from the norm. Those better versed in archival history could probably identify the theoretical veins of archival theory that are the source of tension in the corporate archives. Apart from how we got here, I am concerned when I hear a well-regarded corporate archivist look at SAA, the largest professional "big tent" in North America, and remark, "There's nothing there for me." I am equally concerned that some other archivists, normally dedicated to the diversity of documentation, cannot fathom how to extend the archival tent large enough to cover corporate archivists.

An analogy to this situation was the establishment of the National Association of State Archives and Records Administrators (NASARA) in 1974. According to Bruce Dearstyne, "it originated out of three trends or needs. One, the state archivists were finding themselves more and more involved with records management issues, or actually extending or strengthening their own authority or programs in that area. They found that they could not do archives very well unless records management was also handled well. The advent and growth of electronic records, with issues in both records management and archives, accentuated this trend. They wanted an association that blended records management and archives, unlike the two existing national organizations, SAA and ARMA, which focused on the issues separately. Two, they believed that their programs, because of their setting in state governments, had a commonality with each other but also traits that made them different from other archives programs. Three, they wanted a forum to discuss their issues, particularly technology and managing in a governmental setting. Ten years later, in 1984, NASARA became NAGARA—the National Association of Government Archives and Records Administrators—and expanded its membership base to include local governments and federal agencies, including NARA."[24] Other informal sources suggest that there were some interesting personality clashes within SAA before this schism occurred. Regardless of the rationale, there are probably archivists on both sides that would admit that SAA and the NAGARA each lost something in the process. Much important work has taken place on both sides since 1974, although the sum of the parts may not quite be the same as the whole.

While corporate archivists are nowhere near as large a group as government archivists, their issues are similar to those described by Dearstyne. They have enough reasons, as illustrated above, to become disengaged. The critical issue is one of professional intent. If other archivists truly feel that the work of corporate colleagues falls outside "the identification, preservation, and use of the nation's historical record," then there is little to tie the groups together. This unraveling would be a shame. Rather than shills and spokespeople, corporate archivists are on the front line documenting the record of the nation, which was Helen Samuels' grand goal (or at least dream): a true national archives as a nationwide virtual archive representing all documented sectors of human society. There are, of course, business collections available in some public repositories, but nothing compares to the documentary view from the inside. And those documentary views are increasingly rare and precious. True, much of this record is not available to the public, but as a profession associated with the events of the past, one would think that archivists would take a long-term view. Many such "inside" collections, with the passage of time, will become open archives rather than landfill because of the current work of corporate archivists.

But corporate archivists need help and support. They are in an internal struggle to demonstrate that their existence does not equate to an increased risk to the company. Although some corporate archives are within the law department, many are not, and are viewed cautiously, even suspiciously, by legal counsel. Archivists argue that evidence is a two-edged sword: while records can harbor a smoking gun, they can also be used in defending the corporation. There is no better example than the Ford Motor Company's transparency in addressing allegations that Ford's American headquarters benefited from Ford-Werke's operation in wartime Nazi Germany. The press charged that slave laborers were used at the Cologne plant under the oversight of the American headquarters. Ford threw open its papers and appointed an investigative team of forty-five people. Simon Reich, independent consultant to the effort, found "no complicity on the part of Ford's Dearborn management" in the affair, and added that the study was a "credible example of a company accepting and implementing the code of 'corporate social responsibility' regarding a most delicate issue."[25]

There are other examples that are not so reassuring. In 2002, the city of Chicago passed an ordinance requiring companies wishing to do business with the city to "disclose any association with African-American slave trading in their company's past."[26] JPMorgan Chase (with its excellent corporate archives assisted by History Associates) discovered that slaves were listed as collateral in defaulted loans of two of its predecessor banks in Louisiana. In 2004, the company issued a disclosure and an apology for its links to slavery. Regardless of one's feelings on reparations, the likely effect of maintaining good historical records on the acquisition of older or predecessor companies could be chilling. Corporate archivists face huge difficulties being at the right place at the right time during an acquisition. Usually they hear about a major acquisition at the same time as the press. If society offers little incentive for corporate lawyers to preserve the record of an acquisition, the heritage of some important, old firms will disappear. For every vindication such as Ford's, there will be real risks in maintaining archives for others. Which scenario will the corporate lawyers remember?

This goes back to the heart of Raisingate. The existence of an archives is a positive indication of corporate social responsibility, going beyond mere compliance and taking calculated risk in a society generally suspicious of big business. While Cox throws public accountability at the feet of corporate archivists and records managers, he does not draw the distinction between accountability and responsibility. Michael Moss, in reacting to the Sun "Mad" Raisin cover, claims this territory, noting the effect of the "the audit culture" in which institutions are required to keep records prescribed by audit needs, but not necessarily related to collective memory. Moss notes that the "accountability of the private sector, despite all rhetoric of shareholder value, does not equate to public responsibility." While Moss finds the cover a metaphor for a record in a corporate audit culture, he accurately extrapolates its effect into the public sector. "Public authorities are no less exempt from seeking to contain liability or, to put it in Derrida's language, to forget," writes Moss, citing the work of Verne Harris with the South African Truth and Reconciliation Commission. Archivists in the public sector should take note: this tension between accountability, responsibility, service to your employer, and service to the public good will eventually visit you.[27]

As corporate archivists look creatively for ways to add value to their company, they are aware of this tension. Most have surrounded their archives with tools and programs to protect the archives. The danger is in forgetting the core, or being pulled too far from it. "Compliance" is a powerful tool for archivists to employ as records managers, but it is a tool with some danger, simply because compliance may not circumscribe those records that actually describe what happened—Moss's theory of audit versus responsibility. This is the discussion that all archivists need to have; it is a complex one that needs to be addressed with some sophistication, and business archivists are capable of offering leadership here. But communication is lacking in the big archival tent. In his SAA presidential address, William Maher attempted to express a core that defines the confederation of professional archivists, looking to the authentic record as an item that we all have in common. Unfortunately, at the same time, he dismissively attacked the entertainment industry, which many corporate archivists interpreted (erroneously, I believe) as an attack on business archives. So it also goes with our poor raisin maiden. The editor of the *American Archivist* thought it was a compelling cover. The corporate archivists interpreted the cover as an advocacy affront. Ashdown interpreted the corporate archivists' letter as censorship, and Cox used it to question their ethics. Moss employed the debate to raise the issue about the record in an audit culture. And now we are into some significant issues, if anyone is left listening or learning.

At stake is the vision of Helen Samuels: the most comprehensive documentation of our society. While diversity is currently at the heart of the strategic plan of the Society of American Archivists, how is it that archivists still struggle to find commonality of purpose with their own colleagues? During the last thirty years, SAA has struggled to give voice to each segment of the profession, but perhaps separate groups (like SAA sections) have fostered fragmentation to the detriment of the archival whole. Real-life tests of documentation strategies suggest that there are too few of us archivists to launch an adequate documentary assault on even one locale, so what is the advantage of defining ourselves apart from each other? Having the perspective of a career in both sectors, I find the world of business contains exciting organizations, full of smart and effective people, capable of great and some ignoble things. Their influence on society is enormous. But justifying archives where the bottom line is measured quarterly will always be a tough sell; no doubt corporate archivists will often continue to be perceived internally as brown shoes in the world of corporate tuxedos. As corporate archivists look to share their perspective in the big tent of archival ideas, and find professional support therein, I hope our shoes are not out of place there as well.

Notes

1 Joan K. Haas, Helen Willa Samuels, Barbara Trippel Simmons, *Appraising the Records of Modern Science and Technology: A Guide* (Cambridge, MA: MIT, 1985).

2 Bruce H. Bruemmer and Sheldon Hochheiser, *The High-Technology Company: A Historical and Archival Guide* (Minneapolis: Charles Babbage Institute, 1989).

3 Gord Rabchuk, "Life After the 'Big Bang': Business Archives in the Era of Disorder," *American Archivist* 60 (Winter 1997): 39; Phillip F. Mooney, "Archival Mythology and Corporate Reality: A Potential Powder Keg," in *The Records of American Business*, ed. James M. O'Toole, (Chicago: Society of American Archivists, 1997), 62.

4 Edward Rider, email communication to the Corporate Archives Forum, January 25, 2006. Used with permission.

5 Mark A. Greene and Dennis Meissner, "More Product, Less Process: Revamping Traditional Archival Processing," *American Archivist* 68 (Fall/Winter 2005): 208–63. See also Society of American Archivists, *Guidelines for College and University Archives*, IV. Core Archival Functions, at: http://www.archivists.org/governance/guidelines/cu_guidelines4.asp.

6 See Timothy L. Ericson's "'To Approximate June Pasture': The Documentation Strategy in the Real World," *Archival Issues* 22, no. 1 (1997): 14.

7 Doris J. Malkmus, "Documentation Strategy: Mastodon or Retro-Success?" *American Archivist* 71 (Fall/Winter 2008): 408.

8 Just as an example, I estimate the 2009 ratio of government archivists to Minnesota state employees to be 1:8, 215, whereas at my own institution it is 1:80,000, an order of magnitude difference.

9 Corporate Archives Forum, minutes, http://www.hunterinformation.com/caf.htm. Arnita A. Jones and Philip L. Cantelon, eds., *Corporate Archives and History: Making the Past Work* (Malabar, FL: Krieger Publishing, 1993); and O'Toole, *Records of American Business*. In the latter work, it is worth noting that none of the authors writing directly on appraisal were archivists working within a corporate archives (although I would be three years later).

10 Christopher T. Baer, "Strategy, Structure, Detail, Function: Four Parameters for the Appraisal of Business Records," in O'Toole, *The Records of American Business*, 117–18.

11 Ibid, 119.

12 Elizabeth W. Adkins, "The Development of Business Archives in the United States: An Overview and Personal Perspective," *American Archivist* 60 (Winter 1997): 19–20.

13 Baer, "Strategy, Structure, Detail, Function," 76; Paul C. Lasewicz, "Riding Out the Apocalypse: The Obsolescence of Traditional Archivy in the Face of Modern Corporate Dynamics," *Archival Issues* 22, no. 1 (1997): 65.

14 Lasewicz, "Obsolescence of Traditional Archivy," 66.

15 The Jenkinson quote was used by Randall C. Jimerson in his presidential address for the Society of American Archivists, "Embracing the Power of Archives," available at: http://www.archivists.org/governance/presidential/jimerson.asp). Maher's words are from his SAA presidential address: William J. Maher, "Lost in a Disney-fied World: Archivists and Society in Late Twentieth Century America" (manuscript, September 3, 1998), 5; Jacques Derrida, *Archive Fever* (Chicago: University of Chicago Press, 1996), 2; Rabchuk, "Life After the 'Big Bang'," 41.

16 Mooney, "Archival Mythology and Corporate Reality," 57; Rabchuk, "Life After the 'Big Bang'," 41.

17 James O'Toole, "What's Different about Religious Archives?" *Midwestern Archivist* 9, no. 2 (1984): 99; Richard J. Cox, "Professionalism and Archivists," *American Archivist* 49 (Summer 1986): 223.

18 The cover appeared on the *American Archivist* 66, no. 2 (Fall/Winter 2003). The letter from corporate archivists appeared in the "Forum" in volume 67, no. 2 (Fall/Winter 2004), as well as a letter by Mark Greene and commentary by the editor. Letters from Richard J. Cox and Philip J. Ashdown appear in volume 68 (Spring/Summer 2005). Letters from Randall C. Jimerson and Richard Pearce-Moses appear in volume 68 (Fall/Winter 2005).

19 Current codes of ethics are found at the websites of the Society of American Archivists (www.archivists.org) and the Association of Canadian Archivists (www.archivists.ca). Grover's code is contained in Margaret Turner et al., "Implementing the ICA Code of Ethics: Experiences and Challenges," *Internationaler Arkivkongress* 2004, 7-8, at http://www.ifai.org.mx/ica/presentaciones/21.pdf.

20 Richard J. Cox, "Forum," *American Archivist* 68 (Spring/Summer 2005): 10.

21 Under point IX, "Law" in *Code of Ethics for Archivists*, Society of American Archivists, 2005. Interestingly, it was only after I came to the private sector that I was required to affirm annually an ethical code, which includes a statement about obeying all applicable laws.

22 See Adkins, "Development of Business Archives in the United States." The details of the Burroughs case were related to me by their former archivist, Anne Frantilla. For those appreciating irony, I was the archivist at the Charles Babbage Institute who negotiated the Burroughs donation.

23 Phone conversation with Liz Holum Johnson in the 1990s. I needed a historical picture from her collection, and she warned me not to refer to the operation as an "archives."

24 Email correspondence with Bruce Dearstyne, May 9, 2006. Used with permission.

25 Simon Reich, *Ford's Research Efforts in Assessing the Activities of its Subsidiary in Nazi Germany* (Dearborn: Ford Motor Company, 2001), 7–8.

26 Jonathan Swisher, "Chicago's Belated Fight Against Slavery," in *Northwestern Chronicle*, posted October 24, 2002, http://www.chron.org/tools/viewart.php?artid=508.

27 Michael Moss, "Archivist Friend or Foe" (unpublished manuscript), 9; Michael Moss, "The Archives of Business and the Business of Archives" (unpublished manuscript), 7.

A CAUTIONARY TALE ABOUT LAWS, RECORDS, AND TECHNOLOGY: MAKING A CASE FOR ELECTRONIC RECORDS MANAGEMENT

ROBERT HORTON

On May 17, 2004, the *New York Times* reported, "A federal advisory committee says Congress should pass laws to protect the civil liberties of Americans when the government sifts through computer records and data files for information about terrorists." The committee hinted at an inherent tension between the two distinct mandates—security and privacy—but it suggested that Congress could find some balance through a more precise articulation of the issues. In his column that same day, William Safire approvingly described the committee's report, calling for "written findings by top officials before undertaking any [data] mining; appointing a policy-level privacy officer; making data anonymous; creating an audit trail; court authorization; oversight by a single committee of Congress; developing 'technological and other tools for enhancing privacy protection'; and 'a culture of sensitivity to . . . privacy issues.'"[1]

Safire's list is daunting, encompassing not just more legislation, but additionally complex technological, organizational, and cultural change. But while these issues might be new to the debate on homeland security, they are all familiar to the archival profession, which for years has been wrestling with analogous questions generated by our concerns about electronic records. Because of that, archivists and records managers are in a position to contribute to the discussion. There is an opportunity to help resolve a pressing problem, to raise the profile of the profession, and to get some return on all the investment in the research and implementation projects sponsored over the past decade.

Helen Samuels' work has anticipated this opportunity, especially in terms of how we can analyze and learn from it. With her studies of documentation and particularly her emphasis on an archives' place within the framework of a university and its functions, she has pointed to the fact that archivists work in a context—organizational, political, economic, cultural, social—and they are shaped by that experience.[2] For her, archival theory and principles are not simply academic; they are what guide our actions, what we are thinking as we are doing something. But the reverse has to be true as well: if theory informs practice, then practice informs theory. Without that, there are no means to adapt to new situations, as, for example, the widespread introduction of information technology in recordkeeping, nor is there a way to justify the collaboration we require from records creators and users in complex organizations. Archivists do not merely have to understand their context, as Samuels recommends; they have somehow to fit into it. That is an ongoing task, in a dynamic environment, and no trivial challenge—but an unavoidable one if we hope to document society.

That situation demands a mode of analysis that expands our perspective, broadening it to include the myriad factors that will affect our attempts to enact any archival concepts. Simply because we work in complex organizations and arenas, maneuvering among larger social purposes and processes in the interminable debate over resources, we have to understand the costs and benefits of what we do. Further, we have to articulate both costs and benefits in terms that our masters—the resource allocators—understand; we have to speak their language.[3] Increasingly, the language of government is a mix of measurement and emotion, the dialogue of statistical certainties framed by political belief.

A case study can illuminate what happens when we try to translate archival concepts in such an environment. One is at hand: here we will look at what happened in Minnesota when a state legislator learned that government entities secretly provided confidential government records on citizens to a private entity, which provided access to them through a system without adequate security, any provisions for accountability, or statutory oversight. When this happened, there was, of course, a certain amount of surprise and outrage. The system was shut down. The legislator then drafted a bill to make sure nothing like this could happen again and, at that point, discovered how much room there still was for debate. The discussions that followed, and the eventual fate of the bill, demonstrated that no governmental mandate is without some ambiguity, that even in a case such as this, with the laws clearly contravened or ignored, the state could not easily take a position. More importantly, from the perspective of the archival community, it suggests that the mandates we claim and the principles we proclaim need reevaluation. They did not support a compelling and conclusive argument in the debate about laws, records, and technology. We did not speak the right language.

Minnesota's Criminal Justice Information System

In 1992, two cities in Minnesota, Crystal and Minneapolis, started to share criminal justice information in a database run by the Minnesota Chiefs of Police Association (MCPA).[4] Some 175 government entities in two states, Minnesota and Wisconsin, later became part of the network, eventually known as the Multiple Jurisdictional Network Organization (MJNO). By 2003, the MJNO contained approximately eight million records, encompassing a variety of information relating to the criminal justice functions of government, such as arrests, convictions, applications for gun permits, and so on.

Nothing about this is unusual. The value of criminal justice information, especially after 9/11 and the advent of the Department of Homeland Security, has greatly escalated. Many efforts are underway to break down the barriers between the multitude of entities creating, using and maintaining criminal justice information in order to solve and prevent crime more efficiently and effectively. The federal Department of Justice, for example, supports the Global Justice Information Sharing Initiative, which details a sophisticated and complex effort to improve law enforcement through the application of technology. As the project's website notes:

> Global's mission—the efficient sharing of data among justice entities—is at the very heart of modern public safety and law enforcement. Global is a "group of groups," representing more than thirty independent organizations spanning the spectrum of law enforcement, judicial, correctional, and related bodies. Member organizations participate in Global out of

> shared responsibility and shared belief that, together, they can bring about positive change in interorganizational communication and data sharing.[5]

There was an annual conference on the topic, the Government Symposium on Information Sharing and Homeland Security. And, of course, there was the Department of Defense's ill-fated Total Information Awareness project, headed by Admiral John Poindexter, which was one of the catalysts for the advisory committee's report described in the *New York Times* and cited above. Locally, Minnesota has for several years worked on the development of a statewide system, known as CriMNet, devoting almost $200 million from state and federal sources, to improve the ability of all the entities in the criminal justice system to share information.[6]

In this environment, why would the MJNO stand out? One thing to note is that it did not, for a very long time: in operation from 1992, eventually with some 175 entities involved, the MJNO was a going and growing concern for many years before it came to the public's attention. While its activities were not common knowledge, nor publicly advertised, it was clearly not an undercover operation. Indeed, it experienced its greatest period of growth after 1997, when it applied for, won, and then continued to receive federal grant support.[7] Further, in early 2003, the state of Minnesota leased rights to the system, linking it to CriMNet, and started hosting the MJNO on one of the state's web servers. There is no indication that anyone involved thought there was anything wrong with the system and the way it was operating.

Things began to unravel in 2003. In March, a Minnesota citizen named Scott Chapman was engaged in a counter-protest to an antiwar demonstration at the Burnsville, Minnesota, office of Congressman John Kline. As discussed in a Minnesota House of Representatives hearing, a Burnsville police officer noticed Chapman in an "animated conversation," with a former Minnesota House member.[8] On a hunch, the police officer ran the license plate of a car near which Chapman was standing through the MJNO and learned that the owner had been denied a concealed carry permit; the record did not, as was subsequently learned, indicate that the owner had then successfully reapplied and received a permit. On the basis of this database search, the officer approached Chapman, ascertained that he was the car's owner, and asked to search his fanny pack. After some discussion, Chapman handed it over. The officer found nothing of interest and Chapman left.

Later, Chapman (wondering "Why me?") decided to get a copy of the incident report on the demonstration. When he did, a file clerk at the police department apparently mentioned the existence of yet another source of information, the MJNO. Using Minnesota's equivalent of the Freedom of Information Act, Chapman then requested a copy of his record in the MJNO. At first, the MCPA said it was a private organization, not a governmental entity, and did not have to respond to the request. It added that the information was investigative data, which even a governmental entity would not have to reveal. Finally, it directed Chapman to the records creators—the distinct sources of the information in his aggregated record—for access to the information each had separately provided. This last point was seemingly the MJNO's trump card. As Dennis Delmont, executive director of the MCPA, later explained, "[Critics are] concerned why the Chiefs of Police Association collects all this information on them. The answer is we don't. We facilitate the collection by pointing to the data." That role, he added, does not include any verification or warranty of the accuracy of the data collected.[9]

Normally, the complaints of one citizen about a police department's routine recordkeeping practices would not gather much attention. But his concerns were considerably amplified in October 2003, when an unidentified hacker broke into the MJNO and found information on a member of the Minnesota House, Representative Mary Liz Holberg. The hacker then gave her a copy of the record he found. Holberg said, "It was proven to me that an individual that [sic] was not law enforcement beyond a shadow of a doubt, had access to the system."[10] Now Chapman's story gained some force. Raising concerns over inadequate security, inaccurate data, and unaccountable operations, the MJNO caught the attention of newspapers and lawmakers. Holberg later wrote, "Quite frankly, my first impression was that the citizens had it wrong. How could a database exist that the Legislature was unaware of and that had such poor security that the public regularly had access to millions of files containing private information?"[11]

At this point, the state shut down the MJNO. It soon returned to operation—with more significant security and approximately half as many records. But after the state's Department of Administration released an advisory opinion that the network probably violated several laws on the management and sharing of data, it was shut down permanently in December 2003.[12]

Doing Something: The Debate in the Legislature

To Representative Holberg, the moral of the story was that technology had outpaced policy. Laws meant to govern the collection and use of information in government were designed for a system that used paper for recordkeeping. Those laws sought to introduce accountability to the system; that was lost when technology replaced paper with digital records and the traditional procedures and practices were reengineered, some, evidently, right out of existence. But her concerns were met with pleas from government entities that it would be too expensive and cumbersome to change these new systems and reintroduce accountability. So she asked, "Why weren't these issues addressed when the systems were built?" Her idea was that technology should and could facilitate all the policies determined by the legislature.[13]

To make sure this message got across to government agencies, Holberg introduced a bill on information policy in the 2004 session of the legislature. House File 2800 was:

> A bill for an act relating to government data practices; providing for compliance with law by information management systems; providing for classification of, and access to, CriMNet data; providing public defender access to criminal justice data; [and] requiring a report . . .[14]

In its first version, the bill had some nearly apocalyptic implications for government agencies. It introduced no new policies, but, for the first time, it threatened real, draconian penalties for agencies that failed to respect the policies already mandated.

The overall framework for enforcement began with definitions. First, the bill defined information management systems: "a system used or maintained by a government entity for the management of government data, regardless of the form of the system." In effect, this really meant all systems that used government records or data, which, of course, encompassed virtually all governmental functions, transactions, and activities, because they all involve the creation or use of "government data" at some point.[15] Secondly, it defined the "information policy statutes" that applied to these systems, as enacted in *Minnesota Statutes*, chapter 13, section 15.17 and sections 138.103–138.225. These encompassed the state's Data Practices Act, Official Records Act and Records Management Act. These sections in House File 2800 simply pointed to the policies the legislature had already approved and underscored their importance and relevance to all government records and recordkeeping practices. Functionally, the new bill was just the equivalent of a sign that said, "This means *you*."

But, this time, the laws would mean it. The bill ordered that all systems had to be in compliance with all policy statutes within ninety days of the effective date of the law. Further, any citizen who thought a particular system was not compliant could lodge a complaint with the Department of Administration. If the department's commissioner determined that the system was noncompliant, it had to be shut down. There was no provision for appeal or recourse to this decision; the commissioner's determination alone would be "conclusive proof." It was a call for revolution. The absolutely sweeping nature of the definitions, conceivably encompassing every practice from the use of Post-It notes to massive e-government applications, combined with an impossible timetable for remediation and the prospect of what would be summarily enforced death penalties for entire systems, raised the specter of a government in ruins. Since virtually every system in state and local government undoubtedly contravened some aspect of the information policy statutes and since any citizen could start the process to bring it all crashing down, every government entity and government function faced an imminent shut-down.

The simple and obvious fact was that this bill made information policy more important than anything else on the agenda, any other mandate that a government entity had. Obviously, there was no political consensus in support of this radical change in emphasis, which was challenging enough. Even if there were, the consensus would not rest on any practical certainties; government entities would still have to interpret a host of ambiguous responsibilities specified and implied in the information policy statutes. What, in fact, did those mandates precisely mean? And, given the advent of this brave new world of technology, what form should their implementations take?

For example, what were the ramifications of the Official Records Act's imperative to all government officers and entities to "make and preserve all records necessary to a full and accurate knowledge of their official activities"?[16] While that language had been in the statute since 1941, it had never been the subject of any judicial analysis and it certainly had never carried any penalties for those who failed to fulfill its mandate. "Full and accurate" had never been spelled out, either by agency policy, the legislature, or a Minnesota court. In this instance, as in others, the vague abstractions of the "public good" aspects of good information policy contrasted markedly and unfavorably with the extreme clarity of the proposed consequences suddenly spelled out in House File 2800. Basically, the partially enacted policies and often ad hoc practices of paper recordkeeping offered few tangible clues about the costs and benefits of a comprehensive and compulsory approach to electronic recordkeeping.

There was more. In the bill, the Department of Administration was charged, over the course of a graduated schedule, with the government-wide responsibility of reviewing and certifying every extant system and every proposed system, prior to implementation, to be sure that they complied with the information policy statutes. Criminal justice systems came in for additional and specific mandates. They especially had to be accountable, with provisions for responding to requests from individuals to see their files. They had to be accurate and complete, with provisions for detailed audit-trail data on all aspects of usage. Finally, they had to accept clearly circumscribed limits, both on the types of entities with which they could share data and the types of data they could share. Only the legislature, through statute, could allow for exceptions.

Government agencies, naturally, struck back. They followed two tracks. The first emphasized the impact on government services: there was a near certainty that many important functions—indeed, the work of whole agencies—would come to a halt. Critics raised a variety of questions. Did the legislature want to stop funding nursing homes because the Department of Human Services did not have a comprehensive and up-to-date records retention schedule? Did it want to impede criminal investigations across the state because one police department contributing data to CriMNet was not responsive to a prisoner's request for information on an arrest? This bill would make recordkeeping everyone's highest priority. It would make paperwork—so to speak—government job number one.

Secondly, the fiscal impact would be severe, no small consideration at any time, but especially important at a time when the state was running a budget deficit and the governor had made a pledge of no new taxes. The cost of reviewing systems for compliance was going to be high. The state's Legislative Auditor, for example, estimated that each of its systems audits demanded seven hundred hours of the time of some highly trained and highly paid professionals. That was just one part of the cost for preventive care. Rushing all the patients to the ER would cost even more: CriMNet, for example, estimated the immediate cost of amelioration at just under $25 million. The total projected cost of the bill over three years, with only eight state agencies contributing figures, was close to $60 million.[17]

These were costs and benefits that everyone could understand and their aggregation into compelling arguments had an instant effect. By the time the bill wended its way to a second hearing, the burdens were considerably reduced. The companion bill, Senate File 2561, was introduced with some drastic amendments.[18] Now, compliance with the law was defined in terms of seventeen express mandates for government officers and entities, which were simply lifted from the information policy statutes without further elucidation. One, for example, read: "Make and preserve all records necessary to a full and accurate knowledge of the entity's official activities."[19] This just lent additional emphasis to the various responsibilities already on the books.

More notable was the change in the plans for enforcement. Any citizen could still lodge a complaint with the Department of Administration, but the department's opinions were no longer conclusive or actionable. To compel compliance, the citizen had to take the noncompliant government entity into court. This brought the question into the ordinary legal process, where a court could "fashion any appropriate remedy" and where rights to appeal were clear. Last, the scope of the bill was circumscribed to recognize that local government was a special case; before applying anything new to local government entities, the Department of Administration had to convene an advisory board from specific groups to review and plan for the impact of the bill on that level of government. Anyone could anticipate the recommendations likely to result from that. One witness, representing an association of local government officials, said that, at this point, the bill primarily served to reiterate what was already codified. Since these duties were already mandated, the language of Senate File 2561 was mostly redundant. But another stressed that the specific requirement imposed on CriMNet, to compile and maintain detailed audit trails, was a new burden, too onerous and expensive to bear.

With this, the discussion returned to the House, where Representative Holberg brought her bill to the Judiciary Policy and Finance Committee on April 14. Again, the text was offered with some significant amendments. Holberg began her presentation with an eloquent account of the issues, her diligent efforts to meet the needs of government agencies and her strong belief in the importance of the principles under discussion. She emphasized that information technology could support information policy; government could design and build systems that protected citizens' privacy, kept accurate records, provided accountability, and accomplished business needs. In order to make sure that this all worked in the most economic and efficient means possible, she presented some revisions to House File 2800 that would reduce, if not eliminate, its fiscal impact. But she noted, as others had before her, that all the policies in her bill were already in statute and therefore already mandated for government entities. To her mind, that suggested all the additional costs detailed in the fiscal impact statement simply demonstrated the extent to which agencies were ignoring their current legal responsibilities. Her amendments largely echoed the language in the senate version of the bill. The text began with the list of statutory mandates, now numbering eleven, which government entities had to respect. The Department of Administration was obliged to develop a schedule for reviewing information management systems, along with a budget projecting the costs of the effort, but would not actually have to do anything until the legislature had a chance to review the proposal in its next session. Comprehensive audits of information systems to check for compliance with legislative mandates would wait on further legislative action and, presumably, additional funding.

The Legislative Auditor was instead urged to analyze systems, "as resources permit," for compliance with the information policy statutes. Any government entity operating a system determined by the auditor to be noncompliant would have to present a plan for amelioration to the Department of Administration for review. The commissioner of the department could, but did not have to, require a shutdown of the system if she later determined that progress towards compliance was not proceeding on a satisfactory basis.[20]

The bill retained language about CriMNet calling for full audit-trail data. The data had to include the purpose for which data was used and the identity of the person who used it. The bill listed eight licit, permissible purposes for using CriMNet, some of which were quite broadly defined. If, for example, a police officer checked CriMNet for information on a person at a political rally, she would have to identify herself and select from a menu a specific, applicable purpose such as "investigating a crime," or "determining that an individual may be engaged in illegal activities."[21]

This was still too much for the criminal justice community. Several witnesses stepped forward to complain that the audit-trail provisions in particular would unreasonably increase costs, impede efforts to fight crime, and discourage use of the system. The imposition of a ten-year retention period for audit-trail data, for example, would raise the price of records storage to an unreasonable level. As well, no police officer, at night, on the street, in a potentially dangerous situation, had the time—not even the extra seconds—to select a purpose when doing a computerized records search. Finally, an audit trail that included the name of an officer put that officer at risk; a criminal could request the information and take revenge.

Interestingly, at this point, the tide of opinions seemed to change. Throughout the entire session, legislators, including Representative Holberg, had made extra efforts to address and accommodate the needs and concerns of the criminal justice community. That may have generated a sense of overconfidence; these witnesses were clearly ill prepared for any type of a critical reception. When pressed to move beyond generalities and detail their complaints, they were at a loss. How much more could storing audit-trail data cost to a system that already had a price tag of $200 million? Do not officers logging into a system have to provide a name and password? Could that information be automatically captured? Could the system include a default purpose for a records search? Say, investigating a crime? Are not the names of police officers already in the public record, both in incident reports and court filings? There was a particularly aggressive debate over the question of creating "full and accurate" records. As Representative Eric Lipman noted, that requirement was already in the law. Did the complaints about audit trails signify that the police were not creating full and accurate records by failing to document who used the system and for what purpose? Did that imply, then, that no one knew if and to what extent the records were used or altered for illegal reasons? How could CriMNet guarantee the integrity and security of the system?

These were not welcome questions. The witnesses had to expand upon their initial, categorical response that there was no evidence of misuse and no complaints about the integrity of the system. They explained that the process to determine whether someone had illegally gained access to or altered data would follow a complaint. The system operated under the assumption that all transactions were lawful. But some indication of wrongdoing would spark an audit and investigation that would perforce rely heavily on other records kept outside of the CriMNet system. The investigators could determine the who, what, where, when, and why of misuse from a variety of documents and techniques. In other words, "full and accurate" knowledge could be retrospectively constructed, but would not be evident or available in real time. The alternative, witnesses argued—complete and current documentation—would be too expensive and too burdensome.

All in all, it appeared that those testifying against the bill had relied too much on the expectation of a sympathetic hearing. They were not prepared for the detailed questions that the committee members asked. In particular, they were stumped by the policy questions. For once, the criminal justice card did not trump all others; the witnesses had nothing else in their hands to play. In contrast, Representative Holberg carefully presented a cause for concern and emphasized her willingness to negotiate. She again offered some amendments to the bill to address further the criticisms she had heard; and she again expressed her desire to eliminate the fiscal impact of the bill. Toward that latter end, the date by which CriMNet had to be in full compliance with the information policy statutes was moved to 2010, so that the system revisions could be timed to coincide with the ongoing upgrades to the architecture. The committee approved the bill as amended and forwarded it to the Ways and Means committee to assess its costs.

From there, some extraneous political considerations made themselves known. With some minor changes, both the House and the Senate passed versions of the bill that reiterated the importance of the state's information policies and imposed some positive mandates, including the need to retain audit trails, on CriMNet.[22] But no final version of the bill made its way to the governor. For a variety of reasons, the 2004 session ended with very little accomplished. Essentially, the partisan debate over the state's budget and the concern to position candidates for the upcoming elections led to a paralyzed legislature.[23] Along with almost every other issue of substance, the privacy concerns expressed in Representative Holberg's bill were laid on the table when the legislative session came to a close in May. Subsequent efforts to arrange for a special session, in which the legislature would return to deal with a set number of bills, came to naught. A Republican governor, a Democratic Senate, and a Republican House could not agree on an agenda. Representative Holberg did not carry on with her bill in the 2005 session.

But discussions continue. As of late 2006, a CriMNet taskforce had spent close to a year discussing the familiar issues of accuracy, reliability, and privacy. It did not reach anything like a consensus, though; one member noted, "I have never seen a room full of people with more ways to disagree than the last year on this delivery team. It was real creativity. I just don't think we'll ever get everybody lined up behind it."[24] In the sessions since 2006, the legislature did not return to the bill or directly to the questions it raised, although both houses have examined and debated associated concerns. Privacy is always a hot-button topic, but recent discussions have often focused on privacy and medical records, as the concept of reducing health care costs by sharing medical information digitally has gained momentum. Minnesota, with one of the nation's largest health insurance providers, United Health, and one of the most sophisticated health care providers, the Mayo Clinic, has figured prominently in these conversations.[25]

The debate on documenting government has changed focus. In 2007 and 2008, the legislature examined the prospect of mandating the use of an "open document format" for "the preservation of state documents."[26] As introduced in 2007, the original bill ordered, "Effective July 1, 2008, all documents including text, spreadsheets, and presentations of the state of Minnesota shall be created, exchanged, maintained, and preserved in an open, XML-based file format, as specified by the chief information office of the state."[27] The sweeping nature of the mandate, along with the unreasonable deadline, grabbed people's attention. The debate quickly focused on a familiar concern—costs—but had its political aspects too, as the proponents and opponents were clearly linked to major corporations with an economic interest in the decision. The final bill called for a study committee, with representation from the archives and library communities, and a report to the legislature.

The report concluded against enshrining any technology or standard in statute. Essentially, picking one variable from a complex equation of policy, costs, capacity, business needs, options and dynamic technologies, to name a few, and making it the most important, was not practical; a complicated situation could only be addressed through a flexible decision-making process and appropriate solutions.

The Costs of Doing Business

What makes this bill and debate of interest then? What can archivists learn from it all? We need first to understand and accept that the debate about information policy did not occur on any abstract or theoretical level. Many different constituencies, with many different perspectives, contributed to the discussion. To learn how those differences were negotiated and addressed, we have to put these contributions into a political context. By "political," I mean first of all that the debate took place within a particular framework that lent the discussion a vocabulary and structured it with rules. These will be familiar to anyone who has followed the progress of a bill into law. To those that have not, the whole story must seem a bit fantastic. Think of the issues in the debate over House File 2800: laws that have never been interpreted, let alone enforced; the third rail of budget pressures and fiscal impact statements; the subordination of important policy interests to the dictates of an arbitrary calendar that channeled complex debates into impossibly brief periods; and bills that were radically changed and amended on the fly.

More importantly, though, one should note that while the political vocabulary most often dwelt on absolutes, political decisions invariably resulted in compromises. For example, in the discussion over House File 2800, there were at least seven political principles, all more or less sacred, at work:

- the freedom of information, with the consequences of good government and accountability

- the right to privacy, with government's ability to track citizens circumscribed by law, to preserve personal freedom
- no new taxes, keeping the cost of government down and forcing agencies to cut budgets
- e-government, working smarter, cutting red tape, reengineering government
- the need to document government, by making and keeping "full and accurate" records
- the curse of unfunded mandates, the ills of one level of government carelessly imposing responsibilities on another
- public safety, the need for society to maintain law and order

At points in the debate, these mandates explicitly conflicted with one another, yet it would have been politically impossible simply to discard any one of them as unworkable or inapplicable. Instead there was an ongoing process of contention, negotiation, and accommodation. The normal result of that is a situation where all of the principles are lauded, but few of the programs to implement them are adequately funded. There lies the rub: a cost/benefit analysis is always underway, even if discreet, even if tacit. In this instance, since Minnesota's governor and many of its legislators made a pledge not to raise taxes, the exigencies of the budget lent a particular focus to the debate. Everyone appreciated the governor's pledge and its implications. Representative Holberg, too, explicitly meant to craft a bill that would not have any fiscal impact. The principles of "no new taxes" and "no unfunded mandates" could act as trump cards and all the proposals had to respect the legislature's budget targets. But even without the pledge of no new taxes, the budget would inevitably be the focus of the argument because the budget is the common language of government; every different issue is translated into the more familiar terms of dollars and cents.

It is important to note that two of the other principles—the freedom of information and the right to privacy—allied to the concept of accountability, are most often advanced as reasons to support archival and records management programs in government. These principles were all mentioned in the debate over House File 2800, particularly in the questions over the mandate to create "full and accurate records," but they did not lead to any meaningful or substantive analysis of recordkeeping, as the archival profession understands it. In fact, with the seeming acceptance of the concept of retrospectively documenting decisions only as needed, the government has recognized that the need for accountability is an extraordinary demand. Arguably, this could reflect the fact that Minnesota has no central records management function; the Department of Administration let the program lapse during the budget cuts of 2001. No one, then, represented or spoke for records management during the process. Agencies certainly had records management concerns and legislators had records management questions, but these were discussed in terms of related or larger business functions—authentication, for example, or audit trails. In two instances where specific records-related concerns were raised, once when the deletion of email came up and once when the ten-year retention period for audit-trail data was set, nothing about the conversation was impressive. In fact, the proposition that such a retention period would constitute an unreasonably expensive storage burden for a system designed to contain millions of records, at a cost of hundreds of millions of dollars, was simply ludicrous.

What *Is* to Be Done?

Helen Samuels' work has always had its revolutionary aspects. In that spirit, to paraphrase Lenin, analysis is not simply another occasion to theorize, but to act.[28] But in this highly political context, it seems that the capacity for archival action is limited.

On the legal plane, all the mandates referenced in the debate over House File 2800 are conceptually fixed; the Minnesota legislature is not likely to outright abandon the principles of good government as traditionally defined. But adequately funding the mechanisms to support those principles is a different matter, and so, as a result, the responsibility for the interpretation and application of principles will depend on the tender mercies of individual government entities. On that plane, the routine challenges of doing more with less, as the constraints on budgets become more and more pressing, will be exacerbated by the additional challenge of adapting procedures and practices designed for paper recordkeeping to digital recordkeeping. In other words, responsible staff will have to make difficult choices, without the support of traditional models and habits to guide them.

In the best of all worlds, some enterprise-wide guidance would be available. But in both the states and the federal government, despite some notable efforts to develop architectures and policies, the politics of technology governance has been daunting.[29] American government is intentionally and constitutionally fragmented, with authority, responsibilities, resources, and mandates distributed across multiple entities and levels. Traditional practices push the responsibilities for budgets and functions to single agencies. This makes for an "agency-centric" approach to technology and helps sustain the information silos that characterize the e-government landscape. Projects that focus on the whole enterprise across an entire government (or multiple governments) often mean increased costs and unwelcome change to an individual agency. And change represents risk: there are still many archaic systems in the back offices of government and, while they may not facilitate enterprise-oriented projects, they do work locally and they do manage the function for which they were originally designed. As well, they do so within familiar budgets and personnel structures.

This puts archivists into a quandary. An enterprise approach offers them the chance to push for broadly applicable standards and solutions that support the sort of "public good," "good government" principles that promise something for the whole at the expense of the parts, such as accountability, freedom of information, and so on. If an archives can get the support of a leader in the executive branch—say, a governor—who will persistently direct agencies to move in this direction, then the miracle happens. There is no indication, however, that this will occur in all places.[30]

While we keep our fingers crossed, we have to ask: if a major and well-publicized systemic failure to address records-related mandates will not lead to increased support for archives and records management in government, what will? What should we learn from this example? What impact should practice have on theory? As always, one option is to do nothing—we stay the course, stick to our guns, refuse to compromise our principles. While that approach would meet our means test, it offers scant hope of progress. Simply confirming that records mandates are routinely ignored by government and that the costs of compliance may well be prohibitive will not effectively further the cause. Nor is it much of an argument for preventive care—that is, answering the lament, "if only someone in CriMNet had contacted an archivist or records manager earlier." It is important to remember that the criminal justice community was not significantly inconvenienced by any of this. At no point did anyone agree or admit that the system needed a redesign; only the persistence of one legislator, Mary Liz Holberg, kept the debate alive through the legislative session. And, of course, even if the final version of the bill had passed, CriMNet would still have had until 2010 to implement a scheme for creating and preserving audit trails. While there may have been some embarrassment at times, there was never cause for repentance.

Doing nothing, then, should have little appeal. As noted above, this need to understand and to play a part in a larger organization, to learn how it works and how its members communicate, really demands a different approach. Archivists have to expand our perspective, broadening it to include the myriad factors that will affect our attempts to enact any archival concepts. Two points are critical: First, given the budgetary problems of government and the consequent orientation toward financial concerns, we have to address, persuasively, the question of costs and benefits. Secondly, to speak the language others will understand, we have to learn the nuances of "good e-government," to articulate the principles—call them political or emotional—that will inspire support in the digital age.

The first point is probably more important. To a great extent, the message archivists tend to deliver is weighty with vague references to the public good and notably light on the subject of costs. This will have little resonance in a political debate dominated by catch phrases such as "doing more with less" and "using technology to realize cost savings." In that context, it is problematic for archivists to design solutions that just cost more and, simultaneously, push that fiscal burden on agencies that have other mandates to fulfill. Policies that stress unfunded mandates and implement punitive regulation will not go anywhere. Sadly, those features often characterize what we have to offer. To be persuasive, anything we advocate has to provide some tangible return on investment. From that perspective, the business drivers for the implementation of archival standards that ensure the preservation of digital content could better be defined in terms of what values the archives can add to the enterprise. That points directly to the concept of information as an asset, phrased particularly within the framework of e-government.

The argument here is that the most important case for investments in information technology is the value of the information. For excellent reasons, most e-government projects tend to focus on the immediate goals and functions of the agency managing the effort. But increasingly, there is a strong emphasis on a broader perspective that allows not just for the integration of other entities and constituencies into the project's architecture, but also for the realization of the potential value of the information at the heart of the project itself. That effectively means creating the potential for additional functionality. Minnesota's enterprise technical architecture, for example, states that information is the state's most important asset because it supports decision making.[31] This broader perspective will support work on cross-boundary projects and the integration of systems, data, and functions across entities and organizations.[32] This is the basis of an effective political argument, one that echoes the mandates expressed in such laws as the Uniform Electronic Transactions Act, the E-Government Act of 2002, and the Electronic Signatures in Global and National Commerce Act. This broader perspective also provides a way to demonstrate and measure a return on investments in technology. All electronic records management schemes have some costs, whether measured as additional investments in software and hardware; in systems analysis; in user training and time; or in application interface and maintenance. These investments could result in some counterweight of benefits that stress efficiency, meeting customer expectations, and lowering costs—all arguments we hear, for example, in debates over the development of electronic medical records.[33] In sum, the concept of information as an asset seems the best bet to add value, particularly in the framework of a more collective view of the government enterprise that promotes data sharing and data enhancement.[34]

Overall, the trend toward e-government, which assumes information and functions shared across traditional agency boundaries, will inevitably support the allocation of resources to efforts that maximize the value of information. That, in fact, is the lesson of CriMNet: some $200 million to share information, because it supports law enforcement across the state, but virtually nothing to correct deficiencies in records management.

How do archivists fit into this context? A focus on e-government can be viewed as opportunistic, strategic, rhetorical, or all three. As it would be virtually impossible to find a government official these days whose stated mission did not include some priority on reengineering government by building on technology, it is just common sense, however you define it, to echo those concepts. Yet we have mountains to climb just to articulate, let alone implement, projects based on the concept of information as an asset. Certainly, there is little to indicate that the average archives can contribute to a single effort on the scale of Minnesota's CriMNet, much less to the multiple, ongoing information technology projects occurring across every government.[35]

On a practical basis, one approach that makes sense is one that emphasizes education and collaboration. Education would be mutually beneficial for archivists and their constituencies, ongoing and designed to build the communities described by John Seely Brown and Paul Duguid in *The Social Life of Information*.[36] Education, moreover, is an affordable, manageable function for most archives, strapped as they are for funding. Archivists can identify, help develop, and promote tools that others can put to use. Collaboration would be based on the fundamental recognition that information technology projects increasingly have such broad impact and demand such diverse skills that archivists have to form and work in teams that cross geographical, organizational, and professional boundaries. Archivists would develop special expertise, services, and products that would facilitate and complement the efforts of other entities.[37] To build the infrastructure to support digital archives, they would share costs and overhead with partners in other institutions, states, and professions. Such a collaborative approach—working with partners, and focusing on education, especially—has its roots and inspiration in the documentation strategy of Helen Samuels more than twenty years ago, even if the strategies and the nature of the documentation are ever changing.

Finally, and perhaps most important, archivists should set and reset priorities as opportunities develop and contingencies affect us. As Mark H. Moore wrote, any government entity's "mandate for change is both ambiguous and vulnerable to change, and . . . an efficient response to that reality may require organizations to be adaptive and flexible rather than rigidly focused on achieving a clearly defined objective."[38] An archival program in that context would be:

- focused on the value of information, particularly in terms of data sharing, reuse and protection;

- conversant with developing technologies, enough to speak the language, if not to build the applications;
- opportunistic and flexible in its approach to concepts, mandates, practices, and partnerships;
- cost-effective, with an overriding concern to promote widely applicable standards and practices; and
- collaborative, open to partnerships with new constituencies that are designed to be mutually beneficial.

Altogether, such characteristics do represent a much different prospect for the archival community. Based as they are on an essentially political outlook, they comprise qualities that will foster negotiation and accommodation. Enactment means polishing a corresponding set of "soft skills," to establish and smooth the relationships and partnerships, as well as to manage the ad hoc and ongoing collaborative projects that will dominate the agenda.

That all makes for a cautionary tale, an ambitious strategy for a profession that normally shuns active intervention. But as Helen Samuels wrote, archivists have to do something: their "most important roles are as analyst, planner and agent who create an awareness about documentary problems."[39] We still have an opportunity with technology; we need to broaden our perspective to develop solutions. The alternative, if we take CriMNet's example as a harbinger, might be an archival program existing simply as an unfunded or underfunded afterthought to somebody else's plan.

Notes

1 Robert Pear, "Panel Urges New Protection on Federal 'Data Mining,'" and William Safire, "Security with Liberty," *New York Times*, May 17, 2004, sec. A, 12, 25.

2 Her best known work in this regard is *Varsity Letters: Documenting Modern Colleges and Universities* (Metuchen, NJ: Scarecrow Press and Society of American Archivists, 1992).

3 Two recent studies address how archivists could speak such a language: National Electronic Commerce Coordinating Council, *Digital Archiving: From Fragmentation to Collaboration* (NECCC, 2006), at: http://www.ec3.org/Pubs/2006NASS_WhitePaper.pdf; and Anthony M. Cresswell, G. Brian Burke, and Theresa A. Pardo, *Advancing Return on Investment Analysis for Government: A Public Value Framework* (Albany, NY: Center for Technology in Government, 2006), at http://www.ctg.albany.edu/publications /reports/advancing_roi.

4 Information on the MCPA is available at http://www.mnchiefs.org/.

5 The home page for the Global Justice Information Sharing Initiative is at http://it.ojp.gov/topic.jsp?topic_id=8.

6 The CriMNet project is fully described at http://www.crimnet.state.mn.us. Minnesota's Legislative Auditor's Office recently produced two very interesting and detailed analyses of the project: Program Evaluation Division, *CriMNet*, Report Number 04-05 (2004), at: http://www.auditor.leg.state.mn.us/Ped/2004/pe0405.htm; and Financial Audit Division, *CriMNet Financial Audit*, Report Number 04-08 (2004), at: http://www.auditor.leg.state.mn.us/fad/2004/fad04-08.htm.

7 Patrick Howe, "Growing Use of Private Police Network Raises Some Concerns," *USA Today*, October 30, 2003, www.usatoday.com/tech/news/techpolicy/2003-1-30-mn-cop-database_x.htm.

8 House Judiciary Policy and Finance Committee, April 14, 2004. Rep. Mary Liz Holberg recounted the events.

9 Howe, "Growing Use of Private Police Network."

10 Patrick Howe, "Police Day Network Closed for Now," *St. Paul Pioneer-Press*, November 1, 2003.

11 Mary Liz Holberg, "Why One Legislator Cares about Data Practices," *FYi: From the Information Policy Analysis Division* 3 (2004): 1, at http://www.ipad.state.mn.us.

12 Patrick Howe, "Minnesota Private Police Network Permanently Shut Down over Privacy Concerns," *North County Times*, December 18, 2003.

13 Hearing, Committee on Judiciary Policy and Finance, Minnesota House, April 14, 2004.

14 H.F. 2800, introduced March 4, 2004; see http://www.revisor.leg.state.mn.us/cgi-bin/bldbill.pl?bill=H2800.0&session=ls83.

15 Minnesota law draws some sweeping and impressionistic definitions of data or records in at least four separate laws: *Minnesota Statutes*, ch. 13 and sections 15.17, 138.17 and 325L.01. Conceptually, data and records are different, although it is not entirely clear how, as the definitions of each tautologically includes the other. Content and function intertwine. As Helen Samuels pointed out in 1999, the point really is moot: "A diverse group of professionals was talking about the problems of managing 'information.' As the discussion proceeded I realized that each participant had a different mental model of the 'information' we were discussing based on their work and their own perspective. . . . What we must acknowledge is that each perception is correct. In actuality, 'information' is all of these and more. For academic institutions 'information' encompasses the full spectrum of the information the faculty, staff and students generate, manage and use." Helen Samuels, "Why Should We Care about all this Stuff?" (paper presented at Preservation and Access for Electronic College and University Records, Tucson, AZ, October 1999), http://www.asu.edu/it/events/ecure/bak/ecure1999/samuels-presentation.html.

16 *Minnesota Statutes*, section 15.17.

17 Minnesota House Research Office, H.F. 2800, consolidated fiscal impact note, April 5, 2004.

18 Minnesota Senate, Committee on Judiciary, Hearing, March 23, 2004.

19 S.F. 2561, A-1 amendment, introduced March 23, 2004.

20 H.F. 2800, E7 amendment, April 13, 2004.

21 Ibid.

22 The House bill, H.F. 2800, was folded into an omnibus data practices bill, H.F. 2087, during a floor session, as moved by Representative Holberg.

23 For a contemporary review of the situation, see Kevin Duchshere and Dane Smith, "Pawlenty Silent about Special Session," *Minneapolis Star-Tribune*, May 17, 2004.

24 Dan Gunderson and Elizabeth Stawicki, "Criminal Justice Information Sharing Raises Questions," Minnesota Public Radio, December 28, 2006, at http://minnesota.publicradio.org/display/web/2006/12/11/crimnet2/.

25 For an example, see Marisa Helms, "Your Medical Records Are Leaving Town and Some Privacy and Health Advocates Aren't Happy about It," *MinnPost*, March 10, 2009, at http://www.minnpost.com/stories/2009/03/10/7276/your_medical_records_are_leaving_town_and_some_privacy_and_health_advocates_arent_happy_about_it.

26 For background and details, see Minnesota Office of Enterprise Technology, *Preserving the Present: Creating, Accessing and Maintaining Minnesota's Electronic Documents. Report to the Minnesota Legislature,* January 15, 2008, at http://www.state.mn.us/mn/externalDocs/OET/2008_Legislative_report_to_the_legislature_021208010207_Electronic%20doc%20study%200108.pdf.

27 Ibid., 4.

28 V.I. Lenin, *What Is to Be Done?* (1902), http://www.marxists.org/archive/lenin/works/1901/witbd/.

29 See, for example, Peter Weill and Jeanne W. Ross, *IT Governance* (Cambridge, MA: Harvard Business School Press, 2004); and the report from the 2004 symposium of the National Electronic Commerce Coordinating Council, *Government in the Digital Age: Myths, Realities and Promises,* at http://www.ec3.org.

30 Although it did work in the state of Washington: see the case study in Cresswell et al., *Advancing Return on Investment Analysis.*

31 See *Minnesota Enterprise Technical Architecture,* chapter 1, Conceptual Architecture, at http://www.ot.state.mn.us/architecture. Or consider CriMNet's current motto: "Putting the right information in the hands of the right people, at the right time in the right place" (http://www.crimnet.state.mn.us).

32 For a recent description of cross-boundary projects in e-government, see, for example, the report from the 2003 symposium of the National Electronic Commerce Coordinating Council, *XBI – Cross Boundary Integration: the Key to Successful E-Government* (2003) at http://www.ec3.org/Downloads/2003/XBI_Report.pdf.

33 *Wikipedia,* interestingly, has an entry for "electronic medical record," which notes both archival concerns about preservation of digital content and the principal public policy criticism (privacy) of such records. See http://en.wikipedia.org/wiki/Electronic_medical_record.

34 See Peter Hirtle, "Archives or Assets?" *American Archivist* 66 (2003): 235–47.

35 A recent National Academy of Sciences report even raised questions about the National Archives' ability to manage a single large-scale technology project: Committee on Digital Archiving and the National Archives and Records Administration, Robert F. Sproull and Jon Eisenberg, eds., *Building an Electronic Records Archive at the National Archives and Records Administration: Recommendations for Initial Development* (National Academy of Science, 2003), at http://books.nap.edu/catalog/10707.html.

36 John Seely Brown and Paul Duguid, *The Social Life of Information* (Cambridge, MA: Harvard Business School Press, 2000).

37 For a description of such a program in Minnesota, see Robert Horton, "Obstacles and Opportunities," in *Effective Approaches for Managing Electronic Records and Archives,* ed. Bruce Dearstyne (New Jersey: Scarecrow Press, 2002).

38 Mark H. Moore, *Creating Public Value: Strategic Management in Government* (Cambridge, MA: Harvard University Press, 1995), 70.

39 Helen W. Samuels, "Improving our Disposition: Documentation Strategy," *Archivaria* 33 (Winter 1991–92): 137.

KEEPING RECORDS IN CHANGING ORGANIZATIONS

Rick Barry

Organizations are born and live their own unique, complex lives, and build their own special cultures and behavioral patterns.[1] Each has substrata in the form of people (real organisms); relatively fixed (hierarchical) or fluid (flat, virtual) structuring of their tasks and work groups; a "nervous system" in the form of functions, processes, subprocesses and activities that give stimulus and meaning; information and the wherewithal to communicate it, well or poorly; and physical structure (buildings, locations, regions), to house the component parts of the system, all factors which may work for or against one another or the whole organic body.

Every organization is born, grows, gets sick when its individual organs (or larger systems) malfunction, attempts recovery by adapting to changing environments over time, and struggles to survive in its present form, or to transform into something else, when management imposes new behavioral expectations, or else its functions survive but in a new organizational structure (through mergers, downsizing, takeovers, and so on), or it dies. Sensitivity to behavior of the modern organization as an organic system suggests behavioral clues, analytical tools, and technological insights for professional archivists and records managers that can reinforce current approaches or suggest improved practices to face the challenges of the digital age. This essay will explore these, against four broad suppositions.

First, organizations are organic beings, each with a look and a feel of its own. Each has its own structures and cultures and behavioral patterns. Use of this knowledge can help to inform strategic alliances and tactical approaches for documenting their lives and activities. Secondly, archivists, records managers, enterprise architects, and others can profitably use organizational analysis to sort out what an organization does and possible ways to at least partially capture and preserve its essence for legal, recordkeeping, knowledge-seeking, historical/cultural, or reference purposes. Information tokens in numerous analog and digital formats—principally records that are produced by such organizations during their normal business operations—can offer photo-frame shots of what is very much a moving and adapting target. These tokens can be analyzed and classified in ways useful to build surrogate models based on the actual work processes and living systems of the organization. Such models, in turn, can effectively support a top-down descriptive metadata approach and macroappraisal scheme for identifying the value of records for their appropriate dispositions, in some cases including prior to their creation. Business systems analysis is a tool for carrying out such top-down decomposition and thus understanding an organization's functions and activities. Third, a better appreciation of how information technologies have changed and been used over the years can help to discern their impact on user behaviors and the archives and records management landscape. It can also suggest how some of the very same technologies might effectively be applied to the business of recordkeeping.

Finally, by understanding organizations as complex systems, we can sharpen our sensors for recognizing future challenges before they are on our doorsteps and rethink the way we are delivering recordkeeping services. Lessons from past behavior can offer a lens through which to review our current plans and practices.

* * * * *

Organizations and the individuals within them are like molecular representations in the societies in which they live. We know how individual human behavioral patterns—likes, dislikes, dreams for the future, fears, and routines of living to maintain comfort levels—can cause people to act in different ways. Likewise, organizations create their own complex cultures and behavioral expectations. Deciphering these patterns by records managers and archivists may be relatively easy when statements of corporate aims, values, expectations, and policies are well articulated, communicated and reinforced with employees, and made part of the corporate culture. It becomes thornier when consultations with employees reveal differences between what the organization projects in its corporate documentation from the boardroom and the stark reality on the office floor. This too often becomes apparent to newcomers only after their employment.

Former Department of Defense historian Shelley Davis lived such an experience after accepting a position in the Internal Revenue Service (IRS) as its first and last historian. She later wrote about its dysfunctional recordkeeping and the organizational clues underpinning it.[2] Walking down the building's corridors, Davis noticed the absence of any kind of symbolic tokens of where she was and what important things were carried out there. Unlike her past experience, there were no framed historical documents on the walls, no pictures of iconic activities such as Prohibition-era raids on secret moonshine stills, no portraits of former IRS commissioners depicting its leadership history. She subsequently learned that the policy-related records that she sought in support of her duties were nowhere to be found. Davis reports discovering a long-standing pattern in which the commissioners' administrative records were kept separately in a remote room and, for over thirty years, were denied to the National Archives and Records Administration (NARA), with a poorly trained records management unit facilitating this practice in contradiction of the Federal Records Act. She also pointed to evidence of numerous cases of theft of original signatures of historical figures from records without any negative consequence for staff involved, indicating either managerial ignorance of or serious disregard for the inviolateness of records ethics or theft. After years of failed attempts to work within the system to have archival records transferred to NARA where they belonged, she ultimately left the IRS on ethical grounds.[3]

The American automotive giant General Motors was born as an organization in 1908 and became by 1931 the largest manufacturer of automobiles in the world, until 2008 when its ranking was unseated by Toyota. It is an example of a hundred-year life cycle gone awry, leading up to GM's struggle to survive past 2009 through cash injections and ultimately partial government ownership, and a massive downsizing and restructuring. Whether it will survive, let alone flourish again, remains to be seen at the time of this writing. If it dies, or survives as a much-transformed entity, it will surely become the subject of many organizational studies, where the adaptability of its entrenched culture to changing environments will no doubt draw major attention.

Organizational structure has always influenced how information management—and within it archives and records management—has been practiced. That focus on structure has long been the key element in the description of fonds in a vertical, hierarchical way, underpinning no few records management and archival concepts and practices. Structure can help provide clear lines of accountability, linking records to offices, position numbers, and to other related records. Until recent years, less attention has been paid to such cultural and behavioral factors as management style, trust and loyalty, organizational history, values, incentives and disincentives, and attitudes toward the inviolateness of records and recordkeeping practices.

For the archivist to document organizations through macroappraisal, one does not start from the bottom with mountains of records, but rather with research and analysis into the organization's top-level aims, the business processes created to carry out those aims (including whether they produce appropriate records), and the cultural factors that surround how they are carried out. Likewise, on a supra-organizational level, as Helen Samuels urges in the documentation strategy,[4] archivists should aim to document whole sectors or portions of societies not at the record level, but by starting with common underlying purposes, functions, and shared activities across organizations—say in fields like scientific research or education or in shared beliefs in portions of society—that define and determine both the context and much of the content of those records.[5]

* * * * *

Business systems analysis is a tool for modeling organizations. Such tools also may be applied to other social or virtual entities with common interests. It has enormous potential for facilitating the description, macroappraisal and disposition management of records, either manually or with the aid of computer applications. It provides a means for decomposition and analysis of an organization from its highest order elements—in the forms of its stated vision, aims and objectives—to the lower structured and unstructured entities it establishes, and the processes it puts in place to achieve its goals. Documenting these elements may further be used to create a framework, map, and model of how records or most other major assets (dollars, human resources, real estate) can be keyed to one another and up the chain to the organization's aims. Where business systems analysis is already being used or being contemplated for other corporate purposes, it offers an excellent opportunity for engagement to ensure that recordkeeping needs are included.

I differentiate between the concepts and terms *business systems analysis* and *business process reengineering*. The latter is often used to optimize individual processes, usually revealing along the way how processes are rarely the domains of one department or organizational unit. In many cases, processes can weave among multiple units and stakeholders, in leading or supporting roles. With business systems analysis, complex relationships are mapped both within and among business processes. This characteristic makes such processes natural groupings for macroappraisal.

An important aim of business process reengineering is to automate human interventions or "handoffs" where possible and eliminate paper. This requires interviewing people at every process stage to learn all they know about the process and how to improve it; with what units they undertake or share the process; what records they create, receive, or share; and what makes the handoff necessary. It takes only one such exercise for employees to discern (alas, often accurately) that the real question is: how can part or all of their role within the process be automated or their positions eliminated? Not surprisingly, as valuable an efficiency tool as it may be, business process reengineering has acquired an often well-deserved bad name in human terms. On the other hand, if a records manager is presented with budget cuts that include loss of positions, business process reengineering techniques can be employed to help determine how such cuts might be taken while retaining the service through automation of certain steps.

Business systems analysis views the organization as a goal-driven whole—action-wise and information-wise—mapping all of its processes from its highest core aims that describe its *raison d'être* to its functional, subfunctional, process, subprocess, and transaction/activity levels, with corresponding definitions and even mandates for each step. Processes are named and defined by analysts, then vetted and fine tuned with all process stakeholders. Definitions begin with verbs, because they represent actions that reflect what people (or systems) are actually doing rather than the thing that is done. Each requires information from itself or other processes for its retention schedule to be resolved.[6] Each, in turn, produces information for itself or others. And what are records if not the documentation of such actions at every process and functional level?

Business systems analysis can lead to more systemic improvements among all processes in managing records and other information along functional lines: identifying and designating record-worthiness before and after record creation; creating enterprise-wide metadata databases and interrelationships; facilitating macroappraisal; leveraging auto-classification and enabling computer-assisted or automated disposition management. Process is also a much more stable platform for recordkeeping than organization structure, not to the exclusion of that to be sure, but as the key lens through which structure and other variables are viewed. Matching the frequency of changes in a given structural entity with corresponding changes in business processes over a given period usually discloses that, unless the organization has significantly changed its aims or taken on or dropped an important line of business and its related processes, its process suite persists despite frequent structural changes. This occurs because organizations change structure for nonprocess reasons, such as to create checks and balances, solve sensitive personnel issues, redistribute power, deal with expanding (or shrinking) numbers of clients, cases, or regional offices, consolidate multiple units due to budget cuts, and so on. It would not surprise most people to find that, for example, their human resources department had undergone numerous reorganizations in the past two decades. However, it is likely that, in each structural incarnation, the human resources function remained involved in the same processes: recruit staff, hire staff, train staff, transfer/promote staff, care for staff, terminate staff, retire staff, and so on.

Unlike paper-based systems, unless replicated in two separately organized collections, process/function and structural views of an organization are not mutually exclusive in digital systems. Moreover, being oriented to process can help make the management of records easier, more consistent, and enduring. This is a major positive consideration in the design of electronic recordkeeping systems, both for highly structured organizations struggling to adapt to rapidly changing times and for virtual organizations that are designed explicitly for such adaptability.

This description of business systems analysis may appear to imply that it serves a restricted view of recordkeeping for evidentiary purposes, with little concern for the historical or social memory values of records. This is in no way intended. These important roles that records play can, and should, equally be served, with use of this kind of analysis and modeling, as demonstrated in the above discussion of Samuels' strategies for documenting society and social memory.

Since technological changes are often initiated at the process level, a process orientation can also help dampen negative effects of technology on recordkeeping. The reverse is also true. Embedding information technology within processes can greatly facilitate recordkeeping. Technically, it is difficult to imagine how macroappraisal and disposition management can be automated in the absence of such an approach. This is no small consideration in times of a growing pace of organizational fluidity.

* * * * *

Technology has always both confounded and enlightened information managers over the ages, including remembrancers and archivists. The Renaissance humanist Abbot Johannes Trithemius noted in his *In Praise of Scribes*: "The word written on parchment will last a thousand years. The printed word is on paper. How long will it last? The most you can expect of a book of paper to survive is two hundred years. Yet, there are many who think they can entrust their words to paper."[7] Many assume that current concerns over the likely future loss of fragile digital records with the onset of the "paperless office" is unique to modern times, but the venerable abbot, in challenging the idea of the "parchment-less abbey" over five hundred years ago, uses the same argument as those who now cling to paper rather than digital objects as the best record for longevity. James O'Donnell sees the abbot's technology-based concerns as a harbinger of our situation today:

> [T]he technology of writing had worked its way deeply into the social and economic structure of the community . . . perhaps not essential to the monastic ideal, but . . . integral to its practice. It is the undermining of the monastery that Trithemius most feared.

> And of course he was right . . . the ability of the institution to survive depended on its ability to adapt itself to the new technological environment (universities did much better, until now at least, than monasteries, after all, though in the fifteenth century they shared many common traditions) and that was an adaptation that Trithemius could not bring himself to theorize. If in practice he approved of print and used it, he could still not find a way to bring print into his picture of the monastic life. . . . In practice, print was a business that flourished in less salubrious parts of town, among grubby businessmen unafraid of dirty hands. It was there that a new information order was created, and the [older, monastic] social order found itself wrenched, sometimes agonizingly slowly, sometimes shockingly quickly, to align itself with what technology had created.[8]

We may not yet face the envisioned paperless office, but we do confront offices where paper (except for legacy records) has become a secondary product used mainly for personal convenience and reference, and the primary records essential to organizational health and its memory continuity, as well as to history, are increasingly born-digital in various electronic formats. Some of these electronic or digital records are required to be preserved for many decades for organizational purposes if its systems are to flourish or, as in the case of NARA, for the many centuries that will form "the life of the Republic." As the abbot feared, however, our new technologies have not yet exhibited the ability to last for centuries—perhaps not yet even for a few decades.

This prospect has stimulated thinking and planning for electronic records and a postcustodial model of recordkeeping and enterprise-wide maintenance of such records, as well as functions-oriented macroappraisal concepts and strategies. However, recordkeeping practices remain relatively unchanged between twenty-five years ago and today. Paper-based practices are very much alive, if not well, given the flood of born-digital records. There are some notable exceptions, including large financial institutions and others making increasing use of SharePoint, a software many records professionals consider lacking in robust records functionality. This is something likely to change with increasing focus on electronic records by system developers, NARA and other national archives, and numerous other research institutions in many disciplines and sectors of modern society.

The slow pace in postcustodial electronic records uptake is primarily because archives and records managers have failed to justify the business case for the resources required. Senior managers and budget analysts are accustomed to the notion that introduction of new technology should be accompanied by corresponding financial tradeoffs between more capital for technology and less labor for staff positions. We know this does not work for recordkeeping where, as a practical matter, traditional custodial activities will have to be continued for legacy systems and the mountains of inherited paper, microform, and other analog records they produced, unless and until they are digitized. With the introduction of new electronic records systems, most resources for electronic systems will be additive; and most of the added staff will require different, more expensive skills, some possibly justifying higher graded position levels than the recordkeeping unit manager. (Among other good reasons for employing archivists with university graduate-level credentials as chiefs of records management units, and for consolidating records management and archives functions under an archivist, these steps may eliminate the position grading issue.) Failure to move forward may also rest on uncertainty of how to implement a postcustodial model for electronic records. Perhaps as well it is difficult for executives and even some records managers and archivists to notice the incremental (but highly significant) changes in the legal, risk, and technological landscapes that have taken place over the past two decades and now dictate a fresh look.

Despite disappointing outcomes in the past, some very successful electronic records systems have been implemented that give evidence that records managers can be adept in making their cases to management, or possibly vice versa. Where postcustodial models are successfully introduced, the physical location of records, in particular electronic records, becomes moot, so long as they are properly controlled and maintained, including archival records under the right conditions, especially favoring highly structured forms, transactional, and other data-based records.[9]

With postcustodial models, the corporate recordkeeping function and staff skills for electronic records must shift emphasis from the physical to the logical control of records, including policy making; participating in design of enterprise architectures for information and technology; standards setting that includes minimal standards for the design and implementation of content-based systems; establishing and linking directories of records assets; creating and managing metadata and meta-meta-databases, including embedded records; monitoring and assessing decentralized controls and disposition practices; carrying out business systems analyses and embedding the results of macroappraisal into the disposition process; partnering with auditors to ensure that recordkeeping considerations are routinely covered in audits, with appropriate penalties for noncompliance; and ensuring easy cross-unit access to records to facilitate enterprise-wide knowledge management and, where access restrictions permit, access by scholars, journalists, and the general public.

What can we learn from the generational changes in technology over the past two decades and the different behavioral environments we associate with them? Before the personal computer stormed the workplace beginning in the early and mid-1980s, most executives focused cost controls for mainframe computing on the initial, high costs of the hardware itself. Little attention was placed on costs associated with mostly in-house application software development and programming language standards. Much less attention was given to related technical staff and user training costs until much later. As it turned out, the longer-term human costs of software development, documentation and maintenance, technical support and training, and especially continuing user training were and are now by far the principal costs of computer usage. This is particularly true for user training for large, complex systems, such as one installation for an American Navy/Marine Corps project to put recordkeeping software on four hundred thousand desks, where training costs were greatly underestimated in the bidding process.

The hardware and software generating these costs remained the province of the highly centralized Computing Department. Large mainframe computers and the people who managed them behind glass walls reigned supreme. It was the era of "heavy metal" or "big iron." Less time and resources were given to the data or information produced by these machines, and even less to transforming the transient and ever-changing *data* into electronic *records*, having qualities of fixed, trustworthy, reliable evidence.

This is a harsh assessment, but one that was too often true before personal computers became available and created major competition for dollars, and thus CEO attention. Internal users in "line" operations in organizations, at the mercy of mainframe central computing unit, recall those days as the dark ages, but they were the good days for records management: tight central production controls and mainframe processes that printed out mountains of records on fan-fold paper, or in computer-output microform, were easy to identify, obtain, and manage. Where some of these datasets had long-term archival value, such archival pioneers as Charles Dollar, Margaret Hedstrom, and Harold Naugler developed good guidelines to offload and preserve software-independent "flat files" of the data for preservation in electronic rather than paper-printout format.

When personal computers began to arrive in the workplace in small quantities in the early 1980s, users were eager to get their hands on them to take control of much of the computing power needed in their work. Line managers decided to put these machines on the desk of virtually every knowledge- and support-worker in government and private-sector organizations of all sizes. The spread of the use of these personal or desktop computers across whole organizations in the course of two or three years is surely one of the fastest technological transitions ever.

But most mainframe gurus were not listening, or at least did not comprehend the behavioral revolution in these "line" and "support" business units. At the same time that the mainframe computer technicians were using personal computers as mainframe programming and control tools, end-users across the organization were beginning to find innovative ways to use personal computers for their own business needs in jobs supporting almost every business operation. The personal computing software industry certainly did not miss that trend. It provided new desktop tools—such helpful (or attractive) accessories as calculators, calendars, graphics packages, spreadsheets, and games—and word-processing programs that some thought better than the one used elsewhere in the office. Since they all produced paper, these software tools were brought into the workplace without anyone asking about standards or compatibility, or in fact being much noticed, let alone integrated into work processes in strategic ways. Soon enough, there was informal swapping of experiences and user choices emerged. By the end of the 1980s, therefore, users were de facto dictating the terms of enterprise standards.

* * * * *

The magnitude of the problem rests with the hard reality that, by the beginning of the 1990s, everyone was an end-user. The term remains with us today because it is synonymous with empowerment. In many organizations, large numbers of centralized information technology staff members, formerly assigned to run the mainframes, were redistributed from the central office systems group into scattered end-user units to provide embedded technical support across the entire organization. They would now work shoulder to shoulder with end-users and learn in much greater depth the specific business processes in operational units and how to serve those needs better. Archivists and records staff also had the curtains pulled back on technology, with both its possibilities and limitations exposed. At first, the focal point was largely on choosing the best information technology to meet user needs—the personal computer hardware and software—and much less on managing the informational content produced by the technology. The ascendancy of information technology over information management forced recordkeeping professionals to see the real problems of digital products from all the emerging, incompatible, noninteroperable technologies, often functioning (unlike their mainframe antecedents) without any centralized controls or policies.

In this new world, how should digital information be captured and integrated, as reliable evidence, into the enterprise's corporate record and memory systems? Too often the initial solution was to keep it all in paper format, treating the personal desktop computer like a wonderful automated typewriter, the end-products of which were not born-digital records to be managed in new ways, but familiar paper printouts to be placed in files within the traditional records management system.

The age of the end-user gave way, in the late 1990s, when many changes in large-scale office computer systems were made as risk-reduction measures in the lead-up to the anticipated Y2K crisis and the new business needs of the early 2000s. The focus was now on organizational information content and away from end-user information technology. Attention shifted to the increasingly difficult problem of the management of corporate data of all kinds, both structured in major databases and unstructured in office desktop systems, and in many disparate digital forms. Chief Information Officers (CIOs) soon learned that their jobs now were about content—the message—and not just the medium. Demands for corporate-wide information to respond, as new laws required, to freedom of information requests, and growing legal e-discovery processes, created hurry-up policies or practices. End-user creators were designated to decide on the recordness of the word-processed or email documents they produced and were directed to "print to paper" and forward to the records center. It was, and remains for many, at best a stop-gap measure.

It was also a practice that was, and remains for some, fundamentally flawed. Repeated downsizing had gutted records management operations, leaving few professionals there to classify huge backlogs of printouts—even where records management staff remained at full strength. Overworked end-users, themselves often in downsized offices and forced to "do more with less," often ignored "print to paper and file" policies. These twin factors, and the existence of some newer multimedia and compound born digital records objects that could not ever be printed to paper, combined to render the traditional paper files incomplete and untrustworthy as evidence of business processes. Moreover, the World Wide Web had grown from a single host in 1990 to millions of web pages and domains by the end of that decade, and from a few blogs then to estimates of nearly two hundred million today. One blog-monitoring firm indexed over one hundred million of them in 2008 alone. Others estimate their numbers doubling every six months. Increasingly, much of the information produced using such technologies by business and government constituted important business records. Not surprisingly, the principal focus during this time was on how to manage diverse files from office suite software, such as word processed documents, email, presentation graphics, spreadsheets, and instant messages, in varying proprietary file formats, into an integrated corporate-wide resource. But the digital office world would not stand still. In the 2000s, intranet and website records and, for some, voice and moving digital media have been added to the mix. Where electronic document management systems (EDMS) were designed mainly for textual information, enterprise content management systems (ECMS) were implemented to manage multimedia content together. Once ECMS developers understood this, they began to build or acquire recordkeeping components into their office software suites, especially in the United States when these software applications could be certified by the government (which carried for manufacturers a procurement-friendly commercial advantage) as being compliant with the DoD 5015.2 (now 5015.02) Records Management Application standard, endorsed by the Archivist of the United States for all federal agencies. ECMS certified by this standard offer an opportunity for putting computer technology to work for recordkeeping. It still requires resources, training, and a large measure of still-absent central control.

The most recent development on the growing born-digital mountain is "user-generated content"—such as MySpace, Second Life, Facebook, Flickr, YouTube, Twitter, mobile phone texting, and other social networking, personal journal, and "presence" tools—which form what is loosely called "Web 2.0 computing," or interactive websites, and "social networking."[10] This development was spurred by the development of wireless hand-held computing devices and "smart phones," which made powerful computing capacity entirely mobile and not tied by wires and cables to a desktop. Like many other innovations targeted first at the individual private-user market, use of social-networking systems—in such applications as blogs, wikis, texting, tweets, image capture and sharing—soon found their ways into business and government uses. Virtually all network and local television organizations, for example, now routinely use social networking as part of their toolkits, inviting viewers to send mobile-phone text messages or videos of breaking news stories, weather events, highway conditions, or even crimes in progress. Network commentators often set up their own blogs and invite users to participate on them.[11] Government institutions, and even a few archives, followed this trend, using tweets to alert clients to new programs, service changes, recent acquisitions, and so on, and inviting interactive "social tagging," photographs or commentary on some of their web pages. These developments have introduced a whole new generation of "lay journalism" with advantages (quick, on-the-spot, citizen-based, democratic) and drawbacks (often unprofessional, highly biased, unsourced "reporting") for representing real events or establishing new aspects of the societal record. Either way, whether viewed as positive or negative, "everyman" is now her or his own author, publisher, musician, film-maker, photographer, journalist, critic, reviewer, and archivist. To state the obvious, a new recordmaking reality has dawned that poses both wonderful opportunities and deep challenges to organizational recordkeeping, societal documentation, and archival appraisal and description.

* * * * *

With the advent of every new computing modality, therefore, radical change is not just happening in organizations, but also in vast transformations of communication patterns and information generation in the world around them. How many records professionals take the best advantage of these changing environments? How many are able to seize the opportunities, and recognize the risks, presented by this enormous societal-technological change? How many are able to keep senior management aware of these important technological and societal developments, and articulate accordingly their critical implications for organizational opportunity, risk, accountability, profitability, public relations, and positive citizen or client engagement? If not now able to access senior management, how many are able within their organizational cultures to keep the subject visible, and thus future change possible?

There is now the opportunity, in this environment of transformed organizational cultures and communication patterns, for archivists and records managers to take a fresh look at how they operate. Nine suggested steps, adjusted as may be necessary for local conditions, may help to change the calculus and reverse the trends of recordkeeping failures detailed in the previous sections:

1. Focus on service rather than simply administration. In the past, many records professionals justified their programs by citing legal and managerial mandates, and saw top management as their client. This put the highest premium on excellence in administration. Today, this approach is not enough. Managers want to know what is in it for them *and* for their over-extended staff. Good administration of records cannot be diminished, but today it has to come with high-quality service, and services that exploit fully the new communications technologies to make work easier and more productive.
2. Orient recordkeeping operations to facilitate enterprise-wide functions and business processes rather than to reflect mainly internal organizational structures or subject headings. Doing so will also assist in more effective macroappraisal and orderly retention and disposition of electronic records.
3. Learn how your stakeholders may have changed in recent years. Seek their endorsement by supporting their needs and opportunities for more effectively using records. Who are they—all of them? For example, when we depend on end-users to designate

evidence-bound records amid the myriad information and data they create daily to ensure good recordkeeping practices, such as supplying certain key elements of metadata, that process alone makes them key stakeholders. How happy are they with the computer interface they must use to do those tasks? Does the records unit know? Is it interested? Is it able to adapt to changing user needs quickly and flexibly? What have records managers and archivists done for them today?

4. Make chief information officers and senior information technology staff aware that, if they are considering mainstream enterprise content or document management systems, there are now many such systems with add-on recordkeeping components certified to have minimal recordkeeping functionality, possibly including ones of interest to them.
5. Get to know your procurement officer. Argue that requests for proposals for planned new computer technologies should include recordkeeping certification, and address the full costs for migrating legacy data to the new systems from the older systems that they are intended to replace.
6. Get to know your facility managers. Show how digital records support open space plan. Provide them with, or ask them to ponder, the full real costs of paper records storage, not just the obvious cost of central storage (using the average rental cost per square foot for your central business district available from area commercial real-estate associations)—but off-site records storage (using comparable warehousing costs); and often overlooked costs such as office furniture, cabinetry, shelving, and desk storage space; related purchase, maintenance and repair, and replacement costs, floor-space, and corresponding costs of facility staff salaries, benefits, and training.
7. Integrate analog and digital files in all descriptive systems so that online searches on current business issues direct users to current electronic and relevant earlier analog records, and to related archival records. Integration can be facilitated with common or cross-mapped file plans, metadata directories and finding aids, as well as links to the context-rich results of the functional/process

research that has been undertaken in business systems analysis projects for planning, accountability, macroappraisal, and other organizational purposes. (See also step 9, below.)

8. Consider innovative ways to reach out with new services to stakeholders who may well become your strongest allies, such as Vermont State Archivist Gregory Sanford's very innovative and highly successful "Continuing Issues" program. This provides online examples of records, and rich context around them, to government officials, media and journalists, historians, and others. It includes commentaries on the history of ideas and issues currently being publicly debated in Vermont.[12]
9. Encourage establishing (or updating) an enterprise architecture, such as the Service-Oriented Architecture (SOA) and related web services, to provide a road map of corporate business processes and existing and planned information technology that supports those processes; that offers a path to capturing records from disparate computer-based legacy and new systems; and that makes the strong case for embedding recordkeeping services in that architecture as its animating lifeblood.[13]

Just as in decades past when archivists and records managers lamented that information systems were being designed without the benefit of their knowledge and input, the same danger exists today, although at the higher and riskier levels of business process and enterprise-wide systems architecture. At these levels, the key players are not middle managers and information technology professionals, but CEOs and CIOs, and their senior manager colleagues. By linking records issues to the broader, strategic concerns of senior management, archivists and records managers may find the best opportunities to address and resource some of the more difficult electronic records issues—records capture, metadata management, data migration and long-term preservation, macroappraisal and orderly disposition, records as tools for staff and citizen/client engagement and productivity enhancement, and accountability and risk management. A few archivists have become adept in business systems analysis and process modeling, positioning themselves for the macroappraisal and architectural steps. Among them is Phillip C. Bantin at the Office of University Archives and Records Management, Indiana University.[14] For their numbers to significantly increase, it would require archivists and records managers to embrace a more activist and directing role, such as those suggested in the nine steps above.

Despite the rising tide of new workplace and societal technologies and thus of radically new kinds, formats, and meanings for records, there remains a sharp dichotomy between the postcustodial model of recordkeeping (now so familiar and well received in the arguments of our thought leaders in the modern discourse of our professional literature and graduate-level records management and archival studies programs) and the traditional custodial model still predominantly observed in the world of recordkeeping practitioners across organizational landscapes in the public and private sectors alike. This dichotomy is perhaps no more sharply seen than in those very same teaching universities, where faculties are raising student sights to envision careers influencing, and then occupying, higher places in the recordkeeping universe at the peak of the context/content/structure pyramid, exploring and stimulating functional analysis and use of macroappraisal tools to facilitate this. The harsh reality is that most of these graduates will be employed in traditionally managed records organizations.

The starkest examples are near them. Across the very same campuses, we too frequently see that university administrative records are still dominated by paper-based systems with few fully implemented enterprise-wide electronic records systems, despite pervasive use of desktop, mainframe, and hand-held computers and smartphones in almost every dimension of university business. Even mission-critical databases, such as student records or findings of major research projects, often are not under the purview of any university archives. How can this be? Do university archivists not seriously engage members of their records management and archival studies teaching faculties to seek their assistance in making the business case to university management necessary to obtain budgetary resources to implement such systems? Or do they struggle and languish with endless electronic records planning projects, while waiting hopefully for management to finally "get it" through some embarrassing records-based legal scandal or physical calamity? Do faculty archival educators in turn offer their assistance before being asked? Would university archivists consider such offers as intrusions? Do senior graduate students propose such assistance or internships to such ends, or choose theses in these areas?

Do these people dine in the same cafeterias or engage one another professionally at all, beyond surface social niceties? Perhaps so, but it is difficult to find the evidence in implemented and fully operational university electronic records systems. A small number of others are following Bantin's admirable lead in such areas as the use of business systems analysis and partnerships with corporate audit programs. Bantin continues on his own campus to advance efforts toward electronic records solutions through means short of enterprise content management systems with recordkeeping functionality by slotting some record categories, such as annual and budget reports in the open standard PDF/A format, into the university's institutional repository system—all while working with management as it moves toward an enterprise content management system to ensure that it will have DoD 5015.02 certified extensions for managing electronic records.

Though academia offers a stark contrast between our leading theories and actual practices, inability to implement enterprise-wide electronic records systems is certainly not the exclusive domain of institutions of higher learning. It is all too prevalent even amongst such highly interested players as those companies that develop records management and archival software, and in many national archives around the world, or indeed in most other archives, with respect to the management of their own electronic records. Examples of noteworthy exceptions include many large financial, pharmaceutical, and consulting institutions, where management does "get it." Management gets it in terms of legal and other forms of risk management; it gets it in terms of competitive advantage and better services; and it gets it in terms of the potential opportunities afforded by the repurposing of legacy information, much of it now resting in their digital archives.

To illustrate the point, most tenants occupying the World Trade Center during the first terrorist attack on February 26, 1993 suffered substantial (some permanent) losses of their paper records. One major accounting firm, then the largest occupant of the center, because of redundant computer software and replicated data in records systems in another location, was able to reconstitute its vital records the following week in temporary office space elsewhere and was back in operation within a few days, assuring its institutional customers that they would meet their April 15 deadline for tax services and fiscal obligations. Others, without such business continuity plans and systems, were not so fortunate and either went out of business, suffered irreparable loss of customers, or faced other long-term problems.

Following the bombing, the archivist of one of the other major tenants of the center sent a posting to the archives and records management listservs appealing to all archivists and records managers whose organizations had had dealings with his organization to check their own records and send him copies of any and all relevant communications to assist in the reconstitution of his organization's seriously compromised records repository. One may imagine the incomplete results and consequent trustworthiness of the recordkeeping system.[15]

* * * * *

Now may be the critical moment for archivists and records managers to address the electronic records predicament and recapture the high ground, employing intellectual control over function-and-context-based digital recordmaking and recordkeeping systems. Such value-added contextual linkages can transform data and information into knowledge, now seen by senior management as a critical process and product of most organizational systems. If organizations are to remain healthy and indeed flourish in the digital age, such revitalization of their systems is not a frill, but an organic necessity, for records provide the lifeblood and nervous system necessary for robust operations. Given the evolution of organizational cultures and communications technologies outlined in this essay, timing may finally be on our side for seriously addressing both analog and digital recordkeeping in our organizations within a functional or process-based model. This may be the moment for archivists as specialists in deep-level context to step out of the shadows and more actively engage in organizational behavior and its ongoing change.

Notes

1 The author is most grateful to Terry Cook for his valuable comments and suggestions on earlier drafts of this chapter.

2 Shelley Davis, *Unbridled Power: Inside the Secret Culture of the IRS*, with forward by Mary Matalin (New York: HarperBusiness, 1997). For a brief commentary on this book, see "Thinking about

Accountability, Recordkeeping and Shelley Davis' *Unbridled Power:* a Commentary," by Rick Barry at www.mybestdocs.com/barry-r-on%20sdavis.html. All website references and URL links in this essay were accessible as of March 25, 2010.

3 Despite having made some serious allegations in her book, including mentioning names, to my knowledge no one has yet charged her in a court with libel or other charges.

4 Helen Samuels, "Who Controls the Past," *American Archivist* 49 (Spring 1986): 109–24. See especially the general conceptual statements about adopting a documentation strategy to guide the appraisal and acquisition of records of modern society and its complex institutions. The concept that detailed research and careful analysis of the recordkeeping or documentary landscape should underpin all work by records managers and archivists is central to Samuels' writings. This concept was applied first by Samuels for documenting science and technology across many institutions, and then for education and learning functions within one large modern institution, providing case studies to demonstrate the value of her approach. The first chapter of her *Varsity Letters: Documenting Modern Colleges and Universities* (Metuchen, NJ: Scarecrow Press and Society of American Archivists, 1992) is her clearest theoretical statement on the importance of conceptualization preceding collection; understanding functions, programs, and activities as the context for documentation strategy and all appraisal activity; and basing such appraisal first on analyzing record-producing functions rather than looking for potential research value through massive volumes of individual records.

5 For the best summary of macroappraisal as both concept and practical, implemented strategy, set against its historical background and changing organizational culture, see Terry Cook, "Macroappraisal in Theory and Practice: Origins, Characteristics, and Implementation in Canada, 1950-2000," *Archival Science* 5, nos. 2-4 (2005): 101–61.

6 For example, records emanating from one process may be designated with an event-driven, rather than date-driven, retention schedule, the former presenting greater difficulties for computer-based disposition management. This difficulty may be resolved by the existence of another process that produces evidence of such events having indeed happened.

7 Johannes Trithemius (1462-1516) was the Abbot of Spondheim and St. James at Wurzburg in the northwest part of present-day Bavaria. For the quotation, see his *In Praise of Scribes (De Laude Scriptorum)*, ed. K. Arnold, trans. R. Behrendt (Lawrence, KS: Coronado Press, 1974), 64.

8 James J. O'Donnell, "The Pragmatics of the New: Trithemius, McLuhan, Cassiodorus," presentation to "The Future of the Book" conference, organized by the International Center for Semiotic and Cognitive Studies in the Republic of San Marino, 1994, at www9.georgetown.edu/faculty/jod/sanmarino.html.

9 Multiple physical locations for electronic records stores, whether as a replication of a corporate digital store or as distributed portions of the only corporate store, can be an important way to guard against the risk of total loss from natural or human-made disasters, as part of a well-conceived corporate business continuity plan, sometimes termed disaster preparedness strategies.

10 Twitter is a "microblog" that is limited to 140-character messages, called "tweets." It is commonly used for "presence" messages, but is not limited to that usage. Some news media outlets, for example, use the technology to report headlines with links to the related stories. The *New York Times* has the leading number of Twitter followers for American newspapers—over 17,000—while CBC TV News has over 20,000 followers. "Presence" technology was first used by teenagers to keep one another informed of where they were and what they were doing day and night. Now it is used by their parents in serious business functions. Even senior executives in large firms use auto-reply voice-mail messages such as: "I am out of the office at a client site until approximately 4:00 PM EST today. I am on my cell at..."

11 See http://blogs.washingtonpost.com/washpostblog/ for an excellent example that the *Washington Post* established initially as a simple news blog, but which has been further extended to provide columnist-specific discussion groups to engage readers and to offer avenues for users to set up their own "My Page" profiles.

12 See http://vermont-archives.org/govhistory/governance/index.htm. This project is discussed in detail in Sanford's chapter earlier in this book.

13 Barbara Reed, "Service-Oriented Architecture and Recordkeeping," *Records Management Journal* 18, no. 1 (2008): 7–20, accessible in the Guest Authors section of www.mybestdocs.com. This seminal paper was honored as the *Records Management Journal* outstanding paper of 2008 and, as far as I know, is the first published paper dedicated to this subject.

14 For a brief discussion of business systems analysis and modeling for recordkeeping, see Philip C. Bantin, *Understanding Data and Information Systems for Recordkeeping* (New York: Neal-Schuman, 2008), 21–22, 40. The table of contents and figures, foreword, and preface of the above landmark book, along with a number of papers on the Indiana University Electronic Records projects, may be found at www.mybestdocs.com in the Guest Authors section under Bantin's name.

15 A study of the recordkeeping impact on occupants of the 1993 World Trade Center bombing and the lessons learned that were subsequently acted upon before the 9/11 attack on the same location, and the fate of companies who did learn those lessons versus those who did not, would make a marvelous subject of serious research.

THE TOWER, THE CLOUD, AND POSTERITY: DOCUMENTING IN A DIGITAL WORLD

Richard N. Katz and Paul B. Gandel

There can be no doubt of the astuteness of Marshall McLuhan's observation that "the medium is the message." Those of us who have had the great fortune to concern ourselves with the care and maintenance of the historical record during Helen Samuels' career do so at a time of unprecedented change in the number and nature of media. The thesis of this essay is that the emergence of multiple digital media, ubiquitous networks, virtualization of computation and data storage, open educational resources, open-source software, social networks, and the evolving "cloud" of network-mediated services is changing the nature of human interaction, the messages that comprise our collective memory, and therefore the mission, programs, and services of cultural institutions like archives, libraries, museums, colleges, and universities. For the sake of convenience—and because the metaphor works well on many levels—we refer to such cultural institutions collectively as "the tower." Extending this thinking, we refer throughout this essay to that complex of contemporary or recent technological innovations that extend the individual's or the institution's existing information technology (hereafter IT) capabilities by "virtualizing" IT services (or through acquiring IT services on a subscription or pay-per-use basis over the Internet) as "the cloud" of digital context increasingly enveloping us.

This essay therefore focuses on the impact of the cloud on one critical aspect of the tower's mission—the identification and preservation of the spoken or written record of human activity. Helen Samuels has long urged that we must think strategically about our records and archives. As more and more of our messaging, our personal, scholarly, social, and business activity, and our recordkeeping, move from institutions to a variety of loosely tethered service providers in the Internet cloud, her message takes on even greater urgency.

Among other things, libraries, archives, museums, and academic institutions are storehouses. Gates and towers—in architecture and in metaphor—have served not only to isolate the life of the mind from the hubbub of the marketplace, but to preserve and protect scarce and sacred knowledge artifacts.[1] This is among our oldest and most precious charges. Indeed, archives in medieval and early modern Europe were often stored in the towers of royal castles, the safest and most secure places. Like the monasteries and scriptoria that preceded western universities, the modern archives, library, museum, or academic institution is an arbiter, transmitter, and guardian of culture and of the record that comprises a great deal of humankind's shared memory. The question that arises, therefore, in the context of this volume, is: whither posterity? How does the emergence of the cloud affect both the identification and preservation of society's shared memories and the role of today's towers of knowledge preservation—archives, libraries, museums, and academic institutions—in identifying and preserving this new digital material? Does the emergence of a globally connected cloud of people and information resources herald the unprecedented expansion of our institutions' collective reach, or does limitless access to seemingly unlimited information threaten to undermine long-cherished ideas about truth, knowledge, and history? Does the cloud connect us to one another and our historical record and promote shared values, or will the radical democratization of knowledge result in hopeless fragmentation?

The question of whither posterity, to a great extent, has defined the roles of archivists, librarians, curators, and others for centuries. The authors believe that not only is this question of great import to the future of these noble professions, but that the identification and preservation of shared memory is in fact the glue that holds culture together. Harvard University professor Chris Dede makes the case that the tacit epistemologies that underlie the technologies and behaviors characterized collectively as Web 2.0 "differ dramatically from the 'classical' perspective—the historic views of knowledge, expertise, and learning on which formal education is based." At stake, according to Dede, is a likely rethinking of the classical view of knowledge as consisting "of accurate interrelationships among facts, based on unbiased research that produces compelling evidence about systemic causes."[2] In our view, humankind's assumptions about the nature of collections—what to collect and what to preserve—are rooted in what Dede calls classical epistemology.

Recordkeeping and Human Memory Sharing

To parse and address the issues of identifying and preserving shared memory that are raised by the cloud, it may be helpful to think of recordkeeping and human memory sharing in broad sweeps or epochs. Each epoch is defined to a very great extent by a new and disruptive technology or family of technologies.[3]

Archivy 1.0

The selection and preservation of knowledge for the purpose of creating shared memories is not only a precondition for the development of culture, but a survival skill. Preliterate humans survived by documenting, on rocks and in caves, the existence and location of watering holes, dangers, religious places and objects, and hunts. Beyond survival, however, many early human groups engaged in a specialized and purposeful form of storytelling. Oral speech was in many preliterate cultures the dominant instrument for preserving and sharing human memory. This memorized form "was not the vernacular of casual conversation but an artificially managed language with special rules for memorization, one of which was rhythm."[4] In the oral tradition, selecting knowledge for preservation was frequently a responsibility of a tribe or clan's religious or secular leadership. The preservation of this knowledge involved an amazing, complex, and evolving web of social relationships and responsibilities, ranging from inheritance of responsibility for storytelling from father to son, to the emergence of the epic tradition in poetry in ancient Greece and elsewhere. Even after the introduction of writing, vestiges of this oral tradition persist. Official transmitters included the ancient Greek heralds, Roman stentorians, and medieval jongleurs and town criers who traveled the European countryside and cities. Even contemporary religious sermonizers or present-day political campaigners might be included.[5] Officially sanctioned speakers have long been employed to entertain, transmit news, or generate guidance for contemporary and historical events. As a process for creating shared knowledge or wisdom and for preserving this wisdom, the oral tradition was highly effective and represents an important layer of the foundation on which much prehistoric civilization was built. The "recorded" oral knowledge was remarkably durable. Individuals who were charged with transmitting socially constructed knowledge were taught things verbatim and it was typically a responsibility that was only passed on to genetic heirs or to people who merited trust. Deviating from a script or improvisation was prohibited. Unless carriers of this knowledge died unexpectedly, the knowledge was reasonably secure and credible. Moreover, the source (provenance) of the information was also very clear. The village voice was always a designated person who was trained by his father by his father by his father, or, in matriarchal societies, by a similar succession of mothers. The community could be really sure "where this information came from," in modern archival terms, confident of its provenance or origins and its authenticity.

The durability of knowledge preserved in this fashion, however, was eroded by the emergence of writing. Some of the old stories were recorded and preserved, some have morphed into folklore and legend, and some disappeared altogether as oral traditions fell into disuse in the wake of an emergent written tradition.

Archivy 2.0

If humankind's first efforts to create and preserve shared memory consisted of chiseling a historical or mythological record in pictures in stone, or transmitting spoken words to transmit culture, survival skills, and values, then the invention and adoption of writing can be thought of as Archivy 2.0.

The creation of written language may be viewed in this context as the substitution of, first, one set of symbolic representations for another (written words, characters, or radicals for painted or etched pictures) and, secondly, one storage medium for another (animal skins, vellum, or papyrus for cave walls, human memory cells, or vocal chords). The invention of writing and of storage media outside the human brain was revolutionary. The capacity to store shared memories increased immeasurably, now across time and space, thus allowing for remarkable civilizations to flourish.

Archivist Oliver W. Holmes describes this as permitting the "beginning of a passive reservoir of knowledge."[6] With this expanded capacity came the need to systematize both shared memories and the physical artifacts that contained them and the need to create a cadre of people skilled in the creation and interpretation of such recorded knowledge. As well, shared memory now had physical mass and thus could not be carried from village to city in the minds of storytellers, elders, or other icons of the oral tradition. The challenge of these new realities gave rise to the emergence of libraries, like that in Alexandria, and of bibliophylakes, a special and influential class of officials charged with the creation, collection, care, protection, and interpretation of this precious reservoir. Likewise, in Greek city states, there emerged the centralized archive, with their archons or magistrates, as places of law, of consolidation of power by controlling records and public memory. Central to the stature of bibliophylakes and archons—and their various successors such as librarians, archivists, clerks, and others—was trust. The oral tradition was rooted in the notion of verbatim transmission of information. While there were, no doubt, lapses of accuracy, the oral tradition depended to a very great extent on the shared belief that knowledge that was officially transmitted by personally known agents was accurate. The emergence of writing and the limited spread of literacy meant that social trust needed to be spread farther than ever and that the risk of inaccuracy would also rise. Those charged with creating, collecting, and preserving the human record occupied high positions of trust, and writing—as a representation of reality—became subject to the corruptions of memory lapse, linguistic nuance, legibility, omission, miscopying, and fraud. The rarity of human written recordings and their vulnerability to a variety of threats makes scarcity the defining characteristic of shared memory in this epoch. Other terms that characterize the period (ending around the invention of moveable type) might include *durable* (but vulnerable), *instrumental* (serving largely the power elites), and *tightly controlled.*

Archivy 3.0

Archivy 2.0 centers on mediating human communications and recording knowledge through writing on portable media. The central features of Archivy 3.0 are our efforts to produce repeatable verisimilitude in the printed word and image through mechanical means, to enlarge shared memory by proliferating recorded knowledge, and to expand the reach and influence of human activity through the spoken and written record. These shifts were tectonic in magnitude and shook the foundations of both how societies think about shared knowledge and how they determine what knowledge is to be preserved.

The cause of faithfulness in recorded information was aided by the emergence of the craft of printing. And, of course, the politics of information are continually changing in the face of the increasing abundance of printed materials, the ever-expanding rates of literacy throughout the world, and the emergence of English as the global language of business. The impact of printing and in particular of Gutenberg's moveable type and the commercialization of abundant and ever-cheaper paper are well documented. These tectonic shifts resulted in changes in recordkeeping priorities and skills from a primary concern over protecting scarce texts to the concerns surrounding knowledge management—finding and evaluating information of value amidst an increasingly abundant documentary record. Two later technologies added to the disruptions that define this third epoch: photography and xerography. And, of course, this epoch witnessed the emergence of motion picture film, radio, and television, whose impact on human communications cannot be minimized, but which will not be examined in this essay.

In 1872, Leland Stanford hired the photographer Edward Muybridge to settle a bet about whether there was a point in a horse's gallop when all four hooves leave the ground. Four years later, Muybridge succeeded in capturing a horse in motion using a series of fifty cameras. The photographs were published in a series called "The Horse in Motion" and show quite clearly that, contrary to popular belief, a horse did indeed lift all four hooves off the ground. Muybridge continued to perfect his method of freezing motion into smaller and smaller pieces of time. He produced hundreds of thousands of frozen images of motion of people and animals, including himself.

Photography revolutionized the way we thought about the world and our notions about what we could capture and keep. Photographs rendered their subjects more faithfully than words and drawings and could be reproduced faithfully. Photographers traveled the globe capturing, and thus preserving, monuments and artifacts from far away lands for people who would never be able to witness these scenes firsthand.

And for those who did venture far from home, photography made it possible to take family and home with you in the form of the family picture album. Moreover, as Muybridge first demonstrated, photography made it possible to capture that which was seemingly invisible, such as an instant in a horse's gallop, the microscopic world, and the far distant galaxies. Photography unleashed a revolution and passion for capturing the world around us. It was, perhaps, an innovation that was perfectly suited to western society that had embraced empiricism, positivism, and scientific method. The picture, it seemed, was worth a thousand words, and especially so when it could be shared through new printing processes in books, magazines, and newspapers with millions of viewers.

In 1937, sixty-five years after Muybridge captured the collective imagination with his photographs of horses in motion, American law student Chester Carlson invented "a copying process based on electrostatic energy."[7] Carlson's electrostatic process faithfully reproduced words on a page in minutes. The importance of this innovation cannot be understated, as the essay by Richard Cox in this volume clearly shows. This invention simultaneously gave scaling and verisimilitude huge shots in the arm and changed fundamentally the very nature of the "posterity problem." As David Owen puts it, "It gave people an extraordinary means of preserving and sharing information and it placed the rapid exchange of complicated ideas within the reach of everyone, becoming the biggest breakthrough in written communications since Gutenberg."[8] Photography and xerography, then, made it possible for an enormous number of people to share identical knowledge in different places at roughly the same time. For those charged with preserving a meaningful record of shared memory and human experience, these innovations represented a shift from an era of scarcity to one of abundance, indeed of massive duplication and redundancy. This shift demanded fundamental changes in the philosophy and craft of the archivist. With the proliferation of records came attendant needs to focus on the arrangement of records and on the clarification of their more complex provenance. As well, this proliferation fostered a growing need for people and for methods that could be trusted to facilitate the appraisal of newly abundant resources and selection for preservation in archives of those very few records (typically 1 to 5 percent of the total) that would faithfully serve society's need for shared memory and historical documentation.

Is the Past Prologue?

The essence of the history of recordkeeping over the millennia to this point can be reduced to a series of broad concerns:

- Can esteemed and valuable information be recorded and then collected?
- Can we select, from among such records collected, those that will create a meaningful documentary record for society?
- Who selects what becomes shared memory, and based on what concepts of value?
- Can this information be protected and preserved over time (measured in centuries, or longer)?
- Once collected and appraised for value, can the information then be found?
- Who has access to the information?
- Under what conditions?
- Who mediates this access?
- How easy or affordable is it to gain access?
- Can the information be trusted?
- Is it credible?
- Is it authentic?
- Can we certify its authenticity?
- Can we ascertain its provenance, and understand its complex contexts of creation and subsequent uses and re-creations?

The shifts that we have described are truly monumental, from Archivy 1.0, through Archivy 2.0, to Archivy 3.0. They are summarized in part in table 1.

Table 1. From Archivy 1.0 to Archivy 3.0

FROM	TO
Human record is oral.	Human record is written.
Knowledge is scarce.	Records are abundant.
Archivists are scarce.	Archivists are less scarce but not numerous.
Recorded knowledge is durable.	Recorded knowledge is relatively durable.
Recording of knowledge is representational (reasonably credible).	Recording of knowledge is literal or facsimile (highly credible).
Preoccupation with preservation.	Preoccupation with selection and appraisal.
Information is accessible by elites.	Information is accessible by many.
Information is easy to find (if extant).	Information is difficult to find.
Information is tightly controlled.	Information is increasingly distributed.
Provenance is clear.	Provenance is often traceable.

The shifts from Archivy 1.0 to Archivy 2.0, from oral to written cultures for recordkeeping, set humankind on a fundamentally new path, and in many ways humanity's past did not in fact prepare us well for the future. The shift from information scarcity to information abundance cannot be understated in either importance or extent. And study of the history of ideas tells us that the democratization of information must be viewed as a change of enormous magnitude whose far-reaching impacts would have been hard to predict. Archivy 3.0, the expansion of Archivy 2.0 to its pervasive modern manifestation by the mid-twentieth century, sets the stage for an even more potent change: Archivy 4.0.

Archivy 4.0: The Digital Revolution

This latest shift is likely to be as potent, and potentially more potent, than the shift from Archivy 1.0 to 3.0. This most recent era, and the one in which we now live, has witnessed the shift from paper-based to digital recordkeeping. While it has been only sixty years since the first electronic computers appeared in the 1940s, today virtually all information is created by computers and stored on optical, magnetic, or flash memory, tape, or other digital media. Digitization changes things profoundly.

New Economics

The economics of digital recordkeeping derive not so much from avoiding the ever-increasing costs associated with labor, harvesting trees and refining paper, transporting logs, pulp and paper, developing dyes for ink, recycling expended materials, and constructing and maintaining file offices and huge record centers, but from the economics of innovation we call Moore's law. The cost of computing, storing, and transmitting digital information has declined by about 50 percent each passing eighteen-month period since the invention of the semiconductor. Using this formula, it is likely that, in less than ten years, it will be possible to store the complete collection of the Library of Congress on one's personal storage device. Within eighteen years, we will be able to store the Library of Congress holdings on a key fob–sized memory device.[9] The changing economics of information storage and access are changing the behaviors of those who create, manage, and preserve information. The complexities and storage costs of Archivy 3.0 gave rise to the archival dictum of the later part of the last century: "When in doubt, throw it out." What does the dictum become, and what is the standard of appraisal for retention, when the marginal cost of storing a complete record of human activity approaches zero?

Information Is Superabundant

While the unit costs of storing information are in constant decline, computer industry analyst IDC reported recently that the world produced 281 exabytes of data in 2007.[10] This amounts to nearly thirty-thousand times the holdings of the Library of Congress. The amount of information published each year continues to grow. Nearly three hundred thousand books were published in 2006 alone, an increase of 0.5 percent on 2005 figures.[11] On July 31, 2006, Technorati tracked its 50 millionth blog, and about 175,000 new blogs are created each day.[12] Podcasts, videos, blogs, wikis, and digital archives further expand our information sources, and 2.7 billion Google searches are performed each month; 6.4 billion searches per month on all search engines. Despite the changing economics, the cost of storing all information created was estimated by one writer to approach $7 trillion annually.[13]

Everything Is Connected

Information stored digitally can be viewed or otherwise shared simultaneously by anyone with a computer, compatible software, a web browser, a digital display, and a network connection. The cost of transporting information has dropped to nearly nothing. Digital information can be copied infinitely, stored inexpensively, viewed at virtually no cost, and disseminated for pennies. The interconnection of everyone to everything at photonic speeds shortens the latency time needed to create shared memory and changes the behavior of those using information. These changes, of course, make other changes likely, but unpredictable.

Scientific research has already been profoundly changed by the interconnection of resources of all kinds on the network. The scale of scientific research has grown thanks to these interconnections. It is now possible to leverage the cost of enormous scientific instruments such as telescopes and particle accelerators over global scientific communities and to provide simultaneous access to primary research data anywhere on earth.

The role of *place* in the interconnection of people and information stores is changing and, in fact, diminishing in importance. Notwithstanding the changing role of *place,* the global network is increasing the capacity of repositories to make their collections and data available and to provide great remote support for researchers, seamless access controls, libraries of software tools, and sophisticated data management (storage, metadata, and ontology). The capacity to deliver world-class remote services virtually will likely determine the fate of the modern repository in the future. But what does "world class" mean in the cloud when the tower loses control? Who provides the research and understanding of the complex contextual knowledge needed to transform mere data and information into knowledge and wisdom?

Everything Can Be Found

In the era of Archivy 2.0, recorded information was more abundant (when compared to the Archivy 1.0 period) and resulting archival collections were precious and professionally managed. In the era of Archivy 3.0, paper-based information became evermore abundant, and the duplication and collaborative nature of work evermore complex. Accordingly, tools were developed to produce a coherent collection and to extract value for posterity, including records disposition schedules, archival appraisal concepts and strategies, better arrangement of collections, and the production of automated finding aids using computers and incorporating descriptive standards. The outputs of these activities include magnificent collections, acres of distilled knowledge, epic backlogs of unprocessed collections acquired for preservation's sake, and finding aids that often provided detail only at the upper level of the collection, record group, or fonds or perhaps the record series.

In the Archivy 4.0 sphere we are now entering, digitization, the Internet, social tagging, and the unimaginable investment in search technology are making it possible to search at the document level or at even finer levels of detail. These capabilities are a source of (and the result of) enormous private capital, but also a consequence of "lifting all boats," including that of the historical researcher. These capabilities call into question the meaning of document arrangement and description (for example, contextualization) in the digital context and indeed the value of the archival appraisal function itself: if everything can be kept and everything searched and found, with relative ease and trivial cost, what future use has appraisal and description? These capabilities in the digital world also raise profound questions of public policy as the dependence for discovering archival materials shifts from largely public to largely private (Google, Microsoft, and so forth) providers, and from broad motives of service to profit.

Digital Media Are Ephemeral

Until the twentieth century, paper was a remarkably durable storage medium for critical information. As the records of government and business exploded in quantity, durable high-quality paper was replaced by acidic, inexpensive paper. Notwithstanding the special and very real challenges posed by the introduction and widespread use of nondurable paper stock, it is important to understand the profoundly ephemeral nature of digital media in the effort to preserve shared memory and the historical record. Digital collections can be destroyed with a keystroke and can be altered easily without a trace. Even if not changed by such human intervention, the fragile nature of digital magnetic or optical storage media and their dependence on specific software and operating systems to be rendered intelligible makes them extraordinarily transient for long-term preservation needs. The ephemerality of digital media reverses the trend toward verisimilitude enabled by photography and xerography, and efforts to lock down digital content via electronic date stamps, watermarks, digital signatures, and other measures are meeting only partial success. At risk is the evidentiary value in records inherent in photographs, photocopies, and other fixed, hard-to-tamper-with, and thus trusted, media. The ephemeral nature of digital media is also enabling changes in the very nature of the record, the nature of authorship, and the nature of provenance.

The Social Life of Information Is Undergoing Significant Change[14]

If Web 1.0 was chiefly about the posting of a great deal of the world's current information on the web, Web 2.0 refers to changes in how web developers and users use the web. Increasingly the web is shifting from a place of document discovery and self-expression to a place for social interaction, including collaboration, as well as business and government transactions. New collaborative tools such as blogs and wikis are making it possible for people to convene around common interests and purposes. Importantly, these tools, along with open-source software and open educational resources, are leveling the playing field. From an educational perspective, the web is emerging as perhaps our most open university: a virtual place where people can gather around common interests, review supporting textual, graphic, and data resources, and engage in common discourse and action—social, learning, commercial, or otherwise.

The unique qualities of digital media, though, are making it possible for informal groups—often characterized as "crowds"—to engage in work that had been previously individual or institutional in nature. Wikipedia is perhaps the most noteworthy example. Content co-creation is one of the most important concepts and social behaviors to emerge in Web 2.0 and a development that has the potential to rock the very foundation of archival thinking about authorship and provenance. Similarly, Web 2.0 social behaviors, such as social tagging, will also challenge long-standing professional ideas about the roles and nature of authority control and value-added description in facilitating access to information.

Finally, we will need to grapple with the concept of Internet time. The collaborative nature of the web makes it possible to witness the rapid emergence of more and more versions of information on the web. Establishing provenance is a quixotic task. Even more important will be developing and socializing methods of asserting or otherwise establishing the credibility, validity, standing, and reliability of information produced often by anonymous crowds in the "fullness" of Internet time. As Farhard Manjoo puts it, "The limitless choice we now enjoy over the information we get about our world has loosened our grip on what is—and isn't—true."[15]

Establishing Identity Is Hard

Just as it is becoming increasingly difficult to establish the credibility, validity, standing, and reliability of information, it is increasingly difficult to establish the identity and truthfulness of those seeking to use digital ideas and documents. Colleges, universities, and their archives have long traditions of standing apart from the bazaar, in part to place scholarly coaching and personal reflection in the service of truth seeking. The Internet and the web, however, inherently erode such professions' boundaries. The institution's ability to provide its community members with broad access rights—while at the same time mediating others' access to institutional information resources and collaborative spaces—will demand greater care and investment over time. The new media and the ease of movement across Internet territories is necessitating a rethinking of what constitutes community membership and of the rights and authorities of those who are members of a community, those who are interested stakeholders in the community, and those who are not.

Everyone Is an Archivist

As mentioned, information is now superabundant and the capacity to store it and connect to it is widespread and inexpensive. Social forms are emerging that engage interested amateurs and professionals in tagging information to facilitate its eventual retrieval in multiple and varied ways. Everyone can be a journalist, commentator, expert, and even video star on the Internet. Mundane aspects of life appear every day on sites like YouTube and Facebook, taking so-called reality TV to a whole new level. Take the case of George Bell, a research scientist for Microsoft, who has taken Muybridge's notion of easily recording the moment one step further—he is recording his entire life. Bell carries miniature cameras and recorders at all times to record everything he sees and hears and speaks. The sensors he carries even record changes in light and temperature. Bell, now seventy-one, began storing his life digitally as an experiment to push the boundaries of information technology. He began by scanning books and important papers he wanted to keep. The project then mushroomed into his recording of all the details of his life, from conversations with plumbers to the scholarly papers he writes. Bell's digital database is known as "MyLifeBits" and presents an interesting challenge in determining how to manage information over a human lifetime. Perhaps even more amazing than Bell's recording is the fact that he is also personally storing the 1,300 videos, 5,067 sound files, 42,000 digital pictures, 100,000 email messages, and 67,000 web pages that make up his version of "My Life Bits." The creation of such personal digital repositories is now technologically possible, and Microsoft researchers believe that anticipated advances will enable most individuals to store the complete digital record of their lives.

Will the Cloud Block the Sun?

The introduction of the digital record, and the emergence of richly interconnected data communication networks, low-cost digital storage devices, ever-more-nuanced search engines, and a common user interface (the web), are changing how people create, retain, dispose of, value, use, and preserve information. These technical changes and these shifts in the patterns of information use almost certainly will disrupt the long-standing tradition of the archival community, with possible serious consequences to human shared memory and to scholarship. These changes are partly summarized in table 2, which compares the archival world of the later twentieth century, coping with paper abundance symbolized by the photocopier (Archivy 3.0), and the new era into which we are now well advanced, marked by the digital computer (Archivy 4.0). The implications of these shifts are deeply potent, and must challenge us to ask whether knowing the past truly prepares us for the future.

Table 2. From Archivy 3.0 to the Digital Revolution (Archivy 4.0)

FROM	TO
Information is abundant.	Information is superabundant.
Recorded knowledge is relatively durable.	Recorded knowledge is very ephemeral.
Information discovery is a public service, usually mediated by archivists.	Information discovery is a privately financed search engine without mediation.
Finding information is hard.	Everything can be found.
Repository is physical—a building, office, or cultural institution.	Repository is virtual—a network address without walls.
Related collections across institutions are disconnected.	Everything from multiple sources and locations is connected to the network.
Archivists are a small, elite profession.	Everyone is an archivist.
Access to information is mediated by institutions and professional standards.	Access to information varies widely, with little or no mediation possible.
Document authorship is knowable, as is the context of creation, based on the archivist's research and description work.	Document authorship cannot be easily known or reconstructed, and conveying context about data online is still uncertain.
Archival appraisal is an art, based on the archivist's research and contextual knowledge, strategic planning, and active choosing of the best records.	Archival appraisal may be an algorithm based largely on use popularity, number of site visits, or positions within hierarchies of structure or function.
Preservation across decades and centuries is possible, if sometimes costly.	Preservation beyond the immediate creation technologies is unproven and very uncertain.

There is little doubt that the digital revolution on balance is contributing in magnificent ways to world literacy, to research, and to the democratization of knowledge. There is no doubt that technologies will cut their own channels in most of our institutions, including colleges, universities, libraries, museums, and archives. It is hard to imagine the implications of a single scientific instrument such as the Large Hadron Collider producing nearly one hundred million channels of data streaming from each of the two largest detectors and filling one hundred thousand CDs every second. These CDs would produce a stack to the moon in six months.[16] Or try to imagine the digital artifacts and ephemera of George Bell and the implications of the remorseless recording and storage of unedited human experience by millions or soon scores and hundreds of millions of human beings similarly wired and recorded.

Notwithstanding the daunting nature of the challenge, those of us charged with the collection and preservation of the human record must endure. More than this, we must advocate in the name of shared memory and assert standards for the appraisal, selection, and valuation of the evolving historical record. As University of Manitoba Professor Terry Cook put it, "If there is no such place [as archives] in society where knowledge and meaning can be discerned, where things can be true or not true, where accountability through transparent evidence of actions and ideas by those in power can be readily achieved through good recordkeeping, where the records themselves in transient digital formats can be certified and locked as authentic and reliable, not tampered with, created when, where, and by whom so asserted, and trusted, then we will enter a new dark age."[17] As we all, like George Bell, create our own "presidential libraries," how many of us will withstand the temptation to "tweak" our autobiographic record so that our shared memory can be a bit rosier or more flattering? Not only do the archival and scholarly communities need to advocate for scholarly rigor and for standards, we must strive to popularize these qualities, embed them throughout the education system, and instantiate them in search engines and throughout our own presence and advocacy on the Internet.

What may be the emergence of a new and superior epistemology, as suggested above by Chris Dede, could equally become what Alexis de Tocqueville feared as the tyranny of the majority.[18] Will our capacity to be arbiters of our cultures be enhanced or endangered by subjecting all matters great and small to wiki-ization or to popular, instant, online voting? Will the "American idolization" of facts, trends, taste, and truth crush independence of thought? Will we, as Cook wonders, abandon existing professional standards or fail to construct new ones, leaving a human record possessed of "too much scrambled, meaningless trivia of information where discerning anything of value or having context-rich value statements at all becomes impossible." This state of being is guided by what philosopher Alasdair MacIntyre labeled as *emotivism,* a doctrine holding that all evaluative judgments, especially moral judgments, are merely expressions of preference, attitude, or feeling.[19] It is ironic that just as we became awash in information and wealthy in the tools of discovery, mining, and analysis, the term "truthiness" was coined to describe things "that a person claims to know intuitively or 'from the gut' without regard to evidence, logic, intellectual examination, or facts."[20] Is it possible as information becomes so voluminous, the standards of selection so pluralistic, and the content of information so nuanced, that intuitive feeling will replace research analysis as the social barometer of truth?

Perhaps, then, the past may, sadly, be prologue indeed. Cook observes that it is possible that the cloud will envelop and overwhelm the tower, returning us to a dark age. Medieval Europe's scarcity of information and literate souls left many people in the dark. Today's superabundant but decontextualized information environment—filtered, mashed up, Photoshopped, crowd-sourced, and opaque—contains the potential for leaving people in the dark, or at the very least, so awash with facts and opinions without authenticity, reliability, or trustworthiness, or so controlled (often invisibly) by "Big Brother" for commercial or nationalist purposes, that a metaphoric darkness of meaning will descend. As but one example, the filtering of politically unacceptable search results by Google's China-version of its search engine indicates what is possible.

What Is to Be Done?

The stakes in the game of how the tower and the cloud interact in the context of the identification and protection of the human historical record are high. The issues regarding the future of those modern-day bibliophylakes and archons are similarly momentous. How the game will play out is completely unclear.

What is clear is that we who were stewards of the historical record in the past must now give voice to this great debate. We must present ourselves neither as uncritical enthusiasts of everything shiny and new nor as change-averse curmudgeons protecting a declining turf. It seems clear, too, that the turf of the modern day bibliophylake and archon is not shrinking, but changing. To remain relevant and to continue to serve our great purpose, we must separate those principles that will guide our future actions from the methods and structures that have served these principles in the past. Some of the methods and structures will survive; many will not.

We must conceive of a new professional ecosystem and of our place in such a new tangle of relationships. In Archivy 2.0, the bibliophylake and archon was likely a member of the religious order and a spiritual brother or sister of the scholar-scribe. In the xerographic era of Archivy

3.0, records managers and archivists were linked, as were archivists and historians, and historical-research trends. The new media are rendering old social and professional relations ineffectual and are opening the doors for new relations. This new ecosystem needs to be described and new professional communities and networks need to be formed.

The ephemeral nature of digital media is a vexing problem from a preservation viewpoint. Digital technologies create masses of information and conflicting goals for selection and preservation. A key question is: who determines value and for what purposes? Is it the crowd in the cloud? Furthermore, most digital media are themselves subject to easy alteration (that is part of their virtue) and are not durable. And if the storage media were to be made more durable, digital data still must be rendered readable by software to be usable. The issue of preserving digital data in forms that can be retrieved and read over centuries, but still be authentic, trustworthy surrogates of the "original," is enormously problematic, particularly in the sciences, where files of petabyte size are being produced and captured at an expense of billions of dollars. This is a problem of epic size that demands the attention not only of the archival community, but of foundations and governments.

One of the major issues associated with preserving shared memories is the identity management issue. Substantial progress is being made in constructing a layer of middleware tools and federation practices that will help ensure that record users are who they claim to be and are authorized to do what they assert they are authorized to do. As well, this middleware infrastructure goes far in protecting the traditional privacy of the researcher. Institutions associated with preserving information need to be engaged in this work and must adapt these tools to the archival context.

Archivists will also face especially complex challenges concerning the protection of privacy. Management systems, for example, now make it possible to capture and preserve the classroom contributions of tomorrow's Albert Einstein or George W. Bush. Many faculty members and students might be very uncomfortable if their conversations and interactions in an online class were preserved indefinitely by their institutions. Classrooms are traditional bastions of free speech and for the testing of ideas. "Half-baked thoughts" are encouraged as part of the learning process. Knowing your every thought or proposition might be preserved forever would certainly inhibit the free-wheeling conversations associated with university and college classrooms. Health records are another area of potential conflict between archival preservation and individual privacy. It is clear that the broad standardization and sharing of digital medical records can have some significant benefits, not just increasing medical knowledge, but saving actual lives. However, this capability also raises some controversial issues about privacy and ownership, especially with regard to who can keep and use medical records of deceased individuals—records which could prove to be valuable historical and medical research resources. New community standards, policies, and laws will need to be considered as social conduct in the digital context changes. The archivist needs to be engaged in this public policy debate. Otherwise, we run the risk of violating public trust or, worse, we begin to censor our history to the point where valuable records are destroyed through self-censorship in the fear that they may be used inappropriately.

And we must move closer to where history is being made. This is a reintegration, for the librarian and archivist have long been associated with those creating the shared memories. In many ways, the history of archivy and librarianship is a history of shifting attention from the creators of knowledge to the artifacts themselves and to the great secular temples we have built to house them. In a world of scarcity, those who sought knowledge had to travel to these sources of knowledge. In an era of superabundance, those who wish to preserve the knowledge must now do the traveling, back to the well-springs. The archivist cannot likely remain a creature exclusively of the tower. The values we share and the standards that we must promote, and the rich contextual knowledge about records in which we specialize, must be instantiated when and where the future historical record is being created, as well as into the culture of those technology providers whose products are reshaping the landscape of shared human memory. The librarian and archivist must not simply be part of this new cloud of digital information artifacts. They must take a leadership role in guiding its policies and practices. We need nothing less than a new literacy to guide ourselves and our students through the exciting and sometimes frightening new terrain. Perhaps this is Dede's new epistemology. Perhaps this is the emergence of new standards of critical thinking for digital information rendered "in a cloudy world."

Going digital may be the most significant inflection point in the history of human recordkeeping. Never before has so much information been available to so many people. The implications of having more than a billion people with persistent connections to the Internet and exabytes of information freely and openly available cannot be overstated. With every significant innovation come unintended consequences, and amidst the plentitude that we now enjoy in this arena are found a host of new cautions, threats, and risks. We can never turn back. And even if we had a choice, we would never turn back, for the global benefits of the digital-cloud world are inestimable. The cautions, threats, risks, and other unintended consequences of going digital, however, together do comprise the central challenge for the modern bibliophylakes and archons. Our ancestors and we have protected the record of human achievement through wars, revolutions, fire, flood, and past changes in recording technology. Our fundamental charge remains the same; the stakes likewise remain the same, but are now monumentally high.

Notes

1 Nancy Cantor and Steven Schomberg, "Poised between Two Worlds: The University as Monastery and Marketplace," *EDUCAUSE Review* (March/April 2003), http://net.educause.edu/ir/library/pdf/ERM0320.pdf.

2 Chris Dede, "A Seismic Shift in Epistemology," *EDUCAUSE Review* (May/June 2008): 80.

3 The authors adopt the term "disruptive" as used by Clayton Christiensen to describe a new, low-cost, often simpler technology that displaces an existing, sustaining technology. See Clayton M. Christiensen, *The Innovator's Dilemma* (Cambridge, MA: Harvard University Press, 1997).

4 Eric A. Havelock, "The Alphabetic Mind: A Gift of Ancient Greece to the Modern World," *Oral Tradition* 1, no. 1 (1986): 134.

5 Joseph J. Duggan, "The Social Function of the Medieval Epic in the Romance Literatures," *Oral Tradition* 1, no. 3 (1986): 728.

6 Oliver W. Holmes, "History and Theory of Archival Practice," in *University Archives: Papers Presented at an Institute Conducted by the University of Illinois Graduate School of Library Science*, November 1–4, 1964, ed. Rolland E. Stevens (Champaign, IL: Board of Trustees of the University of Illinois, 1965), at http://www.archive.org/stream/universityarchivalstev/universityarchivalstev_djvu.txt.

7 Mary Bellis, "The History of Xerox: Xerox Photocopiers and Chester Carlson," *About.com: Inventors*, at http://inventors.about.com/od/xyzstartinventions/a/xerox.html.

8 David Owen, *Copies in Seconds* (New York: Simon and Schuster, 2004), 12.

9 Thom Hickey, "Entire Library of Congress," *Outgoing: Library Metatdata Techniques and Trends*, http://outgoing.typepad.com/outgoing/2005/06/entire_library_.html.

10 Lucas Mearian, "Study: Digital Universe and Its Impact Bigger than We Thought," *Computerworld* (March 2008), http://www.computerworld.com/action/article.do? command=viewArticleBasic&articleId=9067639.

11 "Bowker Says Title Output Close to 300,000," *Publishers Weekly*, May 31, 2007, http://www.publishersweekly.com/article/CA6448228.html.

12 "How Many Blogs Are There? 50 Million and Counting," CyberJournalist.net, posted August 7, 2006, http://www.cyberjournalist.net/news/003674.php.

13 David Rosenthal, "Petabyte for a Century," DSHR's Blog, posted July 17, 2007, http://blog.dshr.org/2007/07/update-to-petabyte-for-century.html; for statistics on search engine use, see http://searchenginewatch.com/2156461.

14 The term "social life of information" was coined by John Seeley Brown and Paul Duguid in their book, *The Social Life of Information* (Cambridge, MA: Harvard University Press, 2000).

15 Graham P. Collins, "The Large Hadron Collider: The Discovery Machine," *Scientific American* (January 2008), http://www.sciam.com/article.cfm?id=the-discovery-machine-hadron-collider&page=2.

16 Farhad Manjoo, *True Enough: Learning to Live in a Post-Fact Society* (Hoboken, NJ: John Wiley and Sons, 2008), 4.

17 Terry Cook, email letter to Richard Katz, July 3, 2008.

18 Alexis de Tocqueville, *Democracy in America* (1835), Chapter XV.

19 "Political Philosophy of Alasdair MacIntyre," *Internet Encyclopedia of Philosophy*, at: http://www.iep.utm.edu/p/p-macint.htm#H5.

20 Dick Meyer, "The Truth of Truthiness," CBS News, December 12, 2006, http://www.cbsnews.com/stories/2006/12/12/opinion/meyer/main2250923.shtml. "Truthiness" was coined by comedian Steven Colbert in 2006, in the definition given.

Representing Archives / Being Archival

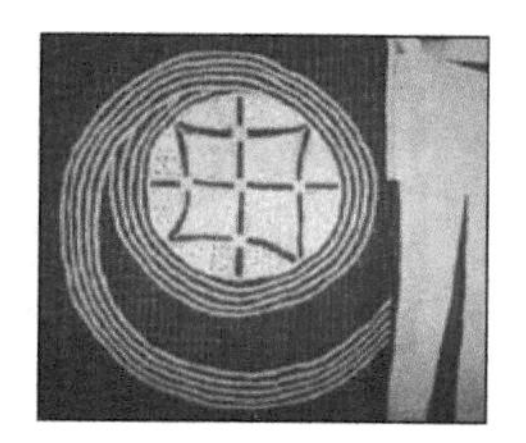

STRUCTURAL FORMALISMS IN DOCUMENTATION: REFLECTING FUNCTION AND SUPPORTING MEANING

DAVID BEARMAN

In the early 1980s, Helen Samuels, Dick Lytle, and I spent many hours talking about organizational functions and the way they shaped records. I remember Helen sitting in Dick's Smithsonian Archives tower window one afternoon as we debated whether appraisal decisions could be made by knowing the organizational function that generated the records. Sometime later, Helen was knitting as I pored through dictionaries in search of active verbs denoting functionality, both of us surrounded by bagels and lox at a table with about a dozen archivists I had invited to a weekend retreat in my offices on the other end of the Arts and Industry Building. We collectively thrashed out the first draft of the "functions vocabulary," an alternative means of accessing records by provenance.[1] In the twenty-plus years since, the question of how function dictates form in documents has rarely been far from my thoughts.

Documents are tools. I would argue that they are the most important tools humans have discovered in the past five thousand years. They have enabled us to communicate over time and distance for millennia long before phones or the Internet. Like all tools, documents have been shaped over the years to work best at specific tasks. Since they first emerged, documents have taken distinctive forms to perform specific functions: proclamations were large, bold documents with ostentatious seals designed to be read aloud in public places and to be seen as important, while accounts were spare, repetitive documents structured to permit their sums to be extracted and computed. Innovations in the design of documents have vastly enhanced their usefulness, as archivists are well aware. Numerous studies have documented the importance that changes in physical form have had for supporting business functions, such as how the replacement of hospital daybooks by patient transaction records in the late nineteenth century made way both for statistical medicine and for the notion of the individual patient with a medical history.[2]

Printed documents are likewise designed to suit changing purposes. Since the advent of printing five hundred years ago, published documents have evolved greatly from their origins as re-presentations of hand-written manuscripts. Printed books demonstrate an increasingly specialized functionality associated with their forms, achieved over time through a dialogue between printers or typesetters and the literate public. It seems that the designers of print pages taught literate people to recognize a huge number of forms of documents from afar and instantly anticipate the character of their content and their function. This meta-encoding of texts has advantages to the reader and to the authors, as will be seen, and so has been reinforced, and become more refined over time.

This relationship between the structure of presentation and the function of the text has been especially fully developed in the design of value-added scholarly tools—indexes, concordances, commentaries, catalogues raisonné, and critical editions, for example—which are a subset of document types designed for highly specialized purposes. Because they have been very expensive to create, requiring the lifetime work of many monks or scholars, only the most culturally valued documents have been afforded this treatment. Yet such value-added documents comprise a foundation on which scholarly cultural discourse in the humanities is conducted and knowledge is built.

We know that some of the massive energy required to create scholarly tools such as concordances and comparative editions is easily obviated through computer-based methods. With the advent of mass digitization, it seems that it might be possible to combine what we know about document formalisms with the technologies of scanning and word-search functions, to make a form of value-added document the norm for all printed literature. If so, a new platform for reading the world's literature—a base-level scholarly edition of all printed works—could be achieved. Such a foundation for the reading of texts would, I believe, revolutionize access by lay people to cultural artifacts that have become remote to them over the course of time. This essay explores how such a new platform for universal knowledge of published culture could be achieved and how the foundations of that capability would in turn impact our methods for managing the contemporary archival record.

Formalisms and the Design of Print

Anyone who reads uses the form of documents to aid in decoding the meaning of text. Printed texts are particularly formal in the sense that they obey a large number of rules of design that permit their readers to swiftly identify their most significant features. This has not always been the case, as readers of incunabula are well aware. Early printed books imitated the conventions of manuscripts and are therefore difficult for those acquainted with modern publishing conventions to understand at a glance. Recently, I have become interested in the consequences of the processes whereby typesetters taught readers, and readers taught other readers, the clues that now distinguish one documentary form from another. Over centuries this has led to implicit conventions in printed publications that aid knowledgeable readers to interpret text not just as words, but as classes of statements with particular functions in a stream of words. My curiosity is driven by a highly practical question about whether we could teach learning systems connected to scanners and neural computers the same tricks literate readers have learned, so that they could read texts more meaningfully than they can from semantic clues alone.

Consider a thought experiment. Your mail today includes an envelope in which you find a printed, folded, eight-page document. On opening its fold, you find the date and salutation "Dear Electricity Consumer," followed by many paragraphs of dense prose. Turning it over, in the final paragraph before the signature, you see several bolded phrases which include the words "open public hearing," a date and time, and an address. You immediately understand that you have received a "cordial invitation" from your utility company to attend a public meeting on a proposed rate hike they have notified you of (as required) and justified exhaustively (in case you actually read the letter). You know that you are not expected to RSVP. Indeed, they do not really want you to come, and normally people would not attend such a meeting unless they were activists involved in public utility matters. Although I have provided several important semantic clues in my account, you could have known all this without reading a word of the text.[3] At a glance you will have taken in the full social function of this documentary form—the mandatory regulatory notice—and moved on to read the rest of your mail. And it, like everything else you read that day, contains numerous other instances in which form telegraphs to you instantly, from the layout of the printed page, and the nature and import of the text.

To what degree do we "read" our mail, or books, even some documents, without reading the actual words? Often we use a combination of layout clues and semantic content to determine whether we need to read more carefully, but frequently it is possible to easily decipher the entire meaning of a document without recourse to "reading" any words at all. In order to fully understand the power of document formalisms, we need to establish the degree to which totally abstracted text conveys meaning, and only then look at the way in which semantic and syntactic information confirms or refines that meaning. By using a book held at too great a distance to read individual words, or a digitized page in which the alphabetic characters have been replaced with Xs and the numeric characters with 0s, we can establish which structures on the page inform a reader knowledgeable about the form of the meaning of their content without requiring the reading of words. This establishes the limits of meta-semantic meaning, but of course does not determine whether that meaning has been conveyed. For example, if we can do something similar with books from other cultures and periods of time with which we are unfamiliar, the actual meanings of the conventions that are less well-known to us may be obscure, and perhaps even seriously misinterpreted, although we will be able to identify where structural semiotics are invoked.

Several questions arise from this thought experiment and more systematic investigations of printed document structures. What is it that we as readers are "reading" and how do we know it? We cannot find, in dictionaries of the language or even in encyclopedia articles on printing or typesetting, the definition of these signs. Apparently we have learned them by personal experience because there is virtually no acknowledgement of this learning requirement in the literature of education and literacy, and hence no formal program for teaching them.[4] Yet we share with others in our print culture a definite understanding of their meaning.

Because the signs we are "reading" are visible to us even when, as is the case when reading pages written in a foreign language or from a different age, we do not understand their import, it is clear that they can be seen. Font size and characteristics (boldness or italics) and line treatment (indentation and margin size), as well as special characters, such as bullets or underlines or headings, are used to convey meaning. But it seems that it is not the specific font, indent, or character that signals meaning, but rather "change" in what otherwise is the background noise of the page as printed, or typed. This change constitutes a signal that we should pay attention to a new structure.[5] If the text were all laid out the same way, with the same margins and fonts, we would be obliged to read every word on its own as an equal. Instead, since there are these changes in the layout, our eyes move to where the change occurs. Small variations in the size and font of print, margins, line spacing, and line justification and alignment are designed to convey differences in intellectual content and authorship, and as "literate" people we read these variations in structure just as we read the words themselves.

But how do we know what the changes mean? Can the various signals we read today be catalogued as meta-properties of some kind of texts? Are they defined by rules, and if so what kinds of rules are they? By studying how we perform this trick of meta-reading, can we learn things that it would be useful to have automated reading tools know? I think so; our blindness to layout formalisms has had serious consequences for the development of programs to automatically read printed texts and structured documents. It should be no surprise that since we have not acknowledged the role that form plays for humans in extracting meaning from text, we have been unable to apply it to machines that read text. So we have developed Optical Character Recognition (OCR) devices that read at the level of letters and we have enhanced their accuracy by looking up character strings in dictionaries and even employed the sophisticated fuzzy logic of semantic context to discriminate likely choices when the characters we have need to be associated with a word. But we have not used automatic mechanisms to mark up texts based on where words occur, what they are likely to denote, or what their referents are based on formal properties of typography. This failure is about to become very costly.

Huge Corpora of Texts, including Archives

Printing is a 550-year-old technology that has built a huge body of practice of how to encode meanings in texts. At every level in a printed book we encounter different kinds of encoded meaning; the title page, for instance, tells us the title of the book, its author, the publisher, place of publication, and date. Much of this "descriptive cataloguing" metadata will be reiterated in contemporary books in a printed section of an early page of the book that actually includes the library catalogue entry, or "cataloguing in publication" (CIP) data. Books of certain genres will contain tables of contents, back-of-the-book indexes, and references or citations. Some books will contain glossaries, editor's commentaries, biographies of contributors, lists of other books published by the publisher, figures, tables and illustrations, or raw data. Reference books typically contain numerous entries organized in a systematic fashion (alphabetically, geographically, temporally, by classification, etc.), in which each entry has a quasi-structured content and the presentation of each entry signals through typography, spacing, and other means the category of information that follows. Our expectations about the content of each of these distinctive sections of the printed book enable us to read more quickly and accurately than would be the case if we were truly to read the book, word by word, from upper left to lower right, and from the first to last page.

In the near future, much, if not most, printed text could be available online in the form of page images. While this will be a huge step in making the knowledge of our civilization more accessible to more people, it will still require either that humans read images of texts to discover their meanings and the connections between them or that machine processes read the digital decoding of the page. Currently, the processes we use to decode texts depend on Optical Character Recognition (OCR); even when it performs well (which so far is limited to reasonably modern printing in western languages), it yields the full text of most words on a page, but obscures their contextual significance. Thus, when we search "full text," our retrieval does not distinguish words that appear in the title of a work, in the author's preface, in the headings and subheadings, in captions on images, or in footnotes or index, from words appearing in the paragraphs of the actual body of the text, though the meaning of the words for our purposes could be quite different depending on the context in which they were used and where they are placed. Out of context, the *Berlin* on the title page (where the book was published) and the *Berlin* at the end of the author's introduction to the second edition (where the author was on that date), are not distinguished from each other nor useful by themselves for geo-locating events without knowing their structural placement in the text.

By analyzing regularities in printed texts, it appears that structural clues could enable us, minimally, to mark up the elements on a title page, in tables of contents, glossaries, indexes, footnotes, and references, in captions on tables, maps, charts, and images, and in the outline structure of the text as presented. Adding this structural knowledge would permit linking of machine-generated bibliographic metadata to other metadata sources to identify the text, its links in a citation web, and the context of any quotation from the full text. Such a navigable network of intertextual connections would be very exciting—especially if it can be achieved on the scale of the world's literature—since, for very large corpora of texts, any filtering of content helps reduce the volume of unwanted results.

The next step in making the digital library of the future a resource for scholarship requires that we can enable machine "readings" of texts to generate rich mark-up of their internal content and create links between them.[6] The preferred mark-up for scholars has long been defined by the Text Encoding Initiative (TEI), which has defined rules for digital texts that identify the meta-significance of units of the text—headings, captions, footnotes, annotations, stage directions, and the like. In automatically marking up texts, we would of course want to use the same conventions. This raises the question of the nature of the relationship between what automated methods could perceive from the "raw" structure of the text and what scholars "mark up" in their sophisticated analyses of textual structures. If we first examined texts that have been marked up with TEI, we could also establish the degree to which the scholarly value-added process has been marking elements that are signaled through visual clues and which aspects of the scholarly mark-up cannot be assisted by machines.[7]

By defining the combination of layout, syntax, and semantic clues used by people to characterize the function of blocks of printed text, the path to automatically marking those elements as part of the processing step following scanning is clear. But this is not all we could reasonably expect to obtain through the deep analysis of print conventions. More subtle clues embedded in printed texts, involving some reliance on syntax and semantics, could expose those portions of a printed volume that are attributable to editors or publishers, or which are the authors' acknowledgments, edition notes, and other paratextual elements.[8] Much additional knowledge revealed in print conventions will be inaccessible, however, unless we can exploit knowledge of layout conventions used in particular genres of texts, periods in the history of printing, and traditions that evolved in particular language communities. This means we need to first identify the regularities of the high-level encoding that signal that a text is of a certain genre, period, or culture.[9]

Genre: Form Predicts Content

As educated readers, if we see a book that has numbered smallish print at the foot of a page and a multicolumn list of words in alphabetical order followed by page numbers at the back, we read the first as footnotes and the latter as an index and know to expect the work to be nonfiction, and probably somewhat scholarly nonfiction. If we see a printed page with numbered lines of differing lengths, we expect poetry or drama.[10] If at the rear of such a book we find quotations from these numbered lines, with paragraphs of prose attributed to the editor rather than the author of the numbered lines, we know we have stumbled on scholarly annotation or commentary in a book of poetry. Even in the odd case that we are "wrong" in making this assumption, as in reading the novel *Pale Fire*, we are still right, since Vladimir Nabokov's novel assumes the form of a scholarly edition as a device of the fiction. These categories of print that we have thus distinguished by form—nonfiction, drama, scholarly annotated poetry, and many more—are called genres.

The fact that sometimes these different genres of writing are distinguishable at a glance from their typography and layout is, of course, no accident. The semiotics are important to our understanding of the words—how else would we know, in a dictionary, which word was being defined and which words were doing the defining? And the semiotics have been developed, one might say honed, over a long time. One of the difficulties we have in reading early printed texts, in addition to the strangeness of the language and the unusual typefaces and somewhat uneven nature of the inking, is that the conventions that we expect to have marked the meanings of words are not present, and other conventions, unfamiliar to us, seem to be operating.

But what genres are, and what genres there are, is not without contention. The term *genre* is often used to distinguish types of writing based on the style of the prose rather than on the broad categories suggested above; thus we might say something is an "essay" or a "valedictory." Likewise, we could read a newspaper and characterize some of its content as "reportage" and some as "editorial." We could make some of these distinctions without reading the texts, based on structural clues, but as often as not, the actual content, not simply the interpretation of content, is frequently dictated by genre. Just as the salutation in a personal letter is likely to be led by the word *Dear,* the "signature" at the end of an author's introduction or preface to a book will typically include a geographical name and date (Berlin, 1946). This is the same content (Berlin, 1946) appearing in the dateline of a newspaper article from that year and place, albeit at the start rather than the end; this enables us to distinguish it from editorial matter in that same paper that will not have a dateline and typically will be signed by the name of the editorial writer.

The concept that genres are powerful predictors of discrete elements of content is no new idea to archivists. Indeed, it is an essential, if usually unstated, assumption of archival appraisal. If regularities in form did not strongly correlate with regularities in content, the record series would not support retention scheduling. Strong programs to tease content out of form can be the basis for historical research methodologies.[11] If Dutch history masters' students can identify regularities in genres of records and use these to guide their search for historical facts, what kinds of cues would our scanners need to find to mark up knowledge from structure?

No empirical studies of the degree to which genre formalism predicts content seem to exist. Indeed, there is not yet a predictive literature of what specific elements of content might be derived from an analysis of structural cues. A preliminary assessment by the author of a variety of art historical publication genres, such as *catalogues raisonné* and exhibition catalogues, suggests that within works nearly all the content characteristics can be predicted from structure. One open question is how content cues can be correlated in analyses between works. We know that precisely the same semiotics will not be applied between works, yet the commonality of the semiotics must be high enough that humans find that reading meaning from structure is possible.

Systematic study of a sample of printed texts to identify the elements that are "marked" by changes in typography and layout would expose the TEI Document Type Definitions (DTDs) or structural "fingerprints" for each volume. These could then be compared. If there is a correlation between structure and genres, a group of printed works that have similar DTDs as encoded by machines should subsequently be judged by human readers to constitute a common genre. Some of the debate about what constitutes a genre, at least with respect to what can be recognized as belonging to a genre using structural clues, would then be resolved.

Similar research in archives could enable our systems to enhance the low meaning conveyed by folder identifications in finding aids (whether EAD marked-up or not), with richer indications of the probable character of their item-level contents. In a world moving toward knowledge browsable with "semantic web-like" (or even Semantic Web) functionality, such content clues would enable connections to be made between documentation distributed in many discrete fonds that would not otherwise be discovered by researchers.

Making Form Explicit to Enhance Content and Function

A small scholarly industry, once comprised of monks but now consisting largely of academics, manufactures *apparatus criticus.* In the digital age, critical apparatus is generated from output instructions based on metadata available in texts marked up according to scholarly guidelines. The mark-up makes explicit structures that are implicitly encoded and annotates the relationship between words in the texts and the critically linked meanings and usages. Computers can generate a variety of different views of texts marked up according to these guidelines. Since these scholarly undertakings have adopted digital technologies, their methods have undergone rapid change accompanied by substantial rethinking. Scholars will continue to debate what knowledge to represent in marking up texts, and we can expect to see an evolution in the forms of critical apparatus as they no longer need to be products that can be printed in hard copy. A range of value-added scholarly tools that exist only as digital analytics could be the future of critical apparatus.

This is especially the case since we can build a specification based on the practices that have generated scholarly critical apparatus in the past for a baseline of metadata that should be represented in digitally processed documents. We should begin with additional information that scholars, like archivists, acquire from particular genres to which they have devoted further study by abstracting the practices that have developed in the study of texts.[12] Many other tasks of the scholarly or archival editor, such as clarifying the usage of terminology and identifying people and places referenced in the text, are also within reach of computing services, though still sufficiently challenging that articles describing methods for such tasks still have a place within the computing-in-the-humanities literature. In the aggregate, these scholarly practices constitute a statement of requirements for what we would minimally want to do with a repository of digital texts. With these requirements as a basis, we can analyze a representative body of texts to determine the extent to which images of texts can be decoded by computers using structural clues, semantic indicators, syntactic markers, and a combination of these expressed in algorithmic methods.

The full range of tasks of scholarly editors that could be relegated to computer processing has not yet been defined. For those decoding and meaning-making practices that were not susceptible to preprocessing, we could further analyze what support could be provided to scholars engaged in these tasks in a digital library or archives through some advanced functionality, possibly harvesting the results of collaborative annotation. In this we can hear technology capabilities echoing and amplifying the functions once imagined by Helen for collaboration in development of documentation strategies.

What functions would it be useful to have in a fully digital library of the world's published literature? To begin with, in addition to classic bibliographic metadata, we could expect to see and navigate through a full table of contents of any book. We could both explore the index prepared for the book and compare it with a full concordance view. And we could examine all the footnotes and references and follow them to their sources. All these are functions, of course, which we could perform now with a digitized and marked-up version of a text.

The architecture of a scholarly re-presentation of all digitized texts could be very different from the present architecture of libraries, including digital libraries, which have the volume as their unit of information. Some things that would be accommodated by a network of textual elements, however, cannot be achieved with mark-up of individual volumes. For example, just as we now follow citations *from* a work, we could, in an environment of networked text elements, follow references *to* a work, made after it was published. Works that have many entries that are structurally similar, as is the case with many reference books, could be viewed and queried as we would a database, so we could view words from Old English roots, or objects sold at auction in France, or drugs containing a particular chemical in more than 5ppm. Books published with keys to abbreviations—whether the initials of contributors to an encyclopedia or short-hands for journal titles that were familiar to nineteenth-century German chemists—can be searched, or viewed, with the full values of these abbreviations shown. (Terry Cook suggests this would be very much a kind of modern paleography, in which archivists of medieval documents are well versed.) Similarly, books with foreign-language terms in glossaries, or alternative spelling lists for geographic place names and the like, can be viewed as if these values were present in the text. We could even reorganize the contents of texts as graphical visualizations that highlight statistical similarities within content. In these respects, the digital library of textual elements is radically different from a digitized library of volumes.

Full-text access to large volumes of books is made much more useful when we have metadata to indicate where in a volume particular words are found. If we assume contextual knowledge in addition to simple OCR reproduction of the text *per se*, we enable new and more precise forms of query. No longer will we unwittingly retrieve works based on words in the editor's preface or in a dust-jacket gloss written by someone other than the author, when we are seeking the ideas of authors themselves. We can decide to look for works in which certain words are, or are not, found in citations. We can include only words found in back-of-the-book indexes, or exclude them (especially if the word itself does not appear as such in the text). We can seek words that appear in chapter headings when they show up in other chapters. And in many other ways we can qualify our searches, both within and between volumes.

Functionality that is now relatively labor intensive can be provided quite simply in this environment. For example, a citation index or collective bibliography (eliminating duplication if desired) can be generated from any group of works and produced as a unified index. In addition, some kinds of scholarly studies that were previously unthinkable, such as comparative analysis of the evolution of genre characteristics over time and across linguistic groups, could be supported in an environment such as this with little difficulty.

Coming Full Circle: Using Form to Drive Functions

In the early 1980s, when we were imagining that organizations performing specific functions generated documents of particular types which years later archivists appraised for their content by analyzing the context of their animating functions, and that our existing record schedules, reflecting the decisions that archivists had reached (ostensibly about certain types of documents), actually addressed the need to document certain functions, we were implicitly arguing that function predicted form and content. What we tried to do was to identify functions at a level of generality that correlated directly to specific forms so that we could make appraisal decisions before records were generated and without the need to wade through billions of pages or files one by one. Subsequently, I would argue that this approach would allow us to record retention metadata within documents as they were generated and, in an electronic environment, to appropriately manage the retention and access to records from the moment of their creation.[13]

Some form-function links were easy to make. Personnel offices received resumes and made job offers in their hiring function. Security officers filed shift incident reports and logs of visitors. Most of the bureaucratically organized functions of modern organizations were enabled by strong formal document types that had equally strong ties to retention periods, often mandated in law or formal organizational policy.

But there were also many much looser associations and what seemed to be more open document types. We could not decide to keep or destroy memoranda *per se*—though memoranda generated from certain functions and transactions, and directed to particular other functions linked in a business process, were often highly predictable in terms of their content, and thus of their need for long-term (or not) retention for business or archival purposes—without having to read all or even any of the individual documents (very much like not having to read the "invitation" from your friendly electrical company). My interests turned to the fine-grained functions that dictated these relations. Helen's turned to the macrofunctions that explained the context of what organizations as a whole were up to. The commonality in these endeavors was our mutual commitment to finding explicit structural relations flowing from implicit functional associations.

Today we are turning the observation on its head and asking ourselves how, if we recognized the forms of documents, could we drive their functions as documents (or parts of documents and books) in a digital environment? Specifically, we imagine that the world's published literature will be largely digitized in a decade and that most archives will be born-digital from now on, but that the nature of the post-processing that will be applied to bit-mapped images has yet to be determined. If we automatically mark up this text using knowledge of document formalisms, we need criteria to assess what features we should document to support the digital library or archive of the future as an integrated scholarly knowledge-base rather than just a repository of "fast paper." Since the objective is to create a base platform for published text of the "scholarly edition" view, we look to that model for functional requirements. The scholarly editions ought, minimally, to link all citations and allusions back to source made by the work in hand. Other essential functions would include providing contextually sensitive dictionary, encyclopedia, and gazetteer look-ups for all the words used in the text, identifying subsequent references to the text, and comparing the edition in hand with all other printed editions, among other things.

When we have succeeded at automatically marking up text in this fashion, it will be possible for a system to generate a page image view, a full-text view if OCR has been applied, and a scholarly edition view of any text. Of course, we need to be clear that such a scholarly edition view is not a computer-generated critical edition; that is, the computer is not going to add analysis that has not been provided by humans elsewhere. The system simply compiles relevant information from other sources. Still, a well-designed environment of integrated scholarly mark-ups from millions of texts would produce an impressive amount of new knowledge. What could such a scholarly edition view expose?

We still need to research how far machine-generated mark-up can take us toward creating a universal, integrated, *apparatus criticus* and what tools we will need to exploit it. Insofar as we succeed, however, the base platform on which all other scholarship rests will be raised to a plateau that previously required teams of scholarly editors or archivists and many centuries to compile. Scholarship will then focus on making novel connections and developing fresh insights, starting from a much higher level of cumulative knowledge.

Archivists might be asking themselves whether this has relevance for them. While some part of the existing paper archival record will doubtless be digitized in coming decades, the real significance, of course, lies with whether we can work from content to function with the vast bulk of the contemporary and future record, which is and will continue to be in electronic formats. I would argue that we can, and must, because no other method of deriving meanings from documents, or determining their appropriate retention and disposal, is likely to be cost effective and scalable. Making the function (in full, rich, functional decomposition, including subfunctions, programs, activities, actors, and transactions) part of the embedded format of documents opens the door for archival participation in these exciting possibilities.

As we develop techniques for teasing meaning from these structural features built into documents, we will want to re-present this new-found (and cumulative) functional knowledge back into the documents (today we would choose RDFa for this) and develop application programming interfaces to archival services that can digest these marked-up documents, ensure their authenticity, represent their functional characteristics, migrate their format dependencies over time, and display them to end-users in context with other documents of the same provenance, time, and place, and subject or activity. In this way we can exploit our ability to read meaning in document structure and use it to construct not just an electronic record of humankind, but the semantic web in which that archive resides and through which knowledge is revealed, and indeed created.

Notes

1 This work stimulated an RLG (Research Libraries Group) Government Records Project vocabulary and played a role in my engagement with functions vocabularies in Australia. See also Alden N. Monroe and Kathleen D. Roe, "What's the Purpose? Functional Access to Archival Records," in *Beyond the Book: Extending MARC for Subject Access*, ed. Toni Petersen and Pat Molholt (Boston: G.K. Hall, 1990), 157–70; and David Bearman, "'Who about What?' or 'From Whence, Why and How?'," in *Archives, Automation, and Access*, ed. Peter Baskerville and Chad Gaffield (Vancouver: University of British Columbia, 1986).

2 See work by Charles E. Rosenberg (such as *The Care of Strangers: The Rise of America's Hospital System* (1987), or *Explaining Epidemics* (1992); and by archivist Barbara Craig, "Hospital Records and Record-Keeping, c. 1850–c. 1950 Part I: The Development of Records in Hospitals," *Archivaria* 29 (Winter 1989-90): 57–87, and "Hospital Records and Record-Keeping, c. 1850–c. 1950 Part II: The Development of Records in Hospitals," *Archivaria* 30 (Summer 1990): 21–38.

3 Which is a good thing, because if we actually try to read this kind of document, we immediately discover that it was written by lawyers, is full of mandatory clauses of little meaning to most people, and is obscure in the extreme.

4 This may, indeed, be a significant contribution to why our teaching of reading fails, but I must leave that for some other researcher to discover.

5 Classical information theory defines information as the signal in what otherwise is noise—change in continuity.

6 Clifford A. Lynch, "Open Computation: Beyond Human-Reader-Centric Views of Scholarly Literatures," in *Open Access: Key Strategic, Technical and Economic Aspects,* ed. Neil Jacobs (Oxford: Chandos Publishing, 2006), 185–93.

7 I am currently conducting research to establish the degree to which existing TEI marked-up texts reflect structural properties that might be "visible" to post-processors of scanned images.

8 Gerald Genette, *Paratexts: Thresholds of Interpretation*, trans. Jane E. Lewin (Cambridge: Cambridge University Press, 1997).

9 This direction of research reflects a vast unexplored intellectual terrain that has, to date, been overlooked by historians of the book. Initial probes suggest, not surprisingly, a variety of traditions tied to differing traditions of publishing in different languages.

10 If these numbered lines were all right justified, we'd probably expect to be reading a legal document.

11 David Bearman and Peter Sigmond, "Explorations of Form of Material Authority Files by Dutch Archivists," *American Archivist* 50 (Spring 1987): 249–53.

12 See, for example, Sheila Muldaur, *The Proficient Reader Record: Genre Assessment for Informational, Biographical, and Procedural Text* (Katonah, NY: Richard C. Owen, 2004). The Modern Language Association has issued Guidelines for Scholarly Editions, http://sunsite.berkeley.edu/MLA/guidelines.html, with revisions proposed at http://jefferson.village.virginia.edu/~jmu2m/cse/CSEguidelines.html.

13 David Bearman, "Towards a Reference Model for Business Acceptable Communications," web-published proposal, December 6, 1994, http://web.archive.org/web/19970707064048/ http://www.lis.pitt.edu/~nhprc/prog6-5.html.

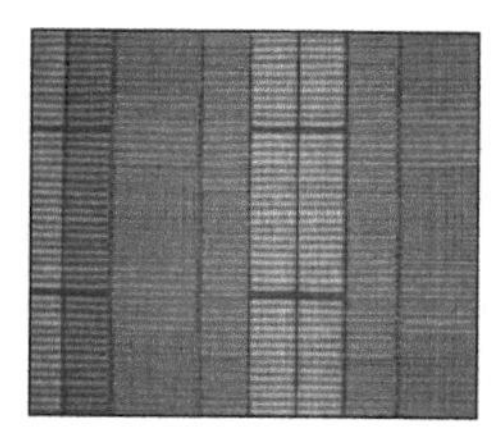

WHO REPRESENTS THE PAST? ARCHIVES, RECORDS, AND THE SOCIAL WEB

ELIZABETH YAKEL

The era of control is over: You can either stay in the bunker, or you can try to participate. And to not participate is criminal.[1]

Who Controls the Past Controls the Future

Even after twenty years, Helen Samuels' article, "Who Controls the Past,"[2] continues to resonate in my head. It holds cautionary notes and at the same time poses ideals which are now part of the archival ethos. In Samuels' article, she argues both that archivists should become more active in seeking, shaping, and developing collections and that we should engage stakeholders in this process. The sharing of control over the shaping of the collecting plan and the selection of materials in collaboration with stakeholders from specific interested communities is a key tenet of documentation strategies. Yet the envisioned participation was carefully controlled and modulated; the archivist was still in control. Archivists defined the collecting themes and scope, convened meetings of the interested parties, performed the majority of the research into a project's feasibility, interpreted the results, and translated those results into action.[3]

While Samuels' article addressed collection development and appraisal and its relationship to controlling the past, archivists' control over collections (and the past) extends as well to their representations of archival materials. In the advent or perhaps the wake of Web 2.0 technologies,[4] it is timely to contemplate opening up archival representation and engaging the researcher in these processes, not unlike the ideal of the documentation strategies.[5] The applicability of shared authority and distributed curation to archival representation—in terms of descriptive practice (what is highlighted, subject analysis, revised descriptive notes, contextual research into the records-creating processes, and so on), the selection for digitization (truly re-presentation of analog in digital form), the creation of surrogates, and the development of interfaces to display all this information—has not been widely explored.

These topics have not been examined, I think, because many archivists have approached Web 2.0 technology as I first did—as a means of designing a better and more user-friendly finding aid or of crowd-sourcing metadata in an era of diminishing resources where "more product, less process" reigns. These are inherently the wrong approaches for thinking about the social web. Web 2.0 is about connection, collaboration, community. For archives, Web 2.0 connects communities with collections or, maybe even more conceptually, communities with their history and identity. What is more, it invites collaboration about that history: what it means, how it should be presented, and what we know. Shared authority and distributed curation are the point. Yet Web 2.0 technologies can be implemented and the community can be integrated in many different ways. This raises questions about how much authority we as archivists are willing to share and how to manage the voices of all those distributed curators.

This essay will discuss controlling the past in the context of online archives, records, manuscripts, and their surrogates. It is loosely based on my five-year odyssey with the Polar Bear Expedition Digital Collections.[6] As the oldest archival experiment in Web 2.0, this research project has given me the opportunity to think about these issues and to consider how to best connect communities and collections. The Polar Bear Expedition was an American military intervention into northern Russia at the end of World War I. Due to the composition of army units at that time, many of the servicemen were from Michigan. As a result of donations from these men and their families, the Bentley Historical Library at the University of Michigan now has approximately sixty-five manuscript collections consisting of diaries, letters, photographs, and other memorabilia documenting this event. These have all been digitized and form the content for the website.

Simply transferring the representational products and the current archival norms of descriptive practices from the repository to the web will not work. Researchers on the web demand more. Also, different communities have also demanded more inclusion in the actual processes for the curation of collections. This essay considers, then, the idea of shared authority and distributed curation in archival representations and virtual systems. It argues that archivists could benefit by moving from a model of mediation and controlled descriptions to one of collaboration and shared authority. It also envisions how distributed curation could benefit communities that have traditionally felt disenfranchised and left out of the archives by enabling multiple voices and perspectives to provide context for the records. There are both potential benefits and challenges in shared authority and distributed curation. Yet I argue that the benefits of increased accessibility and providing users with the ability to reuse and re-create their own archives outweigh the costs. Enabling this type of use is also essential for the continued viability of archival organizations.

Archival Information on the Web

There is incredible access to archival information on the web in terms of developing virtual presences, MARC records, findings aids, and digital images. The University of Idaho's Repositories of Primary Sources website links to over 5,000 websites of archival and manuscript collections' homepages world wide.[7] The WorldCat bibliographic network run by the Online Computer Library Center (OCLC), now merged with the Research Libraries Group (RLG) Union Catalog, contains 1.5 million entries for archives and manuscripts.[8] ArchiveGrid hosts an additional 900,000 descriptions of primary source materials from over 2,500 libraries, museums, and archives worldwide.[9] Other consortia, such as the Online Archive of California, the Rocky Mountain Online Archive, and the Northwest Digital Archives, to give but three examples, contain thousands of additional finding aids available for searching.[10] Additionally, there are thousands of individual repository websites that contain online guides and finding aids.

In terms of digital collections, numerous archives and special collections feature some sampling from their collections. Other sites hold considerably more. American Memory at the Library of Congress is one of the largest, displaying nine million items that document American history and culture, grouped into more than one hundred thematic collections.[11] The Online Archive of California contains over 120,000 images and 50,000 pages of documents, letters, and oral histories.[12] Taken together, these sites provide substantial availability to a wide variety of primary sources. While there are undoubtedly peoples, events, and ideas that are not represented, this level of universal availability of archives in the last ten years is unprecedented and should be celebrated.

Who Represents the Past?

In spite of vastly different interfaces and the underlying databases, websites, and collections previously mentioned, these sites all share a model of using the web as a one-way communication mechanism. Most of our current representations on the web are heavily mediated. They have been created and published by archivists who control what is selected for display, what is said about the collections, all access points to the collections, and how they are indexed. They also represent archival information—contextual and content-oriented—as static (with some updating by the archivist), rather than as dynamic social entities where materials are actively reused and, yes, potentially re-created and jointly curated by archivists and visitors to the site.[13]

There are opportunities and challenges inherent in changing this model of communication and moving toward shared control and distributed curation. Primary sources need to be treated differently in the physical and digital worlds. I will explore two directions in which archives and special collections could move in which shared control might be beneficial and provide examples where some of these mechanisms are already in place. The first, the transition from physical context to virtual interlinking, concerns the context of the collections. The second, changing from mediation to collaboration, refers to the context of the user's interaction with the materials.

From Local Context to Virtual Worlds

Archivists are very aware of the importance of creating both physical and intellectual context for their collections. A basic text on archival arrangement and description notes that:

> It is necessary to discover how the collection was originally organized (if it was organized at all); the context in which the collection was generated; and the relationship of the collection's content to other collections, people, and historical events. The archivist analyzes the content and structure of the collection, gathering information that will form the basis of the finding aid. In addition, research in sources external to the collection provides information about the context in which it was created, which will also become an integral part of the final documentation.[14]

In the physical world, such context is derived in two ways. First, administrative/biographical history and scope and content notes provide, respectively, or perhaps mutually, intellectual context about the creator/provenance and about the contents. Adrian Cunningham even refers to authority control for the creator as context control.[15] Secondly, context emanates from the physicality of the collection, for example, the location in a file, box, series, etc., as part of some larger whole or aggregate, or from its materiality, for example, watermarks, stains, types of inks or fasteners.[16] Intellectual and physical context are possible in the digital world, but they offer different challenges. Intellectual context can be expanded and refer to information within and without a repository from formally designated "authoritative" sources as well as from other curators whose trustworthiness and reliability is less known. Physical context is somewhat harder to represent online. The physical archives world relies on a tactile sense of the materials as the major means of capturing that kind of context. These elements are less apparent in the virtual world, although computer visualizations used in other arenas could come to bear on this problem quite nicely and include the ability to scan folders for thickness, provide visual cues denoting certain types of documentation, and to move back and forth seamlessly between parts of the collection.

In the virtual world, linking provides a means not only of bringing in information to the finding aid, as suggested by a Michael Fox and Peter Wilkerson, but also of linking out to other contexts or sources rather than summarizing and filtering them through the finding aid. Few archivists have taken advantage of this. Yet there are other forms of context that have been important to different communities of archival researchers. For example, professional scholars derive context from citations denoting use by previous researchers. Recent research has documented that academic researchers still rely on peers and citation tracing (both forms of contextualization) as the primary means of identifying collections; this form of contextualization is still strong in spite of the increasing amount of information about archival and manuscript materials on the web.[17] Archivists' linking of primary and secondary sources in the context of the finding aid would be an interesting experiment. Current citation software is a desktop application. A scholar or student amasses his or her own personal citations and shares these in published works or academic papers. Recent online tools, such as Zotero, allow scholars to seamlessly pull citation information from web sources, including primary sources on the web, and share these with others.[18] Researchers who cite collections do not consistently inform archivists that these collections have been cited. Citation databases, such as the *ISI Arts and Humanities Citation Index*, do a poor job of tracking the use of primary sources due to inconsistencies in the formatting of footnotes. Incorporating citations into finding aids by both archivists and researchers would leverage these assets and would engage the researcher and harness his or her knowledge about collections. Finding aids could also link to emerging sites such as CiteULike[19] allowing different user communities to fashion citations specifically for their purposes.

Creating a different type of online context can be done with an image map using simple HTML. Richard Lehane has done this with the finding aid for the papers of Sir Arthur Tange (1914–2001). His website enables virtual users to move about the office and select files and piles. Once selected, the user is shown a description in the finding aid.[20] In the process, we understand more about original order than we would if presented with the finding aid and the boxes alone. This is the best illustration of Brien Brothman's argument that retaining original order is impossible, that it essentially "caters to institutional requirements for a serviceable, idealized archival intellectual order rather than original order."[21]

In the case of representing materials online, scholars are debating how much and what context is required. Andrew Prescott argues that high-quality digitization of full collections provides essential evidence for historians interpreting primary sources.[22] However, the structural context that archivists provide is not always appreciated by scholars, perhaps because, as Brothman implies, it is difficult to navigate as well as misleading. Tim Hitchcock envisions functionalities in systems containing digitized documents that transcend archival context:

> The impact of the digitization of archives in combination with the fundamental deracination of knowledge implied by the use of keyword searching on the corpus of digitized printed text, frees us from the habit of mind implied by the structures of the archives.[23]

The physical location or arrangement of records is just one example of how context influences our perceptions of archival materials, and how they can (or cannot) be assessed for use. Archivists also create context through metadata. Some of this metadata is quite basic, such as Dublin Core. Other metadata, such as Encoded Archival Context (EAC), attempts to communicate a much richer context about the creator. The best example showing the potential of EAC is Bright Sparcs[24] which links biographical information to both primary and secondary sources about a scientist. The context needed by users, however, varies by their information need and intended use. Teachers, for example, might like grade-reading levels indicated against primary sources targeted for school use; parents might want some indication such as a PICS (Platform for Internet Content Selection) visible in the HTML header. Still, despite the large number of official metadata schemas generated by different user communities,[25] these will still fail, even if all combined, to incorporate all the potential access points and context desired by users.

The web also allows the intellectual integration of collections or fonds that are split between several institutions. Bibliographic networks do this by returning search results that show the same creator attributed to dispersed collections. Again it is up to the researcher to do the integration. In the case of the William Muschenheim architectural drawings and papers, the Bentley Historical Library at the University of Michigan and the Avery Architectural and Fine Arts Library at Columbia University have taken advantage of the integrative possibilities of the web and jointly curated a site that intellectually combines their collections.[26] In this model, authority is shared between repositories and curation is only minimally distributed; however, it does allow each institution to place its records into a new context that better hints at some "original order" and provides a more integrated intellectual context for researchers to interact with the materials.

Distributed curation in terms of shared citations or reuniting provenance allows all researchers to consider records in a larger context or in multiple contexts. This new context provides the same internal focus on the records as well as virtually interlinking them to other contexts. Re-creating the context of creation decreases the gap between the creator's original context and archivist's original order or "structure." Archivists can make use of broader, shared contexts through the use of web tools that take advantage of existing metadata and utilize new ways to enable a rich context of links, collaboration, and shared authority.

From Mediation to Collaboration

The underlying premises of Web 2.0 tools are community, collaboration, and connection. For archivists who have long mediated the representation of descriptive content about records, the professional model is that such information about collections largely flows in one direction, that is, from archivist to researcher. Making this process a genuine two-way collaboration is, therefore, a paradigm shift. I acknowledge that archivists have talked to researchers and gained knowledge of collections from them, and from time to time have amended finding aids in response to information from researchers. But by and large, the latter is an exception to the rule; there has been no formal mechanism to capture the knowledge of researchers and integrate that into the archives. Moving from mediation to collaboration is a large step. There are three aspects to this shift: from physical space (reading room) to social space (online); from authority control to collaborative constructions; and from archival authority to distributed curation. Archivists are already experimenting with these ideas and their projects can teach us a lot about the implications of these changes.

From Physical Space to Social Space

Moving from the physical space of the reading room to collaborative social space on the web is a difficult transition. This transition should not be mistaken as a change from control to freedom or one of totally giving up authority. Social spaces, even virtual social spaces, embody modes of acceptable behavior and rules. Depending on the tools, differing degrees of control can be shared and curation distributed in different ways. In addition to explicit rules, how archivists select Web 2.0 functionalities determines how communities and collections will interact in cyberspace.

Virtual archives employing Web 2.0 functionality are social spaces. Implicit and explicit rules are at play in these sites. When launching the Polar Bear Expedition Digital Collections site in January 2006, we relied largely on implicit rules. One implicit rule was embedded in the registration function that required a valid email address for individuals who wanted to contribute comments. As the site matured, we found we needed to develop more formal rules, which we posted. For example, in response to sexually explicit postings, we created and published a rule stating that we would remove postings that we judged to be malicious or out-of-scope. Implicitly, we also technically disallowed in the comments or biographies sections the inclusion of URLs that automatically forwarded visitors to other sites. While some may see this as censorship, we asserted our authority to maintain a certain atmosphere in our social space. Maintenance of the social order occurs in other sites featuring social interaction, such as Wikipedia. In fact, Wikipedia visitors themselves repair pages after malicious tampering, often within minutes.[27]

Making the leap into the Web 2.0 environment may require what Darlene Fichter calls "radical trust":

> Radical trust is about trusting the community. We know that abuse can happen, but we trust (radically) that the community and participation will work. In the real world, we know that vandalism happens but we still put art and sculpture up in our parks. As an online community we come up with safeguards or mechanisms that help keep open contribution and participation working.[28]

Commenting, tagging, and annotation denote very different types of relationships between archivists, online visitors, and collections. Commenting appears to be the most popular form of Web 2.0 functionality for archives. In a system that allows commenting, visitors can add information to the official archival description, but not change it. The relationship between comments and the official description varies by site. In some sites, these are separated, in others comments are presented alongside the archival descriptions contradicting them or other comments, leaving it up to future researchers to weigh the evidence for themselves. For example, the Haags Gemeentearchief website encourages visitors to help describe photographs.[29] As a result, visitors describe and even contradict the archivists' versions and those of other visitors. Project Naming at Library and Archives Canada (LAC) takes a different approach.[30]

Project Naming enables Nunavut youth to connect with elders by soliciting information about photographs of Inuit people from the elders by bringing digitized CDs of images to them. Images on the web can also be identified by filling out a form. These descriptions are then incorporated by LAC staff into their official descriptions. It is unclear whether there is any filtering process done by LAC staff. While seeking additional descriptive metadata or comments is common, the Archives of Manitoba solicits more general comments about its Rearview exhibits, which can in turn lead to additional donations of like material.[31]

On my own site, the Polar Bear Expedition Digital Collections, visitors are given the choice of commenting publicly or privately to the archivists. Comments can be added at any level, for example, to the archival descriptions as well as on individual digital images on the site. The comments are searchable and search results indicate when hits in the comments portion are by other visitors. The site has generated hundreds of comments describing unidentified photographs, correcting misspellings, adding names of men who fought in the campaign, and offering additional digital resources for inclusion on the site. Comments add context while preserving the official (dare I say authoritative) archival description, while also bringing in diverse perspectives (and admittedly more accurate information). As Katie Shilton and Ramesh Srinivasan have pointed out:

> Involving community members in archival arrangement and description could help acknowledge and preserve context and embedded knowledge architectures in the self-documentations of historically marginalized communities.[32]

Annotation creates a greater degree of shared authority than commenting and allows visitors to actually change the underlying archival description. I am not aware of any archival site that currently implements this functionality to the actual archival information, although the National Archives of the United Kingdom comes closest with its Your Archives site. This site is a wiki where visitors and library staff can add, delete, and link to information on the official National Archives site or beyond. Visitors can comment on records, inventories, or add information about events. Entries also link to the actual National Archives catalog.[33] In its introduction, the National Archives explains its process:

> Welcome to Your Archives, The National Archives' online community of records users. These pages are for you to contribute your knowledge of archival sources held by The National Archives and by other archives throughout the UK. The content on these pages has mainly been contributed by users and is designed to offer information additional to that available in the Catalogue, Research Guides, Documents Online and the National Register of Archives. The National Archives does not vouch for the accuracy of the information held within Your Archives.[34]

It is interesting that the National Archives finds it important to say they do not vouch for the accuracy of information on this site. The implication is that they vouch for other information! Yet, in the wiki environment, no one owns the information and everyone owns the information or, perhaps more accurately, everyone shares responsibility for the information on the site. Self-regulation in Wikipedia is an achieved state and participants spend considerable time working on this process.[35]

The type of shared authority on Wikipedia entails cooperation of a large community. In terms of archives, a community this large may be difficult to sustain. Logistics aside, shared authority brings with it shared responsibility within a community. There has been considerable talk in the archival circles about the ownership of records, particularly records documenting persons and peoples in government archives and the need to develop some type of parallel provenance.[36] Retaining these types of records in government custody, but allowing for more community-based description "acknowledges the context of community knowledge, avoids distorting marginalized voices and enables community records be more fully understood by a wider public."[37] This quotation should make us pause to consider whether the contexts that we now select and promulgate for the records are the most relevant. At the very least, archivists might acknowledge that the contexts are selected or incomplete, and that they alone do not have the knowledge or resources to make them more complete.

From Authority Control to Shared Authority

Sharing authority and distributed curation do not begin with posting on the web. Authors such as Verne Harris and Wendy Duff have argued for more collaborative archival description with those who enabled the creation of records (both the records' creators and the records' subjects).[38]

Michelle Light and Tom Hyry are proponents for greater transparency in the development of descriptions and in divulging the biases of the processing archivist.[39] Their call for transparency harks back to Samuels' "Who Controls the Past," and was originally articulated by Terry Cook who first translated this discussion from the appraisal literature, where it had been previously centered, into the realm of description:

> Archivists would engage openly with their clients and respect their needs, rather than forcing them to accept professional metanarratives of how records should be described. Descriptive architecture based around the fonds would be exploded for complex institutional records-creating settings from its relatively flat, mono-hierarchical, and static fixation on a final creator into much richer, multi-relational, many-to-many contextual linkages.[40]

Other archival writers have long called for greater transparency and accountability in the appraisal decision-making process. Several key incidents, such as the FBI records appraisal case, the Enron case, and the Heiner affair, have highlighted the costs and the benefits of transparency.[41] However, decision making in the archival representation process has been far less transparent until recently. While many archivists have blogs that generally comment on professional issues, Stephen Fletcher and Elizabeth Hull's blog, *A View to Hugh: Processing the Hugh Morton Photographs and Films*, invites archivists, researchers, and others into the actual processing and digitization of the Hugh Morton collection:

> This blog is intended to provide information about our progress, to provide glimpses into how photographic archivists work, to highlight interesting discoveries we make along the way, and to foster discussion and input from the many "Friends of Hugh"—residents of the state to which he devoted his life and any other interested parties.[42]

Thus far the postings discuss everything from identifying photographs to commenting on the actual work of processing: "I am very interested in reading of your HUGE AMT. of work to organize this great resource" (February 28, 2008). While the comments about the process are few at this point, the reflection on the work and the transparency of the process is a welcome glimpse into one of the archival world's "black boxes," breaking down the (allegedly) objective, faceless, unbiased authority implicit in most archival descriptions, and explicit in no little traditional archival theory. Interestingly, Morton's wife Julia, the donor, is an active participant on the blog, adding context, observations, and corrections. This engagement of many voices with the processing process exemplifies Cook's claim that "description is continually reinvented, reconstructed, reborn"[43] and shows how transparency in the representational process can lead to new insights, different perspectives, and a more complex and subtle contextual grounding for the records.

The archival authors previously mentioned seem to assume that authority for description is a fixed commodity. Thus, if I share my authority with you, my authority diminishes, yours increases. Borrowing from economic theory, I pose that authority might be a non-rivalrous good. What this means is that consumption or use by one person does not stop others from using the same good. The classic example of a rivalrous good is food: if I eat an apple, you cannot eat the same one. However, the air we breathe is non-rivalrous; my breathing (in normal cases) does not diminish your ability to breathe at the same time.[44] Authority (in our case authority surrounding archival collections) may be like air: archivists, researchers, communities all have and can use it—for better or worse, correct or not, leaving it up to others to judge its merits.

From Archival Authority to Distributed Curation

Distributed curation implies a shared responsibility for collections as well as allowing a range of uses and reuses of materials. This includes allowing visitors to repurpose and personalize materials and enabling user contribution to the collections, thus sharing not only in describing the collections, but shaping the collections.

Curation also implies the purposeful collection of records or objects to be saved by someone or some group. Thus curation is linked to memory: organizational, personal, collective. José van Dijck refers to personal collective memory, "*the acts and products of remembering in which individuals engage to make sense of their lives in relation to the lives of others and to their surroundings, situating themselves in time and place*" [italics original].[45] Personal collective memory is highly bound in objects of remembrance: letters, photographs, ribbons, baseballs, whatever. Sites, such as Facebook and MySpace, allow one to share personal collective memory by creating a virtual scrapbook or diary, identifying with groups, and then inviting one's friends in to visit and participate. Archives can also provide a space for this type of interaction because they stand in the nexus between the personal and the cultural. The Ohio Historical Society's Ohio Memory: An Online Scrapbook of Ohio History provides digital images of books, manuscripts, photographs, and natural history objects. Visitors can view items, and can also save them to a personal scrapbook and add notes. The scrapbook can also be shared with others. This is both a form of curation and re-creation of the archives in one's own image.[46]

The interaction between the personal and the collective is also evident in a number of sites that allow visitors to contribute content. Some of these sites featuring the greatest degree of authority for creation are not run, or are only partly hosted, by archives. The earliest instance of this phenomenon was the Science and Technology in the Making (STIM)[47] site, but more recently the September 11 Digital Archive[48] and the Mozilla Digital Memory Bank[49] continue in this vein, mixing stories and images contributed by visitors to actually create a new virtual archive. While "real" archivists may deride this as a collection without clear provenance and lacking context, to deny virtual visitors the opportunity to contribute to the collective memory is a dangerous tactic for archivists. More recently, some archival sites have allowed such visitor contribution. The National Archives in the United Kingdom has used this most extensively in different sites, such as Moving Here[50] and Your Archives.[51] Moving Here provides links to records to trace family history in the United Kingdom, and has a focus on specific ethnic groups. The site

> explores, records and illustrates why people came to England over the last 200 years and what their experiences were and continue to be. It offers free access, for personal and educational use, to an online catalogue of versions of original material related to migration history from local, regional and national archives, libraries and museums. Moving Here gives visitors to the site the opportunity to publish their own experience of migration. The vision for Moving Here is:
>
> - To overcome barriers to the direct involvement of minority ethnic groups in recording and documenting their own history of migration
> - To ensure this history is passed on to the next generation through schools.[52]

There are a couple of interesting things about the National Archives' site. First, it is one of the sites that overtly provides information concerning its vision. Quite interestingly, the vision is not about archives *per se*, but about enabling co-creation, authority over collections, and encouraging distributed curation. Secondly, by encouraging the adding of stories and images to the site, the National Archives contextualizes the materials in a new way.

The ability to add collections is a powerful draw. The Public Relations and Development Department at Wright State University sponsors the site 1967–2007—40 Years of Wright State University and urges participation:

> We invite you to add comments and remembrances to these photos and also submit personal photographs of your WSU experiences. Share your memories and Raider Pride to make this a live, accessible commemoration of WSU's 40th anniversary. The more you participate, the greater this online celebration becomes. Join the celebration today.[53]

Interestingly, their appraisal policy is more explicit than many of the archives sites. "We reserve the right to reject images and comments that do not comply with the stated criteria. Images and comments submitted on the website will be processed within 72 hours of submission. You will receive an e-mail confirming that we have received your submission."[54] When constructing the Polar Bear Expedition Digital Collections, we planned for corrections and amendments to our text, but did not anticipate or plan for contributions. Our visitors, however, had other ideas and we have accessioned over fifteen additional collections. In no way have we been able to promise a seventy-two-hour turnaround, which has been problematic because not only do contributors want to see their materials online, but they want to see them fast!

Getting to Participation

Archives are one of the last bastions of individualized mediated service. While mediation between archivist and user will be a mainstay in the near future, and perhaps longer for certain specialized kinds of archives, this will not remain the norm. Peter Hirtle hints at a decline in mediation as a consequence of increased digitization.[55] Whether the current archives model of heavily mediated reference services is sustainable is an open question. It also goes against expectations of users of web-based information and social interaction protocols.

Isto Huvila discusses the idea of participatory archives using two Finnish case studies. He argues that participatory archives have three elements: decentralized or shared curation, a radical user orientation which makes usability and resource discovery the first priority, and contextualization of both records and the entire archival process, which includes the context of the user.[56] Some archival sites give us a glimpse of what a future with less mediation and greater participation might be like. Beyond Brown Paper features images from the Brown Paper Company Photographic Collection. The website allows visitors to add comments, which can be done online or telephoned in and then entered by archives staff. Brown Paper was the major industry in Berlin, New Hampshire, from the late nineteenth century through the mid-1960s. As such the collection has a strong community connection. One of the interesting phenomena on this site is that online visitors are talking to each other as they comment on the photographs.[57]

Yet getting to participation is hard. Subject-specific websites, such as Beyond Brown Paper and the Polar Bear Expedition Digital Collections, have devoted, but limited, followings. Looking through a broader lens at cultural heritage institutions, the Flickr Commons experience of the Powerhouse Museum in Australia, as reported by Sebastian Chan, is enlightening:

> In the first 4 weeks of the Commons we had more views of the photos than the same photos in the entirety of last year on our own website. It wasn't as if we made the images on our own website all that hard to find—they were well indexed on our own site by Google, they were made available to the national federated image search/repository Picture Australia, and they also existed in our OPAC. Still, that was no match for Flickr.[58]

Understanding and assessing participation in cultural heritage sites, specifically in archives, requires further study. Achieving "critical mass" to enable visitors to sustain conversations without the intervention of the archivist is important; however, success should not be calculated by raw numbers alone. The open questions are "what level of participation provides sufficient mass to sustain a participatory archive?" and "how do archives assess what is the most appropriate venue for participation around their collections?" Participation is not a given. I have done substantial searching on WorldCat for archival and manuscript materials and have never found one with any tags assigned to it. An "if we build it, they will come" mentality is not good enough. This is a result of thinking about building a site; the goal of social media is to build communities. The questions above should be answered in light of building a community around collections and fostering a quality of engagement.

Heather MacNeil argues that finding aids are "socio-historical" texts which are subject to influence by one's cultural, institutional, and individual philosophy. They are also changeable.[59] In the United States, archivists completing retrospective conversion projects to MARC and EAD have updated many finding aids. Yet these web-based access tools, such as the Beyond Brown Paper site, raise new issues about the socio-historical context of the materials and remind us that the socio-historical context does not end with a finished finding aid, even when use does not involve user annotation or comments; it continues as materials are reused and reinterpreted. Finding aids, records, and contexts all have their own ever-changing histories.

This type of collaboration has also happened sparingly on the Polar Bear Expedition Digital Collections.[60] In designing the site, the perhaps all-too-omnipresent persona, "The Archivist," may have inadvertently drawn most of the comments. I also positioned "The Archivist" apart from, rather than in, the online community. "The Archivist" was an authority above all others, rather than a participant with equal standing. In future designs, I would position the archivist differently, although he would still be there, but in a more participatory role and thus less likely to become the addressee for most comments. Encouraging collaboration while not having the archivist totally blend into the woodwork, as she does in a traditional finding aid, is hard to balance. Perhaps archives can learn from other types of sites how to manage the social dynamics and engage the audience in this process more seamlessly.[61] No archival site seems to have this balance exactly right quite yet.

In addition to fostering explicit participation and collaboration, implicit collaboration is also seen in recommender systems which are a less popular way of connecting people with content in archives. The Everglades Digital Library, a composite digitized collection of primary and secondary sources (including lesson plans) about the history and ecology of the Everglades, from a variety of sources, encourages visitors to rate its materials.[62] Thus later visitors can select more highly rated items and returning visitors can get recommendations based on their own ranking of items.

A different type of recommender system is in use in the Polar Bear Expedition Digital Collections. The Link Paths items are generated as visitors follow different paths around the site. When there is sufficient overlap, the link paths are populated. The more people using the site, the stronger the linkages that are displayed. Still, the link paths have caused confusion and therefore a tag line based on Amazon.com was inserted: "Researchers who viewed this collection also viewed . . ." These are unobtrusive, but these rating and recommender systems take advantage of the actual interaction on a site and are dependent on the behavior of the user community.

Who Controls the Present Controls the Past

In his discussion of the New Deal Network, Tom Thurston writes:

> I'd like to suggest a third category of websites, "associative portals," or aortals. An aortal is a site that enables the creation of social networks. . . . Its structure is designed to foster the creation of distributed networks of academic communities. If a website aims to be more than an archive, an online exhibit, a virtual textbook, it must consider how it can nurture similar dynamic relationships.[63]

An aortal is also a site that enables multiple contexts to coexist, interact, and reemerge as something new, richer, and greater than the sum of its parts. Linking collections to communities is difficult and requires a different type of advocacy than archivists have done in the past. The aforementioned tools primarily focus on connecting communities to collections. I wonder whether this is the correct approach. Should archivists focus their social media sites on community rather than collection building? In order to make this possible, archivists need to reorient their priorities from content building to community building.

This paradigm switch comes at the same time that other social pressures are pushing archivists in the opposite direction. Considerable discussion has been made about hidden or obscure or unprocessed collections and the need to gain greater control over these materials. It is ironic that this striving for greater control is occurring at the same time the era of control may be over. If archivists ever had control over the records, it was always incomplete.

Moving from archival authority to shared authority may help us as archivists to embrace better approaches to processing, such as more product, less process. This would allow archivists to focus on providing rich contexts for records while enabling visitors to help describe the content. The act of sharing control is important; there might just be an unlimited amount out there but we will need "radical trust" to take advantage of it. In the Web 2.0 environment, simply providing access is not enough. Accessibility extends beyond viewing digital objects; it requires interaction on a personal or intellectual level that includes re-creating materials in collections outside the archive and on the desktop. This notion of representation goes even further than that of Laura Millar, who argues for a records continuum approach to description.[64] Although the web makes it possible to separate content and context (and broaden context in the process), it also creates a space where context and content are both continually changing and enlarging throughout all stages of the continuum, even and perhaps especially during continual reuse in the archival dimension (or phase) of the continuum.

These changes imply a fundamentally different type of relationship with our users. This new relationship is one that sees them less as patrons or clients and more as community members, of which we as holders of the records or providers of the service, are now also, even nominally, members. While we have always tried to locate records for researchers, the more active connecting of communities with records, and thus creating communities around records, requires a different set of skills. The former is a more intellectual process; the latter allows for a more affective approach to the records. The former implies that we are gatekeepers; the latter participants, along with our researchers. Social skills and social interactions are at the heart of the emerging web. The web itself, in many ways, presents a self-creating and self-describing world of documentation needing an appraisal and preservation strategy, and, as Helen Samuels counseled, one that archivists should be able to facilitate. "Who controls the past" was defined for Samuels not by "the archivist" alone, but by the collaborative documentary team. Collaboration on the social web now has the potential to engage user communities and archivists in new ways. The answer to "Who represents the past?" is that we all share this responsibility—creators, archivists, and users.

Notes

1 Ed Dilworth, *Wired*, December 2006.

2 Helen Willa Samuels, "Who Controls the Past," *American Archivist* 49 (Spring 1986): 109–24.

3 See, for example, Richard J. Cox, "A Documentation Strategy Case Study: Western New York," *American Archivist* 62 (Spring 1989): 192–200; and Timothy L. Ericson, "To Approximate June Pasture: The Documentation Strategy in the Real World," *Archival Issues* 22, no. 1 (1997): 5–20.

4 Web 2.0 refers to a second generation of Internet services that are more interactive and collaborative, and feature shared control, examples being social networking sites, wikis, and folksonomies.

5 In many instances in this paper, I will use the term *archival representation* instead of *arrangement and description, processing*, or *archival cataloging* because I think this more accurately encompasses all of the activities, goals, and products within this archival function. For more information, see Elizabeth Yakel, "Archival Representation," *Archival Science* 3, no. 1 (2003).

6 Polar Bear Expedition Digital Collections, http://polarbears.si.umich.edu (accessed February 14, 2010).

7 University of Idaho, Repositories of Primary Sources, compiled by Terry Abraham: http://www.uidaho.edu/special-collections/Other.Repositories.html (accessed February 14, 2010).

8 Online Computer Library Center (OCLC), http://www.oclc.org/worldcat/statistics/default.asp (accessed February 14, 2010).

9 OCLC, ArchiveGrid, http://www.lyrasis.org/Products-and-Services/Catalog/A/ArchivesGrid.aspx.

10 See the Online Archive of California, http://www.oac.cdlib.org/; the Rocky Mountain Online Archive, http://rmoa.unm.edu/; and the Northwest Digital Archives, http://nwda.wsulibs.wsu.edu/ (accessed February 14, 2010).

11 Library of Congress, American Memory, http://memory.loc.gov/ammem/about/about.html (accessed February 14, 2010).

12 Online Archive of California, http://www.oac.cdlib.org/ (accessed February 14, 2010).

13 An excellent discussion of the ramifications of this appears in Andrew Prescott, "The Imaging of Historical Documents," in *The Virtual Representation of the Past*, ed. Mark Greengrass and Lorna Hughes (London: Ashgate, 2008), 8–22.

14 Michael J. Fox and Peter Wilkerson, *Introduction to Archival Arrangement and Description: Access to Cultural Heritage*, ed. Susanne Warren (Los Angeles: Getty Research Institute, 1998), available at http://www.getty.edu/research/conducting_research/standards/introarchives/ (accessed February 14, 2010).

15 Adrian Cunningham, "Harnessing the Power of Provenance in Archival Description: An Australian Perspective on the Development of the Second Edition of ISAAR (CPF)" in *Respect for Authority: Authority Control, Context Control, and Archival Description*, ed. Jean Dryden (Binghamton, NY: Haworth Press, 2007), 15–31.

16 Ala Rekrut, "Material Literacy: Reading Records as Material Culture," *Proceedings of the First International Conference on the History of Records and Archives* (I-CHORA), October 2–4, 2003 (Toronto: Faculty of Information Studies, 2003).

17 Helen Tibbo, "Primarily History in America: How U.S. Historians Search for Primary Materials at the Dawn of the Digital Age," *American Archivist* 66 (Spring/Summer 2003); and Ian Anderson, "Are You Being Served? Historians and the Search for Primary Sources," *Archivaria* 58 (Fall 2004).

18 Zotero: http://www.zotero.org/ (accessed February 14, 2010).

19 CiteULike is a social bookmarking cite where people can keep track of their own citations and share them with others: see http://www.citeulike.org/ (accessed February 14, 2010).

20 Richard Lehane, "Picturing Original Order: The Image Map Finding Aid," http://sites.google.com/site/richardlehane/arrangement-and-description/picturing-original-order/image-map-finding-aid (accessed February 14, 2010).

21 Brien Brothman, "Orders of Value: Probing the Theoretical Terms of Archival Practice," *Archivaria* 32 (Summer 1991): 85.

22 Prescott, "The Imaging of Historical Documents," 13.

23 Tim Hitchcock, "Digital Searching and the Re-formation of Historical Knowledge," in Greengrass and Hughes, *Virtual Representation of the Past*, 89. In Hitchcock's view, the decontextualization of archival materials or even parts of archival records allows us to look at each one anew and without preconceived notions about authenticity and reliability. Yet without the structuring elements, such as provenance, original order, and finding aid organization, records also lose meaning.

24 Australian Science Archives Project, Bright Sparcs, http://www.asap.unimelb.edu.au/bsparcs/bsparcshome.htm (accessed February 14, 2010).

25 For a review of some community-generated metadata standards, see Sheila S. Intner, Susan S. Lazinger, and Jean Weihs, *Metadata and its Impact on Libraries* (Westport, CT: Libraries Unlimited, 2006).

26 Finding Aid for the William Muschenheim Architectural Drawings and Papers, http://quod.lib.umich.edu/cgi/f/findaid/findaid-idx?c=bhlead&idno=umich-bhl-02160 (accessed February 14, 2010).

27 Fernanda B. Viégas, Martin Wattenberg, and Dave Kushal, "Studying Cooperation and Conflict between Authors with *History Flow* Visualizations," *Proceedings of CHI 2004* (Vienna, Austria: April 24–29, 2004), 575–76.

28 Darlene Fichter, "Web 2.0, Library 2.0 and Radical Trust: A First Take," http://library2.usask.ca/~fichter/blog_on_the_side/2006/04/web-2.html (accessed February 14, 2010).

29 Haags Gemeentearchief, http://www.denhaag.nl/smartsite.html?id=42061&zoekwaar=ketelaar (accessed February 14, 2010).

30 Library and Archives Canada, Project Naming, http://www.collectionscanada.gc.ca/inuit/index-e.html (accessed February 14, 2010).

31 Archives of Manitoba, Rearview: Emma Louisa Averill, http://www.gov.mb.ca/rearview/averill/index.html (accessed February 14, 2010).

32 Katie Shilton and Ramesh Srinivasan, "Participatory Appraisal and Arrangement for Multicultural Archival Collections," 8, http://polaris.gseis.ucla.edu/srinivasan/Research/Proofs/Shilton%20Srinivasan%20Multicultural%20Archives%20final.pdf (accessed February 14, 2010). Also published in *Archivaria* 63 (Spring 2007).

33 National Archives of the United Kingdom, Your Arthives; for example, see the entry for MT 9/1219: http://yourarchives.nationalarchives.gov.uk/index.php?title=MT_9/1219 (accessed February 14, 2010).

34 National Archives of the United Kingdom, Your Archives, http://yourarchives.nationalarchives.gov.uk/index.php?title=Home_page (accessed February 14, 2010). The underlined phrases in the quotation are all hyperlinked to those other descriptive tools.

35 Fernanda B. Viégas, Martin Wattenberg, Jesse Kriss, and Frank van Ham, "Talk Before You Type: Coordination in Wikipedia," *Proceedings of the 40th Annual Hawaii International Conference on System Sciences* (2007).

36 For representative articles, see Sue McKemmish, Anne Gilliland-Swetland, and Eric Ketelaar, "'Communities of Memory': Pluralising Archival Research and Education Agendas," *Archives and Manuscripts* 33, no. 1 (2005): 4; Laura Millar, "Subject or Object? Shaping and Reshaping the Intersections between Aboriginal and Non-Aboriginal Records," *Archival Science* 6 (2006): 329–50; and Krisztina Laszlo, "Ethnographic Archival Records and Cultural Property," *Archivaria* 61 (2006): 299–308.

37 Shilton and Srinivasan, "Participatory Appraisal and Arrangement for Multicultural Archival Collections," 8.

38 Wendy M. Duff and Verne Harris, "Stories and Names: Archival Description as Narrating Records and Constructing Meanings," *Archival Science* 2, nos. 3–4 (2002): 263–85.

39 Michelle Light and Tom Hyry, "Colophons and Annotations: New Directions for the Finding Aid," *American Archivist* 65 (Fall/Winter 2002): 216–30.

40 Terry Cook, "Fashionable Nonsense or Professional Rebirth: Postmodernism and the Practice of Archives," *Archivaria* 51 (Spring 2001): 32.

41 See Chris Hurley, "Recordkeeping, Document Destruction, and the Law (Heiner, Enron, and McCabe)," *Archives and Manuscripts* 30, no. 2 (November 2002): 6–25; and Susan D. Steinwall, "Appraisal and the FBI Files Case: For Whom Do Archivists Retain Records?" *American Archivist* 49 (Winter 1986): 52–63.

42 *A View to Hugh: Processing the Hugh Morton Photographs and Films*, http://www.lib.unc.edu/blogs/morton/index.php/about/ (accessed February 14, 2010).

43 Cook, "Fashionable Nonsense," 34.

44 Yochai Benkler, "Coase's Penguin, or, Linux and 'the Nature of the Firm," *Yale Law Journal* 112 (2002): 369–446.

45 José van Dijck, *Mediated Memories in the Digital Age* (Stanford, CA: Stanford University Press, 2007).

46 Ohio Historical Society, Ohio Memory: An Online Scrapbook of Ohio History, http://www.ohiomemory.org/index.html (accessed February 14, 2010).

47 Science and Technology in the Making (STIM), http://sloan.stanford.edu/index.htm (accessed February 14, 2010).

48 The September 11 Digital Archive, http://911digitalarchive.org/ (accessed February 14, 2010).

49 Mozilla Digital Memory Bank, http://mozillamemory.org/index.php (accessed April 29, 2009).

50 Moving Here, http://www.movinghere.org.uk/ (accessed February 14, 2010).

51 Your Archives, http://yourarchives.nationalarchives.gov.uk/index.php?title=Home_page (accessed February 14, 2010).

52 Moving Here, http://www.movinghere.org.uk/about/default.htm (accessed February 14, 2010).

53 1967–2007—40 Years of Wright State University, http://www.libraries.wright.edu/40th_wsu/ (accessed February 14, 2010).

54 Ibid.

55 Peter B. Hirtle, "The Impact of Digitization on Special Collections in Libraries," *Libraries and Culture* 37, no. 1 (Winter 2002): 42–52.

56 Isto Huvila, "Participatory Archive: Towards Decentralised Curation, Radical User Orientation, and Broader Contextualization of Records Management," *Archival Science* 8 (2008): 25.

57 Beyond Brown Paper, Comments on item 860: http://beyondbrownpaper.plymouth.edu/item/973#comment-8990 (accessed February 14, 2010).

58 Sebastian Chan, "Commons on Flickr—A Report, Some Concepts and a FAQ: The First 3 Months from the Powerhouse Museum," July 21, 2008, http://www.powerhousemuseum.com/dmsblog/index.php/2008/07/21/commons-on-flickr-a-report-some-concepts-and-an-faq-the-first-3-months-from-the-powerhouse-museum/ (accessed February 14, 2010).

59 Heather MacNeil, "Picking Our Text: Archival Description, Authenticity, and the Archivist as Editor," *American Archivist* 68 (Fall/Winter 2005): 264–78.

60 Polar Bear Expedition Digital Collections, comments on A.O. Mowat: http://polarbears.si.umich.edu/index.pl?node_id=4768&lastnode_id=7328 (accessed February 14, 2010).

61 Derek L. Hansen, Mark S. Ackerman, Paul J. Resnick, and Sean Munson, "Virtual Community Maintenance with a Collaborative Repository," *Proceedings of the American Society for Information Science and Technology* 41, no. 1 (2007): 1–20.

62 Everglades Digital Library, http://cwis.fcla.edu/edl/SPT--Home.php (accessed February 14, 2010).

63 Tom Thurston, "Building Social Networks with Computer Networks: A New Deal for Teaching and Learning," http://www.historycooperative.org/journals/ht/34.2/thurston.html (accessed February 14, 2010).

64 Laura Millar, "An Obligation of Trust: Speculations on Accountability and Description," *American Archivist* 69 (Spring/Summer 2006): 60–78.

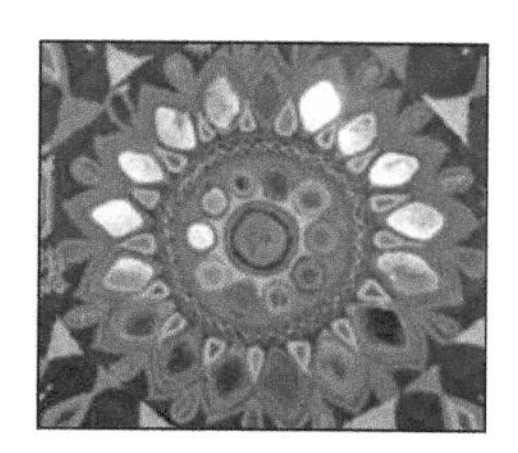

DESIGNS FOR RECORDS AND RECORDKEEPING: VISUAL PRESENTATION IN DIPLOMATICS, THE RECORD CONTINUUM, AND DOCUMENTATION STRATEGY

Brien Brothman

If a three-dimensional map could be made of the different types of records that occupy an imagined archival consciousness, the place name "Text" would undoubtedly arch over the largest expanse and penetrate deepest into the profession's psyche. It almost goes without saying that the archival profession's theories, methods, concepts, and practices have been and largely remain text-driven. Its perspectives on the meaning of "record" along with the contemporary framing of recordkeeping's mission and methodology all bear a "writerly" stamp. Hugh Taylor's picturesque language effectively captured something of this predisposition: "Archivists are reared for the most part on the heavy gruel of text."[1]

One might refer to this as archives' textual conditioning. This conditioning has actually manifested itself in two ways. Not only in the kinds of records that preoccupy them in their writing and practice, but also in how they choose to express their ideas about recordkeeping, archivists have traditionally drawn on and been drawn to verbal forms of expression. In recent years, however, this has started to change. Not only have archivists become increasingly attuned to the significance of visual (and aural) documents, they have also begun to discover the power— the published archival literature, conference presentations, and archival institutions' websites provide ample evidence—that visual forms of expression can impart to their own representations of the archival realm.

This essay explores the significance of the second of these trends. It investigates the increasingly prominent strategy in records and archival discourse of using visual tools—especially geometric figures—to effectively transform a complex universe of actions, events, objects, relations, and processes related to keeping records and, more generally, information, into entities that are identifiable and so, more manageable, manipulable, and measureable. These visual representations are helping to imprint in the minds of archivists mental pictures and narratives that influence the planning and conduct of their work, and also to justify it to themselves and to outside interests. The power of these symbols partly resides in their aesthetic appeal, for they provide a simplified, accessible, single-point perspective on archival work. This perspective is set in a two-dimensional visual rendering of a world of order, uniformity, controllable precision, categorical purity, and implicitly idealized proportionality, and, indeed, uncluttered objectivity.

It is also important for text-habituated archivists to realize, however, that these representational tools, no less than their textual counterparts, have clearly emerged from very specific socio-cultural contexts and orientations. More specifically, as we shall see, beyond their instrumental and didactic functions, these are aestheticized symbols that carry iconic power. Archivists using these tools have drawn on the representational vocabularies associated with a certain dominant culture of scientific professionalism, along with its ideological orientations. As the Canadian communications and media theorist Harold Innis and many who followed him have observed, every form of mediation carries biases about its presentation of space and time, and favours certain forms of power.

The above arguments are advanced by examining the visual presentation techniques employed by three recordkeeping research projects: the University of British Columbia-led InterPARES I project (IP), which was sponsored by the United States Department of Defense and several other partners and funders; the Australian Record Continuum project (RC); and the Documentation Strategy initiative (DS), in whose development Helen Samuels played such a central role. The focus of the essay is on how visual modeling variously served to advance each project's agenda for the archival profession. The three projects undoubtedly share certain features and, indeed, in some respects, complement each other. These commonalities have been temporarily bracketed in order to better elucidate the particular perspectives and priorities in each project that have attracted attention in the archival community over the last ten or fifteen years. Indeed, notwithstanding their compatibilities, these three projects, in their content, context of development, and modeling methods, are not only distinctive but also different at certain points. Each one's aesthetics, ideological assumptions, and intellectual commitments embody potentially incompatible, even conflicting, points of view. Indeed, this essay lends support to the increasingly accepted Kuhnian view of archival science: historical contexts shape not only the materials archivists work with—arrange and describe and appraise and distribute; historical contexts likewise help to shape the very means and methods archivists develop to conceptualize and present those same materials. In a sense, the message in these projects is partly in the medium of representation.

It has not been very long since the archival profession started using modeling techniques—not in any formal sense, at least. Yet it is already impossible in a single essay to cover all the instances in which diagrams, modeling, and other visual means have been used to present ideas about various aspects of archives, recordkeeping, and what is now emerging as the coming field of information management. In the last few years, visual modeling has spiked dramatically in archival discourse. Not only is there insufficient space for a detailed discussion of the variety of modeling methodologies; there are already too many examples of graphic modeling in archives to cover within a single essay. In truth, there is not even time to adequately address all the aspects and versions of the three modeling efforts that are discussed. The growing number of images and diagrams populating archival publications—in print, in power-point presentations, on the web, and in other forums—needs critical attention. Reading graphic information requires a particular vigilance. This is certainly the case for those of us whose primary knowledge and experience has resided in the analysis, processing, and use of textual materials.

At a time when visual imagery is displacing text as the primary tool of expression in many contemporary venues for public and private communication, visual literacy is becoming a required tool of the archival trade. In cyberspace, for example, iconic imagery is assuming an increasingly dominant position.[2] It is becoming necessary to adjust our sensory equipment by learning to look at texts as image-like, and also to recognize that pictures carry verbal freight. Indeed, a more nuanced perspective seems in order: it is important to acknowledge the iconicity of many contemporary texts. Textual documents have always carried iconic qualities; however, it is becoming especially common today for textual documents to be expressly designed as imagery and to exhibit pictorial, "glyphic," visual rhetorical qualities. In fact, the traditional differentiation between "visual" and "verbal"—graphic and typographic—records may preclude the recognition and analysis of deeper complexities in documentary expression.[3]

This essay, once again, also briefly shows how the appearance of graphic modeling in the archival profession is beholden to broader historical and cultural phenomena. The architects of the information society have relied heavily on visual modeling to present, explain, and promote their designs for a world of myriad document and information systems and networks. Information modelers themselves, however, are heirs to a legacy of socially and historically conditioned ideas and practices.

Recordkeepers, like many other professions, have become implicated in this representational trend. It is always risky to propose historical equivalencies. Yet the contemporary proliferation of visual strategies of presentation invites comparison with other moments in history when societies adopted alternate forms of expression. The current turn from textual to graphic representation suggests, paradoxically, the functional equivalent of the ancient turn from pictorial signs to alphabetic forms of writing. The development of alphabets in place of pictures emerged as a response to the need for simple and fast means of communication in increasingly complex institutions and societies. Current social forms had simply overtaxed existing pictographic means of communication. The adoption of purely abstract symbols of expression (or so they seem now) relinquished the direct representation of worldly objects in favor of "the desire to have signs easy and quick to write, but [which are] less needful that they should be self-explanatory when once the writing community has unanimously adopted the local conventions."[4]

Alphabetic means of expression emerged from a long evolution of gestural, visual, and oral means of communication (gesturing, imitating, drawing, and vocalizing what we think, see, want, need, and feel) to a heavily phonocentric form of inscription (inscribing on a durable medium signs representing the evanescent sounds humans make and hear). At the core of the history of alphabetization is a story of increasing simplification through the reduction of the number of signs. The infinite manipulability of a limited number of signs provided ancient societies with the referential power necessary to cover myriad social objects, ideas, relationships, and transactions.[5]

Along with many other professions, recordkeepers have been finding it useful to use a small number of images available in various modeling languages to develop and communicate their ideas. And they are probably doing so for some of the same reasons that ancient societies turned from pictographs to the alphabet. Today, the vast amount of available textual information on recordkeeping and information systems is overwhelming us, notwithstanding specialists' various efforts to confront this deluge of textual documentation with indexing, filtering, discovery, channeling and other tools. All this has engendered a rather ironic propagation of methods to find dry metaground, and "to freeze energy into representation."[6] Increasingly complex information systems and sophisticated explanations of archives and recordkeeping may also be overrunning verbal description. This, too, has undoubtedly prompted the adoption of more economical visual design tools to simplify the presentation of various aspects of archives.[7]

Visual modeling's most basic purpose is didactic and explanatory, and its main virtues clarity and economy. Good diagrams and models represent not only raw information, but also, the standard texts say, sound reasoning and effective communication. The ideal graphic model provides a nonliteral presentation of terms, concepts, objects, and processes that a verbal interpretation would impoverish.[8] This suggests that even the best literal representations can sometimes confuse or distort highly complex situations and processes. Not unlike medieval illuminations of texts, we have begun to use visual cues to help us cope with mountains of computer-generated, network-disseminated, textual information—information that is simultaneously seducing us and overwhelming us. The best models can convince reviewers that economy of exposition has not sacrificed a good approximation of phenomena whose complexity or detail would be beyond the powers of text to explain effectively.[9] For this reason, and several others, we may be witnessing not merely a "pictorial turn,"[10] but a pictorial *return*, the rise of a secondary pictography.

No less than other forms of communication, however, visual presentation techniques are not merely descriptive; they are interpretative instruments, artifacts of their cultural and historical setting. Notwithstanding their scientific, explanatory intentions, diagrammatic tools take on the shape, so to speak, of their contexts and concerns. Moreover, contextual conditions have influenced the strategic choices of particular visual forms and methods of representation. Diagrammatic rhetoric also tends to represent horizontal relations and, at the same time, to eliminate the temporal intercession in social structures. In other words, it achieves a flattening of social relations and institutional life by reducing the tensional dynamics that occur at the intersection of space and time. For example, the context of a record remains constant only by arbitrarily specifying the limits of an event—the beginning and ending moment, hour, year decade or "age"—of a record or "record series" creation. In addition, such rhetoric (indeed, any kind of rhetoric) can serve effectively to deflect critical attention. That is, beyond their cognitive and didactic functions, abstract visual representations potentially offer their authors refuge from detailed written argument, a path of escape from "the vineyard of the text,"[11] and from the risks and exactions of verbal engagement. Whatever their scientific intentions may be, visual representations can coincidentally disarm readers by relieving them from the burden of processing linear text. This they do by moving individuals from an engaged readerly attitude to one of passive "spectatorship."[12] Pictorial representation, in other words, can circumvent readers' critical, rational processing of information, which textual matter tends to evoke. Indeed, our brains may be predisposed to respond positively to the clean lines of geometric figures.[13]

The three projects examined in this essay merit our attention for several reasons. First, they currently rank among the most familiar and influential research initiatives in contemporary recordkeeping.[14] Indeed, these projects have evolved to a point where each one arguably embodies an example of what Thomas Kuhn called a "scientific paradigm." The knowledge each project encompasses, in other words, stands as, or at least aspires to become established as, what Kuhn dubbed "normal" knowledge. That is, they are positioned to attain the status of conventional professional and textbook wisdom.[15] Second, the projects place diagrams and modeling at center stage in their respective presentations, though this is far less the case for the DS initiative, an absence that deserves comment. Third, each project tries in radically different ways to take advantage of the diagrammatic virtue of simplicity. To anticipate, the IP project gets the lion's share of our attention. Not only does it represent a powerful influence in contemporary archival thinking, it has garnered more material support than many other research projects, and, most pertinently, it seems to have gone farther than the other two initiatives in embracing graphic tools in order to develop and communicate its research. The IP project employs a series of diagrams to simplify the presentation of increasing levels of process detail. By way of contrast, the RC relies on a single image to cope with conceptual complexity, and the DS features only a few heavily textual diagrams to present some fundamentally challenging ideas about the role of archives and archivists in society. Finally, these three efforts represent very different, potentially conflicting, preoccupations. The IP focuses on the development and codification of a diplomatics-inspired scientific methodology for institutional recordkeeping; the RC's images embody something like a social theory of recordkeeping, seeking to address broader questions of recordkeeping as a social phenomenon. In this light, the DS might seem out of place here, for the literature on DS features very few graphic representations. Yet the DS is included here precisely as an obverse sort of evidence: its intriguing ideas and strategies might benefit today from more visual modes of representation.

Helen Samuels' work, in particular, promotes a social activist role for archivists. Her corpus of work represents among the most explicit and complex efforts to find hospitable ground for archivists in the potentially contentious terrain between their virtuous political-citizen role in society and their professional obligation to serve specific institutional interests. Indeed, her work anticipates the growing focus among archivists on the development of inter-institutional collaboration and community documentation development.

Before examining the three projects, a little background context on information/record/system modeling is in order. Modeling methods remain idiosyncratic, narrowly focused, and rather disparate. This is the case notwithstanding well-known standardizing efforts such as the Uniform Modeling Language (UML) and Business Process Language (BPL), to name just two. In addition, good histories of information modeling are hard to find. Such histories as there are have been produced largely from the inside, that is, by members of the information modeling profession. These bear the characteristic strengths and weaknesses of such works. A number of these histories are personal retrospectives,[16] others serve as brief prefaces to presentations of the technical dimension of current modeling challenges and practices, others recount histories as part of contemporary methods development, and still others seem to function as brief *pro forma* backgrounders that dignify a proposed methodology with a dash of historical cachet. As in histories of science written by scientists, these histories have the advantage of offering insights and testimony by practitioners who have been on the spot. However, in their current state, histories of information modeling remain narrowly focused, minimally researched, and exhibit little theoretical sophistication. That is, they show no critical awareness of the explanatory importance of setting methodologies and practices within a broader social and historical context.[17] A second problem is that information modeling to some extent has been replicating the very problem it is meant to solve. At a glance, one might easily conclude that the field of information modeling seems to have contracted the very virus it is meant to overcome. So many information modeling methods and modeling systems already exist today—models, metamodels, and even meta-metamodels—that the challenge of developing a critical account of the phenomenon is not only important, but also already overwhelming.[18]

What about the use of modeling and visual resources in published archival writings? Archivists have been using visual materials to support written text for some time. The earliest examples in the *American Archivist* and *Archivaria* consist of reproductions of records—maps, photographs, three-dimensional artifacts, manuscripts, and other archival materials. Archivists' writings have frequently featured reproductions of the records, holdings, or facilities they were discussing to support or illustrate textual argument and description. The volumes in the SAA's Archival Fundamental Series are similarly sprinkled with matrices, photographs, hand sketches, tables, and text boxes. Nothing that could be called an abstract model or diagram, however, appears in the archival literature until the late 1970s. This arguably marked the beginning of a sporadic interest in the representation of recordkeeping methods and processes, a shift from an almost exclusive concentration on documentary content and its value, to an awakening interest in organizational management science, along with a turn to the visual representation of organizations, systems, methods, and processes.

In 1978, Charles Dollar employed the visual vocabulary of structured systems analysis to deal with the appraisal of machine-readable records.[19] For several years, no one followed his example. A few articles in the early 1980s featured some elementary diagrammatic representations, most often to deal with topics related to information control and retrieval. The use of geometrical shapes, frequently arranged top down, came into favour in the 1980s as a means of highlighting certain aspects of information retrieval. Organizational charts, too, with boxes and arrows representing hierarchical relations, made an occasional appearance. A return to Frank Boles and Julia Marks Young's landmark 1985 article on appraisal, "Exploring the Black Box," held a surprise. Instead of representing a process of inputs and outputs of appraisal separated by unknown factors or processes of transformation, as the "Black Box" of the title leads one to expect, the work contains diagrams looking more like traditional vertical representations of organizational structures. The representations suggest hierarchical relationships, with rectangular boxes each representing an aspect of record evaluation.[20] Other authors decided that framing pages of bulleted text in bolded black boxes or rectangles offered representational advantages—perhaps a primitive precursor of power-point thinking. A few articles similarly framed examples of SGML and EAD text-tagging to illustrate the new possibilities of automated description. In any case, whatever the form of abstract visual representation, vertical orientation tellingly structured many diagrams in the 1980s and 1990s and the representation of archival processes is virtually nonexistent.[21]

It was in the late 1980s that diplomatics came onto the scene in North America. Its prominence in contemporary archival thinking and its integral importance to the IP modeling effort make it necessary to briefly consider its status in the archival profession before moving on to a consideration of the IP diagrams. After a number of years of searching and self-doubt in the mid-twentieth century,[22] the traditional science of diplomatics found renewed vigour in the late 1980s.[23] It was shortly thereafter that the IP modeling project was born, in the mid-1990s. Both have remained powerful presences in the archival world. The concepts of diplomatics have proven invaluable to recordkeepers. At least in the short term, the steadfast promotion of, and focus on, a particular notion of *record* has equipped archivists with a coherent working concept of *record.* This is an important accomplishment, for it has enabled archivists to confront a maelstrom of technological inventions and innovations that significantly traumatized the archival world. Diplomatics has described and reaffirmed the centrality of the concept of authenticity[24] in considerations of record worthiness. Perhaps more crucially, it publicized authenticity's importance outside the recordkeeping profession, particularly among organizational managers and information and computer specialists. Not only has diplomatics been a boon to electronic records management, then, but also the challenges of electronic records have arguably breathed new life into diplomatics.

The light that diplomatics has shone on recordkeeping, however, may have been too brilliant by half. Its beam has certainly shed light on important recordkeeping issues, but may also have blinded some of its most ardent devotees to the exorbitance of its more ambitious claims. Its response to the daunting challenges of electronic records, and the diplomatics-based IP modeling effort, displayed considerable methodological prowess. At the same time, it has also imported with it some of the biases of its historical pedigree. Briefly, it has parlayed its success in addressing a specific problem in electronic records management into a far-reaching gospel of a unified archival science. The glittering prospect of total physical and intellectual control undoubtedly has a strong appeal for many in the archival profession. Its highly prescriptive, scientific pretentions proffer an alternative to the suppler and more complex accounting for archives as a social practice—ideas coming from the likes of Hugh Taylor, Terry Cook, Tom Nesmith, Eric Ketelaar Bernadine Dodge, Verne Harris, Joan Schwartz, Richard Brown, and myself, among others, in their explorations over the last twenty years. And, finally, as we will see in more detail, the IP, impelled by computer technology, has been inculcating in current archival theory a record creator's point of view. In a limited sense, as will be further explained, diplomatics has been transformed from one of several possible critical document-reading methodologies, where it has much to offer, into a document-authoring methodology, where its assumptions are much more problematic.

Diplomatics' professional influence today has a story, doubtless many stories, behind it. In the wake of a number of "crises" in the last part of the twentieth century (a term employed by individuals concerned with diplomatics), European recordkeepers in the field began to call for an expanded "contemporary diplomatics." This signaled an acknowledgment that an epistemological revolution in the modern documentary world was underway, and that it was threatening to overtake diplomatics. Several scholars also began to urge their colleagues to abandon diplomatics' narrow juridical, legalistic perspective on documents, along with the notion that factuality and truthfulness are necessarily the marks of valuable records.[25] To do this, however, it seemed necessary to consider the methods and insights of a host of other disciplines, including social history, social science, linguistics, literary criticism, and, not least, archival science.[26] For the second time in thirty years, a number of experts expressed concern about diplomatics' unduly constricted legal-juridical focus and urged their colleagues to look beyond "la diplomatica tradizionale, storico-erudita e di matrice giuridico-positivista" and to consider "altri ambiti del sapere, alla storia sociale, appunto, e alle scienze dell'uomo…" and "elementi che concorrono a determinare il sociale."[27]

What we have come to recognize as diplomatic knowledge in the archival world may be scientific, but scientific in a way that other scientific endeavors have proven to be scientific. Historical pedigree, professional negotiation, loci of economic resources, and social and cultural conditions, in other words, along with rational choice, timely solutions, and scientific validity, have helped to account for diplomatics' prominence in the archival world.[28]

In North America, proponents of diplomatics, principally Luciana Duranti of the University of British Columbia, have emphasized the view that records, by definition, are products of the force of law, of legal systems. Leaving it at that would be oversimplifying her position, for the terms *juridical* and *legal system* have been redefined more broadly to encompass the concept of *social rules.*[29] The introduction of the idea of *social rules* to bolster diplomatics, however, discounts the long discourse among social scientists and legal scholars about the respective power and influence of laws[30] social rules, and organizational rules.[31] Diplomatics' centuries-old privileging of a juridical (that is, legal) perspective on recordkeeping, then, has reasserted and in some sense re-invented itself in the realm of archives and recordkeeping—and seems to be winning the day—and the IP project has been serving as a powerful vehicle for embedding diplomatics perspectives in archival discourse.

The IP project is one of the most impressive archival research endeavours in the last twenty-five years. Indeed, as archival research goes, it recalls, on a reduced scale, a phenomenon described some fifty years ago as "big science,"[32] for it encompasses projects supported by significant financing, multiple players, several institutions, and many subprojects, each undertaking a piece of a larger research agenda. The scale of the projects and their purpose extend beyond the resources and knowledge of any single scientist or institution.[33] The IP drew together experts from institutions located around the world.[34] Led by Duranti, this group set as its mandate the reaffirmation and renovation of archives to meet the challenges of contemporary technology. It has succeeded in drawing a great deal of attention and praise for its wide-ranging work of research, literature synthesis, and data gathering.[35] For the IP I project, the University of British Columbia had established a partnership with the United States Department of Defense to develop a model of record genesis and preservation. There is much to say about this very influential research project. However, we will focus on two of the project's many diagrams. The two diagrams illustrate the entry of archival research into a broader stream of twentieth-century thought and information design. More precisely, this project marks an intriguing convergence of twentieth-century systems thinking, technology design, and managerial ideology with a seventeenth-century documentary methodology.

Designers, it has been said, are great borrowers. They may draw on resources that fall outside their own borders. That is, abstract models, as pure and rarefied as they may appear, are incompletely understood unless the social and historical context of their design choices is known.[36] Archival system designers are no exception. Duranti, for example, has occasionally invoked the name of theoretical biologist Ludwig van Bertalanffy (1901–1972), the commonly acknowledged father of general systems theory.[37] Understandably, she makes no attempt to place systems thinking in any historical context. Her aim undoubtedly was to position the project within a distinguished systems theory lineage, and also to set the project's methodology within the presumably secure sphere of science, not to engage in historical analysis and criticism.[38] Beyond this, personnel from the Georgia Institute of Technology contributed crucially to the IP's modeling methodology. Especially notable is a paper entitled "System Analysis and Modeling for Archival Scientists."[39]

The rise and entrenchment of systems approaches and systems analysis in contemporary organizations drew much of its early impetus from the U.S. military's effort to develop complex weapons as well as other military manufacturing systems after World War II. One such initiative was the Integrated Computer-Aided Manufacturing (ICAM) project. This was a systems management initiative dating from the early 1970s. It was managed by the United States Air Force at Wright-Patterson AFB Materials Laboratory and was part of a technology modernization effort. This project included the Computers in Manufacturing (CIM) project. Dennis E. Wisnosky, an entrepreneur with longstanding ties to the military, is commonly mentioned as the founder and creator of the ICAM program.[40] The ICAM project was brought about by the advent of state-of-the-art technologies, the pressure of economic restraint, the inability of project managers to cope with increasing aerospace design and manufacturing complexity, and the specter of economic and military competition from abroad. It embodied a practical business improvement effort to reduce the time span for incorporation of compatible and standardized manufacturing techniques and to provide unified direction for industry.[41]

It was out of ICAM that the IDEF modeling methodology emerged and it is this methodology that the IP eventually chose in order to develop its model. The IDEF has enjoyed considerable popularity in recent years. It was first developed for a subproject of ICAM known as the Integrated Information Support System (IISS) project. IDEF stands for ICAM DEFinition, and actually encompasses a family of sixteen modeling methods, though fewer than half have seen the light of day. The IP project used IDEF Ø, a "functional" modeling method.[42] The federal government's National Institute of Standards and Technology (NIST) adopted it as its modeling standard in 1993.[43] Its declared purpose was to address "the need for better analysis and communication techniques for people involved in improving manufacturing productivity."[44]

The IDEF, then, like many important American technological creations, is a spin-off product of military-industrial research cooperation. It arose from collaboration between government and private institutions and systems centered on manufacturing and technology. It was meant to answer the needs of conventional manufacturing environments seeking to control the myriad factors of production in disparate locations. To do this, it relied on an engineering methodology built for institutions handling largely stable objects. IDEF incidentally furnishes a good illustration of the argument advanced that, since the Second World War, America's militarily-based national technological superiority has produced a stream of products that now rival, if they have not already displaced, the country's political icons—the Declaration of Independence and other political documents—as the predominant symbols of American culture.[45]

By the 1960s and 1970s, the systems approach, or systems analysis, had entered the American mainstream. To social scientists, systems analysis seemed to offer a way to bolster disciplines perennially accused of scientific slack. It was not long, however, before critics of systems perspectives also began to make themselves heard. Some suggested that the systems phenomenon, while providing a means for coping with project or production complexity, could also cover projects with a rhetorical veneer of rationality and comprehensiveness.[46] Others saw in the systems movement a new kind of perfectionist utopian thinking. It offered a way to find scientifically respectable ways to solve social problems. As systems analysts were quick to find out, their theories tended to reflect closed environments, where variables were known and controllable—not the best model for dealing with social change, which is usually highly politicized, economically constrained, and unpredictable. It was not long before the use of systems-based approaches also became a subject of critical historical investigation.[47]

By the late 1960s, government and Department of Defense scientific projects had lost their appeal for some scientists, evidenced by an increasing reluctance to sit on defense panels, or to collaborate on military projects. The Internet's origins, for example, are usually traced to J.C.R. Licklider and the ARPANET project. Though connected to the military, it operated at arm's length from the government. Established by the U.S. Department of Defense in 1969, it was a product of the cold war. It is worth pointing out, too, that some of its early developers described ARPANET not as an information project, but as a communication project; it was a wide-area, packet-switching network, meant to build system redundancy that could survive a Soviet nuclear attack. In this sense, it began as a national security project. Its earliest diagrams depict a system topography showing widely dispersed computers located in multiple facilities linked by a text-messaging and information-sharing capability.

The conceptual development of the World Wide Web (WWW) took place largely beyond the confines of military environments, farther from cultures of command and control, and, indeed, outside the United States. Most sources agree that Tim Berners-Lee, an English scientist under contract to CERN (Conseil Européen pour la Recherche Nucléaire) first developed the web concept. The first website was built at CERN and put online in August 1991. It was meant to solve the problem of project information and communication management within CERN. Three years later, the story goes, Berners-Lee founded the World Wide Web.

For our purposes, it is important to note that the objects and processes that appear on the Internet are less amenable to the institutional cultures of centralization, command, and control that gave rise to IDEF. Systems had heretofore been designed for stable environments where control of all factors of production is possible. The traditional hierarchical, military-industrial culture from which IDEF sprang is hardly obsolete. However, freezing energy into representation has become a trickier affair on many levels. The IDEF's built-in cultural assumptions limit its ability to envisage structurally amorphous information and the circulation of increasingly boundary-indifferent flows of highly dispersed information. IDEF modeling ignores, or at least suspends inclusion of, the web of webs, the network of networks, that are intersecting with and impinging upon historically stable, distinct, and hierarchical information-laden formations such as institutions, structures, and documents. In fact, Berners-Lee's early sketch diagrams and proposals, his "distributed hypertext system," prominently feature cloud icons, which are network symbols of uncertainty. His web network model is in a sense "hypercontextual"; it explicitly aimed to overcome the obstacles of hierarchical (vertical) information (and organization) structures and to promote information fluidity and widespread (horizontal) communities. Indeed, the idea of a web was meant to cast off the "restraints on information" that hierarchical order had imposed.[48]

The IDEF and the WWW appeared within a few years of each other. Yet their virtually simultaneous appearance, rather than evidencing a single contemporaneous vision or context, symbolizes a historical encounter between two opposing, but mutually implicating, social-cultural drives: an emerging culture tapping into the excitement and stimulation of constant circulation of social energy tending toward instability and recurrent re-creation, reinvention, and reconfiguration, and an enduring traditional culture of centralization, hierarchy, and control tending toward absolute order, object stability, and dynamic equilibrium—toward persistence. To risk accuracy for succinctness, one might suggest that a latent tension exists between webs (networks) and systems, and between texts and their contexts. Attempts to overcome a technical *communication* barrier in the 1990s spawned a period of profound social change that bears the rather misleading—one might argue, ideologically obfuscating—label of *information revolution.* Indeed, the ideas and language embedded in the discourse of *information* and *information revolution* have prevented many archivists, at least until recently, from more explicitly recognizing recordkeeping within the radically different hermeneutical terms (and images) of a *communication* revolution.

The IP project, then, occupies a place within a history of partnerships between United States military operations research and private scientific expertise. The IP is progeny of systems and cultures immersed in institutional settings. Its roots, its genealogy, run long and deep in environments of centralization, hierarchy, stability, and control, whether in seventeenth-century Bourbon France or twentieth-century corporate structures and organizations.[49] And the IP's modeling method of choice rests on assumptions about distinct, highly structured environments of informational command and control. Commensurately, the Department of Defense–University of British Columbia model starts from the position of what it calls the "record creator point of view."[50] Under this description, the author is king, so to speak. In other words, the IP model, like most other recent recordkeeping research initiatives, rests on the assumption that an archivist's or recordkeeper's primary responsibility is to ensure and support continuing and perpetual author control. This is the starting point from which this model's design, and many other models, proceeds.[51]

In its vocabulary and visual appearance, the IP model of document production bears the marks of its diplomatic, scientific, and system-engineering design history. It organizes its information hierarchically, as each entity or object and process is exploded into increasing decomposition, taking readers downward through levels of increasing detail of administrative and functional and process granularity. This bears rough comparison with the adoption by medieval institutions of documentary formulae, one of whose purposes was to impose uniformity and routine on the details of document preparation and, thereby, to constrain the incidental creative, editing, and interpretive impulses of scribes and copyists.[52] Utter consistency of form and rigid, structured, record-creating discipline, in addition to signifying greater efficiency and conferring legal advantages, projected an image of absolute (self) control and power. (Imagine these records as parading in military uniform!) Beholden to diplomatics' formalist ideology, the IP, at its core, specifies a formal, legal scripting of record creation's meaning and process. As William Leatherdale cautioned:

> Too doctrinaire an axiomatization, or literal reconstruction, even supposing this were possible in any neutral untheoretically-infected way, might free science from the infection of error due to uncritical reliance on a model or metaphor, but it would kill it stone dead in the process.[53]

Once implemented, its technicity is amenable to self-creation and self-discipline, indeed, to automation, which may mask but does not eliminate this formulaic narrowness. True to its IDEF heritage, the model's scope, its self-described context, encompasses a production-control system. That is, the "record creator point of view" represents recordkeeping as a manufacturing process whose inputs (juridical system, various professional standards, organizational mandates and function, and professional knowledge) together comprise codified scripts for a creation/production-side methodology. As such, the model is, potentially, an engineering design for a system of virtually automated archival functionality.[54] It is worth noting, however, that in figure 1, *juridical system* is merely one of four kinds of input that go into the making of a record.[55] One cannot help but wonder whether there is a disjunction here between the diagram and the textual discourse on juridical systems. For consistency's sake, at least, would Duranti's expansive juridical system not require that the three other forms of input be subsumed by the juridical system, which would serve as a sort of "metascript" or codification for the manufacture of records (a fond) at the behest of the record manufacturer's interest?

Figures 1 and 2 contain all of the symbolic elements of an IDEF Ø diagram. The syntax and semantics of its arrows and boxes, carefully defined in the standard, are all here. As figure 2 indicates, the act Create Record encompasses not only the act of writing a document; the *act* actually encompasses several *subsumed actions* set out in a neat sequence, as

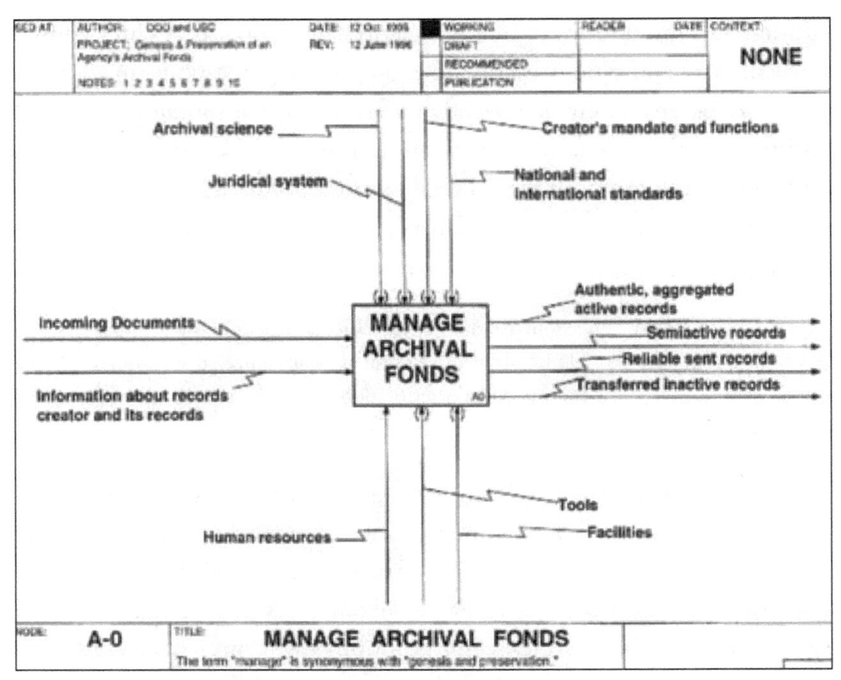

FIGURE 1: "Manage Archival Fonds" diagram from *InterPARES 1: The Preservation of the Integrity of Electronic Records, 1994–1997.*

the numbering of each box indicates—receive, classify, register, and so on. In the language of the IDEF standard, the directional arrows represent "pipelines" or "conduits," a common metaphor of communication design that has not been without its critics.[56] At the same time, this imagery is suggestive of the standard's soothing rhetoric of flowing water or, as the lightning bolts seem to indicate, the movement or flow of electricity. These two images, which typify the project's many modeling diagrams, implicitly evoke the contemporary business-process designer's expression of smooth, well-programmed, and controlled *electrical flows* and *electronic work flows*.

The IP model also draws some of its power from less apparent features. The images exude an appealing rhetoric of objectivity[57] and scientific authority. At a glance, the images evoke an aura of engineering design, step-wise programmable logic, and blueprint precision—down to each diagram's unadorned, neutral, sans serif font.[58] This look serves

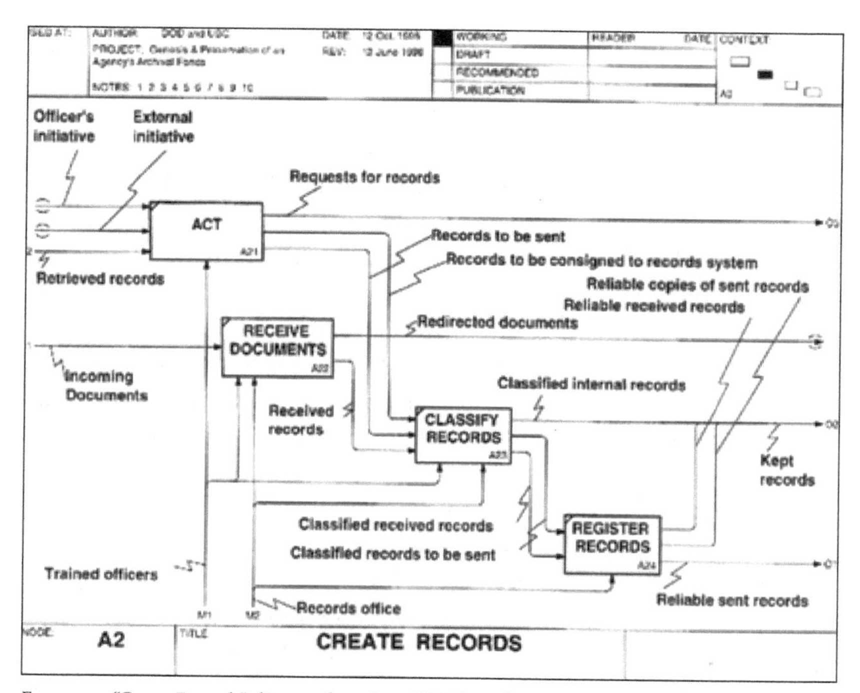

FIGURE 2: "Create Records" diagram from *InterPARES 1: The Preservation of the Integrity of Electronic Records, 1994–1997.*

effectively as a signature that underwrites, that certifies, the Jenkinsonian author's (manufacturer) control. In effect, the IDEF symbolization provided the IP project with new rhetorical tools to achieve several purposes: the images connote currently authoritative professional language and imagery; they simplify the detailed representation of well-established archival concepts and ideas; and they translate these ideas into a symbolic notation familiar to socially influential experts outside the records profession (as does the Open Archival Information System Reference Model), namely information system scientists and technology experts.[59] Set in a visual ambience created by a system-engineering aesthetic, archivists are no longer the handmaidens of history and cultural expression; they are what Duranti and others imagine them to have been throughout their long historical "odyssey," the handmaidens of virtually automated public and private corporate institutions and organizations, thereby placed near the loci of economic and political power.[60] Indeed, one of this project's underlying arguments or assumptions also surfaces in much other current research: authorial hegemony and control over the interpretation of texts. The IP's explicit privileging of the record creator reserves to the creating institution exclusive, that is, monarchical, dominance over the meaning of "its" products. Indeed, the IP diagrams themselves are both performative and illustrative; they simultaneously provide the method for and exemplify the making of a perfect record. This model endows the record creator ("the record creator point of view") with absolute, that is, complete and continuing, control over interpretive choice; it creates the establishment of writer sovereignty over meaning and truth in perpetuity. Diplomatics today rests on a presumptive assertion of what one might call the "divine write" of the absolute author-sovereign.[61] Contemporary diplomatics concerns first and foremost acts of authorship; it entails writerly-producer infallibility.[62] Authors, to the exclusion of readers, remain sole document producers.

Finally, the resurgence of diplomatics in the IP evidences the enduring importance of modern corporate and state formations to contemporary ideas of record making and recordkeeping. The making, managing, and keeping of records and information in accordance with diplomatics' principles, and the concentration of power in modern bureaucratic formations, suit and sustain each other. That is, a particular parity and affinity exist between absolutist social or organizational structures, notions of absolute authorial sovereignty, and the IP project's diplomatically inspired species of document-engineering model. The IP project represents a powerful convergence of several contemporary and historical factors: a homegrown mythology of professional origins, the invocation of the authority and assumptions of engineering and information design, contemporary business/manufacturing perspectives, the "technologization" of archiving, the enlistment of generous corporate support, along with a hallowed 350-year-old document reading-cum-creation methodology. Beyond this, the power of the project's visual rhetoric undoubtedly instances an accurate reading of the emerging cultural predispositions of professional opinion makers and contemporary audiences.[63] Presented in words as an objective precision science, and connoting in pictures a systems engineering-backed and technologically neutral effort, the IP might easily lead readers to forget that, for all of the undoubted benefits it has bestowed, it speaks—and draws—with a particular outlook, one that lacks the suppleness to accommodate the many other sites of record formation that archivists have been investigating at least since the appearance of the idea of societal documentation strategies. It is built on longstanding, constrained and constraining institution-bound notions of record creation context that simply forego more complex understandings of contextuality. Diplomatics' contemporary emplotment of records and recordkeeping bears the influence of its historical development as well as the institutional and socio-cultural conditions of its recent self-reinvention and inventors.

The Record Continuum (RC) sets recordkeeping down in a radically different world. Its imagery has little, if anything, in common with the IP's. Where the IP model consists of many diagrams, the RC features a single image (though a number of additional images elaborating on the same initial one were eventually produced). Also, the RC's iconography is more distinctive than the IP's. Remove the textual labeling from the IP diagrams and one would be hard pressed to guess what kind of system or business line or process is being depicted. Without the labeling, the IP could be representing any production system. It is heavily dependent, in other words, on text for its identity. Remove the textual tagging from the RC, however, and many people in the field could still likely identify it. Its uniqueness makes it immediately recognizable; its iconic power, at least, may turn out to be more enduring than the IP's. Lastly, unlike the IP project's engineering iconography of finite systems and systems analysis, the RC developed imagery that recalls the illustrations of early modern astronomy, of orbits and cycles, of a vast universe, and of documents traveling in some less readily recognizable dimension of time and space.[64] This is not the science of "archivology"; in its imagery and rhetoric, this project gestures toward something between a religious and scientific cosmology. The web version's deep blue tone suggests some heavenly region, and the objects and phenomena it depicts seem to dwell and move in some sort of mysterious deep space. Indeed, Frank Upward, principal progenitor of the RC, wrote that its "dimensions and axes clarify the threading outwards to deeper reaches of time and space."[65]

The RC earns high marks for iconic and conceptual originality. The IP's strength resides in the way its modeling method helps to steer readers steadily through increasing levels of functional detail. To do so, it uses well-known modeling tools. The presentation is detailed, systematic and clear; this is part of its appeal. It effectively entrenches long-standing, though not always uncontested, ideas of records and recordkeeping. The RC, on the other hand, leaves more work for readers to do. Not only does this single, seemingly simple, image hold far more conceptual complexity than does the IP's highly articulated model; it also sets recordkeeping down in a vast and rich, but rather unfamiliar realm.

The IP project's context is bounded by institutional settings of record manufacture. Indeed, the context for its top-level context is, rather unsatisfactorily, "None" (see figure 1), which some have considered a shortcoming of the IDEF system.[66] The RC includes record creation, but places the making of records in the temporally expansive, and more complex, context of social and collective memory. In fact, this is probably selling the RC short: the RC's ambition—boundless ambition, one might say—is to open our eyes to unsuspected levels of documentary reality, to uncover for us temporal and spatial dimensions of recordkeeping that have hitherto remained largely invisible to us in our traditional and (as it turns out) parochial documentary world. Its authors' subsequent interpretation and elaboration on the original image have lead its creative director, Frank Upward, to introduce the notion of a *spacetime continuum,* a concept taken from the early twentieth-century Viennese mathematician Hermann Minkowski.

Upward's dense presentational style can discourage readers from giving a serious hearing to his complex vision of archives. Spacetime is a counter-intuitive concept, as it asks us to forego our comfortable linear notions of time. In addition, Upward's proneness to grandiloquent rhetoric and intellectual turgidity, along with his occasionally glib dismissal of those who cannot grasp his sometimes-opaque exposition of the RC's spacetime complexities, have surely limited its influence. It would be a mistake, however, to underestimate the continuum's conceptual brilliance. At the same time, it would also be wrong to overlook its seemingly willful dismissal of the social and cultural context that sets limits on its scientific pretensions. The IP project brackets the *reading of records* as part of the context of their formation. Upward, on the other hand, seems to ask us to set aside the historical context from which the RC emerged. This seems like special pleading for an exemption from contextual analysis of the RC—an especially curious demand for an archivist to make.[67]

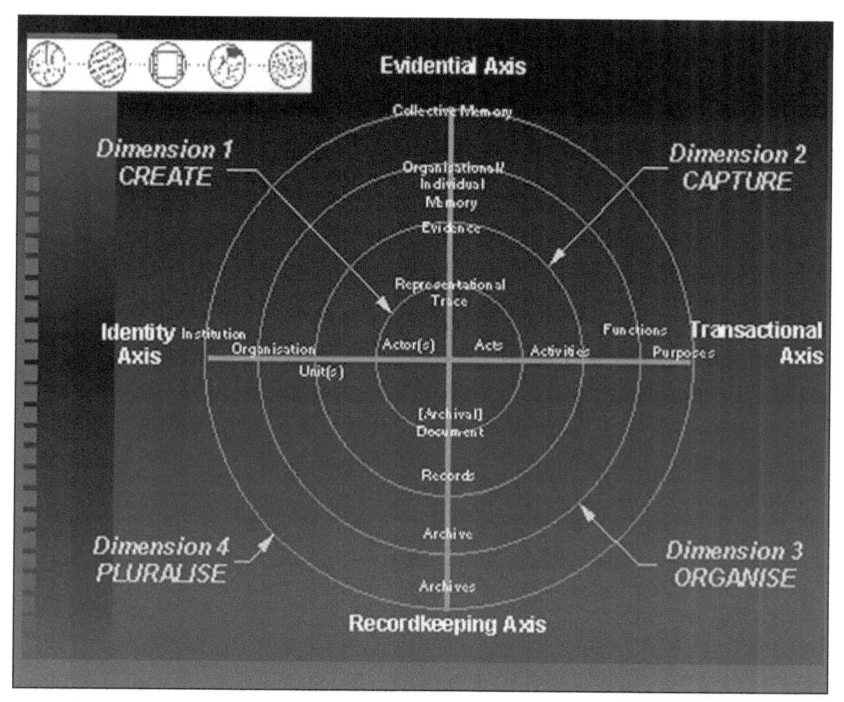

FIGURE 3: *Records Continuum Diagram, 1997.*

To be fair, the IP and the RC projects have different goals. The IP, staffed by individuals from a highly operational culture, succeeded in developing a detailed scheme for an automated, system-friendly record-creation program. The RC provides a plausible theoretical explanation of recordkeeping. The IP describes a systems environment and provides pertinent specifications, but ignores the social context, the boundary forces that can condition the behavior of ostensibly juridically controlled, diplomatically informed, information systems. The RC's impact, on the other hand, may be limited by the leap of imagination it takes to comprehend its cosmological scale, and also by the many interpretive possibilities its opaque language licenses.[68]

It is not entirely surprising that Upward himself has only gradually arrived at a notion of continuum that satisfies him. In his early work, the writings of social theorist Anthony Giddens inspired him to examine the issue of space and time. Later, he supplemented his thinking with

Minkowski's notions of spacetime and continuum as well as the mathematician's revolutionary idea of *four dimensionality.* This latter notion posits that physical objects possess not only discrete spatial parts, but also multiple observer-dependent temporal dimensions.[69] Unless one can grasp the ideas of spacetime and four-dimensionality, the more radical and unsettling ramifications of a record continuum setting will not be appreciated.[70] And finally, the concentric circles might leave one with the impression that the innermost circle represents a dominant centre or core. Yet this would be misreading the text, for the continuum, by implication at least, precludes the existence of any completely determinant point at which "recordness" appears once and for all time.[71]

So where does Documentation Strategy (DS) fit into all this? DS is an approach to recordkeeping that came into its own in the 1980s. It provided archivists with a powerful and, for many, appealing vision of what recordkeeping might, or should, become. Among those who led the way was Helen Samuels. DS remains *de rigueur* in archival studies curricula. To a degree, however, events seem to have overtaken it and obscured its early ethical and political undercurrents. Yet the DS's vision falls somewhere between the RC and IP models. Between the RC's recognition that archivists need to remain sensitive to the broader socio-historical context in which institutional records are made and kept,[72] and the IP's emphasis on the importance of improving the means individual institutions and organizations use to deal with their records, lies the DS.

Helen Samuels was a major progenitor of and publicist for these efforts. At this time, her name is the one that probably remains most closely associated with the DS. Based at the MIT archives, she reached out to colleagues in other institutions with a vision that anticipated and combined the RC's broader conception of recordkeeping in society and the IP's more focused and legal-juridical perspective on administrative-institutional record creation. Her contribution to the articulation of the DS, combined with her later work on functional analysis in university environments,[73] joined with an ability to present her ideas in a concise and accessible manner, stands as an enduring contribution to archival discourse. Even *Varsity Letters*, which focused on the documentation of individual academic institutions, continued to emphasize the importance for archivists to look beyond their own institutional boundaries and interests and to take heed of the complex organizational, technological, and social relationships in which institutions and their records are inevitably embedded.[74]

The DS has experienced variable success, for reasons some critics were quick to point out. First, attempts to implement it have sometimes encountered logistical challenges (and funding problems) inherent in gathering together in one place records managers, archivists, and subject specialists, as well as users from multiple institutions—often in different cities and states—to articulate the scope of the documentation topic, a common mission, and a research agenda that could accommodate multi-institutional interests and efforts. The irony is that the emergence of networking technology has enabled people from outside the field of archives to develop tools that could make Samuels' vision possible. The advent of research on collaborative computing technologies, "federated" information environments, and collaborative software are providing the means to conduct inter-institutional research in multiple fields, disciplines, and locations exactly as Samuels counseled for the DS's research agenda. In this sense, her visionary approach may be seen as "right idea, wrong timing," but now the timing is much better. Second, the DS, at its inception, incorporated a political agenda into its work. This involved a determination to document individuals, classes, and groups that traditional archives had neglected.[75] Samuels' opus has aimed to address a difficult challenge—to somehow bridge the gap between the necessarily self-interested records management focus on the well-being of individual institutions (and the records therein) and the archival consciousness of participation in a broader collective socio-historical process. The DS stands astride the legal and business charge to preemptively create and keep protective (probative) documentation and the archivist's intellectual and moral burden to understand the creator's self-defined (and often self-interested) context, but also to identify the broader social and cultural processes of which individuals and organizations and their documentation form a part. Finally, her work emphasized the importance of understanding how archival records might be described, organized, and presented in a way that promotes the documentation of society, and contributes to the shaping of the collective memory. In her article "Improving Our Disposition," for example, Samuels ambitiously set out to articulate a position that mediated between the potentially conflicting roles of working on behalf of individual institutional interests and trying to engage in documentation strategy's broader perspective on adequate documentation of communities and society. It was this intention that drove her to insist that archivists must take an active role in establishing a documentary record for those who might otherwise be deprived of one.[76]

Helen Samuels' work anticipated and presented, often with greater clarity, much that both the IP and RC now proffer. Hand in hand with the urgency of addressing an increasingly diffuse information landscape, her writings manifest a keen awareness of the increasingly crowded information management landscape, where many other social actors are playing an important role in the creation and control of information. In "Who Controls the Past," for example, she sounds a warning that proper documentation, whether of institutions or issues, increasingly depends on a mastery of the "technologized," that is, networked information landscape. This requires rethinking the division of labor among disparate institutions.[77] The DS has done much to awaken the archival consciousness of recordkeepers. For the time being, it has been overshadowed by more recent work whose presentation is marked by greater technical sophistication, perhaps, but which demonstrates no greater—and often less—theoretical acumen.

Those who have participated in the development and presentation of the DS have used visual imagery sparingly. At most, bulleted text was placed in text boxes. The one exception is an article by Larry Hackman and Joan Warnow-Blewett, which used visual tools to present a DS "process model."[78] The effort was a rudimentary one. Showing its age, even its visual presentation was heavily text-dependent and hardly taps the power of visual exposition. This was a good beginning that needed follow-up, a thread that was dropped prematurely. Ironically, however, the DS may be an ideal candidate for visual modeling. With the increasing availability of collaborative workspaces, net communication tools, standardized record description and description interchange standards, not to mention sophisticated visualization tools, the DS seems like an idea that is well suited to take advantage of collaborative research and business tools. In a sense, documentation strategy may have appeared a few years too soon, but only a few. Perhaps all that documentation strategy needs is an effective, memorable visual rhetoric now that network technology has potentially solved the logistical problems it encountered early on.

There is undoubtedly some truth in the adage that a picture is worth a thousand words. However, the research we have reviewed points to a number of other truths: a single picture can also hide a thousand words—and a single term can evoke a thousand images. The three projects discussed above represent some of the most advanced thinking about recordkeeping. The use of visual representation, especially in two of the cases, bolstered already powerful agendas and rich perspectives on the meanings and methods of keeping records. Spatial representation of information management and recordkeeping, however, can also often obscure the complex temporality that constantly disturbs a document's settling comfortably into the fixed state that "recordness" alleges for it. This aspect of record formation must be brought more into view in our models of archives and archiving. Visual models tend to highlight the movement of information across space, across structures. Such representations can vitiate the representation of archives' principal role and function, which is not merely to control *information*. Rather, it is their principal, and inevitably creative, responsibility to engage in the *communication* of messages in the historical process across time.

Recordkeepers certainly have responsibilities to record producers. Yet, beyond this point, archival theory—arrangement and description, appraisal, preservation, and so on—seems to fade to a whisper. Current theories of recordkeeping allow little room for the overlapping and tensional aspects of producer, distributor, and consumer perspectives and interests. Creator, transmitter, and reader all play a part in what has been described elsewhere as "record formation."[79] Archives—archivists—are bound to engage in transmissive and creative-interpretive social action. Archives form part of a process of intergenerational shaping of documentary meaning. Within the framework of social communication across generations, the clear lines of difference among author, deliverer, and reader lose some of their sharpness. Yet some of the most dominant contemporary models of records and archives, especially the IP, tend to shield their work from these disruptive dimensions of the socio-temporal life of documents.

Recordkeeping is now being firmly embedded in information systems, which are being built to create, capture, and disseminate mathematically accurate and reliable testimony to "truth." Those who aim to design perfect records and flawless systems ignore an inconvenient truth:

archivists, as preservers, are situated in a creative-transmissive relationship with record creators. Archivists form part of a hermeneutic, that is, an interpreting chain. As such, as a community of actors whose approach to information artifacts is marked by professional, organizational, institutional, national, ethnic, philosophical, and other biases, assumptions, commitments, goals, and values, it cannot be otherwise. The tendency of contemporary archival theory to deify the (record) producer, and, perhaps incidentally, to occlude the reader from its concept of record formation, is understandable; the fragility of electronically created records seems to have impelled us toward what has been called an up-front, preemptive approach. This is a reasonable and appropriate response to the information technology revolution. Indeed, our profession is having its say about the contours of that revolution.

This does not absolve us, however, of responsibility to recognize that computer technology, like all previous media, arrive at archives' portal already carrying social, linguistic, symbolic, political, and ideological baggage. Thus, the information revolution is itself already a mental and social construct, nothing more and nothing less than a historical artifact. Like all revolutions, the information revolution has both impelled archivists to rewrite their past and marked the archival profession's own destiny and direction.[80] These events have elicited some remarkable innovations and adaptations from the archival profession, including those reviewed here. By its spatial horizontal bias, however, current research in information and record science has also too often entailed a foreclosure on, a foreshortening of, archival spacetime. It is important for archivists to apprehend the many *meanings* of past, present, and future. A new temporal sensibility will compel us to rethink the relationship between the concepts of creation, keeping, distribution, and use, and to enhance a peculiarly archival consciousness of records in the flow of time. It is important to acknowledge and promote the particular temporal complexity and extension in the archival imagination of notions like community, institution, and nation.

Finally, archivists need to rethink the habitual differentiations between textual and visual forms of expression. This is one more longstanding categorical differentiation that website environments and digital media appear to be putting under strain. With respect to archives, it is emerging that giving content and structure and context to records is—perhaps always has been—a sort of exercise in graphic design, and that the power in even textual record lies partly in their imagistic qualities. Conversely, graphic images have always been invested with verbal freight; seeing, in a way, involves a semantic processing of information. Thus, notions like content and structure are perhaps less distinctive than once thought, or, at least, once were. One can speak of the content of record design and the design of record content, or, perhaps, the genres of various documents. Design choice—the often invisible rhetoric of representation—occurs in all documents: bureaucratic *forms*, private *letters*, corporate websites, layout of reports and studies, films, photographs, and so on. But this also includes graphic representations of archival methods and processes themselves, and schematic textual representation of an archives' hierarchical, clustered, or networked system of arrangement of context, content, and structure. And so the phenomenon of "mixed media" may have a longer and more complex history than has been recognized. The archival brain needs to recalibrate its conceptualization of seeing/reading/hearing. It needs to refresh its critical theories, philosophies, and semiotics of records design, both for the records it encounters and, as we have seen in this essay, for the designs of the archives itself.

Notes

It is with pleasure that I express gratitude to Terry Cook for sharing with me his unsurpassed knowledge of the archival literature as well as his numerous suggestions for sharpening the argument of the essay. Any errors of fact or interpretation remain entirely mine.

1 Hugh Taylor, quoted in Elisabeth Kaplan and Jeffrey Mifflin, "'Mind and Sight': Visual Literacy and Archivists," *Archival Issues* 21, no. 2 (1996), 119.

2 Jay David Bolter, *Writing Space: Computers, Hypertext, and the Remediation of Print* (Mahwah, NJ: Lawrence Erlbaum, 2000), ch. 1 passim. The increasingly imagistic look and feel of textual documents is well discussed by W. J. T. Mitchell in various works. One need only enter the phrase "information visualization" in Google to get a rough idea of the scope of interest—admittedly in a biased medium with a self-selecting population.

3 For an interesting account of the imagistic aspects of writing, see Ann-Marie Christin, "L'Ecriture et l'Image," in *Collège* 8, no. 1 (1997): 1–33.

4 As George Rawlinson observed of the alphabet, "Its primary merit was that of simplicity." *History of Phoenicia* (Longmans, Green, 1889), 377; David Diringer, *Writing* (Frederick A. Praeger, 1962), ch. 5; and A.C. Moorhouse, *The Triumph of the Alphabet: A History of Writing* (Henry Schumann, 1953), 13. Interestingly, Peter Chen, a pioneer in information modeling and the developer of Entity-Relationship modeling in the 1970s, explains that he perceived a relationship between Entity-Relationship modeling and ancient Egyptian pictographic languages: "That's the reason I spent a lot of time looking at ancient Egyptian languages in the last few years. Actually, I have probably 20 books on Egyptian hieroglyph languages." Marianne

Winslett. "Interview with Peter Chen. Peter Chen Speaks Out," *SIGMOD Record* 33, no. 1 (March 2004).

5 Eric Havelock, "The Oral-Literate Equation: A Formula for the Modern Mind," in *Literacy, Language, and Learning: The Nature and Consequences of Reading and Writing*, ed. David Olson and Nancy Torrance (Cambridge: Cambridge University Press, 1985).

6 W. F. Garrett-Betts and Donald Lawrence, "Thawing Frozen Image/Word: Vernacular Post-modern Aesthetics," *Mosaic* 31 (1998).

7 Interestingly, early system modelers from the 1970s later judged their own work to have been "ponderous tomes" weighted down with too much textual description, like massive "Victorian novels." Ed Yourdon, "Just Enough Structured Systems Analysis," ch. 7, at http://www.yourdon.com/PDF/JESA/JESAchpt7.pdf (Dec. 2006). An MIT-trained computer scientist, Yourdon is a renowned consulting software engineer and among the active model developers from the 1970s. He remains a prolific author, conference speaker, and consultant.

8 Stuart Peterfreund, *Literature and Science* (Boston: Northeastern University Press, 1990), 61–67. See also W. H. Leatherdale, *The Role of Analogy, Model and Metaphor in Science* (Amsterdam: North-Holland, 1974).

9 T. E. Rihll and A. G. Wilson, "Modelling Settlement Structures in Ancient Greece: New Approaches to the Polis," in *City and Country in the Ancient World*, ed. John Rich and Andrew Wallace-Hadrill (London: Routledge, 1992), 62.

10 "Pictorial Turn" is a phrase coined by W. J. T. Mitchell in his *Picture Theory: Essays on Visual and Verbal Representation* (Chicago and London: University of Chicago Press, 1994), 11.

11 Ivan Illich, *In the Vineyard of the Text: A Commentary to Hugh's Didascalicon* (Chicago: University of Chicago Press, 1993).

12 Susan Reilly, review of *Picture Theory* by W. J. T. Mitchell, *Other Voices* 1, no. 2 (September 1998). "When humans see simple shapes and forms or orderly arrangements they tend to be attracted to them and focus on their qualities."

13 Derek Hodgson, "Understanding the Origins of Paleoart. The Neuorovisual Resonance Theory and Brain Functioning," *Paleoanthropology* (2006), 54–67.

14 A number of obvious and significant omissions from this article are the Reference Model for Open Archives Information System, whose intervention in archival discourse with a new visual and verbal semantics has exerted significant influence on how archivists conceive of and speak about records and information systems. In fact, OAIS is one of several initiatives that form part of systems analysis's—information science's—conquest of archival discourse. One might also make a strong argument for the Pittsburgh Project as well as writings on macroappraisal for inclusion. For a comparison and critique of the Pittsburgh and UBC modeling efforts, see Paul Marsden, "When is the Future? Comparative Notes on the Electronic Record-Keeping Projects of the University of Pittsburgh and the University of British Columbia," *Archivaria* 43 (Spring 1997), 158–73.

15 Thomas Kuhn, *The Structure of Scientific Revolutions* (Chicago: University of Chicago Press, 1962). For a history of archival research that laments archival scholarship's failure to achieve the status of a universal, unified science, see Luciana Duranti, "The Future of Archival Scholarship," University College Dublin, October 1998, http://www.ucd.ie/archives/html/conferences/luciana-notes.htm.

16 For example, James Rumbaugh, *OMT Insights* (New York: SIGS Books, 1996), reprinting essays that appeared in the *Journal of Object Oriented Programming* between 1992 and 1995. The chapter on "Black Boxes" is particularly useful.

17 See Ted Codd, "A Relational Model of Data for Large Shared Data Banks," *Communications of the ACM* 13, no. 6 (June 1970); Peter Pin-Shan Chen, "The Entity-Relationship Model—Toward a Unified View of Data," *ACM Transactions on Database Systems* 1, no. 1 (1976). See also John Mylopoulos, "Information Modeling in the Time of Revolution," *Information Systems* 23, nos. 3–4 (June 1998). Of tangential interest are the many scholarly works on the history of scientific visualization and technical illustration. See Brian Baigrie, ed., *Picturing Knowledge: Historical and Philosophical Problems Concerning the Use of Art in Science* (Toronto: University of Toronto Press, 1996). Edward Tufte's intriguing works on visualization, though more theoretical and practical than historical, are worth mentioning. There is also an abundance of information

covering the influence of computer technology on design practices. Finally, it might have been useful to explore the emerging field of design history. A brief excursus, however, failed to reveal any significant attention to information system design. Rather, *design history* and *graphic design history* tend to refer to commercial advertising design, the design of industrial and consumer products, as well as software that captures and records the steps and progress of current system designs, See, for example, the *Journal of Design History* (2004–2007).

18 To get a good sense of the range of contemporary information modeling techniques, see the excellent overview in the *Periodic Table of Visualizations* at the Information Aesthetics website. It includes seventy-two modeling methods, with visual examples of each one: http://infosthetics.com/archives/2007/01/periodic_table_of_visualization_methods.html. Another somewhat useful source is Alan F. Blackwell and Yuri Engelhardt, "A Taxonomy of Diagram Taxonomies," http://www.cl.cam.ac.uk/~afb21/publications/TwD98.html. Also of interest is Alan Blackwell, *Metaphor in Diagrams* (PhD thesis, University of Cambridge, 1998), http://www.cl.cam.ac.uk/~afb21/publications/thesis/index.html.

19 Charles Dollar, "Appraising Machine-Readable Records," *American Archivist* 41 (October 1978), 423–30.

20 Frank Boles and Julia Marks Young, "Exploring the Black Box: The Appraisal of University Administrative Records," *American Archivist* 48 (Spring 1985).

21 Notable exceptions are John MacDonald's graphics, which, though visually lacking explanatory power, nevertheless manage to provide some prescient bits of information; see his "Managing Information in an Office Systems Environment. The IMOSA Project," *American Archivist* 58 (Spring 1995). See also David Bearman's "Description Standards: A Framework for Action," *American Archivist* 52 (Fall 1989).

22 Many years earlier, in the 1960s, diplomatics had also experienced an identity crisis. See Leonard Boyle, "Diplomatics," in *Medieval Studies: An Introduction*, ed. James M. Powell (Syracuse: Syracuse University Press, 1992), 82–113; as well as Robert-Henri Bautier, "Leçon d'ouverture du cours de diplomatique a l'Ecole des Chartes," *Bibliothèque de l'Ecole des chartes* CXIX (1961), 194–225; and Heinrich Fichtenau, "La situation actuelle des études de diplomatique en Autriche," Conference faite à l'École des chartes, le 10 novembre 1960. Fichtenau and Bautier's papers were again presented at a 1962 conference at L'Ecole des Chartes on the status and future of diplomatics. Armando Petrucci provided an important review and commented on the crisis discussed at the 1962 conference; see his "Diplomatica vecchia e nuova," in *Studi Medievali, 3rd series* (1963), 785–98. This article was republished in *Scrineum* in 2002. For a convenient summary of the internal "crisis in diplomatics" in the late-twentieth century, and recent responses, see Michele Ansani, "Diplomatica (e diplomatisti) nell'arena digitale," in *Scrineum* 1 (1999): 1–11. The article discusses the process of negotiation that culminated in la Commission internationale de Diplomatique's *Un complesso di norme* di *edizione* and the 1994 *Vocabulaire International de la Diplomatique*. The commission, created in 1970, ultimately affirmed that diplomatics addressed "les actes écrits (on disait volontiers au XIXe siècle les "chartes") où se trouve consigné soit l'accomplissement d'un acte juridique, soit l'existence d'un fait juridique, soit encore éventuellement un fait quelconque dès lors que l'écrit est rédigé dans une certaine forme propre à lui donner validité," cited in "Notions de diplomatique," a web-published syllabus for an online course at L'Ecole des chartes, given by Olivier Guyotjeannin. See *Theleme. Techniques pour l'Historien en Ligne : Études, Manuels, Exercices*, http://theleme.enc.sorbonne.fr/document14.html. Other significant contributions to the discourse include Alessandro Pratesi, "Diplomatica in crisi?" in *Miscellanea in memoria di Giorgio Cencetti* (Torino, 1973), 443–55; Olivier Guyotjeannin, "La diplomatique et l'élargissment de son champs," *La Gazette des archives* 172 (1994), 12-18; Caroline Williams, "Diplomatic Attitudes: From Mabillon to Metadata," *Journal of the Society of Archivists* 26, no. 1 (April 2005): 1–24; Giovanna Nicolaj, "Originale, authenticum, publicum: una sciarada per il documento diplomatico," *Scrineum* 2 (2000); Michele Ansani, "Diplomatica e nuove tecnologie. La tradizione disciplinare fra innovazione e nemesi digitale," in *Scrineum* 1 (2003); Antonella Ghignoli, "La definizione dei principi e le metodologie diplomatistiche: innovazioni ed eredità," in *Scrineum* 1 (2003).

23 Luciana Duranti's series of six articles entitled "New Uses for an Old Science," the first appearing in *Archivaria* 28 (Summer 1988), and the others in the next five successive issues, marked the emergence of diplomatics to prominence in North America.

24 For a critical discussion of documentation and historical authenticity, see Giovanna Nicolaj, "Sentieri di diplomatica," *Scrineum* 2 (2002), which first appeared in *Archivio Storico Italiano* CXLIV (1986), 305–31. For this article, Nicolaj drew on Armando Petrucci's, "L'illusione della storia autentica: le testimonianze documentarie," in *L'insegnamento della storia e i materiali del lavoro storiografico*. Atti del Conv. di Treviso, 10-12 Nov. 1980, Messina 1984. Nicolaj's writings provide among the most informed and thoughtful analysis and commentary on diplomatics.

25 The kinds of records that diplomatics traditionally placed lower in the hierarchy of documents—for example, inauthentic, unreliable, inaccurate, false, or forged documents—can prove invaluable to historians and other users of archives. Rita Costa Gomes, "Letters and Letter Writing in Fifteenth Century Portugal," in *Reading Interpreting, Historicizing: Letters as Historical Sources*, ed. Regina Schulte and Xenia Von Tippelskirch (European University Institute, Florence, EUI Working Papers), HEC 2004/2, http://cadmus.iue.it/dspace/bitstream/1814/2600/1/HEC04-02.pdf.

26 Heather McNeil, "Providing Grounds for Trust II: The Findings of the Authenticity Task Force of InterPARES," *Archivaria* 54 (Fall 2002): 28.

27 Nicolaj, "Sentieri di diplomatica." See also Nicolaj, "Lineamenti di un diplomatica generale," *Scrineum* 1 (2003). Roughly translated, Nicolaj's point is that diplomatics needs to move beyond its traditional concepts, which are filtered through historical erudition and positive law, and begin to consider other areas of knowledge, particularly social history and the humanities, including those factors that help to determine the nature of social life.

28 Diplomatics' claim to scientific status dates back to the era of the scientific revolution. At that time, professions and crafts beyond the traditional physical sciences began to embrace the rising epistemological status (and political utility) of scientific methods, and to invoke them in their own fields. By the late nineteenth century, it was being claimed that diplomatics dealt with the kinds of documents that could serve as an ultimate test or control on the veracity of all other social documentation: "...contrôle perpètuels des autres sources...," from Arthur Giry, *Manuel de Diplomatique* (Paris: 1894), 4. Duranti's insertion of the term "archivology" into the English professional lexicon, implying a value- and contingency-free body of knowledge, an ahistorical scientific methodology, is in keeping with this tradition. It is interesting to note, too, that Duranti's uses of and views on the history of recordkeeping serve to entrench this scientific status. This is implicit, for example, in her complaint that current historical knowledge of archives "far from being organized in a systematic and rigorous conceptual construct, was passed on irregularly, without a definite form." In other words, rather than coming down to us as a consistent set of principles, as a unified body of scientific knowledge or laws, the lineage of our archival concepts, language, and theories have been marked by inconsistency and lack of coherence, misshapen by the forces of historical contingency. Duranti, "The Future of Archival Scholarship."

29 Duranti's use of the words *juridical* and *legal* deserves a brief look, as these terms are integral on many levels with the IP project. Along with a number of earlier writers on diplomatics, (Tessier, Cenetti, Bautier, and others), Duranti recognized that diplomatics must expand its purview beyond the world of individual documents and also draw on other disciplines to address broader issues that preoccupy archival science. However, she did so in a peculiar way. Rather than acknowledging that diplomatics' juridical-legal focus precludes important perspectives on documentary issues and that this focus thus limits our understanding of records, she seems instead to have broadened the meaning of the notions of *legal* and *juridical* to encompass other theoretical and analytical perspectives. This has had the effect of preserving a nominally dominant position for diplomatics' longstanding juridical focus. For example, we encounter the following description of a juridical system: it "includes three components: the social group, organizational principle of the social group, and the system of binding rules recognized by the social group (positive law, beliefs, mores, and values)." The parenthetical elaboration on "juridical," indicating that it encompasses something more than "positive laws" and law-governed identity, needs closer scrutiny than it has received. An admittedly limited search in Italian sources on diplomatics failed to turn up any use of *giuridico* that is as broad as Duranti's. In most instances, *giuridico* refers to positive law. Similarly, the French word *juridique* and English *juridical* consistently refer to textually codified laws and judicial systems, not to social rules, communal values, or religious or other beliefs. Elsewhere, in the same newly expansive spirit, Duranti writes that a juridical *system* "is a collectivity organized on the basis of a system of rules.

The system of rules is called a legal system. A legal system is a complex paradigm containing many divisions and subdivisions. It can be broken down into *positive law* (as set out in the various legal sources—legislation, judicial precedent, custom, and literary sources—either authoritative, consisting of statutes, law reports, and books of authority, or nonauthoritative, such as medieval chronicles, periodicals, other books) and all the other *conceptions and notions of binding law* (natural law, morality, orthodox religious beliefs, mercantile custom, Roman/Canon law). *Because a legal system includes all the rules that are perceived as binding at any time and/or place, no aspect of human life and affairs remains outside a legal system.*" "Diplomatics: New Uses for an Old Science (Part II)," *Archivaria* 29 (Winter 1989-90): 5 (emphasis added). See, however, Duranti, "Diplomatics: New Uses for an Old Science," *Archivaria* 29 (Summer 1989), 15. On the differences between English and other legal terminology, see Kenneth Pennington, review of Brian Tierney, *The Idea of Natural Rights: Studies on Natural Rights, Natural Law and Church, 1150-1625*," in *Studies in Law and Religion* 5 (Emory University, 1997). Thus, *legal system* in Duranti's assertion appears to encompass much more than anglophones and francophones (and, it seems, many Italian sources would allow), and to arrogate under the term *legal* things that are not. On the importance of these nonlegal perspectives to understanding archives, see also Eric Ketelaar, "Tacit Narratives: The Meanings of Archives," in *Archival Science* 1, no. 2 (June 2001): 136 and passim; Terry Cook, "What is Past is Prologue: A History of Archival Ideas Since 1898, and the Future Paradigm Shift," *Archivaria* 43 (1997): 17–63; and, especially, Terry Cook, "Are the Administrative and Cultural Values of Archives Compatible?" (presentation to Appraisal Seminar, Monash University, Melbourne, VIC March 16, 1999), http://www.recordkeeping.com.au/march99/terrycookadmincultural.html. See also note 27 on the idea of rules.

30 Archivists need to consider the limits of legal determinism in accounts of the making and keeping of records. That is, it is important to examine the relationship between laws and nonlegal social rules and structures, to what degree each is autonomous and/or influences the other, and to what extent each one shapes individuals, public officials, groups and institutions' motives, reasons, and methods for composing content and keeping records. For a sampling of the deliberations on social rules and law among legal scholars, philosophers, and social theorists, see David Braybrooke, ed., *Social Rules: Origin, Character, Logic, Change* (Boulder: Westview Press, 1996); H. L. A. Hart, *The Concept of Law* (Oxford: Clarendon Press, 1961), especially ch. VII, "Formalism and Rule Scepticism"; Stephen Perry, "Hart on Social Rules and the Foundations of Law. Liberating the Internal Point of View," *Fordham Law Review* 75 (2006): 1171–1209. A skeptical view of the fact-rules-law relationship in individual cases may be found in Riccardo Guastini, "A Sceptical View on Legal Interpretation," in *Analisi e diritto ricerche di giurisprudenza analitica* (University of Genoa, School of Law, 2006) at: http://www.giuri.unige.it/intro/dipist/digita/filo/testi/ and "On Legal Order: Some Criticism of the Received View," *Ethical Theory and Moral Practice* 3, no. 3 (September 2000), 263–72. See also Giovanni Tarello, *Storia della cultura giuridica moderna, Assolutismo e Codificazione del Diritto* (Bologna: 1976). On the need to move beyond consideration of juridical systems and to recognize the circular relationship between written law codes and other forms of writing, see Nicolaj, "Lineamenti di un diplomatica generale": "La prassi documentaria, nel suo multiforme e cangiante profilo, non solo è 'digestione' della legge o consuetudine (in senso tecnico) e perciò fonte di diritto, ma anche, sempre e comunque, agisce e preme sulle altre fonti di diritto (legge e dottrina), nel lungo periodo e quasi in un processo circolare ininterrotto, tanto da costringere quelle fonti stesse ad adattamenti e reinterpretazioni tali che, secondo un noto adagio, "il diritto nasce vecchio.") That is to say, enacted laws inevitably are born already aged by extra-legal influences, and vice versa. For a similar perspective on the relationship between institutions and laws, see Peter Morton, *An Institutional Theory of Law: Keeping Law in Its Place* (Oxford: Clarendon Press, 1998). For two fine examples of the often large gulf between law, regulation, and executive fiat directed at the creation of records and the reality of recordkeeping based on social convention, group identity norms, local customs, and self-interest, see Barbara L. Craig, "Rethinking Formal Knowledge and its Practices in the Organization: The British Treasury's Registry Between 1900 and 1950," *Archival Science* 2, nos. 1–2 (2002): 111–36; and Ciaran B. Trace, "What is Recorded is Never Simply 'What Happened': Record-Keeping in Modern Organizational Culture," in *Archival Science* 2, nos. 1–2 (2002): 137–59.

31 The seminal philosophical text on the concept of social rules is Peter Winch, *The Idea of a Social Science and its Relation to Philosophy* (London: Routledge and Kegan Paul, 1958). Perhaps most

familiar to archivists, however, is Anthony Giddens' notion of structuration, which formed a major contribution to the debate among sociologists on the meaning and scope of social rules. Giddens' work provided an important part of the theoretical underpinnings of macroappraisal in Canada and continuum thinking in Australia. See his *The Constitution of Society: Outline of the Theory of Structuration* (Berkeley: University of California, 1984). See also Karsten R. Stueber, "How to Think about Rules and Rule Following," *Philosophy of the Social Sciences* 35, no. 3 (2005): 307–23; Lorenzo Bernasconi-Kohn, "How Not to Think about Rules and Rule Following. A Response to Stueber," *Philosophy of the Social Sciences* 36, no. 1 (2006): 86–94; Philip Pettit, "Winch's Double-edged Idea of a Social Science," *History of the Human Sciences* 13, no. 1 (2000): 63–77; and Ahilan T. Arulanantham, "Breaking the Rules? Wittgenstein and Legal Realism," *Yale Law Journal* 107 (1998): 1853–84. For a taste of the issues involved in setting out the relations among rules and laws and reasons and acting, see Frederick Schauer, *Playing by the Rules: A Philosophical Examination of Rule-Based Decision Making in Law and in Life* (Oxford: Oxford University Press, 2002). A detailed elucidation of the issue of the relation between top-down and bottom-up rules and social control rules and legal rules may be found in John Griffiths, "The Social Working of Legal Rules," *Journal of Legal Pluralism* 48 (2003): 1-84. For a detailed analysis of the idea of the juridical, see Pierre Bourdieu, "The Force of Law: Toward a Sociology of the Juridical Field," *Hastings Law Journal* 38 (July 1987): 805–53. The western world's long-standing commitment to the legal idea of individuals' contractual and transactional freedom and the (mistaken) reductionist description of individuals as singularly legal constructions receives critical treatment in Alain Supiot, *Homo Juridicus: Essai sur la fonction anthropologique du Droit* (Paris: Edition du Seuil, 2005); as well as in Alain Pottage and Martha Mundy, eds., *Law, Anthropology, and the Constitution of the Social* (Cambridge: Cambridge University Press, 2004). Finally, for a penetrating discussion of the complex relations among law, rules, and scientific method, along with sovereignty, systems, jurisdiction, and diplomatics, see Nicolaj, "Lineamenti di un diplomatica generale."

32 The coining of the phrase "Big Science" is usually attributed to Alvin M. Weinberg at the time he was director of Oak Ridge National Laboratory, and first appeared in *Science* in 1961. Weinberg compared the large-scale scientific enterprises of the twentieth century to the wonders of earlier civilizations. On big science projects, see Thomas Parke Hughes, *American Genesis: A Century of Invention and Technological Enthusiasm, 1870-1970* (New York: Viking, 1989).

33 As Duranti wrote, "[T] he renewed interaction between scholars and practitioners made it clear that the challenge presented by electronic records was not one to be met by individual researchers in isolation, but required partnerships, planning, and financial resources." See her "The Future of Archival Scholarship."

34 The project website mentions "law, history, computer science and engineering, information science, and chemistry." Systems builders, according to one source, are no respecters of knowledge categories or professional boundaries. Bijker Wiebe, Thomas Hughes, and Trevor Pinch, eds., *The Social Construction of Technological Systems: New Directions in the Sociology and History of Technology* (Cambridge, MA: MIT Press, 1987), 1.

35 See the InterPARES web page on Dissemination, http://www.interpares.org/ip1/ip1_dissemination.cfm?proj=ip1&cat=pr-atcl-i.

36 John Seeley Brown, "Borderline Issues: Social and Material Aspects of Design," *Human-Computer Interaction* 9 (1994): 9–36.

37 Van Bertalannfy was a Viennese-born theoretical biologist who held academic positions in both Canada and the United States. His *General Systems Theory* (1969) remains a primary text for anyone interested in the rise of systems theory in the twentieth century. See Mark Davidson, *Uncommon Sense: The Life and Thought of Ludwig van Bertalannfy, 1901-1972* (Los Angeles: Tarcher, 1983).

38 See Luciana Duranti, "The Impact of Digital Technology on Archival Science," *Archival Science* 1, no. 1 (March 2004): 39–55. On diplomatics' history, see Barbara Lazenby Craig, review of *Diplomatics: New Uses for an Old Science by Luciana Duranti*, in *Archivaria* 49 (Spring 2000): 217.

39 William Underwood, "System Analysis and Modeling for Archival Scientists," Version 1.0 (November 1999). This paper, first found at the internet site of the Georgia Institute for Technology, is no longer available online.

40 Wisnosky's story is typical of the American military-information technology sector complex. He spent much of his career moving back and forth between service in the U.S. Department of Defense (DOD) and the private sector. He established the Wizdom Systems, Inc., a company founded as the Process Company in 1986. The company has held several business systems contracts with the DOD. At last word, Wisnosky was reporting to the office of the deputy under secretary of defense for business. He had assumed the post of chief technical officer of the Department of Defense business mission area. His work has evolved from manufacturing control processes to business information architecture systems. See Wizdom home page, http://www.wizdom.com/.

41 Air Force Materials Lab, Wright-Patterson AFB Ohio, "ICAM Program Prospectus. Abstract," Defense Technical Information Center (December 1, 1977).

42 It is interesting to note that the IDEF suite of modeling methods was projected to include IDEF 11, an "information artifact modeling" method. I have been unable to find any evidence for its existence.

43 United States, Secretary of Commerce, Federal Information Processing Standards Publication 184 (December 21, 1993), Announcing the Standard for Integration Definition for Information Modeling (IDEFx).

44 Draft Federal Information Processing Standards Publication 183 (December 21, 1993), Announcing the Standard for Integration Definition for Function Modeling (IDEF øidef0), v.

45 Thomas Hughes, *American Genesis: A Century of Invention and Technological Enthusiasm* (Chicago: University of Chicago Press, 2004); and Daniel Boorstin, *Republic of Technology: Reflections on Our Future Community* (New York: Harper and Row, 1978).

46 Robert Lilienfeld, *The Rise of Systems Theory: An Ideological Analysis* (New York: John Wiley and Sons, 1978); Robert Boguslaw, *The New Utopians: A Study of Systems Design and Social Change* (Englewood Cliffs: Prentice Hall, 1965). On the broader social and political implications of the transfer of engineering methods and systems thinking to organizational management, see Yehouda Shenhav, *Manufacturing Rationality: The Engineering Foundations of the Managerial Revolution* (Oxford: Oxford University Press, 1999). For a longer view of the use of the term system, see Julie Candler Hayes, *Reading the French Enlightenment. System and Subversion* (Cambridge: Cambridge University Press, 1999).

47 See, for example, Wiebe, Hughes, and Pinch, eds., *The Social Construction of Technological Systems*, passim; Thomas Hughes and Renate Mayntz, *The Development of Large Technical Systems* (Boulder, CO: Westview Press, 1988); and Thomas Hughes, *Rescuing Prometheus* (New York: Pantheon Books, 1998), chapter 5.

48 Tim Berners-Lee, "Information Management: A Proposal," http://www.w3.org/history/1989/proposal.html.

49 On diplomatics' absolutist historical lineage, see note 60, below.

50 An issue that bears closer analysis is the significance of the complex change in diplomatics' role as a traditional *post hoc* method for reading old documents to determine authenticity, and its more recent focus, under the influence of changing technology, on providing advice on the *writing* or *creating* of authenticity into documents.

51 Others have argued that archivists and users play an important role in shaping the identity of the record. See among others Cook, "What is Past is Prologue"; Margaret Hedstrom, et al., "'The Old Version Flickers More': Digital Preservation from the User's Perspective," *American Archivist* 69 (Spring–Summer 2006): 163 and passim; and Brien Brothman, "Orders of Value: Probing the Theoretical Terms of Archival Practice," *Archivaria* 32 (Summer 1991): 78–100. See also Tom Nesmith, "The Concept of Societal Provenance and Records of Nineteenth-Century Aboriginal-European Relations in Western Canada: Implications for Archival Theory and Practice," *Archival Science* 6, nos. 3-4 (2006).

52 Thus, the phenomenon of impersonality that Weber found in nineteenth-century bureaucracy actually first appeared many centuries earlier. However, the degree of latitude that medieval scribes had to deviate from a preset documentary type remains an open historical question.

53 W.H. Leatherdale, *The Role of Analogy, Model and Metaphor in Science*, cited by J. J. Bono, "Science, Discourse, and Literature: The Role/Rule of Metaphor in Science," in Peterfreund, ed., *Literature and Science*, 61–67.

54 On diplomatics and the automation of archival processes, see David Bearman, "Diplomatics, Weberian Bureaucracy, and the Management of Electronic Records," *American Archivist* 55 (Winter 1992): 180.

55 Admittedly, the central image of the diagram is labeled "Manage Archival Fonds," not "Create Record." However, setting aside issues raised by the word *archival*, it is worth noting that the diagram's footnote establishes an equivalency between *manage* and *genesis*. Why not simply label the central box "Genesis and Preservation"? This claim of terminological equivalency invites further analysis, to say the least.

56 M.J. Reddy, "The Conduit Metaphor—A Case of Frame Conflict in our Language about Language," cited in *Metaphor and Thought*, ed. A. Ortony (Cambridge: Cambridge University Press, 1979), 284–97; and Celia Martin de Leon, "Metonymic Motivation of the Conduit Metaphor," in *Metaphorik.de* (June 2004), http://www.metaphorik.de/06/.

57 In fact, in a brief exposition of InterPARES, one reads that the project "espouses no epistemological perspective or intellectual definitions *a prioi*," the kind of claim that must always be regarded with a degree of skepticism, if not suspicion. Luciana Duranti, "The Long-Term Preservation of Accurate and Authentic Digital Data: The InterPARES Project," *Data Science Journal* 4, no. 25 (October 2005): 109.

58 The Arial sans serif font, often featured in Microsoft-based graphics, has been the subject of some interesting controversy among typographers.

59 It then fed this notation back to the archival profession as something new. On the rhetoric of engineering design, see Barbara Lewis, "Talking to Texts and Sketches: The Function of Written and Graphic Mediation in Engineering Design," *Business Communication Quarterly* 63 (2000).

60 See Luciana Duranti, "The Odyssey of the Records Manager: From the Dawn of Civilization to the Fall of the Roman Empire," *Records Management Quarterly* 23, no. 3 (July 1989); and "The Odyssey of the Records Manager: From the Middle Ages to Modern Times," *Records Management Quarterly* 23, no. 4 (October 1989). These two articles have been important in providing the archival profession with a past, with a mythology, a storytelling of the origins of contemporary recordkeeping, even if told in such a way as to privilege the alleged juridical primacy of records and their creation across the millennia. Similarly, Duranti's reinvigoration of diplomatics (and "archivology") as a science, as well as her claim that the IP project began with no particular perspective (see note 57), must be received with caution. It has entrenched in the archival consciousness an understanding of records that bears the imprint of its diplomatic origins. Diplomatics emerged on the North American shores of the late twentieth century as a fully formed science of document criticism. However, its methods and concepts carry considerable historical baggage, as this essay and earlier notes show. One can easily dismiss as inconsequential that its contemporary shape represents the outcome of Jean-Baptiste Mabillon's magisterial work on diplomatics, the *De Re Diplomatica* (1683). This work proved a useful tool in the consolidation of monarchical state power, which, in turn, served to promote a particular idea and valorization of records and recordkeeping. On archives, information controls, and "the mechanics of the regime," see James E. King, *Science and Rationalism in the Government of Louis XIV, 1661-1683* (New York: Octagon Books, 1972), chapter 6; Janet Coleman, *The Individual in Political Theory and Practice* (Oxford: Oxford University Press, 1996), 272; Ian Fraser and Patrick Nerhot, *Law, Writing, Meaning: An Essay in Legal Hermeneutics* (Edinburgh: Edinburgh University Press, 1992), 59 and passim; and Orest A. Ranum, *Artisans of Glory: Writers and Historical Thought in Seventeenth Century France* (Chapel Hill: University of North Carolina Press, 1980). On the concentration of power, centralization of bureaucracy, and role of archives, see David Parker, *Class and State in Ancien Regime France: The Road to Modernity* (London: Routledge, 1996), chapter 6. Analogously, Giovanna Nicolaj offers fascinating insights into the relationship between the emerging hegemony of diplomatic, juridical-legal document creation, the notarial class's rise to political power, and the conflict between Latin and vulgar language usage in medieval Italy. Giovanna Nicolaj, "Il volgare nei documenti italiani medievali." Finally, on the unresolved concept of *document* in the diplomatics of Mabillon's time, see Paul Bertrand, "Érudition et diplomatique," *L'érudition, cycle thématique 2002-2003 de l'IRHT* (Paris, 2005), http://aedilis.irht.cnrs.fr/erudition/jeudi_erudition_2_bertrand.htm.

61 What Walter Ong described as "exquisite circumspection," in *Orality and Literacy: The Technologizing of the Word* (London: Routledge, 1988), 104.

62 The IP project, diplomatics, and much other contemporary archival theory and methodology, then, bracket the implications of reader interpretation for concepts and theories of records and recordkeeping. Contributing to the entrenchment of the "record creator point of view" in archival thought, the IP project also explains the following: "Reliability depends on two factors: the degree of completeness of the record's form and the degree of control exercised over its procedure of creation. Therefore, reliability is of greater concern to the record's creator than to its preserver." Luciana Duranti and Kenneth Thibodeau, "The InterPARES International Research Project," *Information Management Journal* (January 2001). Extant histories of reading and the notion of a "confrontation between reader and writer" should alert archivists to the pitfalls of such "silencing readers" and succumbing completely to producer-creator determinism in archival theories and explanations of "recordness." See Jesper Svenbro, *Phrasikleia. An Anthroplogy of Reading in Ancient Greece* (Ithaca: Cornell, 1993); Raymond Gillespie, *Reading Ireland: Print, Reading, and Social Class in Early Modern Ireland* (Manchester: Manchester University Press, 2005); Steven Roger Fischer, *A History of Reading* (London: Reaktion, 2003); and Lisa Block de Bhear, *A Rhetoric of Silence and Other Selected Writings* (The Hague: Walter de Gruyter, 1995), passim. Finally, see also Roland Barthes' seminal *S/Z* on the writer vs. the reader as text producer (Paris: Éditions du Seuil, 1970, trans. Richard Miller, New York: Hill and Wang, 1974), 4. Thomas Hobbes (1566-1679) who, along with Jean Bodin (1530-1596) and Jacques-Bénigne Bossuet (1627-1704), ranks among the primary theorists of absolutism, foresaw the problem of reader participation for maintaining state documentary control. More specifically, he anticipated the threat that publication—a widening readership—posed to monarchical control of textual interpretation: "The legislator known, and the laws either by writing or by the light of nature sufficiently published, there wanteth yet another very material circumstance to make them obligatory. For it is not the letter, but the intendment, or meaning; that is to say, the authentic interpretation of the law (which is the sense of the legislator), in which the nature of the law consisteth; and therefore the *interpretation of all laws dependeth on the authority sovereign; and the interpreters can be none but those which the sovereign*, to whom only the subject oweth obedience, shall appoint. For else, by the craft of an interpreter, the law may be made to bear a sense contrary to that of the sovereign, by which means the interpreter becomes the legislator." *Leviathan,* chapter 26, section 8, "Of Civil Laws."

63 Charles Kostelnick and Michael Hassett, *Shaping Information: The Rhetoric of Visual Conventions* (Carbondale: Southern Illinois University Press, 2003), 6.

64 Terry Cook observed that the RC is the "world's most inclusive model for archives," in "Beyond the Screen: The Records Continuum and the Archival Cultural Heritage," paper delivered at Australian Society of Archivists Conference, Melbourne, August 18, 2000, www.archivists.org.au/sem/conf2000/terrycook.

65 Frank Upward, "Structuring the Records Continuum, Part Two: Structuration Theory and Recordkeeping," *Archives and Manuscripts* 25, no. 1 (1997). Upward's imagination is wide-ranging. Interestingly, he, too, resorts to the popular "conduit" metaphor of controlled water flow when he refers to "data plumbing" to describe an aspect of the project. "Modelling the Continuum as Paradigm Shift in Recordkeeping and Archiving Process—and Beyond—A Personal Reflection," *Records Management Journal* 10, no. 3 (November 2001).

66 As one study dryly notes, IDEF does not represent the conditions necessary to enter into or exit the process. Ovidiu S. Noran, "Business Modelling: UML vs. IDEF," www.cit.gu.edu//~noran.

67 "Naming of the parts is an onerous task in modeling complexity, and defining them always raises the issue of professional or cultural perceptions. The moment professional and cultural factors intrude, persistence is lost." Upward, "Modelling the Continuum as a Paradigm Shift."

68 It should be pointed out, however, that the Records Continuum Research Group (RCRG), incorporated in 1998, has worked hard to develop applications of the RC and to develop tools to make the RC more operational. Based at Monash University in Australia, the RCRG has evolved into an information management consulting service.

69 Minkowski first presented the idea of spacetime in an article titled "Raum und Zeit" (Space and Time) in 1908. The article included abstract diagrams illustrating the idea of four dimensionality. On the idea of four dimensionality, see Theodore Sider's introduction to his *Four-Dimensionalism: An Ontology of Persistence and Time* (Oxford: Oxford University Press, 2001). He makes a crucial distinction between two ideas of object persistence: objects that "perdure"

and objects that "endure." The first chapter also provides an accessible explanation of what it means to say that an object has "temporal parts."

70 The intersection of seemingly space-bound objects with the dimension of time, or, at least Upward's exemplification of it, has much more in common with my notion of *record formation* than I realized when I first developed it. See Brien Brothman, "Archives, Life Cycles, and Death Wishes: A Helical Model of Record Formation," *Archivaria* 61 (Spring 2006). Minkowski's notion of multiple temporal parts forms part of the concept of a record formation. Indeed, I have since discovered that the helical figures I used to model record formation sometimes appear in illustrations of the notion of continua.

71 On the complexity of temporal description in recordkeeping, see, again, Brothman, "Archives, Life Cycles, and Death Wishes."

72 This aspect of the DS seems to anticipate some aspects of Jeanette Bastian's recent notion of "community of record" as well as the collaborative possibilities of archival social networking and "wiki" interactivity, described by Elizabeth Yakel in the preceding essay in this volume.

73 Helen Willa Samuels, *Varsity Letters: Documenting Modern Colleges and Universities* (Metuchen, NJ: Scarecrow Press and Society of American Archivists, 1992).

74 Ibid., 5.

75 New-left historian Howard Zinn was sometimes cited as a source of influence.

76 Samuels, "Improving Our Disposition," 137. See also Richard J. Cox and Helen W. Samuels, "The Archivist's First Responsibility: A Research Agenda to Improve the Identification and Retention of Records of Enduring Value," *American Archivist* 51 (Winter and Spring 1988): 29; Samuels, *Varsity Letters*, 12; F. Gerald Ham, "The Archival Edge," *American Archivist* 38 (January 1975): 5–13.

77 Samuels, "Who Controls the Past," passim; Samuels, "Improving Our Disposition," 126.

78 Larry Hackman and Joan Warnow-Blewett, "The Documentation Strategy Process: A Model and Case Study," *American Archivist* 50 (Winter 1987), 12–47.

79 On "record formation," see Brothman, "Archives, Life Cycles, Death Wishes," passim.

80 One would do well to consider J. G. A. Pocock's admonition concerning the well-worn scholarly rhetoric of "revolution": "To trace the history of a revolution is, almost of necessity, to start with a straw man. The rhetoric of the exercise compels the construction of an account of the way things stood before change began which neglects the extent to which change had begun already and the activities of men under the old regime resembled the activities which were to receive emphasis as a result of the process of transformation." Pocock, *Politics, Language, and Time: Essays on Political Thought and History* (Chicago: University of Chicago Press, 1989), 4.

THE EVOLUTION OF ARCHIVAL PRACTICE AND THE HISTORY-ARCHIVAL DIVIDE

Francis X. Blouin Jr.

On August 18, 1883, Pope Leo XIII spoke to the issue of history as a source for understanding the past. In a letter that led to the opening of the Vatican Archives, Leo, long angered that emerging nationalist-based histories were ignoring the contributions of the popes, argued for the need for "true" history. He saw the need to "show the Italian people what they owe to the popes of the past centuries." For this to happen, Leo advised, "Let men work at the sources; use prudence and not rashness in judgment. . . . Go to the sources. That is why I have opened the archives to you."[1] For Leo, the archives would be the source of the true history so long as historians minded Cicero's admonition that nothing untrue be said and nothing true be unsaid. For Leo and increasingly in the nineteenth century for the new professional historical establishment, the archive was the ultimate arbiter or tribunal of historical truth. The opening of the Vatican archives, as with the opening of new state archives all across Europe in the nineteenth century, laid bare fundamental questions of Church and State, Faith and Reason, Truth and Power. Archives, in close partnership with academic history, became a source of truth and understanding. A partnership came to flourish among archivists and historians based on shared positivist ideas about historical truth, centered around scientific notions about the validity and objectivity of archives. This partnership and mindset dominated academic history for nearly a century after Leo's pronouncement. However, toward the end of the twentieth century, this partnership began to dissolve into what I call the archival divide. History was moving toward new conceptual frameworks that diminished the privileged position of the archives, and so too were archives moving toward new frameworks that would marginalize the authority of academic history in ascribing importance and meaning to archival collections.

In this essay, I focus on North American archival practice in the late twentieth century. In these years, archival practice carefully, and with considerable intellectual deliberation, carved a space that increasingly relies on systematic organization of archival activities. The effectiveness of these systems rests principally on the existence of specific authorities, standards, methodologies, and contextualities. These systematic approaches have contributed much to the organization and accessibility of archives in cost-effective ways. Yet these particular intellectual constructs have found little direction or sustenance from current discourses on historical methodology or from professional circles that explore the nature of "past." By the 1970s, archivists were facing a series of challenges that required new interventionist approaches to the administration of records at the same time that history was increasingly pluralized in its interests and directions by new definitions of what constitutes the past. As a result, the positivism that was the glue that held archives and history as a common enterprise split apart. Common terms such as *authority, evidence, context, system, provenance,* and, of course, *archive* came to be understood quite differently by both professions. This semantic separation signaled the opening up of the "archival divide."

There are two developments, I believe, that have pushed archives in new directions: first, the "postcustodial" interventionist turn of the late 1970s, and secondly, the technical and conceptual turns of the late 1980s. The latter centered around the challenges of computer-based records and the digital revolution and around postmodern theory deeply affecting both archives and history as professions and activities. In this paper I will address the first, because it is the conceptual area where the writings of Helen Samuels have been most influential.

* * * * *

The comfortable, positivist-based, cooperative focus between history and the archive was challenged in the 1970s by the sheer volume of document production and the expanding intellectual reach of historical interests.

While historians saw a limitless conceptual space in what might properly be called "the past," archives faced a significant practical challenge of space of a different kind. Buildings were filling up. Not everything could be saved. How were selections to be made? Could there be derived from study of the new historical authorities and interpretations some direction for new conceptual frameworks needed to guide the process of appraisal, selection, and long-term retention by archives during an era of vast production of documentation? By the late 1970s and beginning of the 1980s, two senior archivists, Gerald Ham and Frank G. Burke, began to ask broad questions about the nature of archives and the role of archival institutions. Moreover, by this time, the National Archives and Records Service (now National Archives and Records Administration) was an enormous institution not only in Washington but with federally funded branches all over the country and a growing system of presidential libraries. Though private historical societies remained, many (like those vast repositories in Ohio and Wisconsin) had been merged with state-based public archives. Other state governments had established state-funded historical archives. The question of archives and collecting was no longer primarily a private or philanthropic matter; because of these funding arrangements and the legislation underpinning them, public archives more than ever were becoming a matter of, and accountable to, public trust. This would be supported by an emerging legal framework that more specifically defined public records, freedom of information, and protection of privacy. All these developments strongly reinforced the new role of archives as publicly accountable administrative entities serving a broad clientele well beyond academic historians.

Ham posited that archives were entering a "postcustodial era." He cited the pressures of the bulk of records now being produced as the major factor in the shift from the traditional custodial model and toward his new conception. For Ham this meant making decisions. Not everything could be saved. Archivists could no longer sit passively in the stacks taking custody of all records passed their way and focus primarily on their curatorship; rather, hard appraisal choices would have to be made. He called on archivists to question new technologies for the storage of information, to identify new systems for records appraisal, and to address complexities derived from right-to-know and privacy legislation. He saw a need to navigate these issues with new approaches and with a new kind of interventionism that would be informed by considered research and reflection on the part of the archivist in areas well beyond the latest trends in historiography.[2] Frank Burke at that same time pushed the idea that archival work should rest on very broad theoretical constructions. He asked, for example: "What is it within the nature of society that makes it create the records that it does?" "What are the sociological aspects of records management?" "What is the nature of history, historical fact, and historical thought?"[3] He argued that archivists would need to focus on these issues in order to formulate collections that would service continuing interest in a historical past. Burke's point of departure was a sense that history was important and informed by documentation, and vice versa. His remarks arose from a long-standing framework that set archives in the United States within the context of historical research. But he tried to redefine the positivist bond in more modern terms within the context of postcustodial thinking. His assertions were bold and set in a kind of new historicism.

Burke sought to revive the history-archives connection in a more complicated framework by revisiting fundamental historical questions about the relationship of documents to the intellectual constructs of the past. His thoughtful attempts to set archival practice within a broader framework of historical ideas received a scathing critique by Lester Cappon, a prominent historian of the day, as well as a leading archivist bent on defending the old positivist order. In the pages of the *American Archivist,* Cappon ridiculed Burke's position, asserting that any of the theoretical concerns Burke was raising were really the "province of the historian." He proclaimed, "History is what historians do." And that is not what archivists do. His arguments in effect drew on the great British archival theorist Hilary Jenkinson, the classic defender of the traditionalist, positivist, curatorial approach to archives, saying that "archives were not drawn up in the interest of or for the information of posterity." Archives to Jenkinson (and to Cappon) have two common qualities of extraordinary importance: "impartiality" and "authenticity." If the student understands their administrative context, "they [the records] can not tell him anything but the truth." He postulated that Burke's query—"should the archivist be concerned that what he is preserving is truth, or just evidence?"—is irrelevant in the context of the origin and continuous custody of the archives. He feared any blurring of archival issues and historical understanding: "Let us not compromise the status of archives as a separate discipline, maintaining the *integrity* of the records as its first principle."[4] This exchange further chilled an already marked divide, with Cappon (and those who followed him) looking backward while historians were rapidly embracing a new historicism (in some ways characteristically postmodern) very similar to what Burke was suggesting.

Cappon's rear-guarded reaction ignored the critically changed context to which Ham and Burke were reacting. The problem of "bulk" forced a kind and level of interventionism that Cappon and Jenkinson could not have anticipated. Cappon wanted to preserve the Jenkinsonian concept of the archivist as the passive custodian caring for documents that could claim authority from the very process of their generation and subsequent curatorship, that is to say from some clear authority derived from a consensual understanding of the past that privileged certain institutions by the very nature of their existence and by their perceived dominance in the formation of societal and political norms. It is that consensual authority that defined the integrity that Cappon sought to preserve. Ironically, the essence of the idea of a separation of historical interpretation from archival authenticity was, in fact, a blurring of the two. Accepted notions of archival impartiality rested on an unquestioned acceptance by historical inquiry of archival processes of selection and of institutional hierarchies.[5]

The dismissal of the Cappon piece by most archivists confirmed that archives and archivists would need to look beyond formal academic history for new conceptual frameworks. The quest was for more defined systems that could be used as an authoritative basis of interventionist and systematic approaches to archives, in effect one that focused on the management of the records of modern society. An important element in this quest was the increasingly diverse source base of ideas from numerous disciplines for the construction of systems for managing the historical record, for assessing its meaning, for defining its authority, and for deciding its long-term value. Selection was a public matter in public institutions. These were the essential elements in the age of postcustodial interventionism.

This conceptual shift toward internal administrative and legal authorities for records retention was also manifest in the business or private-sector community that, with notable exceptions, found an umbrella under the American Records Management Association (ARMA), where the focus was on the maintenance of records in accordance with the legal and administrative requirements of the firm. The founding and flourishing of ARMA, and later the National Association of Government Archivists and Records Administrators (NAGARA), represented the hegemony of institutional values over academic historical values in the administration of both current active records and inactive archival records. Archives, particularly those managing recent records in the private sector of the economy, were closed operations within records management divisions. These new professional organizations represented an intellectual separation from the broad coalition of interests that brought together historians and archivists under the umbrella of the Society of American Archivists back in the days of its founding in 1936, as Bruce Bruemmer discusses in an earlier essay in this volume.

A variety of approaches emerged based on research methodologies in vogue at the time. There were many articles devoted to applying the methodologies of social science to the sampling and selection of records. Herman Kahn and Philip Bauer sparred over the costs of retention. Some strategies focused on specific types of records for various subject areas. Work was done to consider appraisal on specific kinds of records within a context of scholarly use. These studies all acknowledged the bulk of materials and attempted to bridge selection with historiographical issues. Few of these efforts were in any way confirmed, validated, or even engaged by those practising historical scholarship in the related fields.[6]

* * * * *

These efforts were attempts by archivists to underpin the selection process from trends in academic work. But none really succeeded. The 1970s were the days of history from the "bottom up." Historians were moving away from a preoccupation with political and social institutions that had generated the archives to a studied focus on political, social, and cultural forces that challenged those institutions. Thus the older consensus among the historical and the archival professions—that the central importance of those major institutions of the state (and their records) should govern or structure the appraisal process—now broke down. Gerald Ham summarized the intellectual problem of appraisal in his presidential address to the Society of American Archivists in 1974. New paradigms were emerging in historical study. History from the bottom up was to discover and recover the lives of the ordinary and the ignored. But as two historians, Howard Zinn and Sam B. Warner (who did try to engage with archivists) had earlier noted, archives were biased in their appraisal strategies toward elite institutions. Ham attributed this to archival passivity. He cited the "custodial image" drawn from Jenkinsonian principles that led to this unintentional distortion in the historical record. Archivists, he argued, would have to be more active in documenting society. He called for the "active archivist." He argued that "institutionalization, bulk, missing data, vulnerable records, and technology—have expanded the universe of potential archival data, have given a contemporaneous character to archival acquisition, and have permanently altered the job of the archivist by forcing him to make choices that he never had to make before."[7] While there were calls for more intervention in archival selection and more sensitivity to the archivists' conscious shaping of collections, no one came forward with any authority or assurance, derived from a serious study of the past, to suggest with certainty what records could be discarded that at some point would not be of value in the (perhaps distant) future.

History was broadening its concerns, archivists would argue, beyond the practical capacities of the archival infrastructure. Everything simply could not be saved. However, in an intellectual climate where every aspect of life, every story, every life, was worthy of serious academic attention, then every document had potential research value. It was a compelling argument that expanded exponentially the legitimate questions of a historical nature, to the point where trying to answer them by preserving all relevant documentation became an absolute archival impossibility. Moreover, because historical study was moving in so many new directions at such a rapid pace, no historian dared to take on the responsibility for recommending the destruction of vast masses of documentation that modern appraisal required.

Frank Boles and Julia Young, reflecting on the problem of authorities derived from academic historiography, pushed the traditional appraisal framework proposed by the distinguished American archivist Theodore Schellenberg much further than many other archivists by proposing an overall conception of the selection process. Schellenberg had proposed two sets of values for the retention of records: evidential and informational. While his work implied intervention in the formation of archival collections as part of the records management life cycle, his idea of evidence and his concept of what constituted information were derived from the notion that archives are a product of records production in bureaucratic environments. Evidentiary value presumed that the most important documentation would be found at the highest levels of administration. Informational value was a much less-defined category but generally applied to low-level records activity that contained information deemed to be useful for historical or other research. In any case, there was no hint in Schellenberg that these decisions would limit or define the possibilities of historical research using government records. Rather, this appraisal framework was designed to select and preserve records deemed to be of obvious historical significance.[8] Boles and Young coupled appraisal as a theoretical concern with process as a practical matter—not only a matter of the value of information for research purposes, but also the costs of its processing, description, and preservation, the physical condition of the material, the degree of user interest, and so on. Their process diagrams identified nearly fifty different factors to be considered.[9] This article, more than any other to that point, presented appraisal as exclusively an archival problem—a matter of archival theory and strategy and administration. Archivists had to make the decisions and should do so on terms that were in essence archival. A developed consideration of historiography is absent in the work that represented a more practical interventionist turn in the evaluation of archival material. The focus of the many articles on appraisal increasingly saw it as a matter of archival theory independent of historiography.

The integration of practical considerations as equally important factors in the appraisal process affirmed that archives, while understanding the breadth of historical interests, could not fill that conceptual space, could not expand to embrace the idea of providing all documents for answering all questions. Ham and others were arguing that the archivists had to come up with new and more complex systems that would lead to intelligent decisions on the retention and disposition of records. The ever-increasing rate of records production required difficult selection decisions to be made. In this process, the relationship to academic history was increasingly marginalized. No academic historical framework existed that could inform and guide these appraisal decisions. History as a discipline could not accept the responsibility for the destruction of documentary material when virtually everything was of potential research value. Yet Ham argued that appraisal cannot be a random process, "a selection process [that was] so random, so fragmented, so uncoordinated, and even so often accidental . . . [and one that] too often reflected narrow research interests rather than the broad spectrum of human experience. If we cannot transcend these obstacles then the archivist will remain at best nothing more than a weathervane moved by the changing winds of historiography."[10] Archivists then essentially turned to the record itself, and its context of creation, for devising appraisal concepts and methods, thus effectively separating the record's value from its role primarily as the potential source base of scientific history. This meant looking at the record and especially the records-creating processes and contexts, and forming appraisal strategies around them.

By the 1980s, archivists searched to find categories of analysis that would aid in determining records of value in an age of abundance. "Historical value" as a concept was replaced by "enduring value," or just "archival value," implying a broader set of constituencies for whom value was important.[11] As Boles and Young signaled, the whole process of determining value had to be removed from any exclusive reliance derived from academic discourse in history in order to incorporate other issues. This move away from historical analysis in the formation of archival collections took the process of selection out of the historiographical discourse. The process of archival appraisal moved toward an institutional essentialism and a pragmatic kind of universalism, looking for and presenting the essence of documentation as rooted in its origins and in the process of its creation. This emerging framework pushed American archival practice toward then-recent continental and Canadian models, identifying attributes of record values that would be useful and recognizable over time, independent of shifting historical paradigms and knowledge structures. The result was to treat provenance as a functional and value axiom, not as a historical circumstance. History and the historical were subordinated to the essence of the record itself and its functional context of creation and contemporary use.

The work of Helen Samuels was particularly influential in this process. She questioned the archivist's capacities to predict future trends in research. Her book on college and university archives, *Varsity Letters*, is an extensive application of "functional analysis" to the problem of selection. She argued that "rather than relying on subjective guesses about potential research, appraisal decisions must be guided by clearer documentary objectives based on a thorough understanding of the phenomenon or institution to be documented." Critical for this discussion was her further observation: "since archivists cannot predict future research, the best they can do is to document institutions as adequately as possible."[12]

Recognizing that no process is totally objective, Samuels argued that, set in a functional rather than a historical context, records in an institutional archives would best reflect that institution if organizational complexities of the institution itself formed the analytic construct for the selection of records. What follows in the book is a lengthy and nuanced articulation of the functional activities, structures, subfunctional layers, purposes, and aspirations that represent the modern university independent of any historical periodization. This is preliminary to a framework for strategic thinking about what documents should endure as valid representations of the life of an institution in all its complexity, multiple roles, or, as she argues, "not on the specific history, people, events, structure or records . . . but on an understanding of what the institution does—what are its functions."[13] Based on this knowledge, derived by functional research by the archivist, a documentation strategy could be articulated that would identify the records essential to reflect the function and thus to be preserved as archives. When the same function was performed at similar institutions, or shared among two or more institutions, collections could be coordinated so that every institution was not collecting the same type of record. These ideas and strategies were formulated in a way to define essential categories, universally applied, independent of historical constructs that in the end may be fleeting.

This essentialism separates the archival understanding of the process of documentation from broader and shifting interpretive frameworks of history and culture. When there is agreement among historians and archivists on the authorities that determine what is of importance in the understanding of history and culture, then this separation is not a problem—archives are then but one element in the identification of an academic consensus. But when there is contestation on these historical and cultural questions (and these days there is always contestation), then this approach distances the archives from specific constructions of historical meaning. To marginalize historical meaning is to define the archives as evidential—which on one level they clearly are. To limit archives to the institutionally specific argues for authority that is essentialist and does not easily conform to the shifting categories of modern academic historical inquiry. There are then two separate conceptual frameworks at work: archives and history—both broadly historical, to be sure, but in reality quite different, to the point where scholars like Carolyn Steedman find that, for her historical purposes, in the archives there is not "very much there."[14] These essentialist principles became the basis for the new archival interventionism, where a functionalist analytical framework formed the authorities for selection rather than historiographical trends or concepts. Hence the ahistorical character of the interventionist turn by archivists.

This is but one of several developments in the late twentieth century that contribute to the separateness that I argue defines the conceptual space of the historian and that of the archivist. There are great tensions between these two circles of discourse, partly because each still sees the other in mid-twentieth-century terms. Improving this relationship will require a new partnership on the part of academic history to comprehend the intellectual constructs that form the foundation of modern archival administration—and on the part of archivists better efforts to understand the breadth of conceptual frameworks that now constitute contemporary approaches to the study of history, including potentially the history of those functional contexts that underpin the new appraisal theories and strategies.[15]

Notes

This article is part of my larger work with William Rosenberg that focuses on the role of archives in processing the past. It will be published by Oxford University Press in 2011.

1 Owen Chadwick, *Catholicism and History: The Opening of the Vatican Archives* (Cambridge: Cambridge University Press, 1978), 101.

2 F. Gerald Ham, "Archival Strategies for the Post Custodial Age," *American Archivist* 44 (Summer 1981): 207–16.

3 Frank G. Burke, "The Future Course of Archival Theory in the United States," *American Archivist* 44 (Winter 1981): 40–46.

4 Lester J. Cappon, "What, Then, Is There to Theorize About?" *American Archivist* 45 (Winter 1982): 23. See also Richard Cox, ed., *Lester J. Cappon and the Relationship of History, Archives, and Scholarship in the Golden Age of Archival Theory* (Chicago: Society of American Archivists, 2004).

5 For the most devastating critique of this historian-archivist double blindness and the resulting irony, see Hans Booms, "Society and the Formation of a Documentary Heritage: Issues in the Appraisal of Archival Sources," *Archivaria* 24 (Summer 1987; original 1972, trans. Hermina Joldersma and Richard Klumpenhouwer): 69–107. For a parallel, and another non-American, reaction to the huge challenges of appraising the bulk of modern records, one that also firmly rejected the Jenkinsonian custodial paradigm, see Terry Cook, "An Archival Revolution: W. Kaye Lamb and the Transformation of the Archival Profession," *Archivaria* 60 (Fall 2005): 185–234; Lamb was Dominion Archivist of Canada from 1948 to 1969. For an overview of the evolution of archival appraisal concepts, see Terry Cook, "Macroappraisal in Theory and Practice: Origins, Characteristics, and Implementation in Canada, 1950–2000," *Archival Science* 5, nos. 2-4 (2005): 101–61.

6 The literature in English on archival appraisal is truly vast. The particular examples cited here were selected because of their conscious attempt to link appraisal to particular concerns in sub-disciplines of historical study. See Ralph M. Hower, "The Preservation of Business Records," *Bulletin of the Business Historical Society* 11 (October 1937): 37–83; Robert W. Lovett, "The Appraisal of Older Business Records," *American Archivist* 15 (April 1952): 231–39; Francis X. Blouin Jr., "An Agenda for the Appraisal of Business Records," in *Archival Choices: Managing the Historical Record in an Age of Abundance*, ed. Nancy E. Peace (Lexington, MA: D.C. Heath, 1984), 61–80, and his "A New Perspective on the Appraisal of Business Records: A Review," *American Archivist* 42 (July 1979): 312–20; David Klaassen,"The Provenance of Social Work Case Records: Implications for Archival Appraisal and Access," *Provenance* 1 (Spring 1983): 5–26; Lydia Lucas, "Managing Congressional Papers: A Repository View," *American Archivist* 41 (July 1978): 275–80; Paul I. Chestnut, "Appraising the Papers of State Legislators," *American Archivist* 48 (Spring 1985): 159–72; Maynard J. Brichford, *Scientific and Technological Documentation: Archival Evaluation and Processing of University Records Relating to Science and Technology* (Urbana-Champaign: University of Illinois, 1969); Conference on Science Manuscripts, History of Science Association, Washington, D.C., May 5–6, 1960, ISIS 53, no. 1 (1962): 3–157; Joan K. Haas, Helen Willa Samuels, and Barbara Trippel Simmons, *Appraising Records of Contemporary Science and Technology: A Guide* (Cambridge, MA: Massachusetts Institute of Technology, 1985); and Joint Committee on Archives of Science and Technology (JCAST), Clark A. Elliott, ed., *Understanding Progress and a Process: Documentation of the History of Post-War Science and Technology in the United States* (Chicago: Society of American Archivists, 1983). See also the overviews by Booms and Cook in the previous footnote for non-American analyses of the linkage of appraisal and historical studies and historiography.

7 F. Gerald Ham, "The Archival Edge," *American Archivist* 38 (January 1975): 10.

8 Theodore R. Schellenberg, *Modern Archives: Principles and Techniques* (Chicago: University of Chicago Press, 1956). See also his *Appraisal of Modern Public Records* (Washington, DC: U.S. Govt. Print. Off., 1956).

9 Frank Boles and Julia Marks Young, "Exploring the Black Box: The Appraisal of University Administrative Records," *American Archivist* 48 (Spring 1985): 121–40.

10 Ham, "The Archival Edge," 8.

11 Society of American Archivists, *Task Force on Goals and Priorities, Planning for the Archival Profession: A Report of the SAA Task Force on Goals and Priorities* (Chicago: Society of American Archivists, 1986).

12 Helen Willa Samuels, *Varsity Letters: Documenting Modern Colleges and Universities* (Metuchen, NJ: Scarecrow Press and Society of American Archivists, 1992), 8.

13 Ibid., 4.

14 Carolyn Steedman, *Dust: The Archive and Cultural History* (New Brunswick, NJ: Rutgers University Press, 2002), 68.

15 For a parallel analysis of the "divide" found in the present essay, and suggestions of how archivists and historians may form a new partnership centered around the contextual history of records and their creators, see Terry Cook, "The Archive(s) is a Foreign Country: Historians, Archivists, and the Changing Archival Landscape," *Canadian Historical Review* 90, no. 3 (September 2009): 497–534.

THE ARCHIVIST'S PERSPECTIVE: THE HISTORY OF AN IDEA

JAMES M. O'TOOLE

Any profession that adopts as one of its characteristic aphorisms the line spoken by Antonio, the "usurping duke" of Shakespeare's *The Tempest*—"What's past is prologue"—is understandably one that will be interested in its own history. Accordingly, recent years have seen a growing interest in the history of the archival profession. Presidential addresses and other papers at meetings have often looked back on the expansion of the profession in North America. Five separate international conferences on the history of records and archives have been held since 2003, and plans are underway to continue this biennial series. We have had explorations of the historical sociology of archivists as a group (the emergent roles of women and of racial and ethnic minorities, for example) and studies of the development of the institutions in which archivists work, most notably the national archives of both the United States and Canada. Biographies of a few leading archival practitioners of the last couple of centuries have appeared. The Society of American Archivists (SAA) has in recent years reprinted several classic texts, reissuing these seminal titles with new introductions that place them in their own historical context and that of subsequent developments. While there is much yet to be done, this has been, on the whole, a good time for archival history.[1]

One area that has been lacking in this output, however, is what might be called the intellectual history of archives. Terry Cook, in a magisterial essay published in 1997, is one of the few to explore systematically the history of archival ideas and concepts, to describe and analyze the notions that professional archivists have used to frame and organize their work. The historical development of archival thinking about appraisal and the selection of documents for preservation has also been studied by Cook himself and by others. Brien Brothman has explored the idea that records are perceived to have various sorts of values, and that these values are the justification for all the effort that archivists expend in saving, organizing, and making them available, according to varying notions of "order." My own analyses of such familiar concepts as permanence and uniqueness, as applied to archival records, have been done in the hope of understanding the ideas that archivists have in their heads and apply to their day-to-day activities.[2] By making explicit the ways of thinking that shape archival work, these studies can benefit even practitioners who think they have no time for detached, self-aware reflection. Though questions of "how" may be the more routine experience of archival work, questions of "why" always remain relevant.

An archival idea worth exploring as part of this intellectual history is the notion of the archivist's perspective. That archivists have a particular way of looking at things, distinct from that of other people who come into contact with records, is not a new idea. Fifty years ago, T. R. Schellenberg described the "basic methodological differences" between archivists and librarians, differences that derived from the nature of the materials the two groups of professionals dealt with. Methodology is not perspective, of course, but Schellenberg's understanding of archivists and their work was grounded in the belief that there were important distinctions between them and other kinds of information professionals. At about the same time, Ernst Posner, in his SAA presidential address of 1956, voiced a similar belief. "What, then, is the American archivist, this new man?" Posner asked, echoing Crevecoeur. His answer was largely given over to a description of the characteristics of archival practitioners in the United States, based on one of the first demographic surveys of the profession ever undertaken. But then he went on to enumerate a number of distinctive intellectual characteristics, including what he called "elasticity of thinking." Contemporary American archivists, Posner said, were in the habit of taking notions gathered from the still-small body of archival literature and rethinking them so as to apply to unforeseen professional problems. Finally, virtually all of Margaret Cross Norton's writings about archives were built on an insistence that archivists simply approached records in a way that was different from others, particularly historians, librarians, or records managers.[3]

More recently, talk of a singular perspective that archivists bring to their work has become more explicit, and it may be said to have had an obscure starting point. Consider this resolution, adopted at a meeting of the governing council of the SAA in January 1983: "Whereas, the archival profession in North America lacks a clear definition of what an archivist is; and Whereas, the absence of this definition of the minimum components necessary to distinguish an archivist lie at the heart of the majority of the most pressing issues facing the profession today; Therefore, the Council of the Society of American Archivists herewith establishes a study group of no more than five members to draft a statement defining an archivist." The minutes do not record anything of the discussion that ensued on introduction of the measure, and the motion passed, though with two abstentions.[4] Parse some of the phrases in this resolution. It begins with a flat assertion that the word *archivist* is not well defined. No proof is offered—proof is seldom required in "whereas" clauses—but by this time, accounts of confusion about who archivists were and what they did were commonplace. Virtually every archivist had a story to tell of a family member or cab driver who confused archivists with occulists, anarchists, and others. A formal survey conducted by a marketing firm had demonstrated that, even among the employers and "bosses" of archivists, there was often a lack of clarity about just exactly what archivists did.[5] This provided evidence for the resolution's insistence that the lack of clarity was the root cause of the important issues facing the profession. Only the drafting and acceptance of a more useful definition of *archivist* (and, by implication, of archival work) could resolve this confusion. Then the path might be opened not only to greater appreciation for archival work, but also to more substantial support of archival programs.

The resolution had a broader context in several related professional issues of the 1980s. Note the mention of the "minimum components necessary to distinguish an archivist." That was a reference to an extended discussion, then underway, of the proper qualifications for professional archivists and how best to specify and enforce those standards. The discussion usually focused on three related areas. The first was concerned with the establishment of graduate-level programs of pre-employment archival education in universities. A good deal of energy was wasted in debating the proper organizational setting for these programs—whether history departments or library schools—but in most cases they were directed by practicing archivists who also did a little teaching on the side. The number of archival education programs was still small, and their offerings ranged from the adequate to the well-intended but unsatisfactory. In most of them, a single overview introductory course was followed by one or more internships and practica, sometimes accompanied by periodic classroom discussions of what the students were learning and doing in internship placements. Spurred by the writings of some of the faculty who taught such courses and recognized their inadequacy—most notably Frank Burke of the National Archives of the United States and American University, in a seminal essay that was ostensibly about archival theory, but was actually about archival education—these bare-bones programs seemed inadequate preparation for a professional career. To improve them, new questions had to be asked. What should the curriculum of such graduate programs be? How many courses, and what kinds of course content, specifically in archives, should students take? What mechanisms for the formal accreditation of such programs by outside evaluating agencies or the professional societies should be developed? Several universities were beginning to devote greater resources to these programs, including the appointment of full-time archival faculty members. Similar discussions were more advanced in Canada, leading to the establishment of the first master's degree in archives at the University of British Columbia in 1981.[6]

A second focus of professional energy connected to the resolution to define an archivist was the development of a plan to certify the professional competence and abilities of individual archival practitioners. Other professions had well-established procedures to assure both potential employers and the public at large that anyone claiming their mantle was justified in doing so. A certified accountant, for example, was someone whose knowledge and skills had been tested, and could therefore be relied upon, not merely someone who was "good with numbers." Similar programs formally verified the credentials of doctors, lawyers, teachers, and engineers, and so this model was proposed for emulation by archivists. Discussion of this idea at professional meetings was sometimes acrimonious, but the SAA Council approved a certification plan in 1987. Designed to accommodate both archivists who had already been in the profession for some time (often with little or nothing in the way of formal education for their work) and those who were just entering it, this system provided for certification in two different ways. One could present evidence of one's credentials and professional activities and be "grandfathered" into the ranks of the certified, at least at the outset, or one could sit for a certification examination—the parallel to the bar exam or the exam for certified public accountants—and receive the designation. In either case, certification would be for a limited period, requiring periodic renewal, thereby encouraging continuing professional education and development. Work began immediately on constructing the certification exam: what were the things that an archivist should be expected to know and to do? While the number of professionals who take this exam has remained small over the intervening years, it is still administered.[7]

A third dimension of the context for the effort to define an archivist was a less successful effort to articulate the standards that programs calling themselves *archives* ought to be expected to meet. Thus, the 1980s saw some discussion of the possible accreditation by the professional societies of individual archival institutions. This was a time of rapid growth in the profession. Organizations and agencies that had been producing records for a long time for their own purposes, but had never before maintained formal programs to care for those records, were now establishing them, and archivists were being hired to manage them. This growth was particularly apparent in the private sector and in entities that were outside the ranks of traditional historical or cultural agencies. The number of archives of religious bodies—particularly Roman Catholic sisterhoods and dioceses—positively exploded, and businesses, hospitals, and other corporate entities were not far behind. Often founded because of the personal interest of an executive of the parent body, these archives varied widely in scope and program definition. Would it be possible to define the minimum standards that such new archives ought to meet? Could professional tools be developed whereby archivists in those settings could evaluate their own programs, identifying strengths and weaknesses, using the latter to argue for increased support from the people who were somewhat coldly identified as "resource allocators" for the archives? Though some interesting theoretical work was done on behalf of this idea and two self-study instruments were made available, the potential political problems of institutional accreditation proved insurmountable. What would happen if a given program were judged not to meet acceptable standards? Would the appropriate resource allocator be motivated to improve the program, through an investment of additional resources, or merely abandon all attempts and fire the archivist? Institutional accreditation remains today a professional path not taken.[8]

The desire to define an archivist was thus part of a larger effort to articulate more fully the nature and importance of archival work, not only to archivists themselves, but also to nonarchivists. As such, it was an attempt to improve the position that archives occupied—or did not occupy—in the public mind. At another meeting shortly after the defining resolution was adopted, the SAA Council established an Archives and Society Task Force, charged (as President David Gracy, the moving force behind the resolution, explained in his incoming presidential address) with four responsibilities: to draft a statement on the importance of archives to society at large; to propose ways in which archivists could raise the level of "public awareness, appreciation, understanding, and support" for archival work; to set some specific priorities in this area for the SAA to pursue in the near term; and, finally, to serve as a clearinghouse for information and ideas on the subject.[9] This Archives and Society initiative was perhaps the most successful of several efforts in this period that looked to the "consolidation of professional identity" (as I called it at the time), less because it actually accomplished a revolution in how the general public viewed archives than because it accustomed archivists themselves to thinking about how nonarchivists viewed them and their work. As a result, conscious efforts to explain the value of archives became a regular and accepted part of what archivists do.

The task force charged with defining the word *archivist* had less of an impact, but its work was nonetheless a significant step toward clarifying the nature of the archivist's perspective. Though the resolution had called for up to five members, in the end three were appointed: John Fleckner of the Smithsonian Institution; Trudy Huskamp Peterson of the National Archives; and myself, then of the archives of the Roman Catholic Archdiocese of Boston. We exchanged a few preliminary ideas beforehand—in those days, this was done by *letter*, if you can believe it—and then we met in Washington for two days to hammer out a statement. Our document purposely did not begin at what might have been the obvious starting point, namely, to define what an archivist was by describing what an archivist did. That would come later, but we felt it important to put the characteristic professional activities into a larger framework. Accordingly, after some high-flown introductory rhetoric ("The archivist is the trustee of the present and the past for future generations, . . . a saver and a destroyer, a holder and a sharer") we laid out a threefold structure for our definition: knowledge, values, practice. First and foremost, archivists shared a body of knowledge, and they also shared common values derived from that knowledge. Only then did they apply their knowledge and their values in practical situations. Knowledge and values were the keys to the archivist's perspective; practice was what archivists did, and how they did it, because they had that perspective. Knowledge was itself divided into two components: the general knowledge of history, literature, the natural and social sciences that came with a good liberal arts education; and specific knowledge about "the discipline of archives." The latter included "an understanding of the historical development and present status of archival practice, both in the archivist's own country and elsewhere; the origins and functions of archival records, their customary forms, arrangements and contents, and their use as research resources; and awareness of standards for conduct and practice adopted by the organized profession."[10]

The question of archival values interested me most at the time and, as I recall, I took the lead in drafting that particular section of the document. Like knowledge, values could be divided into the general and the particular. Common social and human values such as fairness, honesty, and cooperation were there. If our task force had been working in a more consciously postmodern age, we would probably not have included "objectivity" on this list, unwilling to enter into debate on what that word may mean. More important, however, were those values that were "specific to the archival profession and derive from a unifying belief in the value of historical records to society and of the archival mission to preserve them." To speak of "unifying belief" was to begin getting at the archivist's perspective, and we identified six important beliefs: that records in any form (this was a nod in the direction of the then just-expanding computer technologies) may contain information of long-term value; that preserving the integrity of the information in records was essential and that "continuity of custodianship" helped ensure it; that records were organic and were best understood in their own proper context; that records ought to be managed in a systematic way, encompassing both retention and destruction; that records ought to be organized so that a variety of possible clients could draw on them; and that the use of records ought to be encouraged in ways consistent with the competing demands of their physical preservation, the protection of privacy, and other obligations. Only after all this did we proceed to define archival practice, itemizing a fairly standard list of tasks (though not always using these exact words): appraisal, arrangement, description, access, outreach, preservation, and all the rest.

Our definition was published in the January 1984 issue of the *SAA Newsletter* (a publication now known as *Archival Outlook*), together with a call for comments. Exactly nine members of the profession commented, and excerpts from these were published in a subsequent issue of the newsletter with the hope, the editor said, that they would be useful "as consideration of the concepts of certification of archivists and accreditation of educational programs and/or archival institutions continues." One commentator criticized the document as too vague, maintaining that it offered no specific guidance on what qualifications to look for in an archival consultant, a task which (I say in our defense) we had not been assigned. The opening "poetry" of the document was both praised and reproved; there was objection to use of the word "client" to describe users of archives; and there was some not-unexpected, if tiresome, carping that the statement applied only to big, well-resourced archival institutions and overlooked small single-person operations. Another commentator had hoped for a "historical, etymological" definition so as to distinguish archivists more narrowly from other information professionals, but yet another believed that it should have been broadened so as to apply to both archivists and other records managers. Finally, one archivist criticized the definition for failing to stress the role that archives might play in areas of "major social concern." With those few responses, however, discussion of the definition of an archivist came to an abrupt end, and the whole effort almost immediately disappeared. The SAA Council passed a resolution thanking our drafting group—one member unaccountably voted no on this—and that was that.[11] Work did continue on the drafting of successively more detailed guidelines for archival education programs and on the specification of knowledge areas that would be covered by the certification exam, but "Archivist: A Definition" became one of the great forgotten documents of recent professional history.

And yet the definition—and its early attempt to delineate the archivist's perspective—rose from the dead a few years later when I was asked to prepare the introductory volume in the Archival Fundamentals Series, published by the SAA with the assistance of grant support from the National Historical Publications and Records Commission. That work, *Understanding Archives and Manuscripts*, was intended to provide a general introduction to the world of archives for beginners, and also for nonarchivists who wanted or needed to know something about archives in a preliminary way. It introduced basic concepts of archives and records work and provided a brief history of the archives profession in the United States before going on to describe who archivists were and what they did. The volume appeared in 1990 and was adopted for use in workshops and as a textbook in university archives courses. Its shortcomings became apparent quickly enough. The Internet did not exist in its pages, for example; near-universal use of the World Wide Web, by archivists and by the public at large, came only after its publication. Accordingly, a second edition, written with Richard Cox, appeared in 2006, maintaining the structure and much of the original discussion, but with significant new material as well.[12] In both versions, the old triad from the definition document—knowledge-values-practice—seemed the best way to accomplish the explanatory task at hand and, in a fuller form, that structure became the outline for the second half of the book, originally consisting of two chapters. One of these was entitled "The Archivist's Perspective: Knowledge and Values," the other "The Archivist's Task: Responsibilities and Duties."

Here was a more elaborated and explicit statement of the archivist's perspective. "Just as doctors think like doctors and lawyers think like lawyers," both editions say, "so archivists think like archivists: they analyze and understand archival problems in their own special way." The text proposed that the archivist's perspective was different from that of those who either created records in the first place or those who used them after the fact. Each of those groups viewed records merely as a means to some other end. The former saw records as byproducts of human activity, tools that helped them transact and accomplish certain business, whether personal or collective; it was that business that was most important. The latter saw records as sources of information useful for entirely different reasons, such as historical or genealogical research; those interests took precedence over the question of why the information had been recorded in the first place. Archivists, by contrast, had their own "habits of thinking and analyzing, together with characteristic attitudes that govern and guide their work." For them, records performed "not merely one service but a whole range of them, some of which cannot be anticipated." Making a variety of uses possible was the archivist's goal, and the archivist's perspective made achieving it possible, a perspective "derive[d] from a base of knowledge and a set of shared values, acquired and refined" over the course of an individual's career. The volume's second edition added reference to the role in this of "the traditions and experiences of the archival community," thereby suggesting that the development of perspective was a communal task, not merely an individual one for archivists. This was a way of highlighting the importance of professional involvement beyond one's own institution and of continuing education.[13]

Knowledge as the foundation for the archivist's perspective was now described in more expansive terms than had been possible in the 1984 definition. Four broad categories were discussed: knowledge of the individuals and institutions that produced records; knowledge of records themselves; knowledge of the variety of uses to which records might be put; and knowledge of archival principles. Some examples were offered in each category to show how an archivist looked at things differently from others who encountered records, even as the forms of those records changed. The officer who had kept the record books of a nineteenth-century orphanage, for example, was compared with the clerk who maintained the twentieth-century paper case files of a welfare agency and the twenty-first-century worker who maintained those same records in digital form: each of these was interested primarily in caring for the institution's clients, with the records an aid in doing so. An outside researcher studying those records, now or in the future, was likely to have either a broad historical or narrower genealogical purpose in mind. The archivist charged with maintaining the records, however, was motivated by different interests from either group and therefore asked different questions. Are all the records here, or are there gaps that need to be filled? How were the records kept originally and how, if necessary, could that order be physically reconstructed? How might the changing content of the information in the records be noted and described so that users will be able to find what they want? What impact has the changing format of the records had on how they are managed, used, and understood? Because archivists had these distinct questions, they looked for and saw different things when they encountered bodies of records. "The archivist learns to see through the records to larger insights that ultimately help explain the records, the actions that produced them, and the information they contain. The archivist can see how individuals and organizations reveal themselves, knowingly or not, through their records."[14] This emphasis on archival knowledge as a way of seeing was deliberate; it was a way of describing the foundational elements of the archivist's particular perspective.

Archival values were the other essential component of the perspective, and these too were elaborated more fully than in the original definition document. From a wider list of possibilities, seven values were discussed. These began with the assertion that archives existed in order to be used, not merely preserved for their own sake, and this led to other values that pertained to various aspects of archival work: that distinctions were necessary between records useful only in the near term and those with a more lasting usefulness; that those records which were preserved for the long term should be kept coherently; that they should be organized so as to facilitate their easy use; that sensitive information in records should be guarded from use so long as the sensitivity remained; that archival collections be administered equitably and impartially; and that archival institutions ought to cooperate with one another when appropriate. As with the discussion of archival knowledge, some examples of these values in practice were offered, and contrasts were drawn with the values that nonarchivists brought to their work. On the one hand, for example, a corporate creator of records might want to destroy some of them as soon as possible, fearing the exposure of wrong-doing; an outside researcher, on the other hand, might not recognize the need to guard for a certain time private information about living persons. The archivist had different values and therefore a different perspective. Moreover, even the changing technologies of records did not fundamentally alter the values archivists brought to their work. The importance of separating the permanently valuable from the merely transitory was consistent whether one was dealing with paper files or rapidly expanding digital memory; in fact, that task was all the more important.

This discussion of archival knowledge and values was an attempt to describe the archivist's perspective, and it was presented as a corrective to what many had come to criticize as a too-practical emphasis in contemporary archival thinking and writing. In the first half of the twentieth century in North America, archivists had been more likely to receive training than what could properly be called *education*. There were few formal, semester-length courses in archives as such, though there were a great many short-term workshops. These might be useful in preparing archivists for their first jobs, usually at the entry level, but they were less successful in anticipating a long career. For one or two professional generations, most archivists had learned their tasks and acquired their perspective on the job, after they had secured employment in an archival institution. This had given them a relentlessly pragmatic approach to their work, a disposition that was not entirely bad. Among other things, it encouraged the "elasticity of thinking" that Posner had observed. By emphasizing that knowledge and values preceded practice, however, the two editions of *Understanding Archives* attempted to shift the approach and provide a broader basis for professional education and development. In that, it was part of a movement toward what one writer described as a new "age of archival analysis," an age to which many, including Helen Samuels, contributed. This was also the era of the documentation strategy, an approach to archival collecting—this last word quickly proved problematic in this context—that stressed the importance of planning and inter-institutional cooperation. Samuels' essay of 1986, "Who Controls the Past," outlined the approach broadly, and her 1992 book, *Varsity Letters*, applied it specifically to the records of American higher education.[15] Both were important efforts to employ a broader perspective in the day-to-day demands of archival work.

If archivists have this distinct perspective, however, two questions remain: How do they acquire it, and what difference does it make? In particular, do they carry this perspective with them, perhaps especially after they cease to be archivists and move on to something else? Acquisition of the perspective still develops over the course of an individual archival career, but more now than formerly it is also grounded in the explicit course work of archival education. A number of universities in the United States and Canada have heeded Frank Burke's call for the appointment of full-time archival educators, situated both in history departments and in schools of library and information science. A few doctoral programs to prepare younger faculty to take up these positions have also emerged. Archival education programs (generally at the master's level) allow for multicourse sequences, in which the specific intellectual content of archives work can be examined and analyzed through the familiar methods of other academic disciplines: reading, discussion, original research, writing papers and theses, and so on. Such courses are able to offer archival education properly so called, rather than what Timothy Ericson once termed "education that might benefit an archivist" in such related but distinct areas as history or museum studies.[16] To be sure, this first generation of formal archival education programs has remained very fragile: universities often abandon them when the founding faculty retire or leave, and the job market for new faculty remains uncertain. The archival education glass is both half full and half empty. But the likelihood is greater now than it was a quarter-century ago that archivists-to-be will have the chance to study archives as an independent discipline and to develop their own perspective in a deliberate fashion.

This process has been aided in recent years by the expansion of the scholarly literature on the history and nature of recorded information. Scholars of a wide range of historical times and places have produced studies that show how human societies have captured, stored, and used information in all its many forms. M. T. Clanchy's *From Memory to Written Record* (1979; expanded 1993), a study of the transition from oral to written culture in Norman England, almost immediately became a "cult classic" among archivists, and it was only the first of many studies of writing and documents in the medieval period. Discussion of the customary forms and processes of information in ancient civilizations has also been particularly lively, with *Ancient Literacy* (1989) by William Harris a starting point from which others have proceeded. More broadly still, the cliché that our own is quintessentially an "information age" has prompted scholars to explore earlier ages that were no less so. Peter Burke's *Social History of Knowledge* (2000) and Daniel Headrick's *When Information Came of Age* (also 2000) are contributions to this reconstruction of how any society manages and uses information.[17] The application of these many studies specifically to archivists and their work is not hard to imagine. Archivists are responsible for managing a portion of the information by which our own society operates, and thus a knowledge of how this task has been accomplished elsewhere puts their efforts into a broader historical perspective. To the degree that archival education programs include consideration of such texts in their courses, they expand the base of knowledge that helps archivists develop their own perspective.

Applying their way of seeing things in settings other than archives is also something that archivists come instinctively to do. Like an eye for fine art or an ear for music, a perspective once acquired becomes so ingrained that its bearer applies it unthinkingly in new situations. Archivists who cease to work in archival programs but who go on to other professions have found that they carry their earlier knowledge and values, built up in archives, with them to their new professions. A session at the 2004 SAA annual meeting presented papers (never published) exploring this phenomenon by former archivists who now worked in education, health care, and social service.[18] They agreed that they did their current work differently because they had once been archivists. From personal conversations with Helen Samuels, the honoree of this volume, I know that her own post-archival work in university administration continued to be informed by her studies of the specifically archival dimensions of higher education. For myself, I know that I am a better historian for having been an archivist. Not only am I able to identify possible sources for my own historical research more readily than I might otherwise, but I also believe that I read historical sources differently—better—for knowing that they came from a context other than my own. They were not created to be my source materials, but for other purposes altogether, and I do not begin to understand them until I recognize that. Though now a full-time historian, I still retain my archivist's perspective.

For those who continue to work in archives, finding ways to develop and nurture the archivist's perspective remains an essential task. The daily demands of archival work are always pressing. There are new records to be appraised and acquired; there are users exploring a range of questions; there are issues of personnel, budget, and facilities management. Moreover, all these tasks have become more complex as the world has gone increasingly digital, with archivally valuable information now routinely captured and used in constantly-changing electronic formats that render existing hardware and software systems obsolete in no time. Archivists cannot hope to confront and succeed in the face of such an ongoing information revolution if they approach their work only with a body of practical habits. Theirs must indeed be an "elasticity of thinking" that is built on their broader knowledge and values. In this, Helen Samuels' insistence that conceptualization must precede action is a reliable guide for the challenges ahead. Archivists will succeed in facing those challenges only if they think like archivists before they act like archivists. In that thinking, they will rely on their unique perspective.

Notes

1 See, for example, J. Frank Cook, "The Blessings of Providence on an Association of Archivists," *American Archivist* 46 (Fall 1983): 374–99; Victor Gondos Jr., *J. Franklin Jameson and the Birth of the National Archives, 1906–1926* (Philadelphia: University of Pennsylvania Press, 1981); Richard J. Cox, ed., *Lester J. Cappon and the Relationship of History, Archives, and Scholarship in the Golden Age of Archival Theory* (Chicago: Society of American Archivists, 2004); Michele F. Pacifico, "Founding Mothers: Women in the Society of American Archivists," *American Archivist* 50 (Summer 1987): 370–89; Jacqueline Goggin, "Carter G. Woodson and the Collection of Source Materials for Afro-American History," *American Archivist* 48 (Summer 1985): 261–71. Donald R. McCoy's *The National Archives: America's Ministry of Documents, 1934-1968* (Chapel Hill: University of North Carolina Press, 1978) describes the origins of the National Archives of the United States; a full history of the comparable institution, originally known as the Public Archives of Canada, by Terry Cook and Glenn T. Wright (with Ian E. Wilson) is forthcoming. The first International Conference on the History of Records and Archives was held in Toronto in 2003, the second in Amsterdam in 2005, the third in Boston in 2007, the fourth in Perth (Australia) in 2008, and the fifth in London in 2010. Several titles have been reissued in the SAA Archival Classics series, including Ernst Posner's *Archives in the Ancient World* (2003; orig. pub. 1972); and S. Muller, J. A. Feith, and R. Fruin, *Manual for the Arrangement and Description of Archives* (2003; orig. pub. 1898). See some other titles in note 3 below.

2 Terry Cook, "What Is Past Is Prologue: A History of Archival Ideas Since 1898, and the Future Paradigm Shift," *Archivaria* 43 (Spring 1997): 17–63; Terry Cook, "Mind Over Matter: Towards a New Theory of Archival Appraisal," *The Archival Imagination: Essays in Honour of Hugh A. Taylor*, ed. Barbara Craig (Ottawa: Association of Canadian Archivists, 1992), 38–70; Terry Cook, "Macroappraisal in Theory and Practice: Origins, Characteristics, and Implementation in Canada, 1950-2000," *Archival Science* 5, nos. 2–4 (2005): 101–61; Brien Brothman, "Orders of Value: Probing the Theoretical Terms of Archival Practice," *Archivaria* 32 (1991): 78–100; James M. O'Toole, "On the Idea of Permanence," *American Archivist* 52 (Winter 1989): 10–25; and James M. O'Toole, "On the Idea of Uniqueness," *American Archivist* 57 (Fall 1994): 632–58.

3 T. R. Schellenberg, *Modern Archives: Principles and Techniques* (Chicago: University of Chicago Press, 1956), 23; Ernst Posner, "What, Then, Is the American Archivist, This New Man?" *Archives and the Public Interest: Selected Essays by Ernst Posner*, ed. Ken Munden (Washington, DC: Public Affairs Press, 1967), 165; Thornton W. Mitchell, ed., *Norton on Archives: The Writings of Margaret Cross Norton on Archival and Records Management* (Carbondale: Southern Illinois University Press, 1975). All three of these titles have also been reissued as part of the SAA Classics series.

4 Council Minutes, January 22–23, 1983, in *American Archivist* 46 (Summer 1983): 355.

5 Sidney J. Levy and Albert G. Robles, *The Image of Archivists: Resource Allocators' Perceptions* (Chicago: Society of American Archivists, 1984).

6 See Terry Eastwood, "Nurturing Archival Education in the University," *American Archivist* 51 (Summer 1988): 228–52; Jacqueline S. Goggin, "'That We Shall Truly Deserve the Title of Profession': The Training and Education of Archivists, 1930–1960," *American Archivist* 47 (Summer 1984): 243–54; Frank G. Burke, "The Future Course of Archival Theory in the United States," *American Archivist* 44 (Winter 1981): 40–44. For a snapshot of later developments, see James M. O'Toole, "The Archival Curriculum: Where Are We Now?" *Archival Issues* 22 (1997): 103–16. For an update on Canadian views on this subject, which emphasizes the distinctiveness of archival knowledge, see Tom Nesmith, "What is an Archival Education?" *Journal of the Society of Archivists* 28, no. 1 (April 2007): 1–17; and Terry Cook "'The Imperative of Challenging Absolutes' in Graduate Archival Education Programs: Issues for Educators and the Profession," *American Archivist* 63 (Fall/Winter 2000): 380–91.

7 There has been, to my knowledge, no systematic analysis of the certification process during the two decades of its existence; such a study should be undertaken. On the origins of the program, see "Report of the Interim Board for Certification," *SAA Newsletter* (January 1988): 10-15; see also William J. Maher, "Contexts for Understanding Professional Certification: Opening Pandora's Box?" *American Archivist* 51 (Fall 1988): 408–27. For a look at some recent data

relating to certified archivists, see Anne P. Diffendal, "Certified Archivists in the A*CENSUS," *American Archivist* 69 (Fall/Winter 2006): 419–37.

8 Paul H. McCarthy, "The Management of Archives: A Research Agenda," *American Archivist* 51 (Winter-Spring 1988): 52–69; Mary Jo Pugh and William Joyce, eds., *Evaluation of Archival Institutions: Services, Principles, and Guide to Self-Study* (Chicago: Society of American Archivists, 1982); Paul H. McCarthy Jr., ed., *Archives Assessment and Planning Workbook* (Chicago: Society of American Archivists, 1989).

9 David B. Gracy, "Archives and Society: The First Archival Revolution," *American Archivist* 47 (Spring 1984): 7–10.

10 "Archivist: A Definition," *SAA Newsletter* (January 1984): 4–5.

11 "Commentary on 'Archivist: A Definition,'" *SAA Newsletter* (March 1984): 3-4; Council Minutes, October 2, 1983, in *American Archivist* 47 (Winter 1984): 95.

12 James M. O'Toole, *Understanding Archives and Manuscripts* (Chicago: Society of American Archivists, 1990); James M. O'Toole and Richard J. Cox, *Understanding Archives and Manuscripts* (Chicago: Society of American Archivists, 2006). Hereafter, these are referred to, respectively, as *Understanding I* and *Understanding II.*

13 *Understanding I,* 49; *Understanding II,* 87–88. Former SAA president Hugh Taylor, in a series of provocative essays, tried to "imagine archives," as numerous scholars have tried to imagine commonalities for other communities, whereby archivists in institutions big and small, public and private, textual or visual or digital media, all recognize certain values, concepts, a professional history, and a mission that affords them a shared perspective as a community of archivists, despite their many differences. See Terry Cook and Gordon Dodds, eds., *Imagining Archives: Essays and Reflections by Hugh A. Taylor* (Lanham, MD, and Oxford: Society of American Archivists and Association of Canadian Archivists in association with Scarecrow Press, 2003), especially 16–27.

14 *Understanding II,* 91–92; *Understanding I,* 51, had said that archivists are "trained and practiced at seeing through records." The distinction is not unimportant, emphasizing that archival education is truly a matter of broad "education," not mere "training."

15 Helen W. Samuels, "Who Controls the Past," *American Archivist* 49 (Spring 1986): 109–124; Helen W. Samuels, *Varsity Letters: Documenting Modern Colleges and Universities* (Metuchen, NJ: Scarecrow Press and Society of American Archivists, 1992). On documentation strategies, see also Larry J. Hackman and Joan Warnow-Blewett, "The Documentation Strategy Process: A Model and a Case Study," *American Archivist* 50 (Winter 1987): 12–47; and Richard J. Cox, "A Documentation Strategy Case Study: Western New York," *American Archivist* 52 (Spring 1989): 192–200.

16 Timothy L. Ericson, "Professional Associations and Archival Education: A Different Role, or a Different Theater?" *American Archivist* 51 (Summer 1990): 298–311.

17 So great has been the scholarly output in this area in the last two decades that it is impossible now, as it would not have been just two decades ago, to list all the relevant titles. Those noted here are M. T. Clanchy, *From Memory to Written Record: England 1066–1307* (Cambridge, MA: Harvard University Press, 1979; second edition London: Blackwell, 1993); William V. Harris, *Ancient Literacy* (Cambridge, MA: Harvard University Press, 1989); Peter Burke, *A Social History of Knowledge: From Gutenberg to Diderot* (Cambridge: Polity, 2000); and Daniel R. Headrick, *When Information Came of Age: Technologies of Knowledge in the Age of Reason and Revolution, 1700–1850* (New York: Oxford University Press, 2000). For a useful overview, see also Henri-Jean Martin, *The History and Power of Writing,* trans. Lydia G. Cochrane (Chicago: University of Chicago Press, 1994). At his death in January 2007, Martin was working on a general history of information, which will, one hopes, be published posthumously.

18 The session, called "The Value of the Archivist's Perspective," held on August 5, 2004, at the SAA meeting in Boston, included Jacqueline Goggin (formerly of the Library of Congress), Lawrence Dowler (formerly of Yale University), and myself.

ETHICS AND THE ARCHIVE: "AN INCESSANT MOVEMENT OF RECONTEXTUALISATION"

VERNE HARRIS

Setting Context 1: Helen Samuels

Helen Samuels' contribution to archival theory and practice is inestimable. Her body of work, her corpus, particularly in the late 1980s and 1990s, played a significant role in destabilising what she called "the traditional view of the archivist as the passive assembler of an existing record,"[1] and, together with the work of Hans Booms and Terry Cook, created the possibility of a post-Schellenbergian approach to what we call archival appraisal. Dominant discourses in archives today, in my view, underestimate her contribution. Her interlinked concepts of "documentation strategy" and "functional analysis" are usually noted, if at all, as catalysts for or precursors to the bigger movements of "macroappraisal" which became widespread in many parts of the world from the mid-1990s.

I remember being electrified simultaneously by her work and that of Terry Cook in the late 1980s. Caught in the isolation of apartheid South Africa, and being a practitioner, more or less instinctively, within an "archives for justice" paradigm, I felt the power—and the resonance with my experience—of four primary propositions (and energies) in their work:

- Appraisal is far more than the mere selection of records for preservation. Instead, appraisal is about the documenting of societal processes, and reaches across and into all the traditional archival functions.

- The archivist is not a passive assembler, a custodian, a keeper. Rather, she is an active shaper of social memory, and should embrace the role of memory activist.
- The archivist is not, in the first instance, a reader of and a worker with texts. Rather, she illuminates texts through an intense, critical, and multidisciplinary engagement with contexts. She is a purveyor of context, and of necessity pays the sharpest and broadest attention possible to it.
- The archivist must go beyond merely marking, or bemoaning, the many gaps in the documentary record. She is obliged to seek ways of filling those gaps, of bringing in those voices, those experiences, those memories—in short, those strangers—marginalised in or excluded from the record.

These propositions were and remain far-reaching, even revolutionary. They assumed a fresh epistemological frame for archival endeavour and implied a new politics and a new ethics for such endeavour. At the time, I folded them seamlessly into my own (in retrospect, profoundly positivist and quintessentially South African) experience of the archive in the contexts of struggle for justice in apartheid South Africa. Today, the resonance of the propositions feels different to me, but its power remains. I am still electrified by it. My subsequent readings and rereadings in the work of Jacques Derrida, my prolonged engagement with deconstruction, and, no doubt, my experiences in post-apartheid South Africa, have provided multiple refoldings. Arguably, the propositions are now at once threads in a growing tapestry *and* the remains—the loose threads—of weavings long past.

It is with gratitude to Helen Samuels, and in homage to her work, that I offer this essay. In it I provide a reading of *ethics* and *archive*—ethics and the archive, ethics in the archive, archival ethics. For what electrified me in those early readings of her work was, precisely, its politico-ethical underpinnings and implications. Although, for the most part, she herself eschewed explicit engagement with these dimensions, and diminishes still her work's significance to them, their presence was unavoidable and remains compelling for both archival theory and practice.

Setting Context 2: Verne Harris

For more than a decade now I have, incessantly and almost exclusively, written about ethics. Why that is, and what it might mean, are questions worth pondering, despite the threat of inordinate boredom. Personal contexts are unavoidable. Without (yet) going as far as Derrida—who argued that there is nothing outside context,[2] and who also argued that "there are only contexts without any centre or absolute anchoring"[3]—it is incontrovertible that my thinking of ethics has been shaped by my contexts. Equally, my actions—more precisely, my attempts to take ethical action—have been shaped by my perceptions of my contexts. The verb *shape,* of course, is a word, like all words, without absolute anchoring. Semantically, it stretches across a continuum we could define by the poles *determine* and *influence.* Being *determined by* one's contexts—a condition with obvious Marxian reference[4]—is far removed from being *influenced by* context. I think we would all accept, without hesitation, that our contexts have *influenced* us. And I think we would all hesitate at the thought of our contexts *determining* us. Of course, the questions of what it is I mean by *contexts,* what it is readers understand by *contexts,* and what it is that Derrida understands, as opposed to what archivists understand, by *contexts,* together open up another realm of uncertainty. But enough of marking the uncertainty which haunts even our certitudes—*especially* our certitudes. I begin with a brief autobiographical (re)contextualisation.

I first encountered conventional archives as a student of history in the early 1980s. It was through historiography that I developed a more or less radical, or historical materialist, critique of the apartheid archival system. In 1985 I took up employment in South Africa's State Archives Service (as the country's National Archives was then called), and worked my way up the ranks at the same time as becoming increasingly involved in anti-apartheid structures outside the workplace. I saw my role in the system as one of digging out information for use in the struggles against apartheid. By the early 1990s, as a formal transition from apartheid to democracy was being negotiated, I found myself less in two conflicting streams, and more in two increasingly parallel streams: on the one hand, I was a participant in the state's transformation endeavours; on the other, I participated in the African National Congress-led reimagining of South Africa's archival system. Our country's negotiated settlement determined that state structures and establishments would remain in place after the first national democratic election in 1994, subject to gradual processes of what we still call transformation. As head of transformation in the renamed National Archives of South Africa, and head of liaison between the National Archives and the Truth and Reconciliation Commission, I felt the resilience of these two streams, sometimes running in the same direction, sometimes in opposite directions. In 2001 I left the National Archives for nongovernmental organisations and the academy, and for a freedom I felt was under growing threat from what I call processes of re-bureaucratisation in the post-apartheid state. Needless to say, in the last nine years, I (and the organisations I have worked for) have frequently found ourselves in conflict with organs of the state. We have declined to go with the (main)stream.

Every exercise of contextualisation, autobiographical or otherwise, must take into account that in principle there can be no limit to context. In the words of Derrida: "the finiteness of a context is never secured or simple, there is an indefinite opening of every context, an essential non-totalisation."[5] So, here I merely *suggest* the outline of an autobiographical context, of a crucible of experience in which my thinking about the archive has formed. In this crucible—one of struggle, of conflict, and of contest—I have never considered the possibility that an archivist can be, or should aspire to be, an impartial custodian (or passive assembler, or mere keeper). Arguably, my shaping has not allowed me to think of the archivist in such a way. In this crucible of my contexts, the archivist is called (indeed, compelled) to activism, to the importuning of justice to come, to the telling rather than the keeping of story. Not surprisingly perhaps, in these contexts, "the ethical" has always loomed large. My professional experience has been one not of the occasional ethical dilemma, but of the routine, even the daily dilemma—together with the occasional (and clearly related) drama of litigation, formal complaint, disciplinary procedure, and trial by media. In the early days, I frequently consulted and cited relevant professional codes of ethical conduct; indeed, I was one of the drafters of the South African Society of Archivists' 1993 *Professional Code*. But through the last decade and more, I have avoided such codes. To put it bluntly, in the hurly-burly of the archive at work, I have found them—and I am choosing my words carefully—to be entirely useless.

Ironically, the experience which inaugurated, and defined, this alienation occurred in the same year of the South African code's introduction.[6]

At the time I was working as a records management archivist in South Africa's State Archives Service, and began receiving reports from junior officials in government departments that they had received instructions to destroy certain categories of classified records without authorisation from the director of archives. The apartheid regime was still in place, but engaged in a transition process ahead of the country's first democratic election the following year. My investigation revealed that these departments were acting on instructions in a government-wide circular issued by the state's security secretariat. This was a large-scale destruction of sensitive public records outside the operation of the Archives Act. I briefed the director accordingly and was assured that every effort would be made through official channels to halt the destruction exercise. As days went by and it became apparent that official action was achieving nothing, and that even if it eventually was successful, it would be too late to prevent the loss of huge quantities of records, I was faced with a difficult decision. Should I allow the official process to take its course, or should I act outside official channels in an attempt to stop the destruction? In my struggle with right and wrong, I turned to the newly-formulated national *Professional Code*. One of its provisions asserted that "the archivist has a moral duty to preserve information about the past and present for the future"[7]; another that "the archivist must protect the integrity of archives/information against alteration, removal, damage and theft."[8] Surely this was a powerful mandate to break the rules, to break the law if necessary, in acting against what I believed to be the illegal destruction of public records with archival value? And yet the code also posited the following: "At all times the archivist must act within the parameters of the policy laid down by his/her employer"[9] and "the archivist respects the confidentiality of records in his/her care as determined in consultation with his/her employer."[10] My employer was the apartheid state. For me to disclose what was happening to the press and other outside agencies, especially by providing them with a copy of the circular instruction (which was itself a classified document) would involve defying state policy on confidentiality, breaking public service regulations on proper conduct, and committing an offence in terms of the Protection of Information Act—which at the time carried a maximum penalty of ten years' imprisonment. I was confronted by contradictory imperatives, and had no useful professional guidance on how to resolve them.

Ultimately, I did what was wrong in the eyes of the law, my employer, and the last-quoted tenets of the code. I disclosed what was happening to a journalist and to the nongovernmental organisation Lawyers for Human Rights, and provided them with copies of supporting documentation. My employer was subsequently taken to court and forced to acknowledge that the destruction exercise had ignored the operation of the Archives Act. I had become a whistleblower, someone who exposes wrong-doing, most commonly in the context of an employer-employee relationship. In making my decision, I had been forced to reach beyond articulations of right and wrong provided by law and professional ethics. I had scoured my own sense of right and wrong in an engagement with my understanding of human rights, my identification with a variety of relevant social values, an assessment of risk to me and my family, as well as the consequences of the loss of rich evidence essential to the pursuit of justice in a post-apartheid South Africa. In the end, my moment of decision was an intensely subjective one. It was a debate between me and my conscience, informed of course by many layers of context. And this, I want to argue, is where all of us find ourselves after we have exhausted the space provided by investigation, analysis, and discussion. There is no knowing of right without giving account to personal morality. For each of us has the right, and the obligation, to be true to ourselves. It remains a question, of course, as to whether I made a decision, in the strictest sense. It felt like a decision at the time. But in retrospect, the analysis I undertook made it clear what I *had* to do. I did what had to be done rather than take a leap over the abyss constituted by choice. In the next section of this essay I return to the questions of choice and decision, from a more theoretical perspective.

What have I made of this and a myriad of similar experiences? And what has my experience made of me? Impossible questions to answer beyond a life lived and an opus offered. Experience, of course, is always mediated. My positing of the archivist as an activist, as an importuner of justice to come, as a teller of story, is, in crude terms, a reading of and from my own experience. In my case, and I am sure it is not a coincidence, for as long as I have eschewed professional codes of ethics, I have been (consciously) reading experience within a frame and in the language of what can be called deconstruction. This is not the place for an exploration of what deconstruction might mean. But a preliminary outline of core concepts is necessary, beginning with the word *deconstruction* and the concept archived in it. Jacques Derrida resisted definitions, although he teased his audiences with a relentless semantic flirtation. For instance:

> One of the definitions of what is called deconstruction would be the effort to take this limitless context into account, to pay the sharpest and the broadest attention possible to context, and thus to an incessant movement of recontextualisation.[11]

Deconstruction, whether it is understood in relation primarily to "an incessant movement" or to the *paying of attention* to such movement, has to do with a fundamental opening to what power excludes, or ignores, or marginalises—a fundamental opening to what is closed out. There is always a politics of (re)contextualisation. Power will always expect to determine context. (As I, here, have expected to determine an autobiographical context.) And the call of justice is to trouble this expectation. In the words of Derrida, justice "bears witness to that which will not allow itself to be enclosed within a context,"[12] especially not a predetermined, naturalised context of power.

The phrase *the call of justice,* of course, raises a host of questions. In numerous texts, I have explored what is meant by the word *justice,* what is meant by the phrase *the call of justice,* and what in various traditions is meant by the slogan, *archives for justice.*[13] Space will not allow a reinscription of what are admittedly complex and possibly tedious arguments. My privileging justice is a response to three imperatives, which I do no more than name here.[14] First, I believe—and clearly I'm expressing a belief rather than offering an analysis—that the call of justice is the most important of all calls. It comes from beyond records and archives. It comes through the fabric of injustice which is our experience of life. Obviously the call sounds differentially—it will sound less insistently for a manuscript librarian in a well-resourced private library somewhere in North America than it will for an overworked and emotionally strung-out archivist in the East Timor Truth Commission, for example. But always the call will sound. Secondly, the structural pull in all recordmaking is toward the replication of existing relations of power, with the attendant exclusions, privilegings, and marginalisations. Archivists cannot avoid complicity, for institutionally (and often legally) they are positioned within structures of power. But we can work against its pull and for me it is a moral imperative to do so. And thirdly, those who have power—the elites—use "the archive" as an instrument of power, whether they be elites in repressive states, emerging democracies, or established democracies; whether they be elites in state bureaucracies, large corporations, intellectual establishments, or church hierarchies. If justice is not to be forgotten in the process, if "use" is not to become "abuse," then archivists and other recordmakers are obliged at the very least to trouble such use, to interrogate it, to insist that it disclose itself, to create space for alternative or contrary uses. For me, responding to these three imperatives marks the beginning of a just politics in archives. And the beginning of an appropriate professional ethics.

The beginning has to be about a fundamental opening—an opening to the voice of "the other," to the haunting of context, to the knocking of the stranger, to Derrida's ghosts that flit behind, through, and under the concrete presence of power. The beginning is to invite a fundamental hospitality that values and gives energy to experiences belonging to the stranger. This, in my view, is the beginning of ethics. For Jacques Derrida, it *is* ethics.[15] Of course, the demands of hospitality play out differentially in relation to power. It is easier, for example, for the powerful to be hospitable. But always hospitality demands what is impossible. For it reaches to *every* stranger. And it wants the host to become the guest. And it forestalls any determination of who is the host and who is the guest. This conundrum plays out every time we hear a knock on our door—whether the door be the boundary of a professional discourse, the immigration office of a country, an entrance to a suburban home, or the boxes containing the documents of a new archival acquisition.

Who would ever dare to say they hear with full confidence the call of justice? How can we ever be sure that it is the call of justice sounding in our ears? I do not know the answers to these questions. I do not know that there can be answers. Following thinkers like Derrida and Emmanuel Levinas—and, in a longer and extrapolatory reading, thinkers like Helen Samuels and Terry Cook—I believe that we begin to discern the call when we turn our ears to the strangers knocking at the door and feel thereby the imperative to offer these strangers our archival hospitality.

Reading Ethics

In my reading, the English-language discourses around ethics in relation to recordmaking and the archive are dominated by inscriptions of theory, codifications of principle, and case studies. There is very little articulation of praxis. By praxis I mean the connecting, the binding, the articulating, of theory with practice. I mean a practice of ethics hospitable to theory. In the United States, the commentaries with which the Society of American Archivists supplemented its 1992 Code of Ethics could be read as an attempt to find a praxis. But how do we read the subsequent removal, or separation, of these commentaries? The inordinate influence of lawyers and particular layers of law on professional space? A loss of nerve? A legitimate response to an environment inhospitable to praxis?

The dominant discourse on archival ethics—in the United States, in my own country, and elsewhere—I would argue, far from advocating what I have called "a fundamental hospitality," instead is founded in, and promotes, what I can only call "fundamental separation." It is a discourse determined to keep out what is always already inside and to keep separate what belongs together. It is a discourse unwilling to pay attention—sharp, broad, or otherwise—to the incessant movement of recontextualisation, in the Derridean sense described above. It is a discourse antithetical to hospitality. Clearly, a close reading of the discourse would be necessary to substantiate such assertions, but space is not on my side. Here I propose merely to name three movements, or orders, of separation now informing the discourse, and thus discouraging attention to recontextualisation.

First movement of separation. So much of the discourse is premised on a more or less neat separation of domains—the private and the public, the personal and the institutional, the legal and the ethical, the professional and the nonprofessional. I am *not* suggesting that these distinctions have no validity, nor that they have no influence in the real world, nor that the determination of boundaries is unnecessary or undesirable. I *am* suggesting that the neatness of their separation is highly problematic. For in this neatness, the interpenetration of domains is denied. Complexity is disguised. And the full and true challenge of the ethical is avoided. Let me illustrate such neat separation by simply quoting, without comment, three brief excerpts from Karen Benedict's 2003 book *Ethics and the Archival Profession*, published and endorsed by the SAA. All three are to be found in the book's introductory essay: (1) "Ultimately, each person must answer to his or her own conscience if personal and professional morality conflict."[16] (2) "Confusion frequently seems to arise within the profession between what are *legal* and what are *ethical* obligations. Copyright, intellectual property rights, tax consequences, and privacy are matters of law."[17] (3) "Legal and ethical courses of action do sometimes conflict, forcing individuals to make a choice. In doing so, however, it is a matter of personal conscience...."[18]

Second movement of separation. So much of the discourse constitutes a barricading of "the professional" from the dynamics of power and authority. In this mode, "the professional" must be protected from "the political." To me this is an impossible defence intellectually, and an impossible stance practically, in the real world of daily archival work. For politics is, precisely, the engagement of power with principle, which no archivist can avoid. And this power-principle engagement defines "the ethical." There can be no purely ethical question, nor for that matter a purely political one. The ethical and the political are always implicated in one another. As Derrida argued: "every time the ethical and the political are caught in a knot, in an irreducible intrication, this does not mean that they are simply tangled, but that what seems not to have to be negotiated politically . . . is . . . subject to political transaction: and this political transaction . . . is not an accident, a degeneration, or a last resort; it is prescribed by ethical duty itself."[19] The professional acts ethically not when she keeps politics at bay, but when she finds a just politics in action.

Third movement of separation. The notion of the ethical assumes a decision—a choice for right and against wrong. I think those who have read Karen Benedict's book will agree with me that such "decision" lies at the heart of every one of its many case studies. Rightly so. But I am uncomfortable with the dominant discourse's disregard for the abyss over which every one of us stands when we choose between right and wrong. Strictly speaking, we need to attend to a myriad of questions here, such as the following: Where does deconstruction of the classic right-wrong binary opposition leave us? Who is authorised to declare a decision right or wrong? Is one who chooses the least wrong option making a right decision? An impossible complexity. An abyss. But let us pause at just two questions. If, on the one hand, a right decision, an ethical decision, presupposes the gathering in and analysis of all relevant contextual information; and if, on the other hand, we are right in saying that there is an indefinite opening of every context, that even a particular defined context resists saturation, then does the ethical not catch us in a bind? I believe it does. But not inordinately. Not enough or in a way to justify inaction. While reading the case studies in Karen Benedict's book, I almost always felt that I needed more information, a better understanding of context, before I would be able to decide. I felt caught in a bind, but not paralysed. The imperative is to gather in as much relevant information as can reasonably be expected in the circumstances, deploy the instruments of rational analysis as thoroughly as possible in the circumstances, and then to act accordingly. But what if (and here comes the second question) such a process does not constitute the making of a decision? We gather in relevant information, we do the analysis, and the analysis determines what we must do. For Jacques Derrida, this is not about decision: "It is when it is not possible to know what must be done, when knowledge is not and cannot be determining that a decision is possible as such."[20] The Derridean decision is always a leap. It is the act(ion) of faith when rational analysis fails to make it clear what choice must be taken. Decision happens in:

> situations in which, forced to obey two apparently antinomical imperatives, I literally do not know what to do, . . . and I must then *take* what is called a *decision* and a *responsibility*, a responsible decision . . . . Even if I had at my disposal, or could acquire all knowledge, all possible science or consciousness on this matter—as must in fact be done, this is a duty—an infinite leap still remains before me, because a responsible decision, if it is to be the event of a decision in the face of two contradictory imperatives, cannot simply be dictated, programmed, prescribed by knowledge as such. This is why I am tempted to speak of a *profession of faith*.[21]

An abyss indeed. And the archivist who stands above it is truly caught in a bind. More precisely, a double-bind—for we are bound by duty, a duty clearly ethical through and through, to a full acquisition of relevant knowledge based on thorough research, but the acquisition can never be fully full, and if we succeed to a reasonable degree we are still attended by the spectre of two contradictory imperatives and thus, ultimately, by a leap beyond rational analysis. It takes faith to regard closely the abyss over which every one of us stands when we choose between right and wrong.

As you can tell, my reading of the discourse is an argument for an ethics not of separations, but of bindings. For an ethics which befriends the abyss. An ethics which pays the sharpest and the broadest attention possible to an incessant movement of (and need for) recontextualisation. An ethics, in short, of hospitality.

A Case Study: Nelson Mandela's Prison Archive

What might all this mean—I hear Helen Samuels and Terry Cook asking—for an archivist in the hurly-burly of the archive at work? If we cannot answer this question, then we and our ideas deserve only to be shelved in an ivory tower. So I move toward a conclusion by offering something of a case study, one in the restricted space of a single records accumulation, or archives group, or collection of documents.[22] The case, I believe, speaks to questions like the following: "What does the call of justice mean for someone working all day every day processing archival collections?"

Nelson Mandela was in prison for twenty-seven years. During that time, he was incarcerated in five different prisons, including Robben Island, where he spent nearly eighteen years. He was released in 1990. In the transition period leading up to South Africa's first democratic election in 1994, the state consolidated all the files of political prisoners from the apartheid era at Pretoria Central Prison. Although a mass of state documentation was destroyed ahead of the election, this collection of prison files was passed intact to the new post-apartheid government.[23] Five years later, it was transferred to the National Archives, after strong lobbying *inter alia* from the Truth and Reconciliation Commission. In 2004 Mandela authorised my project team at the Nelson Mandela Foundation to access and study his own files in this collection.[24] While we anticipated a large and archivally rich set of records, what we discovered overwhelmed us: approximately two hundred standard government files, most bursting with documentation, still awaiting even rudimentary processing. The order of the files was arbitrary. The only finding aid was a very rough listing littered with errors. Many of the files were in a perilous condition, with loose documents, no apparent internal order, damaged paper, and fading faxes and other early forms of copied records. The informational content we have encountered is extraordinary. Throughout his incarceration Mandela was kept under intense surveillance, with several state agencies collaborating to document his every move. It seems that copies of every letter he received or wrote, whether or not they survived the censors, were filed after analysis. Here we see represented in exemplary fashion the apartheid system's obsessive recordmaking and the documentary infrastructure of a police state actually at work. This was matched, I must hasten to add, by Mandela's own obsessive recordmaking—this was a man who understood the power of the record. As the elected leader of the most senior political prisoners, he represented his comrades on a wide range of issues, so that the files constitute a window into the experiences of many others. This dimension intensified dramatically in the 1980s, with Mandela inaugurating "talks about talks" with the state on South Africa's future. The files almost explode in scale, with a detailed tracing of every move by the state to assess the broader political environment, to control the negotiations, and to manipulate Mandela.

I am assuming that I do not need to establish further for this readership the importance of these files. I am assuming, too, that I do not need to demonstrate the responsibility carried by the National Archives to ensure their preservation and accessibility. And I am assuming that I do not need to detail the elementary processing required to make this archive both intelligible and usable. So, let us assume an elementary intervention, informed by the highest standards of conventional archival arrangement and description. This alone constitutes a huge task, a task which is not unrelated to justice. However, it is also a task routinely undertaken by archivists using systems (intellectual and technological) which are oppressive. A task, in other words, which can be all about control. So, were we one day to be done with this task in relation to the Mandela files, then the call of justice would only have begun to sound in our ears. Justice would not be done with us, nor, I hope, we with it.

During six years of fitful work with Nelson Mandela's prison files, my team has encountered a host of Derridean strangers, those ghosts haunting the archival world of order and hierarchy. Here I propose merely to name the major categories of *stranger* encountered by us—eleven of them. These are the ones we have learned names for. We are aware of many as yet unnamed or nameless strangers, and in truth have often felt overwhelmed by strangeness.

1. Substantial as this archive is, dense as its documentation of processes accumulated over nearly three decades, we quickly became aware of absences, the records which should have been there but were not: the estranged ones. ("The stranger" is not

a stable category. Every one who is not a stranger can become estranged, and the stranger can find belonging.) We have not begun a systematic search yet, but already we have identified strays: prison files on Mandela located in Cape Town, now transferred to the National Archives in Pretoria; a collection of official photographs of Mandela which went missing from Robben Island; stray prison-era personal records which we located in the African National Congress (ANC) headquarters, with the Soweto Heritage Trust, and in private possession; and a prison occurrence book which went missing from Pollsmoor Prison.

2. It is justifiable to treat the Mandela prison files as a discrete accumulation—a *fonds*— although it was violently removed from a particular institutional context and inserted into a more or less artificial collection of political prisoner files. We have heard the call to explore these recordmaking contexts.
3. Immediately one is overwhelmed by a cacophony of calls. The files are linked into a vast and shifting web of other records accumulations, each, of course, with its own strays. We have, for example, begun to engage Mandela's personal archives. Soon after we initiated this publicly, a former security policeman came forward with two of Mandela's prison notebooks, which had been in his private possession for over thirty years. We have only begun to mark what appear to be the primary strands in the web—the personal archives of Mandela, his family, and all with whom he corresponded from prison; the ANC; legal firms which attended to his interests while in prison; Prison Services head office; the Security Police; the Department of Justice; National Intelligence; the Prime Minister's Office; and so on.
4. Each of these strands comprises a myriad of institutional, political, biographical, and other layers. Let me name just one: the apartheid prison system, with its codes, rules, regulations, cultures, discourses, languages, idioms, personalities, and so on, all changing over time.
5. We have found numerous letters, both incoming and outgoing, which never reached their destinations. Each one, then, is at home in the archive but estranged, belonging elsewhere. Is it

destiny, is it the call of justice, that these letters be released from captivity? Even if their original destinations have changed, possibly irrevocably?

6. Because of Mandela's leadership role in prison, the stories of other prisoners are marked in his files. How can we mark these markings to facilitate access to them by these other former prisoners, their families, and associates?
7. The question of access immediately congregates a throng of strangers. How many strangers need to be consulted, by law and by right, before the archive can be placed in the public domain?
8. Amongst all the codings embedded in the files, one stands out. All of them need to be identified of course, but this one is critical. The prisoners used codes in their correspondence with the outside world—personal, family and organisational. We have only just begun the search for formal ANC organisational codes; recently we found one, dating from the early 1980s, in the archives of former ANC president Oliver Tambo.[25]
9. The vast majority of the texts in these files are either in English or Afrikaans, with a smattering in isiXhosa. What are the imperatives to effect translation? And in what languages should the finding aids and other descriptive instruments be? (I ask these questions in the context of a country which has eleven official languages.)
10. As we invest so much energy in engaging this single accumulation of records, we hear the voices of a host of more or less neglected accumulations. Some are closely connected, most notably the files of other political prisoners, others are not. Is our hospitality to the Mandela files predicated on the neglect of others? Is any act of hospitality predicated on such neglect? Can a turning to one ever avoid a turning away from another?
11. As we have read through the files, documented our findings, posed questions, marked spaces to explore, pursued particular strands, and so on, we have become acutely aware of how the strangeness within each of us is determinative of what we hear and what we do not hear. Unavoidably, the Mandela files have become a terrain in which we are working with our own

> strangers. A question, then, for every archivist: how to mark the personal traces we leave in our work?

What I have described above is the experience of haunting[26]—the experience of being haunted by strangers. Haunted by the infinite reach of strangeness. Haunted by ghosts of absence and non-presence. An experience not unlike, and not unrelated to, the experience of standing over an abyss. An experience suggested—if not named—in the work of Helen Samuels: the archivist confronted by a record rendered meaningful only by analysis, in the documentation strategy she proposed, of an ever-unfolding horizon of context(s), and a record shaped indelibly by those multiple contexts as much as by the manifold absences within the holdings of any one archival institution, or even within a single *fonds*.

Now let me return to the question I posed at the beginning of this case study: "What does the call of justice mean for someone working all day every day in an archives processing collections?" I want to suggest that this case study, like Helen Samuels' corpus, posits an archivist open to being haunted. An archivist, therefore, who while striving to do the possible to the best of her ability, is always aware of the impossible demand facing her. An archivist who, in the face of the strangers haunting her, is reaching for an impossible hospitality, is attempting always to give strangers welcome, is striving to make the archive a home. There is no place here for the faint-hearted, nor for bureaucratic functionaries, even if they be diligent.

Beginnings

I have been haunting readers for long enough. Let me close with three provocations. First, what I am positing is an archivist, or recordmaker, who responds to being haunted by paying the sharpest and the broadest attention possible to context, and thus to an incessant movement of continual recontextualisation. I am positing an archivist not deterred by the abyss, but rather filled with the passion of hospitality. Secondly, I want to suggest that for such an archivist professional codes of ethics would not be of much use in the hurly-burly of daily work. The challenge is to open these codes to the incessant movements that signal haunting. And lastly, I have privileged energies that bind together even as they place in a bind. An ethics of hospitality demands of the practitioner commitment to binding together in an openness to hospitality *while being ceaselessly bound* by both the imperatives and the limitations of such binding. I do not think it is an accident that one of the etymological contexts, if not roots, of the word *religion* is constituted by the Latin word *religare,* to tie or bind. In its Derridean sense, religion is about a fundamental hospitality to the limitless strands of what needs to be bound together, and a consequent determination to be ceaselessly binding strands together. In this deepest sense, the call sounding in our ears is a religious call—a call to what Derrida calls religion without religion.[27] It is here, in responding to this call, in embarking on the spiritual quest which the great Hugh Taylor embraced, that the archivist truly finds her journey.[28]

Notes

This essay began its life as a keynote paper for the conference Archives and Ethics: Reflections on Practice, held at the University of Wisconsin, Milwaukee, November 2007. Significantly, it was at this conference that I finally met Helen Samuels. She was in the audience, and provided me with robust feedback, both from the floor and during my subsequent visit to her Chicago home. A truncated version of the paper was published in the Dutch architectural journal *Volume* 15 (2008). I have used elements of the paper for several conference papers since, and it has inevitably been through processes of refinement. New elements have inserted themselves. I am grateful to Helen and many later listeners and readers for their responses. Particularly valuable were those offered by my mentor of over twenty years, Terry Cook, and the great Norwegian archivist, Gudmund Valderhaug.

1 Helen Samuels, *Varsity Letters: Documenting Modern Colleges and Universities* (Metuchen, NJ: Scarecrow Press and Society of American Archivists, 1992), 265.

2 Jacques Derrida, *Limited Inc* (Evanston: Northwestern University Press, 1988), 136.

3 Ibid., 12.

4 By "Marxian reference," I do not mean Marx himself. Rather, I signal a reference which congregates many competing discourses around the name "Marx," a reference which conjures up Engels, Lenin, and Trotsky as much as it does Marx, a reference which also conjures up Althusser and Sartre, Mao and Gramsci, and even Derrida. All of them have insisted on human agency as positioned within contexts. All of them have either privileged material contexts or at least flirted with such a privileging.

5 Derrida, *Limited Inc,* 137.

6 Here I rehearse a story told previously in my *Archives and Justice: A South African Perspective* (Chicago: Society of American Archivists, 2007), 209–11.

7 South African Society of Archivists, *Professional Code for South African Archivists* (Pretoria: SASA, 1993), section 4.1.

8 Ibid., 4.3.

9 Ibid., 4.6.1.

10 Ibid., 4.6.2.

11 Derrida, *Limited Inc,* 136.

12 Jacques Derrida and Maurizio Ferraris, *A Taste for the Secret* (Cambridge, UK: Polity, 2001), 17.

13 See, for example, many of the essays in my *Archives and Justice.*

14 I draw this from my "Archives, Politics and Justice," in Margaret Procter, Michael Cook, and Caroline Williams, eds., *Political Pressure and the Archival Record* (Chicago: Society of American Archivists, 2006).

15 Derrida made this argument in numerous texts. See, for example, Jacques Derrida, *Politics of Friendship* (London and New York: Verso, 1997); and Jacques Derrida and Anne Dufourmantelle, *Of Hospitality* (Stanford: Stanford University Press, 2000). In the last decade of his life, from the 1994 publication in French of *Politics of Friendship,* Derrida repeatedly engaged the theme of hospitality. For a brilliant reading of Derrida on ethics, see Robert Gibbs, *Why Ethics? Signs of Responsibilities* (Princeton, NJ: Princeton University Press, 2000).

16 Karen Benedict, *Ethics and the Archival Profession: Introduction and Case Studies* (Chicago: Society of American Archivists, 2003), 9.

17 Ibid., 12.

18 Ibid., 16.

19 Jacques Derrida, *Negotiations: Interventions and Interviews 1971-2001* (Stanford: Stanford University Press, 2002), 304.

20 Jacques Derrida, *Points . . . Interviews 1974-1994* (Stanford: Stanford University Press, 1995), 147.

21 Derrida, *Negotiations,* 372.

22 This little case study, which I first recounted during a lecture in Pittsburgh in 2006 and have repeated in a number of other contexts, draws heavily from readings by Anthea Josias (now at the University of Michigan) of Nelson Mandela's prison files. I am indebted to her for her generosity in sharing them with me.

23 *Truth and Reconciliation Commission of South Africa Report* (Cape Town, 1998), vol. 1, ch. 8.

24 A range of people have worked on the project since 2004, but Anthea Josias was the lead researcher.

25 This archives is located in the library of the University of Fort Hare in South Africa.

26 The question of spectrality, of ghosts, of presences in absence, of absences in presence, is central to the thinking of Jacques Derrida.

27 See John Caputo, *The Prayers and Tears of Jacques Derrida: Religion without Religion* (Bloomington: Indiana University Press, 1997), 194–96.

28 Taylor's embrace of this quest can be engaged, for example, in many essays in his *Imagining Archives: Essays and Reflections by Hugh A. Taylor,* ed. Terry Cook and Gordon Dodds (Lanham, MD, and Oxford: Society of American Archivists and Association of Canadian Archivists in association with Scarecrow Press, 2003). Read, especially, chapter 17, "The Archivist, the Letter, and the Spirit" (originally published in *Archivaria* in 1997).

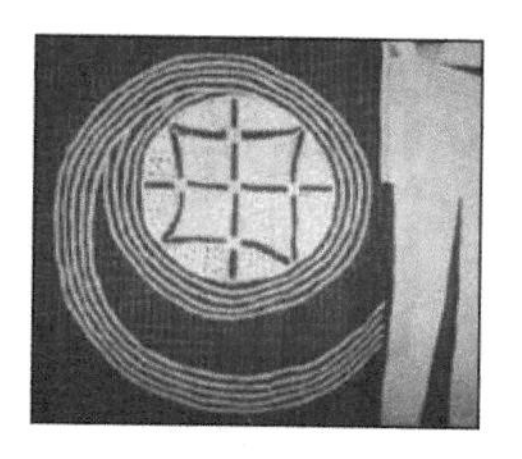

HOW ARCHIVISTS "CONTROL THE PAST"

RANDALL C. JIMERSON

In her seminal article, "Who Controls the Past," Helen Samuels elaborated the concept of documentation strategies as a means of improving how archivists and other information professionals select the documentary traces that will define today's society for future generations of researchers. The article's title, taken from George Orwell's *Nineteen Eighty-Four*, also introduced archivists to the relevance of Orwell's observations about human memory and recordkeeping. This epigraph used by Samuels combines two separate passages from Orwell:

> Who controls the past, controls the future; who controls the present, controls the past. . . .The mutability of the past is the central tenet of Ingsoc. Past events, it is argued, have no objective existence, but survive only in written records and in human memories. The past is whatever the records and the memories agree upon. And since the Party is in full control of all records, and in equally full control of the minds of its members, it follows that the past is whatever the Party chooses to make it.[1]

Orwell's frightening vision of a society without authentic and reliable records framed Samuels' recommendations for documentation strategies to counteract this dangerous possibility. Although widely cited by archivists, the article's title is frequently misstated, turning Orwell's phrase into a question: Who controls the past? In fact, by quoting Orwell, Samuels implies a direct connection between archival documentation of the past and the potential political power and societal influence of archivists. A deeper reading of Orwell's writings—inspired by the Samuels citation and by my 1968 freshman humanities course devoted entirely to Orwell's works—reveals the broad extent of his insights into the importance of archives.

Orwell on Documenting Society

Documenting society has always been a political activity. Since ancient times those in power have strengthened their control through careful recordkeeping. Those lacking power to create, preserve, and use documentary evidence become marginalized and neglected—by history, by historians, and by society. However, the French Revolution introduced the concept that official government records should be created and used to protect the rights of all citizens, not just the political, social, and clerical leaders. George Orwell imagined a society in which this concept has been rescinded and the rulers control all information. This nightmare world—for those concerned about history, memory, and recordkeeping—infuses Orwell's writings. Both in his well-known totalitarian dystopias and in his less familiar essays, Orwell warned against powerful rulers who controlled their subjects, in part, by hiding or distorting the truth through destruction or alteration of records. The only means for preserving accurate accounts of the past, Orwell argued, was through reliable records and human memory. Although he never directly addressed the nature of archives *per se*, his writings about the necessity for authentic written records clearly embed Orwell in the realm of archives. His perspective and his commitment coincide with subsequent efforts to demonstrate the centrality of archives to modern society and the dangers of a world without access to reliable information about the past and present.

Orwell's early writings focused on social and political causes. After serving with the Indian Imperial Police in Burma, Orwell developed a distaste for imperialism and racism, which imbued his novel *Burmese Days* (1934). His personal experience living with the poor and downtrodden led to two nonfictional accounts, *Down and Out in Paris and London* (1933) and *The Road to Wigan Pier* (1937). In these works he articulated his belief in human dignity and his commitment to the goals of socialism (if not to the socialist British Labour Party).

Orwell's interest in history, records, and evidence grew out of his personal experiences as a volunteer fighting against Franco during the Spanish Civil War. In his 1938 memoir of the war, *Homage to Catalonia*, Orwell stated that most of the reporting from Spain amounted to little more than propaganda for one side or the other. He concluded, "It will never be possible to get a completely accurate and unbiased account of the Barcelona fighting, because the necessary records do not exist. Future historians will have nothing to go upon except a mass of accusations and party propaganda."[2] In Orwell's experience, personal memory could expose the falsity of collective memory and historical accounts of events that he had witnessed. However, without records (archival memory), the necessary corroboration could not exist.

Orwell's commitment to historical truth, based on accurate records, emerged again in two essays about the Spanish Civil War that he wrote during the Second World War. "During the Spanish Civil War I found myself feeling very strongly that a true history of this war never would or could be written. Accurate figures, objective accounts of what was happening, simply did not exist," Orwell wrote in 1944. "And if Franco or anyone at all resembling him remains in power, the history of the war will consist quite largely of 'facts' which millions of people now living know to be lies."[3] Even if he were overthrown, Orwell asked in 1943, "What kind of records will Franco have left behind him? Suppose even that the records kept on the Government side are recoverable—even so, how is a true history of the war to be written?" Almost any account was bound to be "a partisan history, unreliable" even regarding minor events. Some kind of history would be written, Orwell predicted, "and after those who actually remember the war are dead, it will be universally accepted. So for all practical purposes the lie will have become truth."[4]

Orwell repeatedly lamented the fragmentary record of the past and the resulting gaps in our knowledge of historical events. His experiences in the Spanish and world wars, however, caused him to recognize that "History is written by the winners."[5] This affected his view of all historical accounts: "When I think of antiquity, the detail that frightens me is that those hundreds of millions of slaves on whose backs civilization rested generation after generation have left behind them no record whatever."[6] These silences of the archives, the absence of records, deeply troubled Orwell.

When faced with the difficult task of distinguishing truth from lies, Orwell concluded, the first recourse to establish what actually occurred is through authentic records. Without reliable records, he warned, "One has no way of verifying the facts, one is not even fully certain that they have happened, and one is always presented with totally different interpretations from different sources."[7] The problem was identifying which of the competing allegations were true and which false. First-hand accounts, accurate newspaper reporting, official records, and personal papers could establish claims to veracity. Such records formed the best antidote to lies and propaganda, as Orwell had recognized from his Spanish Civil War experience.

Once corrupt leaders destroy or alter all available written records, only the memory of eyewitnesses can reestablish a truthful account of events. Personal memory is fallible and can be challenged or undermined. Totalitarian leaders could exploit this weakness to strengthen their control over the population. The malleability of memory thus rendered it less reliable than written records. From ancient Sumeria through the Middle Ages, this was a central argument for those favoring reliance on documents rather than oral tradition. In modern Western societies, it has become a commonplace assumption. For example, taxpayers must produce written receipts to support deductions, students must submit transcripts of academic achievement when applying for jobs, and courts demand that mere "hearsay" evidence be verified through cross-examination of witnesses or proving the authenticity and veracity of documents. Although some societies maintain oral traditions, these are often considered "primitive" or inferior by most Westerners.

The significance of recorded information—whether in textual, visual, sound, or electronic media—rests on cultural assumptions that give validation to particular kinds of evidence. For most modern Westerners, only documentary evidence can be fully trusted. Orwell argued that falsifications and lies about the past enabled dictators to control the present and the future. Authentic records—the very stuff of archives—would provide one of the strongest bulwarks against totalitarianism.

These arguments provide a political justification for accurate recordkeeping. Since this is central to the mission of archival institutions, it endows them with political and societal significance. As Orwell recognized, even without the imprimatur of archival custody, records that can be authenticated provide a basis for constructing truth claims about the past. They offer a corrective to false statements, lies, and propaganda. Citizens can rely on such documents to achieve accurate knowledge and to counter the power of unscrupulous leaders and demagogues.

Animal Farm and the Politics of Memory

Orwell's early essays warning of such dangers reached a limited readership. By turning to fiction, however, he gained a worldwide audience, portraying the dangers of totalitarianism in vivid imagery, especially in his last two novels published in the final five years of his life: *Animal Farm* (1945) and *Nineteen Eighty-Four* (1949). Central to the themes of both novels are the concerns outlined above regarding history, memory, and records. Although it would be a stretch to claim that these are novels *about* archives (Orwell never used the word *archives*), in both works the importance of records is critical in securing the ruling elite's control over public thought. Without the ability to refer to authentic documents, it becomes impossible to contradict political orthodoxy.

In *Animal Farm*, Orwell created a "fairy story" revealing the tendency toward totalitarianism among barnyard animals who escape the tyranny of their human masters only to suffer oppression from their own kind. Central to the development of this allegory is the concept of a written document—a rudimentary constitution—designed to protect the rights of the animals. The ruling pigs alter the written rules to suit their needs. They cover up this falsification of the record by challenging the other animals' memory of the past. When the animals claim that they had all agreed on a resolution never to engage in trade with humans, spokes-pig Squealer asks shrewdly, "'Are you certain that this is not something you have dreamed, comrades? Have you any record of such a resolution? Is it written down anywhere?' And since it was certainly true that nothing of the kind existed in writing, the animals were satisfied that they had been mistaken."[8] Each time a written rule is altered, the animals question their own memory, rather than doubt the validity of the documents. Written evidence trumps memory as an authority, even for the recent past.

When falsifying existing records is not enough, the pigs create or "discover" new documents to solidify their absolute power. In order to discredit the rebellious pig Snowball, Squealer tells the animals that Snowball was a secret agent of farmer Jones. "It has all been proved by documents which he left behind him and which we have only just discovered," Squealer claims. When the noble horse, Boxer, argues that Snowball had been a hero of the Battle of the Cowshed, Squealer replies, "That was our mistake, comrade. For we know now—it is written down in the secret documents that we have found—that in reality he was trying to lure us to our doom."[9] Memory could thus be altered by powerful lies and vivid descriptions as well as by falsified documents. Repeated often enough, and without contradictory documentary evidence, such lies become truth.

The pigs use their mastery of writing to solidify their power and authority. Squealer tells the animals that the pigs "had to expend enormous labours every day upon mysterious things called 'files,' 'reports,' 'minutes,' and 'memoranda.' These were large sheets of paper which had to be closely covered with writing, and as soon as they were so covered, they were burnt in the furnace."[10] (This is what a records manager would call a very short-term retention schedule!) For the pigs of *Animal Farm*, it is simply a way to use written records to mystify and dominate the proletarian animals. Without recourse to their own records, the animals lack any validation for both personal and collective memory of the past.

Animal Farm depicts a totalitarian society in which the rulers consolidate their power through control of both memory and records. With no verifiable records of the past, the animals' memory can be altered or crushed by the domineering pigs. Orwell thus found a fictional setting to illustrate his growing alarm for a society in which absolute power could be wielded not with a gun, but with a pen. Without records, without archives, there could be no authentic and reliable evidence of the past.

Nineteen Eighty-Four and the Destruction of Memory

Orwell brought these concerns to full realization in his final and most famous novel, *Nineteen Eighty-Four*, the very title of which has entered popular parlance as shorthand for the dangers of political oppression. In portraying a bleak totalitarian dystopia, he demonstrated the ability of the rulers to control their subjects through constant surveillance, thought control, and manipulation of language. Central to this power was the Party's control over written records and human memory. As Ingsoc claims, past events "survive only in written records and in human memories." By controlling both the records and individual memories, the Party can define the past as it chooses.[11]

Orwell clearly distinguished memory from records. They are alternative means of understanding and representing the past. Yet it is clear that written records hold primacy in this system of thought control. Orwell did not use the term *archives,* but his message clearly addresses concerns facing modern archives.

Documentary evidence lies at the heart of Orwell's depiction of totalitarianism. The Party gains control over records both by destroying and by altering them. It is significant that Winston Smith, the ill-fated hero of *Nineteen Eighty-Four,* works in the Records Department of Oceania, which plays a central role in solidifying the Party's power. He daily must go back into the archives of government reports, newspapers, books, and party speeches to alter the historical record in accordance with changing needs of those in power. To show the leader's infallibility, Smith and his fellow records specialists would "rewrite a paragraph of Big Brother's speech in such a way as to make him predict the thing that had actually happened." Once a revised version of the record has been substituted, the obsolete records of the past are quickly discarded down the "memory hole"—Newspeak for a chute that leads to an enormous central incinerator.[12] Winston ponders this revision of the past, when the Party controls all written records. "The past, he reflected, had not merely been altered, it had been actually destroyed. For how could you establish even the most obvious fact when there existed no record outside your own memory?"[13] As Orwell recognizes, memory relies on corroborating evidence, on records that provide tangible links to the past.

Total control over records gave the Party absolute power over knowledge of everything outside one's personal experience. "If the Party could thrust its hand into the past and say of this or that event, *it never happened*—that, surely, was more terrifying than mere torture and death," Orwell warned. " . . . And if all others accepted the lie which the Party imposed—if all records told the same tale—then the lie passed into history and became truth. 'Who controls the past' ran the Party slogan, 'controls the future: who controls the present controls the past.'"[14] The power over history thus shapes the political power of the ruling elite, and this power over historical reality comes from control of written records—from archives. The widespread falsification of records requires extensive archival institutions, perverting the proper role of archives. "There were the vast repositories where the corrected documents were stored, and the hidden furnaces where the original copies were destroyed," Orwell explains.[15]

In his efforts to undermine the Party's control, Winston imagines the possibility of a resistance movement, "small groups of people banding themselves together, and gradually growing, and even leaving a few records behind, so that the next generation can carry on where we have left off."[16] Records could link together these rebel bands, who could verify through these records each other's memories of the past. The futility of such hope becomes apparent at the end, when Party loyalist O'Brien interrogates the captured Winston Smith:

> O'Brien smiled faintly. . . . "Does the past exist concretely, in space? Is there somewhere or other a place, a world of solid objects, where the past is still happening?"
>
> "No."
>
> "Then where does the past exist, if at all?"
>
> "In records. It is written down."
>
> "In records. And—?"
>
> "In the mind. In human memories."
>
> "In memory. Very well, then. We, the Party, control all records, and we control all memories. Then we control the past, do we not? . . . . Whatever the Party holds to be the truth *is* truth."[17]

This completes the cycle, perfects the lie. It fills the archives with doctored records and the human mind with false memories. As Winston recognizes, "History has stopped. Nothing exists except an endless present in which the Party is always right."[18] In the end, of course, Winston Smith succumbs to the mind control of the Party and comes to love Big Brother. Yet Orwell did not think the future hopeless for mankind. As he stated in a letter to Francis Henson, he set the story in Britain "in order to emphasize that the English-speaking races are not innately better than anyone else and that totalitarianism, *if not fought against*, could triumph anywhere."[19] The possibility of—the necessity for—resistance to tyranny gave Orwell some optimism about the future. *Nineteen Eighty-Four* was not a hopeless lament, but a cry for action, a call to unseat the forces of totalitarianism wherever they might arise. Read from an archival perspective, Orwell clearly seems to suggest that trustworthy recordkeeping and archival systems could even preclude the rise of totalitarianism.

Orwell in the Archives

If it is true that the victors write history, as Orwell declared, it follows that they often employ archives to institutionalize their power. This has been true throughout human history. Despots, kings, religious leaders, and presidents have legitimized their authority through documents, both symbolic and real. From Greek and Roman archives preserving records of governmental power, to medieval charters, to the American Constitution, such documents have strengthened the power of the rulers. Yet the rights of subjects have also been protected by resorting to documents, from the Magna Carta to the American Bill of Rights, to the French Declaration of the Rights of Man.

In archives, from ancient to modern times, the preponderance of records has documented the activities and interests of the more powerful groups in society. Education, literacy, and access to power have reinforced the entrenched interests of the elite classes. Representation in archives has privileged the stories of these groups, since it is their voices that are most often recorded and thus most frequently heard in historical accounts. Examples abound of societies in which the powerful have ruled by controlling and manipulating information and records. As Noam Chomsky argues, "elites depend on sophisticated information systems, media control, surveillance" and related measures to maintain their positions.[20] Echoing the implicit objective of Orwell's Ministry of Truth, Jacques Derrida explicitly links political power to the archives: "There is no political power without control of the archive, if not of memory."[21]

Even in democratic societies, public officials often seek to control public discourse by manipulating access to information. Government secrecy is the enemy of truth, and the beginning of amnesia. Thus, as we look at the relationships among memory, history, and archives, we should keep in mind that these are vital concerns for contemporary society, not merely for totalitarian regimes of ancient empires or Orwellian fiction. At times the nature of our social and political systems—including our personal and collective liberties—may be at stake.

As George Orwell reminded us, the very act of remembering can be a powerful political statement. What we remember, and how we form and preserve our memories, defines us as individuals, as members of various social groups, and as a society. Confronted by demands for sanitizing the past—for a collective drink of the fatal kool-aid of amnesia—we can join

Winston Smith in resistance, or passively consume what leaders offer us. Faced with the overpowering totalitarian control of the Party, Smith placed his hope in history. When members of a clandestine resistance group offer a toast, the leader asks, "What shall it be this time? . . . To the death of Big Brother? To humanity? To the future?" "To the past," Winston suggests. "The past is more important," his comrade agrees.[22] For Orwell, memory—both personal and collective—provided the only antidote to totalitarianism. The political act of defiance required both personal memory and the corroborating evidence of authentic and reliable records. Orwell found his answer to the dangers of political repression in the archives.

Archival Selection and Appraisal

If archives wield this potential power to contribute to the rights and welfare of all people in society, and thus to resist the documentary hegemony of the powerful, how do they exercise this influence? Unfortunately, the answer often is: poorly. Archivists have not yet become savvy about publicizing their programs, promoting their services, or explaining their expertise. In a few instances, archivists have gained some recognition as advocates for accountability in government, business, and the academy. Archivists have also made significant progress in documenting marginalized groups, such as racial minorities, women, laborers, ethnic groups, and lesbian/gay/bisexual/transgender communities. The terms *archival, archive,* and *archives* have entered public consciousness, but usually in applications that make many archivists cringe—such as the option to "archive" telephone messages for up to ninety days, or as a reference to a place where older website messages are stored indiscriminately.

Although often hidden from public awareness, archivists have made particularly impressive improvements in their methods of selection and appraisal. Societal groups once overlooked have gained a foothold in many archives. The political and social ferment of the 1960s led some historians and archivists to argue that archivists should actively intervene to ensure documentation of underrepresented social groups in American archives, which generally reflected the powerful groups in society.[23] This challenge to the profession not only led to some important new initiatives in documenting minority groups in archives, but also opened a debate over the "neutrality" of archival acquisition. Until recently, defining institutional collecting policies for manuscripts and archives was considered a routine and impartial process, with the archivist passively accepting records offered by others or obtaining only records that matched a narrow band of research trends set by academic historians. This view has recently been challenged by calls for archivists to recognize that the decision to collect some manuscripts and not others is freighted with cultural value systems that privilege certain groups in society over others. Decisions about acquisition of archives and manuscripts have significant implications for documentation of modern society, yet critics charge that, at least until recently, archival selection often occurs without conceptual thinking about purpose and methods.[24]

In recent years an increasing number of archivists have responded to studies of social memory and of postmodernism by recognizing much more consciously and vocally that their role in selection and acquisition does shape the documentary record. Because designating a document as archival endows it with elevated status, archivists must make such decisions deliberately, based on careful research, and then documented transparently for posterity. Records in institutional archives are important as evidence, but they are also important as societal documentation.

One of the most creative responses to these concerns has been the concept of documentation strategy, first proposed in the mid-1980s by Helen Samuels, Larry Hackman, Joan Warnow-Blewett, and others. In response to the call for active engagement in collecting underrepresented sources, the documentation strategy challenged archivists to move beyond their institutional walls to examine sources from many institutions for documenting broad aspects of society. The documentation strategy acknowledged the need for activism in order to "assure the documentation of an ongoing issue, activity, or geographic area," in the midst of an increasingly complicated modern society.[25] This approach encouraged inter-institutional cooperation and consideration of all formats of information and documentation, including print and artifact sources, and provided a planning mechanism for systematic analysis and selection of documents.[26] Although sometimes criticized as unworkable in terms of its logistics, the concept of documentation strategy provided an instructive challenge to archivists weighing decisions about records selection and documentation of society. At the very least, it encouraged archivists to consider archival records as part of the larger universe of information.

It also recognized that, even for a particular theme being documented, archival sources comprised one aspect of documentation in many types of media in numerous kinds of institutions, well beyond the purview of any one archival repository to acquire.[27]

Ensuring adequate documentation for all sectors of society both protects individuals' rights and preserves documentation for subsequent analysis of society's past. Because meaning is something that is always constructed and not inherent in documents, archivists need to think clearly about how they determine which manuscripts and records should be collected and preserved. Archival principles and functions developed largely in the context of nineteenth-century bureaucratic states. The principle of provenance, for example, reflects assumptions about organizational structures and hierarchies that privilege those in power and those with a recognized collectivity and a recordmaking and recordkeeping capacity.

Opening archives to new perspectives, allowing the voices marginalized by the dominant culture to speak freely, requires a broader concept of provenance, and a willingness to modify traditional archival practices. Historian Adele Perry contends that "the absences in the colonial archive are not neutral, voluntary, or strictly literal"; they are "silences borne of and perpetuated by violence and radical inequality."[28] As Joel Wurl argues, archivists should consider provenance to apply to collective social entities, including ethnic groups.[29] Archival significance thus would not depend upon formal bureaucratic and organizational structures, which many marginalized groups lack.

Concern for the "voiceless populations" in society should lead archivists to adjust their procedures for all basic archival functions. In selection and appraisal, archivists need to be conscious of the potential bias in their traditional methods. Archival choices have long been shaped by the constraints of power relations and sources of funding. To counter these biases, archivists should seek opportunities to preserve records of those often overlooked by their collecting strategies and recognize the broader concept of "societal provenance" for an entire community (including those groups often marginalized or silenced in archival collecting policies and appraisal guidelines).[30] For example, even within institutional archives, archivists could also recognize the historical value of records documenting workers, community relations, and other aspects of corporate or organizational activities beyond the legal, fiscal, and administrative requirements. Government archivists could ensure that their records reflect the ideas, concerns, and issues of citizens articulated through their interaction with government agencies, not merely mirroring the activities of the state itself. In making such decisions regarding archival selection and appraisal, archivists run the risk of intruding their own concepts of history and society into the archival record. However, this is an inevitable consequence of archival agency. It is a subjectivity that should not be denied, as archivists often do, but admitted, documented, and entered into the public discourse on memory, history, and archives.[31]

Archival appraisal typically reflects power relations established by state agencies, business corporations, religious establishments, academic institutions, and other power brokers. The archivist making appraisal decisions quite literally determines what evidence and information future generations will be able to see. In this sense, the archivist shapes documentation for the future as much as the original creator of the records. The archivist thereby becomes co-creator of the archival record. The question is not whether the archivist imposes her or his personal interpretation, but whether the action is taken consciously and documented openly, as the archivist actively documents society and its institutions. And it may no longer be enough to select and acquire records that have already been created, even in this more self-conscious and transparently accountable manner. Archivists may need to consider going beyond their custodial role and filling in the gaps, to ensure that documentation is created where it is missing, and to address the needs of those outside the societal power structures.

Controlling the Past

Taking such bold action will not be easy for some archivists to accept. Archivists often seem most comfortable developing technical procedures for organizing records, preparing finding aids to guide researchers, and preserving and managing everything from paper documents to electronic records. These techniques are valuable tools to provide services to our users. Yet too much emphasis on *how* to fulfill our duties can obscure *why* we complete these tasks. It is important to step back occasionally and remember the ultimate purposes that we fulfill, and the societal needs we satisfy, both today and for posterity.

In a democratic system, archival records protect the rights of citizens, hold public and corporate officials accountable, and provide essential evidence of legal, administrative, and financial transactions. In combination with libraries, museums, and related institutions, archives also contribute to documenting and preserving cultural heritage. Despite these significant contributions to the legal structures and cultural heritage of society, compared to libraries and museums, archives remain to most citizens relatively unknown, mysterious, and alien.

In recent years, scholars in many disciplines have examined the memory of society and its relationship to national identity, power relationships, collective psychology, and history. Although many historians have probed these issues, few have examined in detail the relationship between memory and documents. Recent discourses regarding the concept of social memory have challenged our assumptions about objective, neutral, and impartial archives. The archive has become a focal point for analysis and contestation, not simply a hallowed shrine of Truth. Yet most scholars still discuss the archive as though repositories operate with no human intervention or control. Their analysis of the problematic nature of some archival sources rarely acknowledges the role or agency of the archivist.

The information revolution taking place in today's society transforms how data is created, stored, transmitted, and preserved for future reference. Media experts and technology pundits repeatedly declare that the scale and scope of this is "unprecedented" in human history. However, if we look back to previous eras of changing information infrastructure, we can see precedents for today's changes in the earlier introductions of industrial systems, classification schema, the printing press, paper, parchment, the Greek alphabet, clay tablets, cuneiform scripts, and structured language itself.

One of the enduring beliefs regarding archives is that they enshrine "the truth" in unchanging forms that provide accurate evidence from the past. As stated publicly—and attested by their footnotes—historians, legal researchers, and other investigators rely on the integrity of records preserved in archives for much of their contemporaneous sources of information about the past. Given this reliance on documents and archives, the process by which they are compiled and preserved deserves much more careful scrutiny. In recent years, many archivists have begun to focus on understanding and responding to the needs of a multiplicity of users of archival records. At its core, this emphasis speaks to the future. It privileges the usability of archives over simple estimates of their value in documenting the past. Archival memory takes account of the past, but its orientation is to the present and future uses of such knowledge. Far from being lost in the past, archivists constantly anticipate and prepare for the future. As they do so, archivists construct memory and continually re-construct it to meet the ever-changing needs of society.

Although frequently cited as "the memory of society," this metaphor for archival records does not stand up to critical analysis. We need to distinguish between archival documentation and human memory. Archives are both more and less than memory, perhaps an antidote to fallible human cognition—although even that analogy begins to crumble when we consider the malleable and ever-changing nature of archival documentation. In responding to such challenges, it is essential to consider archives as one of several professions dedicated to documenting society and providing essential information to individuals. This was one of the great breakthroughs of Helen Samuels' concept of documentation strategies, which emphasized cooperation among archives, libraries, museums, and other information professions.

Within this broader context of information professionals, archivists have a moral professional responsibility to balance the support that archives have often given to the status quo by giving equal voice to those groups that too often have been marginalized and silenced. Documenting society requires attention both to the leaders and to the common citizens, to voices of power and to victims of oppression. Examples of the use of records and archives to redress social wrongs and support the causes of justice and community consciousness among marginalized groups are growing more numerous. Archivists can become active agents for change, in accordance with their existing professional principles, by taking decisive steps to counter the biases of previous archival practices. Even in democratic societies, public officials often seek to control public discourse by manipulating access to information.

Responding effectively to the challenges of using the power of archives for the public good will require a broad commitment by the archival profession to reflect on underlying assumptions and biases, and to overcome these through a renewed commitment to democratic values.

There are risks involved in such changes. But the stakes are too high not to accept these challenges. Along with librarians, curators, records managers, and others, archivists should commit themselves to the values of public accountability, open government, cultural diversity, and social justice.

Archivists can thus contribute to a richer human experience of understanding and compassion. By documenting the full range of human experience—so far as that is possible—we can help to protect the rights of citizens, and to hold public figures in government and business accountable for their actions. We can provide resources for people to examine the past, to comprehend the present, and to prepare for a better future. This is the essence of our common humanity. It provides archivists with a sense of professional purpose and a social conscience. It also provides society with the best single collective antidote to the possibility of an Orwellian dystopia arising in our midst. Archivists, historians, and others can thank Helen Samuels for making the connection between archival concerns for adequate documentation of society through authentic records and the concerns for truth, power, memory, and records expressed so clearly by George Orwell. By shaping the documentary record of society, archivists indeed control the past and thus the future, at least to some degree. Unless they recognize and accept this power, thoughtfully and transparently, they will fail to meet their most significant professional and societal responsibility.

Notes

This essay is a revised version of "Orwell in the Archives: Memory, Records, and Politics," presented at the International Council on Archives' Section on University and Research Institution Archives conference in Dundee, Scotland (2007). Portions of this essay appeared in *Archives Power: Memory, Accountability, and Social Justice* (Society of American Archivists, 2009), which was written after this essay was submitted for the current volume.

1 Helen Samuels, "Who Controls the Past," *American Archivist* (Spring 1986): 109–24.

2 George Orwell, *Homage to Catalonia* (Boston: Beacon, 1952), 150.

3 George Orwell, "As I Please" column, *Tribune*, February 4, 1944, http://www.netcharles.com/orwell (accessed January 3, 2007).

4 George Orwell, "Looking Back on the Spanish War," in *A Collection of Essays* (Garden City, NY: 1954), 202–204.

5 Orwell, "As I Please."

6 Orwell, "Looking Back," 206. Writing about French Caribbean archives, Laurent Dubois echoes Orwell. Dubois examines "the limits of the archives left by slavery" and "the stories of the slaves themselves—the absences and silences in the archives." Laurent Dubois, "Maroons in the Archives: Uses of the Past in the French Caribbean," in *Archives, Documentation, and Institutions*

of Social Memory: Essays from the Sawyer Seminar, ed. Francis X. Blouin Jr. and William G. Rosenberg (Ann Arbor: University of Michigan Press, 2006), 292.

7 Orwell, "Notes on Nationalism," October 1945, www.netcharles.com/orwell/essays/notes-on-nationalism1.htm (accessed January 3, 2007).

8 George Orwell, *Animal Farm: A Fairy Story* (New York: Signet Classic, 1996): 76–77.

9 Ibid., 89–91.

10 Ibid., 129.

11 George Orwell, *Nineteen Eighty-Four* (New York: Signet Classic, 1950), 213.

12 Ibid., 38–39.

13 Ibid., 36.

14 Ibid., 34–35.

15 Ibid., 42.

16 Ibid., 155–56.

17 Ibid., 248–49.

18 Ibid., 155.

19 Orwell, as quoted in Christopher Hitchens, *Why Orwell Matters* (New York: Basic Books, 2002), 85. Original emphasis.

20 Noam Chomsky, as paraphrased by Verne Harris, "Archives, Politics, and Justice," in *Political Pressure and the Archival Record*, ed. Margaret Procter, Michael Cook, and Caroline Williams (Chicago: Society of American Archivists, 2005), 175.

21 Jacques Derrida, *Archive Fever: A Freudian Impression* (Chicago: University of Chicago Press, 1996), 4.

22 Orwell, *Nineteen Eighty-Four*, 176.

23 For examples, see Howard Zinn, "Secrecy, Archives, and the Public Interest," *Midwestern Archivist* 2, no. 2 (1977): 20–21; and Patrick M. Quinn, "Archivists and Historians: The Times They Are A-Changin,'" *Midwestern Archivist* 2, no. 2 (1977): 8.

24 Timothy L. Ericson, "At the 'rim of creative dissatisfaction': Archivists and Acquisition Development," *Archivaria* 33 (Winter 1991–92): 66–77.

25 Samuels, "Who Controls the Past"; Larry J. Hackman and Joan Warnow-Blewett, "The Documentation Strategy Process: A Model and a Case Study," *American Archivist* 50 (Winter 1987): 12–47.

26 Richard J. Cox, "The Documentation Strategy and Archival Appraisal Principles: A Different Perspective," *Archivaria* 38 (1994): 11–36.

27 Elizabeth Snowden Johnson, "Our Archives, Our Selves: Documentation Strategy and the Re-Appraisal of Professional Identity," *American Archivist* 71 (Spring/Summer 2008): 193–95.

28 Adele Perry, "The Colonial Archive on Trial: Possession, Dispossession, and History in *Delgamuukw v. British Columbia*," in *Archive Stories: Facts, Fictions, and the Writing of History*, ed. Antoinette Burton (Durham, NC: Duke University Press, 2005), 345.

29 Joel Wurl, "Ethnicity as Provenance: In Search of Values and Principles for Documenting the Immigrant Experience," *Archival Issues* 29, no. 1 (2005): 66.

30 Tom Nesmith, "The Concept of Societal Provenance and Records of Nineteenth-Century Aboriginal-European Relations in Western Canada: Implications for Archival Theory and Practice," *Archival Science* 6, nos. 3–4 (2006): 351–60.

31 On the citizen-state interaction as a critical value to be considered during the appraisal of government records, and on the growing recognition by archivists over the past century of the inevitable subjectivity of appraisal, see Terry Cook, "Macroappraisal in Theory and Practice: Origins, Characteristics, and Implementation in Canada, 1950–2000," *Archival Science* 5, nos. 2–4 (2005): 101–61. For the first explicit and still powerful theoretical statement of such archival subjectivity, and its profound implications for forming the archive, see Hans Booms, "Society and the Formation of a Documentary Heritage: Issues in the Appraisal of Archival Sources," *Archivaria* 24 (Summer 1987, original 1972, translation by Hermina Joldersma and Richard Klumpenhouwer): 69–107.

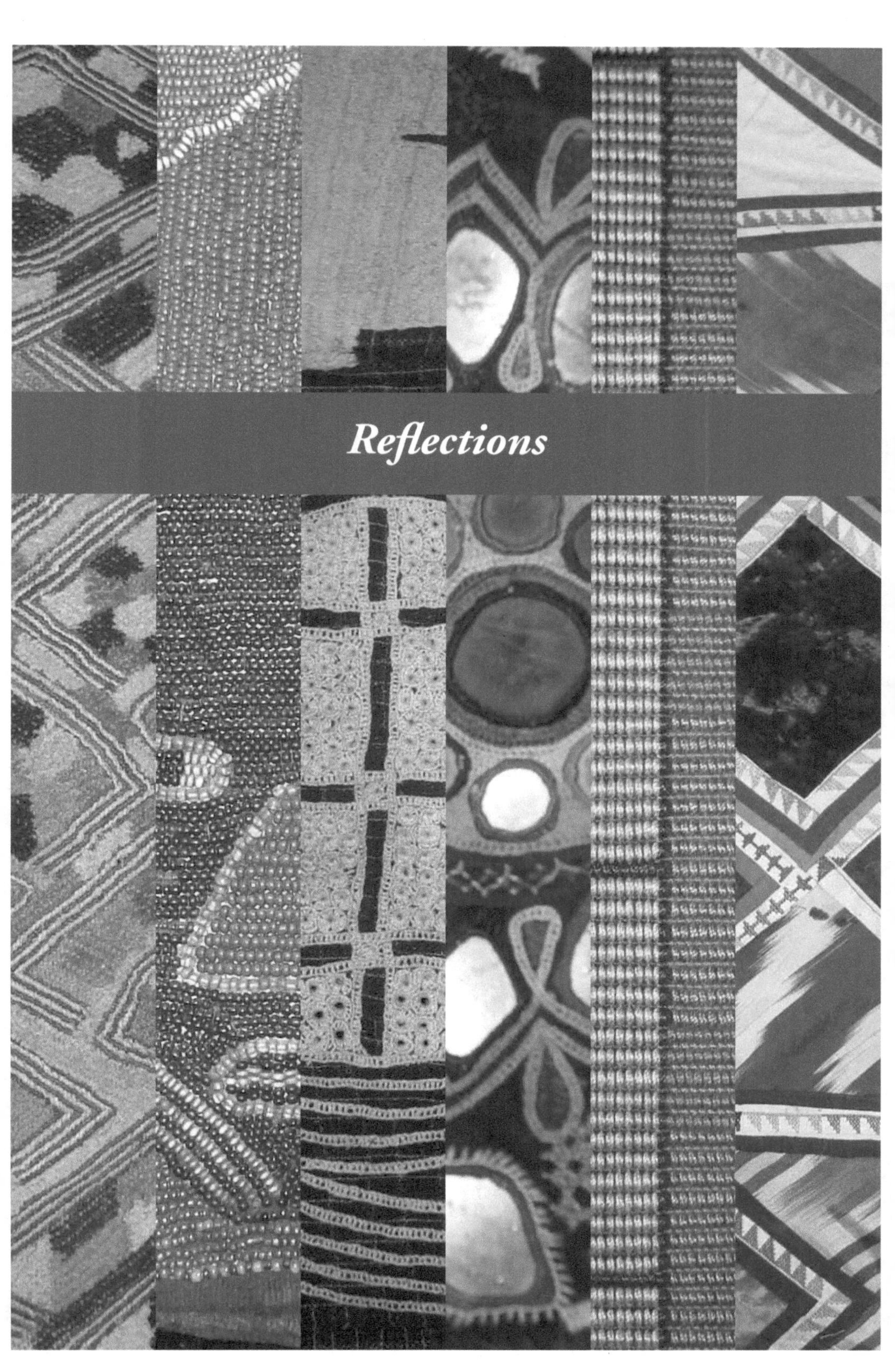

Reflections

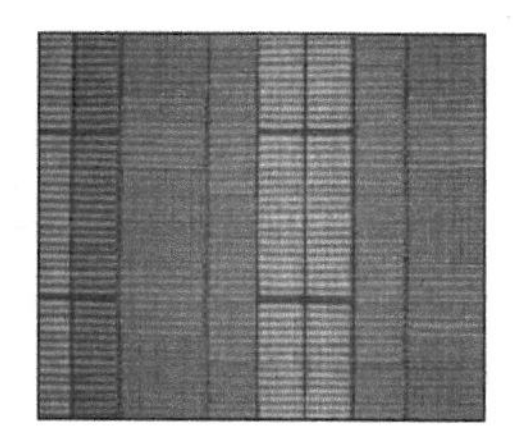

MAKING BETTER PROFESSIONALS: REFLECTIONS ON SELECTED WRITINGS OF HELEN WILLA SAMUELS

ELISABETH KAPLAN

American Archivist editor Eva Moseley introduced an article in the spring 1982 issue in this way: "[the authors] discuss a central part of our work: processing—and put it in the perspective of our intellectual role as partners in determining the range and shape of future research. . . . [They] indicate an enhanced, more interesting and more difficult role for archivists," one in which archivists "become intellectually more active 'brokers' between the creators and the users of records."

Moseley's assessment of the article by Helen W. Samuels and Karen T. Lynch was not only insightful, but prescient. Exploring these early topics around processing led Samuels very quickly to a profound rethinking of core assumptions about archival work. A brilliant thinker, an engaged practitioner, and a committed member of the profession, Samuels' works are all characterized by a conviction that archival practice is enriched and enhanced when it rests on a considered and rationalized intellectual framework, and that hard-won knowledge should be shared, not only in the form of thoughtful writings, but equally important, in useful tools like guidelines and case studies. Hers has been a life of learning and then sharing that learning with others.

The motivation, however, was always grounded in practice. In 1986 Samuels suggested that, "challenged by the abundance of materials, the scarcity of resources to care for them, and the decentralized nature of contemporary society and its records, archivists must develop new intellectual frameworks to guide them."[1] If pragmatic factors motivated her, Samuels was always conceptual in her response, working through new intellectual problems rather than continuing with the often ad hoc practices of the past. With that declaration, she dove headfirst into the intellectually challenging aspects of archival work, with a characteristic optimism and energy. As mainstays in the archival canon, her writings have now inspired generations of archivists to do the same, as the previous essays in this volume undoubtedly make clear.

The following is a highly selective discussion of some of the themes that make her writings influential and inspirational. It is not an exhaustive listing of her reports and papers, but rather an appreciation of and reflection on her work, in the order in which it has evolved over time.

***Processing Manual for the Institute Archives and Special Collections, MIT Libraries* (Cambridge: Massachusetts Institute of Technology, 1981).**

"An Analysis of Processing Procedures: The Adaptable Approach" (with Karen T. Lynch), *American Archivist* 45 (Spring 1982).

"Arguably the most influential writing on processing in the 1980s," wrote Mark Greene and Dennis Meissner of the MIT Processing Manual, in what is certainly the most influential writing on processing since then.[2] The manual's companion piece, which appeared in the spring 1982 issue of the *American Archivist*, proposed an entirely new way to conceive of the basic archival function of processing.

In the course of processing a large backlog of manuscript collections, Samuels and her colleagues became convinced that the automatic application of standardized "rules" for arrangement and description was neither appropriate for the records they sought to manage, nor was it sustainable in a modern institutional context. They sketched out instead a more rationalized approach to processing, beginning with an intellectually rigorous assessment of the materials, an assessment of the options available, a series of deliberate decisions about the appropriate treatment, and the documentation of those decisions in a processing plan. "The ideal level of processing is not the same for all collections," wrote Samuels and her colleagues, and "the processor should assume that his or her work on a collection is all that will ever be done; it is unlikely that there will be time and staff to reprocess collections." The manual broke down the process, step by step, providing the tools for the suggested decision-making process.

Prosaic as this first foray may sound, the *Processing Manual* hinted at what would become a central theme in Samuels' work: the concept of archivist as conscious, deliberate shaper of the historical record, and a persuasive argument for the legitimacy of that approach, where the alternative was clearly archival paralysis, or a sterile clinging to past conventions in hopes that they would still address the new scale and character of modern documentation. From her earliest publications Samuels demonstrates a certain archival self-consciousness and agency, at a time when very few others (notably Hugh Taylor and Terry Cook) were acknowledging the "objectivity problem" in the archival field.

***Understanding Progress as Process: Documentation of the History of Post-War Science and Technology in the United States. Final Report of the Joint Committee on Archives of Science and Technology* (HSS-SHOT-SAA-ARMA), ed. Clark A. Elliott (Chicago: Society of American Archivists, 1983).**

Samuels was a key member of the Joint Committee on Archives of Science and Technology and an important contributor to the JCAST report, as it became known. The committee, composed of archivists, records managers, and historians of science and technology, explored the immense problem for stakeholders in the archival record that was posed in postwar documentation of science and technology in the United States.

The report synthesized a tremendous amount of information on documentation of science and technology—its creators, users, discipline-specific peculiarities, and the resources and institutional contexts that sustain it—and provided specific recommendations for further research and implementation experiments that archivists, manuscript collectors, records managers, and other stakeholder and constituent groups might undertake. With an orientation both pragmatic and optimistic, the JCAST report resembles many of the projects and publications which Samuels helped to steer. As noted in the introduction, for example, the committee members early on "declared their faith in the capacity of guidelines to reform archival practice" and the group "from the beginning adopted the strategy of attempting to generate professional consensus on practice by analyzing the contemporary situation, the nature of scientific and technological documentation, and the requirements of users."

Yet the JCAST committee's work also had implications that challenged the conventional framework of archival thinking. One of the issues highlighted in the report involved the paradoxical problem for archivists facing the vast and over-abundant documentation of some scientific activities, on the one hand, and the absence of any or adequate documentation, on the other. Both abundance and absence required a deliberate and conscious reaction on the part of the archivist. Clearly the neutral keeper of inherited records would not be able to manage the former without imposing some selection criteria on the body of available documentation, and some core activities would not be adequately documented without the archivist's deliberate participation to shape the archive.

***Appraising the Records of Modern Science and Technology: A Guide* (with Joan Krizack Haas and Barbara Trippel Simmons), (Cambridge: Massachusetts Institute of Technology, 1985).**

"The MIT Appraisal Project and its Broader Applications" (with Joan Krizack Haas and Barbara Trippel Simmons), *American Archivist* 49 (Summer 1986).

Appraising the Records of Modern Science and Technology situated the JCAST report's general analysis, findings, and recommendations within a specific institutional setting, Samuels' home base at the Massachusetts Institute of Technology. A contemporary review described it as an "unusually significant addition to a small but growing body of appraisal literature in the field of scientific archives" and predicted that it would be "effective in helping to overcome the archivists' traditional diffidence in this [subject area of science and technology] because of its nontraditional approach." The same reviewer noted the significance of the authors' decisions about how to present the information: "the authors devote much of their text to a very lucid explanation of the basic elements of scientific research projects and professional activity and describe the documentation generated at each stage. Only after this description do they proceed to discuss appraisal considerations."[3]

Indeed, the resulting matrix has proved indispensable to multiple audiences in a variety of circumstances: the archivist encountering an unfamiliar document type and unsure of its significance; the historian considering a new area of research but needing an overview of types of sources likely to support it; the records manager desiring to add nuance to a classification system or develop a new one. Certainly for the archivist paralyzed by a mountain of documentary material and without a clue as to where to start in deciding what to keep and what to destroy, the guide demystified both the activities themselves and the resulting records, and provided suggestions for defining and interpreting long-term value to aid appraisal in this unfamiliar and long-neglected area.

The guide proposed a nuanced approach to appraisal, conducted "through systematic analysis of how records are created and used within a particular discipline or enterprise," eschewing the idea of appraisal simply by record type, position of the creator in an organizational hierarchy, or past trends shown by what researchers requested on the subject in the reference room.

In the summer 1986 issue of the *American Archivist*, the three authors described the project methodology that had resulted in the guide, highlighted some findings, and laid out suggestions for generalizing those findings in other subject or functional contexts. The paper is a great read for its succinct presentation of innovative ideas. "When appraising records, archivists should consider the total body of documentation, not just the material they are appraising." "Appraisal advice cannot be dogmatic and prescriptive." "Uniform appraisal standards should not be formulated because appraisal is a dynamic process that changes, according to the goals, acquisition policy, and financial constraints of each institution." "Appraisal cannot be based on attempts to predict future research trends."

The authors urge their colleagues to analyze "how archivists make and document appraisal decisions and how they communicate appraisal guidance," again anticipating by many years the literature calling for archivists to come to grips with the problem of subjectivity by becoming more conscious and declarative and transparent in their practice.

"Who Controls the Past," ***American Archivist*** **49 (Spring 1986).**

"The Roots of 128: A Hypothetical Documentation Strategy" (with Philip N. Alexander), ***American Archivist*** **50 (Fall 1987).**

"The Archivist's First Responsibility: A Research Agenda to Improve the Identification and Retention of Records of Enduring Value" (with Richard J. Cox), ***American Archivist*** **51 (Winter/Spring 1988).**

The first-published articulation of the concept of documentation strategy, "Who Controls the Past" is one of the most frequently cited writings on archives in the English-speaking world, and is still a constant presence on archival studies course syllabi.

Samuels began the article with what must have seemed a fairly straightforward comment at the time. "Though once perceived as keepers," she wrote, "American archivists, having accepted appraisal responsibilities, perceive themselves as selectors." This assumption about how archivists perceive their role in relation to appraisal was challenged in the United States, Canada, and Europe by a surprising number of traditionalists who did not, in fact, accept this conception of their role.

"Who Controls the Past" presented an as-yet untested approach to appraisal in the context of modern records, although Samuels' earlier work on science and technology had clearly demonstrated the practical possibilities of the strategy. If societal functions were increasingly collaborative and distributed across multiple institutions, then the records of these activities would also be distributed and collaborative. Why not take a collaborative and distributed approach to documenting these areas?

The proposed documentation strategy would be a multi-institutional research and planning process to precede a carefully defined effort to ensure adequate documentation of a particular issue, activity, function, geographical area, or phenomenon. Responsibility would be shared beyond the archival realm, to include records creators, records managers, subject specialists in the field (such as historians, scientists, lawyers, etc.) and likely future users of the resulting archival record.

The documentation strategy would require another then-radical adjustment to the construction of archival roles and responsibilities: as Samuels put it, "archivists' concept of their 'collection' [does] not end at their own doors." Unfortunately, this was interpreted quite literally by many in the archival community, who envisioned in the documentation strategy some level of significant disruption to existing programs and a threat to professional authority and independence.

With her MIT colleague Philip Alexander, Samuels developed a hypothetical case study of a current, real-life situation—the high-tech expansion along Route 128 in Boston—in order to sketch out how a documentation strategy plan might work in an extremely complex, multi-institutional setting. "Reexamined fifty or one hundred years hence, no framework or strategy will be judged perfect. . . . But that is the risk of all selection processes, and archivists have a responsibility at least to try their hand at making the right choices."

Samuels and Richard J. Cox co-authored "The Archivist's First Responsibility" in response to an SAA task force report, published in 1986, that advocated, among other things, that archivists work toward a deeper understanding of characteristics of modern records and the related need to "develop and apply appraisal and documentation strategies." The article is in part an endorsement of archival research—the need for archivists to continually push at the boundaries of archival knowledge that chain them to outdated practices, to learn and share useful information that enriches our understanding of archival work, and, more important, improves its practice: "All archivists hear colleagues describe appraisal as an inexact art or as a function that requires a certain instinctive feel, characterizations which capture the immensely difficult responsibility that is archival appraisal. But archivists should not shortchange themselves by focusing on the mysterious feel or art that appraisal may require; doing so only guarantees that they remain satisfied with groping about in the dark when identifying information that has enduring value. The focus should be on a specific research agenda that enables archivists to move to better and more precise means of accomplishing their first responsibility."

"North American Archival Identity," ***Second European Conference on Archives: Proceedings*****, Ann Arbor, Michigan, 1989 (Paris: International Conference on Archives, 1989).**

Samuels was well aware that as a practicing university archivist—not an archival educator nor a scholar—the invitation to speak to the topic of "North American archival identity" for a primarily European audience at events of the International Congress on Archives was a bit of a departure. Noting her slight discomfort, she began by revealing her own professional identity, including her background as a librarian who had learned archives on the job.

Rather than delve into a discussion of, for example, the ideal institutional placement and credentialing of formal archival education, or the desired suitability or otherwise of a historical or a library background for an archivist, Samuels proposed to explore the notion of archival identity in terms of the concept of archival knowledge. Such knowledge she viewed as a shifting, rather than fixed, body of information based on theory and practice. As a "North American archivist who has been engaged in research on modern documentation," Samuels stated, "this research has forced me to examine modern institutions and their documentation, and thereby to question the knowledge that archivists require to carry out their responsibilities." In describing the areas where archival knowledge could—should—expand, she wove together many of the themes explored in her earlier research and publications, and foreshadowed subsequent works. The talk provided her with the opportunity to present these themes as part of a coherent whole.

The published version of Samuels' address evokes themes noted in this essay—the importance of intentionality in documentation planning; the need for more collaborative approaches to collecting materials created in increasingly consortial ways; the need to consider documentation as a broad whole, rather than pieces of material parceled out to format or media specialists; the need to work closely with records creators and potential users and to collaborate with librarians; and the need for the adoption of standards.

Samuels also discusses the inutility, to records users, of the basic archival principle of original order and even of provenance as a framework for archival description. Advocating an emphasis on subject access instead, Samuels wrote that "acceptance of new ideas adapted from the library profession is improving access to records while altering archival practice." She argued that "traditional archival practice utilizes the hierarchical description of offices as the primary access to records. Researchers working with archivists have to translate their inquiries about a person or subject into an appropriate search of specific office records. Subject access has been spurned because it has been equated with physical reorganization by subject."

"For all of these reasons," Samuels wrote, "I believe archivists need new tools."

"Improving our Disposition: Documentation Strategy," ***Archivaria*** **33 (Winter 1991–92).**

Varsity Letters: Documenting Modern Colleges and Universities **(Chicago: Society of American Archivists; Metuchen, NJ: Scarecrow Press, 1992).**

Functional analysis was one such tool. "What does it take to document an institution?" asked Samuels in the introduction to *Varsity Letters*. This masterwork synthesizes the arguments and findings of the previous publications and presents the newly conceived "functional analysis" to address documentation in the context of a single institution.

"Improving our Disposition" was a prepublication version of what would be the introductory essay to *Varsity Letters,* and provides a useful bridge from the concept of documentation strategy to the proposed functional analysis. "The intellectual approach that underlies documentation strategies is the same as the newly proposed institutional functional analysis: analysis and planning must precede collecting," she wrote, emphasizing that the two are "separate techniques but mutually supportive of one another."

Functional analysis refocused the planning process to an analysis of the institution itself and what it actually does—its functions. Samuels proposed that the modern research university has seven broad functions, and she described and systematically broke each into primary and secondary activities, and then delineated some of the documentary issues associated with them. Though MIT was the subject of her functional analysis, the book's step-by step suggestions for creating an institutional documentation plan could be transposed into any institutional context.

The core ideas presented in *Varsity Letters* were provocative. "Is the archivist's responsibility to manage existing records, or to play a role in ensuring the adequate documentation of the institution?" asked Samuels (it is safe to conclude, rhetorically); "The approach taken in this work suggests a larger, more active role for archivists." Further, she suggests that "to meet the challenges posed by modern documentation, archivists and their colleagues must become active participants in the creation, analysis, and selection of the documentary record." By asking how the archivist can best document some phenomenon or activity in society, rather than which of the surviving traditional records should be kept, Samuels opens up the possibility of appraising and acquiring far richer, inclusive, and reflective archives, with the archivist as their active shaper.

"Drinking from the Fire Hose: Documenting Education at MIT," ***Archives and Manuscripts*** **25 (May 1997).**

"Educational Technology: A Documentary Tool? New Approaches to Documenting Teaching and Learning in Higher Education," ***The Academic Archivist*** **23, no. 2 (Spring 2006). Newsletter of the College and University Archives Section of the Society of American Archivists.**

In *Varsity Letters*, Samuels described the relative shallowness of useful information in the documentation normally generated by the process of teaching and learning. With "Drinking from the Fire Hose," Samuels delved into the previously mentioned problem of gaps in the documentary record. "Archival and records management techniques focus attention on the management of records," she wrote. "The archivist's problem is perceived as controlling the abundance of modern records . . . The documentary analysis in this work suggests that there are other documentary problems for the archivist to address as well, including the problems associated with technological change and the scarcity or even absence of documentation."

"Drinking from the Fire Hose" describes an innovative collaboration, undertaken at MIT, to develop better, richer documentation of the teaching and learning process itself, using a variety of media and techniques, including video recordings and interviews with faculty and students. While the results were inconclusive, Samuels urged others to explore similar projects, and summed up her philosophy that such efforts allow archivists multiple opportunities: to test ideas, to develop techniques, and to examine and share the results—all of which in turn make us "better professionals."

An application to the National Historical Publications and Records Commission Electronic Records Research Fellowship Program delved deeper into the problematic documentation of teaching and learning and the possible responses. In a series of presentations and in the project report, a brief version of which was published in the College and University Archivists' newsletter, Samuels proposed that the burgeoning field of digital educational technology might provide archivists with the tools to fill further those gaps in the record of teaching and learning. Referring to then-novel tools such as wikis and e-portfolios, Samuels suggested that educational technology had the potential to capture not only works, but the more ephemeral ideas and communications developed as byproducts of interaction between students and instructors, in the classroom and online. These inherently collaborative tools might allow for the capture for the first time of the collaborative nature of these social communications and communal activities, in which each utterance gains its meaning from its context. And what could be more archival than that?

Harnessing the array of emerging educational technology tools and their rapid uptake by faculty and students seemed a stretch when Samuels first proposed it. Just a few years later, these tools are ubiquitous in higher education and their capture by archivists is a legitimate and important instrument for just this purpose. SAA programs in the years since Samuels wrote now routinely include sessions on capturing course blogs and websites, but with the issues still being presented either as technological problems or occasionally copyright risks. The concept of these tools as very useful means of capturing legitimate documentation never even comes up, an observation which provides a suitable point at which to close these reflections on some highlights of her published work.

Samuels' writings have extraordinary staying power; they can be read and reread in the light of archival challenges unknowable at the time of their publication. Samuels' works are consistently visionary, based on solid research, and they are intellectually rigorous. They are often provocative and always invite debate as well as experimentation and application. They are courageous, passionate, and generous. Samuels described her ICA talk as "an opportunity to look forward and to suggest why and how our profession should change"—which, come to think of it, is not a bad lens through which to view her larger body of work, and another indication of why this book exists.

Notes

1 Helen Samuels, "Who Controls the Past," *American Archivist* (Spring 1986): 109–24.

2 Mark Greene and Dennis Meissner, "More Product, Less Process: Revamping Traditional Archival Processing," *American Archivist* 68 (Fall/Winter 2005): 214.

3 Review by George D. Teslos in *American Archivist* 49 (Spring 1986): 195.

LEARNINGS: WEAVING IT ALL TOGETHER

HELEN WILLA SAMUELS

To every answer you can find a new question.

Jewish Proverb

During his lifetime [LaRue] had traveled, collecting his people's stories piece by piece. He had wanted to have an expanded understanding of the bloodlines of which he was a part, and to know how to pass his understanding on. He had wanted to be a doorway, and had spent a lot of time trying to get that right, he thought, to understand what was and wasn't his to do. And now he found himself sitting in his backyard thinking over where he had been.

Helen Elaine Lee *(The Serpent's Gift)*

In *The Serpent's Gift*, we follow LaRue from birth to old age as he listens to his family's stories. And in the end, as the family storyteller, LaRue acknowledges all that he has learned from them. Stories are central to archivists as well. We begin by asking questions and listening to the stories we are told first by our professional colleagues, and then by those who are associated with our home institutions. For university archives, where I worked for so many years, the stories come from the faculty, students, and staff. And we find wonderful stories in the institutional and personal records we acquire, describe, and encourage our researchers to use, which they in turn retell across generations to come. In the end, we may have the good fortune to become storytellers ourselves, as we recount careers stimulated and supported by teachers, donors, researchers, and colleagues. All of this rich imparted knowledge informs and guides us. And with some energy and luck, we make this knowledge our own, finding the path that is ours, and the stories that speak to our own journey. In telling these stories, we acknowledge the deep sense of gratitude, and the gifts that have been bestowed. What a gift I was given to be guided and nurtured by so many! These are the archival "bloodlines" of which I am a part. The intellectual support, the generosity, the friendship, and the fun: I will be forever grateful.

Terry Cook and the authors of these essays have so greatly honored me with this festschrift. I am deeply thankful. This afterword gives me the opportunity to acknowledge some of the individuals who made my years as an archivist so stimulating and enjoyable. This cannot be just a thank-you list of endless names. Rather, I hope the stories that follow about just a few of these individuals from various stages of my career will suggest the generosity of many more, and my gratitude to all of them. And like LaRue, I will try to get this right.[1]

In offering me the opportunity to contribute this afterword, Terry sent me back in time as I tried to understand my journey, the leitmotifs that have guided it, and the threads that have bound it together. Central to the beginning of that journey was growing up in a family that so valued learning, not just classroom learning, but learning embedded in every facet of life. I remember our house filled with my parents' friends discussing the arts and politics. And though we were of modest means, my parents took my sister Sara and me to the theater, concerts, and museums in New York City. My father would sit at the piano and treat us to renditions of everything from Beethoven to Irving Berlin. It was a rich intellectual atmosphere that fostered my curiosity and encouraged my questions.

From the time I was a young girl, my father's parents, Nana Gert and Papa Harry, lived with us in Queens. Nana Gert taught me how to knit and cook. But my Papa Harry helped me understand my Jewish heritage, which perhaps laid the foundation for the centrality that learning came to play in my life. My grandfather was a very observant Jew, quietly saying his morning and evening prayers in the privacy of his living room. My own much more limited observance focused strongly on Passover, which remains among my most vivid childhood memories.

By tradition, the Passover Seder, marking the Exodus of the Jews from Egypt, is conducted in the home, with family and friends in attendance. The text of the service is contained in the *Haggadah,* which means "telling," as the Seder service retells the story of the Exodus. But the story is actually told in response to "The Four Questions" asked by the youngest child at the table, most often me, at the beginning of the Seder. The first question is, "Why is this night different from all other nights?" The *Haggadah* contains not only the biblical passages that narrate the story of the Exodus, but also commentaries and explanations of the Passover traditions drawn from the rabbinic literature. We are told that the source of the *Haggadah* was an all-night discussion held by five Talmudic scholars at a Seder table as they discussed the Exodus.

My Papa Harry conducted the service in Hebrew at breakneck speed so that he could get, as quickly as possible, to the delicious meal my Nana Gert had prepared. While these annual Passover celebrations taught me about my Jewish heritage, I believe they also instilled in me the value of asking questions, and listening to and learning from the stories that are told in answer to those questions. And I recognize that like my "First Question" so many years ago, the *why* questions continue to intrigue me more than the *how* questions. Questioning why we do things the way we do them always encouraged me to learn more, and seek alternative paths when the answers to those questions just raised more questions.

An Archival Career Begins in Cincinnati

As I think about this thread of learning, I understand how fortunate I was that my professional career allowed me to work at academic institutions. After receiving my library degree, I utilized my undergraduate studies in music to work as a music librarian at the Hilles Library at Radcliffe College. Then as an archivist, I worked first at the University of Cincinnati, and finally (and for most of my career) at the Massachusetts Institute of Technology (MIT). Higher education, with learning as its core responsibility, was an ideal situation for me. With opportunities to interact with faculty, administrators, and students, and actively partake in both the intellectual and social campus life, there were many times I said to myself, "They are paying me to do this?"

One thing I did get right was falling into archival work at just the right moment. I was hired at the University of Cincinnati in 1972 by two members of the history department, Professors Zane Miller and Henry D. Shapiro, to run a fledgling archival program, which was to be part of the Ohio Historical Society's regional network. To become a network site, Henry and Zane were required to hire an archivist to run the program. I pointed out the minor technicality that I was a librarian, and a music librarian at that, and that I didn't have a clue what archivists did. They said, "No problem, we'll get you trained."

Shortly after I was hired, Zane Miller and I attended the annual meeting of the Society of American Archivists (SAA) which, most fortunately, was held that year in Columbus, Ohio. It was there I heard F. Gerald Ham speak for the first time, and where I met Ruth Helmuth. Ruth was the archivist and archival instructor at Case Western Reserve University, and each summer she held the only training program designed specifically for college and university archivists. She welcomed me to SAA and invited me to attend her program the following summer, which I did.

The members of the class included other fledgling college and university archivists. And what instructors we had: Robert Warner, Philip Mason, William Biggelstone, as well as Ruth. Though we valued all that Bob, Phil, and Ruth discussed with us, we particularly responded to Bill Biggelstone as he was the only lecturer who ran a "one person shop" like ours. As he began his presentation, one of the students interrupted Bill to ask about the size of his staff. "Well," he responded, "there's myself, some student assistants, and an occasional volunteer." Our roar of approval acknowledged a kindred soul, and his lecture proceeded. I felt immediately surrounded by a group of supportive and totally committed archivists who were there to guide me that summer and in the years ahead, and I remain grateful that those teachers and fellow students became both colleagues and friends.

As I was not formally trained as a historian, I was particularly fortunate to work with able historians from the outset, including Zane and Henry, and particularly Professor Saul Benison, and to learn so much from them. Saul, a historian of science and oral historian, had brought Dr. Albert B. Sabin's manuscript collection to the University of Cincinnati, and was conducting an extensive oral history with him about his life and the development of the oral polio vaccine. Saul believed that the integrated use of primary and secondary sources was required to fully inform an oral historian, and he therefore made exhaustive use of Sabin's manuscript collection before each oral history interview. I assumed his approach was the accepted practice, and only later came to appreciate the controversial and often negative opinions about oral history and its place in the documentary and archival record. I believe that what I learned from Saul later informed my own work on documentary issues by broadening my understanding of the integrated nature of documentation to include not just the textual records I had studied in college and library school, but also the institutional and personal records I would work with and come to understand in the years ahead.

Envelopes of Sound contains a transcript of a wonderful panel discussion, "It's not the Song, It's the Singing," recorded at WFMT in Chicago in 1973, in which Saul participated with Studs Terkel, Jan Vansina, and others.[2] In response to a question about how Saul got involved in oral history, he explained that while he was working at Columbia University as Allan Nevins' assistant, Nevins informed him that he was to conduct a series of interviews about medicine. "What the hell do I know about medicine?" was Saul's response. While Nevins encouraged him to take some additional courses to prepare for the interviews, he also said, "The people who you interview are going to become your teachers and you're going to know a hell of a lot, and it all depends on what questions you pursue." And thus, my teacher Saul helped me appreciate the value of learning all that one can about the people you talk with, and asking good questions as the foundation for all archival tasks, whether that talking is with donors and researchers or one's own colleagues when initiating a documentation project.

And finally, it was Saul who encouraged me to apply for the position of institute archivist at MIT, a generous and enormously supportive act during a time of transition in my life.

A Significant Letter—and My Years at MIT

As I think back over the years at MIT, I remember one letter and, later on, one phone call that, in retrospect, became doorways to so much that followed. Though MIT was founded in 1861, there had been no concerted effort to save the Institute's historical records. Dr. Julius A. Stratton, MIT's president from 1959 to 1966, had encouraged the director of libraries, Jay K. Lucker, to rectify that problem by creating an Institute Archives. When I arrived in 1977 as MIT's first institute archivist, my challenge was to build a collection—assemble MIT's institutional records of lasting value and encourage the donation of personal records from members of the faculty.[3]

Shortly after I arrived I received a long letter from James R. Killian, Jr., who had been president of MIT from 1948 to 1959, and who served as President Eisenhower's science advisor.[4] The letter itemized his MIT presidential records, as well as his government and consulting files. A copy of the letter had been sent to my boss, and I remember Jay bounding into the archives saying, "What are we going to do?" My response was to suggest that I talk with Mr. Killian, which I did. The acquisition of this collection brought what is still one of the most significant and heavily used sets of records to the archives.[5] But I also came to understand that this acquisition made so much more possible. Gradually I perceived the deep admiration and love that everyone at MIT had for Mr. Killian. When talking with faculty or administrators, if I mentioned that he had given his papers to the archives, invariably the response was, "Well, if Jim gave you his papers, then I'll do the same." Every door opened. I was therefore delighted that many years later when I had the occasion to visit with Mr. Killian, I was able to thank him for trusting me and our fledgling program, and by his example encouraging his colleagues to do the same.

I arrived at MIT knowing embarrassingly little about the world of science and technology.[6] But I quickly understood that the faculty were teachers, who were more than willing to talk about and explain their work. I therefore had the great good fortune to learn so much from them. In May 1977 I went to see Professor John C. Sheehan to ask him to give his personal records to the Institute Archives. Professor Sheehan was the very first member of the faculty I met with, and as I prepared for that visit I recognized that while I could gather basic biographical facts, I lacked the technical knowledge required to be able to understand his published work and scientific accomplishments. I did learn that he held the patent on semi-synthetic penicillin, and that the patent had been heavily contested in the courts. But my knowledge ended there. My meeting gave me the opportunity to tell Professor Sheehan about the Institute Archives, and explain how we would care for his records. As we talked, Professor Sheehan asked me, "Do you understand why the patent was so heavily contested?" To which I responded, "No, Professor Sheehan, I'm afraid I don't." At that moment, with a huge smile on his face, Professor Sheehan jumped up from his chair, grabbed a piece of chalk, went to the blackboard, and I was treated to a private class, including bonding diagrams, that enabled him to explain the breadth of his patent. And I remember absorbing this lesson thinking, "If this is what MIT is going to be like—lucky me." All I had to do was ask questions, listen, and then learn so much from these generous individuals.

Manson Benedict and Irving Kaplan, long-time colleagues and good friends, might be thought of as an "odd couple." Both were founding members of the Department of Nuclear Engineering at MIT, but of radically different backgrounds and appearances. Professor Kaplan, a native New Yorker, was always attired in professorial baggy pants and sweaters, while Professor Benedict, born in Michigan, had the bearing and dress of a proper New Englander, habitually attired in three-piece suits. Together they developed the gaseous diffusion method for separating isotopes of uranium, and supervised the engineering and development of the Gaseous Diffusion plant (K-25) in Oak Ridge, Tennessee, where fissionable material for the atomic bomb was produced during World War II. One day, as I worked with Professor Benedict, preparing his records for the archives, I asked him about the difficulties of building the K-25 plant. In response he said, "Well that's right, we didn't have the goddamnedest idea if it would work!" I tried not to drop the box I was working on in response to his statement, which soon after I was able to repeat to Professor Kaplan. "Manson said goddamnedest?" was his astonished, amused, and affectionate reply. What I took from this exchange, and so many others I was privileged to be a part of, was the wonder and intellectual excitement the faculty had for their work.

It was through their records that I came to know these individuals more fully, and the more I studied these records, the more interested I became in the nature of the complex and varied documentation they created and used. Initially, my own glib rule of thumb was that engineers created meticulously organized, complete files, mathematicians left no records, and physicists left only piles of paper on every surface, including desks, couches, chairs, and the floors of their offices. But, of course, as I worked to understand the real complexities of modern science and technology, I learned from what our donors told me about how and why they created and used their records.

William Shurcliff founded the Citizens League against the Sonic Boom, a small, grass-roots citizens' movement formed to sway public opinion and influence the decision-making process of Congress on supersonic transport. When Dr. Shurcliff gave his records to the Institute Archives, he told me that the night before deciding to establish the league, he had formulated a classification scheme for the records he knew he would have to create. That classification scheme clearly outlined what he knew he would have to accomplish to be successful—which he was.

Harold E. Edgerton, known to one and all as "Doc," was a professor of electrical engineering at MIT from 1928 until his death in 1990. Doc Edgerton perfected the stroboscope, and developed high-speed photographic techniques that allowed very rapid events to be captured on film. Chronicling his long and fascinating career were the laboratory notebooks he maintained from 1930 to 1990. While most lab notebooks contain endless amounts of data, notes on equipment, and experimental conditions, Doc's are quite different. While they certainly include those elements, they also contain innumerable images that record his experiments using stroboscopic photography to capture a broad range of subject matter including hummingbirds in flight, a baseball batter hitting a ball, and a drop of milk forming a crown as it rebounds off a surface. But these notebooks are also a very personal chronicle, as they contain images of so many who visited his lab, including colleagues, students, and his children. When I asked him about the notebooks and the extraordinary record he had created, he simply shrugged his shoulders and smiled. That was his style. His "points of guidance" might be considered the articulated version of that shrug and smile: "Work like hell, tell everyone everything you know, close a deal with a handshake, and have fun." It is a great philosophy for life, and Doc was its ideal proponent.

While the initial goal for the Institute Archives was to gather and preserve both institutional and personal records, once collections were accessioned and processed, we wanted to ensure that they would be used. Our first efforts were directed toward the MIT administration, to demonstrate the service the archives staff could offer to the Institute. Over the years the archives contributed to the work of many Institute committees, the celebration of anniversaries, and the defense of the Institute in lawsuits. I remain very proud of the commitment the archives staff had, and continues to have, to this service.

Our efforts were rewarded by a growing stream of historians and other scholars who came to use the collections. We learned so much from working with them. What was the focus of their research? What collections had they come to use, and what additional sources could we recommend? Were our finding aids useful? Did they find errors, or have suggestions to make? We shared both their excitement as they discovered rich material that addressed their needs, as well as their disappointment about information not found. They were enormously generous with their insights and became our valued teachers and advisors. From early on, the annual report of the Institute Archives included a bibliography of published works and exhibits that utilized the collections. We gently badgered our researchers about sending copies of their publications to us. I well remember those first annual reports which contained but one or two citations. The staff of the Institute Archives continues to compile what is now a very extensive and impressive bibliography, and it remains something we all regard with a great sense of accomplishment.

Several researchers became valued colleagues and friends, and I was particularly grateful to have their advice during our research projects. Robert Root-Bernstein and Robert Friedel were particularly patient and constant advisors. I first met Robert Root-Bernstein when I was asked to visit the Salk Institute to consult on their plans to create an archives. Bob, a biochemist and a historian of science, was working at Salk on historical projects. We quickly determined that there was no immediate hope of establishing an archival program, and so the conversation rapidly turned to his research on the evolution of scientific theories and institutions. We stayed in touch, and his advice was greatly appreciated during our appraisal studies as we sought to describe research methodologies: how research questions are formulated, and the methods used to seek answers to those questions. His discerning and creative approaches and his ability to articulate difficult concepts were invaluable.

From the time we came to know each other as members of the Joint Committee on the Archives of Science and Technology (JCAST), Robert Friedel was a friend and valued advisor. Our conversations and his insightful publications taught me so much about the history of engineering, and how engineers go about their work. I was visiting Robert just as my book on documenting colleges and universities was nearing completion. I told him that my working title was *Sex, Parking, and Sports,* which was taken from the observation made by Clark Kerr, a former president of the University of California, that a college president's job was to provide sex for the students, parking for the faculty, and sports for the alumni. I also reported that my mother hated that title! It was Robert who then suggested *Varsity Letters: Documenting Modern Colleges and Universities.* As my father was a great punster, I thought the title was perfect.

The archival programs at the University of Cincinnati and MIT succeeded because of the committed team of individuals who staffed both repositories. I was so fortunate to work with so many individuals who made those archives vibrant and successful, including Elizabeth Andrews, Lois Beattie, Bridget Carr, Deborah Cozort Day, Elisabeth Kaplan, Joan Krizack, Kathy Marquis, Jeffrey Mifflin, D. Gregory Sanford, Barbara T. Simmons, Anne Van Camp, and Alice Vestal. They demonstrated great dedication to our archival endeavors, and I remain very proud of all we accomplished.

Gregory Sanford was the very first professional I hired at MIT in 1977, when he joined the Institute Archives to work for a year with MIT's fledgling Oral History Project. The description of Gregory as a gentle giant is most apt, and while he accomplished so much in that short time period, I also remember his stories, jokes, and many laughs. After his year at MIT, Gregory returned to Vermont, where in 1982 he became state archivist, building a remarkable program that is a valued resource for government officials as well as the general public. Among his research projects, Gregory developed ways to manage electronic records through the Vermont Information Strategy Plan (VISP), which utilized, and greatly extended, a functional analysis approach. His exceptional skills as a writer combined with his zeal to use historical documents to inform government officials and the citizens of Vermont, led to the Continuing Issues of Government and Governance, available to all on the Vermont State Archives website. The Continuing Issues service has had a significant impact on public policy debates and state governance. As I have followed Gregory's career, as well as the careers of others with whom I worked, I have been delighted as our relationships have changed from supervisor and staff, to colleagues and friends.

That Phone Call—and Life with Archival Colleagues

Soon after I arrived at MIT in 1977, I received a phone call from Joan Warnow, then associate director of the Center for the History of Physics at the American Institute of Physics (AIP). As we did not know each other prior to this call, we chatted first about our archival backgrounds, and then about physicists at MIT. Toward the end of the conversation, Joan—always direct and practical, as I came to appreciate—asked how old I was. When I told her I was thirty-four, she said, "Damn good thing. You have a lot of work to do!" Throughout my years at MIT, Joan was always there to advise, provide a larger perspective, and make more work for me.

Just a year later when SAA's annual meeting was to be held in Nashville, Tennessee, Joan asked if I would be interested in taking this opportunity to travel to Oak Ridge, tour the National Laboratory, and visit their archives. I jumped at the opportunity to visit what had already become an iconic location. The idea was to meet in Knoxville where we would rent a car, drive to Oak Ridge, and after our visit drive to Nashville for the SAA meeting. It was only when we arrived in Knoxville, however, and proceeded to pick up our car, that Joan informed me that she did not drive. She was at that time, after all, a confirmed resident of Manhattan, with no need to drive! So I happily became her chauffeur, colleague, and friend.

I believe it was thanks to Joan that in 1979 I was asked to serve as one of SAA's representatives on the Joint Committee on the Archives of Science and Technology (JCAST). At first, this appointment was significant more for what I learned than for what I was able to contribute. JCAST focused on documentary issues, particularly the challenge of capturing the history of postwar science and technology. From the 1960s on, there had been several conferences and publications that focused on this theme. JCAST, funded by the National Science Foundation, was comprised of representatives of the History of Science Society, Society for the History of Technology, Society of American Archivists, and the American Records Management Association. SAA chose Joan, Maynard Brichford, and myself as their representatives. The only reason I was chosen, I am sure, was that I was at MIT. Among the other members were David Bearman, Sharon Gibbs, Clark Elliott, and Dick Lytle, as well as several historians of science and technology, including Robert Friedel. What an experience it was for me to work with and learn from such an extraordinary group of thoughtful people. As our work proceeded, they gave me the confidence to contribute more fully, and to take on additional studies of documentary issues.

Several of the recommendations in the JCAST report, *Understanding Progress as Process,*[7] dealt with the need to "undertake serious investigations relating to the documentation of science and technology," and the need accordingly to develop appraisal guidelines. I had come to understand that wrestling with these issues, especially appraisal, intrigued me. I had also come to understand that MIT was a research-driven, grant-dependent environment, and I thought that if the Institute Archives similarly undertook funded research projects and published the results of our studies, our ability to understand and work with the faculty would be enhanced. For the Institute Archives, I therefore applied for and received grant funds to undertake such appraisal studies, which resulted first in *Appraising the Records of Modern Science and Technology* and later *Varsity Letters*.

Throughout the research projects, I maintained detailed notebooks in which I recorded my conversations, readings, and ruminations. One of the first entries, made in June 1981, captures an early meeting with David Bearman and Dick Lytle.[8] I remember sitting in Dick's office in the Smithsonian Castle, on the window sill, happily recording our conversations and their advice. But it might be more accurate to describe these as intellectual skirmishes between Dick and David. I would pose a question and then sit back, listen, and take notes as these "conversations" evolved. These early notes record David's observation that "Appraisal studies normally focus on existing records. Break away from that model and ask what should be documented. Focus on the activity and not the form of the record." It is clear that David's advice greatly influenced my thinking, and I am indebted to him for his guidance and support.

The Mellon Foundation's funding of the Bentley Historical Library's Fellowships for the Study of Modern Archives at the University of Michigan roughly coincided with their funding of the documentation projects at MIT. Fran Blouin and Bill Wallach, the Bentley Library's director and associate director, kindly invited me and the research staff for the two projects to join the Fellows at their summer seminars in Ann Arbor, and report on our work. Joan Krizack and Barbara T. Simmons were my co-authors for the documentary study of science and technology, and Bridget Carr and Beth Sandager were the project staff for the work on institutional functional analysis. We welcomed these opportunities to vet our work in its early stages, and hear the range of reactions from the Fellows and Bentley staff. They always left us with us with much to think about.

Another key early influence was my service on SAA's Committee on Goals and Priorities (CGAP, 1980–1986). The charge to the committee was to carry out a planning exercise for the profession. Our modest mission statement was, "To ensure the identification, preservation and use of records of enduring value." Gerry Ham was the Chairman of the Task Force, whose members included Larry Hackman, Paul Chestnut, John Fleckner, Anne Kenney, and me. I chaired the working group on identification and retention, whose members were Richard Cox, Charles Dollar, Susan Grigg, Alan Negus, and Jim O'Toole. This was a tremendously energizing enterprise. In the end, CGAP not only influenced SAA, but also the work of many of us who were fortunate to engage in this activity. My thinking was particularly influenced by Gerry's critique of past archival appraisal practice, and Larry's emphasis on strategic planning.

I remember one CGAP meeting in Chicago particularly because of a slow amble with Gerry on a cold winter evening. Our meetings were held at SAA headquarters, then located on South Wells Street, while we stayed at a hotel on North Michigan Avenue. I recall the twilit sky and very cold air as we left the SAA offices and headed back to the hotel. As we had been sitting all day, the plan was to walk back. The group took off at a rapid pace, but I hung toward the back to amble with Gerry and share a memorable conversation that blended personal and professional topics, ranging from archival theory to farming.

The opportunity to work with and learn from such engaged and thoughtful colleagues encouraged me to pursue the documentary research that increasingly had come to interest me. JCAST helped me understand the records of modern science and technology, while MIT offered the perfect environment to study one institution's records in depth. And CGAP encouraged me to consider why planning and cooperation were critical to the identification and preservation of the interconnected records of modern institutions. The rationale for both documentation strategies and institutional functional analysis evolved from these experiences. Both of these concepts rest on the premise that the documentation of modern society is dispersed yet integrated, reflecting the complex organization of contemporary society. Therefore, analysis and planning must precede documentary efforts, and institutions must work together to ensure the retention of an integrated record conceptually, if one dispersed physically. These ideas were for me the logical and effective means to meet the challenges posed by modern documentary records.

From 1987 to 1990, Tim Ericson, Richard Cox, and I took to the road and offered a series of seven seminars sponsored by SAA on documentation strategies. These seminars brought together archivists from a single geographic area, and we found the participants quite receptive to documentation strategies, as the process resonated with their desire to assemble a coordinated record of their region. At the same time, the seminars provided an extended opportunity to spend time with Tim and Richard. Tim's responsibility was to find the best breakfast place in town, where we met each morning at the assigned time. They both had to deal with the fact that I did not drink coffee and tended to have too much energy first thing in the morning. I would arrive, raring to go, talking a mile a minute, oblivious to their efforts to eat a good breakfast in silence, and wake up slowly. Ah, the patience of good friends!

As this section on colleagues began with Joan Warnow, so it is appropriate to end with her. Though I may be credited with articulating the concept of documentation strategies, it is important to acknowledge the role Joan and her colleagues at AIP's Center for the History of Physics played in formulating and implementing these concepts, and to understand how their efforts influenced my own thinking. The mission of the center is to ensure the documentation of modern physics. In 1977, when Joan and I first talked, physicists were based primarily at academic institutions, where they taught and carried out research with their graduate students. During that first conversation, we talked about the faculty in MIT's Physics Department who were members of the National Academy of Sciences, and Joan encouraged me to work with these individuals to acquire their records, which I did. But, in the following years, scientific research changed dramatically, as projects became large international collaborations, involving teams of scientists affiliated with many institutions, working in dispersed locations—and the records were scattered accordingly.

Joan, Spencer Weart, and the staff of the center undertook a series of important documentary studies involving scientists, historians, and archivists (including myself) to help them understand these complex, dispersed activities, and plan for the long-term care of the resulting records. The concept of "documentation strategies" was derived, therefore, quite naturally as a useful method to analyze and ensure the preservation of these interconnected but dispersed records. The importance of the work that Joan and the AIP staff carried out may not receive the credit it deserves, perhaps because it is perceived to be subject-focused or applicable only to scientific records. This view overlooks the central core of the work which was essentially a functional analysis, in this case the function of conducting research in modern physics. Joan and the center staff understood that only by achieving a functional understanding could an effective cooperative solution be devised to analyze and plan for the retention of the naturally dispersed yet integrated records relating to that function.

Retirement and Beyond

Retirement has given me the freedom and time to ask new questions—or old questions in new ways—by pulling several threads together and returning to ideas presented in *Varsity Letters*. During my last years at MIT, I worked with the Council on Educational Technology, which was charged "to enhance the quality of MIT education by encouraging the use of appropriate technology." This work gave me an extraordinary opportunity to observe how technology is dramatically transforming the educational process: the way the faculty teach and the tools available to help students learn. And as I studied these new tools, the archivist in me kept focusing on the records that were being created in support of activities previously undocumented or very seriously underdocumented.

In 1992 when *Varsity Letters* was published, the chapter on the core function "Convey Knowledge" concluded that the educational process often remained elusive and difficult to document. College and university archives might receive lecture notes from members of the faculty, class notes taken by the students, and, in more recent years, videotapes of classes. Now, however, technology is altering the educational process in modest to very dramatic ways. And the applications of educational technology are creating new documentary evidence of the process of teaching and learning. I am intrigued with the opportunity to learn more about educational technology and its effect on the educational process, and to consider what the resulting record means for archivists, and the archival record of our institutions. In a larger sense, though, it suggests that functional analyses and documentary recommendations must constantly be revised as an environment, and the resulting documentary record, changes over time.

Weaving It All Together

Threads have multiple meanings in my life. Figuratively, they represent the recurring themes that have guided me. Metaphorically, anything threadlike implies continuity or connectedness, such as following the thread of an argument. What could be more archival than continuity and connectedness over time? But, as my friends and colleagues well know, threads also literally reflect my passion for knitting and textiles.

As I have been observed knitting during many archival meetings, I must include my favourite knitting stories. A perceptive MIT colleague, who did not know much about my personal background, once remarked that I must have come from a musical background as knitting, swimming, and walking—all steady rhythmic activities—were such important parts of my life. It is one of those seemingly simple observations that rings so true. It is perhaps the steady rhythmic quality of those activities that I find so soothing and restorative.

Back in the days when I was at the University of Cincinnati, and Lew Bellardo was at the Kentucky Department for Libraries and Archives, we were both attendees at a particularly exasperating and endless meeting. At the end of the session, Lew said to me, "Okay, now I get it. The faster you knit, the more aggravated you are. And, when you put your knitting down and look up, someone is in serious trouble." I realized this: he was right!

My general rule was that I would knit only at large meetings where I could hide in the corner of a room and not be distracting. But when I had to face a small, all-day meeting of scientists, historians, and archivists, I broke my rule, but tried to hide at the end of the seminar table. Unfortunately, I was seated next to a scientist I did not know, who gave me a withering glance when I took out my knitting. As the day progressed, I watched as his note-taking turned into doodling. At the end of the day, he said to me, "I wish I knew how to knit. You have made a sweater, and I have wasted a day."

Knitting is also related to my passion for textiles. The visual and tactile pleasures I derive from textiles have always been enhanced by studying the people who created those objects. Who made the textile and how was it used in their culture? What fibres, dyes, and techniques were employed? Do the patterns, and objects depicted on the textile have symbolic meaning? Textiles are cultural records that transmit their own stories, and I believe that my studies of these objects encouraged me to broaden my definition of "documentary records" beyond traditional textual or even archival records as normally understood.

A truly wonderful example from the world of textiles of my favourite dictum, "It all comes down to records," is the current research on Incan *khipu,* which are objects consisting of a primary cord, with pendant strings bearing clusters of knots. Until recently, scholars were perplexed that the Incas, known to be a very advanced society, did not have a system of writing. But Spanish colonial documents are now understood to indicate that the *khipu* were used for recordkeeping. Gary Urton, a Professor of Pre-Columbian Studies at Harvard, explains that those documents "recorded the Inka khipu-keeper coming before the Spanish scribe, standing there with his khipu and reading its contents, string by string."[9] Now scholars are creating an extensive database of images of all known *khipu* to facilitate the decoding of this three-dimensional, textile-based system of writing. So once again—it all comes down to records!

Three Special Acknowledgments

I owe two Canadian colleagues a particular debt for their openness to new ideas, their pointed though most polite questions and critiques, as well as their constant support. In 1989 and again in 1990, Hugh Taylor invited me to talk about documentation strategies with the month-long English-language Archives Course sponsored by the National Archives of Canada in Ottawa. Though I sensed that Hugh had reservations about the concept, I was struck that he felt it was important to challenge his students and introduce them to new ideas. Hugh took me to dinner during one of those visits, giving me the occasion to ask his advice about my research. In his dear, gentle, and thoughtful manner, he encouraged me to pursue my work, knowing, I believe, that the work would evolve, be critiqued, and mature.

And the same can be said of Terry Cook. Terry, the consummate colleague, teacher, and friend, has been an ever-willing sounding board, always questioning and prodding, but always in the most gentle and supportive manner. He is the best type of critic, one who always encourages you to do better. But perhaps his most insightful questioning came when I was invited to the Association of Canadian Archivists' meeting in Banff to speak about documentation strategies and institutional functional analysis, and explain the relationship between the two.[10] It was Terry who asked me whether in retrospect I wished that I had done *Varsity Letters* and the work on institutional functional analysis first, and documentation strategies second. His question reflected his understanding that the process of documenting one's home institution provides the grounding and rationale to launch cooperative documentary efforts. So he, I think, was not surprised by my emphatic *yes.* Terry always encouraged me to rise to his challenges by thinking more deeply and speaking and writing with greater clarity and precision. I have learned so much from him.

I wish I had both space and time to add a story about each contributor to this book, but I fear that the editor would not be happy if I doubled the length of this volume. I must, though, acknowledge and thank one additional person—my mentor, colleague, friend, and husband, Greg Anderson, for his endless patience with things archival.

Greg became the associate director for systems and planning in the MIT Libraries while I was still working on *Varsity Letters.* At the beginning of some meeting, while we waited for the other committee members to arrive, Greg asked me about the project. I remember explaining how and why we were using institutional functional analysis, and briefly describing the seven core, broad functions we had identified for modern colleges and universities. Some time later, Greg asked me to work with him on an exercise for the Library Council (the directors and senior staff of the MIT Libraries) in which we would use the functions as a means to explore how the Libraries actually interacted with and supported MIT. With seven flip charts in the front of the conference room, each listing one of the functions, I opened the session by explaining each function. Greg then asked the group to think about how their work supported each function. It was like pulling teeth as we began. But then the head of cataloguing lit up as she understood how cataloguing books and journals supported the "research" function, as well as "teaching and learning," and even "socialize"—after all, they also catalogued the murder mystery collection! In the end, as we worked through the functions, subfunctions, and their supporting activities, it was an eye-opening experience for all of us. I was delighted that Greg chose to use my work in this way, but even more so because he saw the power of functional analysis for uses way beyond what I had envisioned.

Just after we decided to get married, we were both visiting Chicago, Greg for an American Library Association meeting, and I at SAA. Many good friends and colleagues were in town for the SAA meeting, and they insisted on meeting Greg. They had to approve or the wedding was off! So my dear husband-to-be showed up for dinner and "his inquisition." How did he feel about archivists? SAA? Documentation strategies? I am very grateful that he passed his exam, and we received everyone's blessing.

Learnings: *"To every answer you can find a new question"*

The opportunity to write this afterword has provided an unexpected opportunity for introspection. Like LaRue, I am very thankful to have been given this occasion to reflect on my journey, on my bloodlines, and the threads that have bound my life together. In the end, it is very clear that my journey and these stories were only made possible because of the individuals who were there along the way to teach and guide me.

And what a nurturing journey this has been. In reflecting on the centrality of learning as a binding thread in my life, I understand how fortunate I was to become an archivist and, particularly, an archivist in an academic setting. To have found work that *required* that I work with such fascinating people, and to learn from them, was a true privilege. What an adventure to be caught in this endless loop of asking questions and learning, only to realize that the answer resulted in a new question. Perhaps the stories related in this afterword have given me the opportunity to be a doorway as LaRue hoped to be. If in any way I have become a teacher to others, then I can only feel even more grateful and enriched. And if my career contains a lesson for young archivists, it would be this: ask questions, listen, find that next question, and savor the joy of becoming, and then always being, a learning archivist.

And so I come full circle back to my fellow archivists, my colleagues, my friends. To have been supported by so many wonderful people has been a true gift, and I remain so grateful for the guidance, support, and friendship I received. My father told us about George M. Cohan Jr., a vaudevillian, who would end each performance with the same line: "Ladies and gentlemen, my mother thanks you, my father thanks you, my sister thanks you, and I thank you!" And so I do.

Notes

1 As editor, Terry asked me to reflect on my career and its lessons for archivists based on my "personal" experiences. I have tried to maintain that focus, telling the "personal" stories that lay behind my more "public" persona. Terry was also insistent that I see none of the other essays as I was writing, so I would not be tempted to react in this afterword to what may have been written about my career and ideas in the preceding pages of this book.

2 Ronald J. Grele, ed., *Envelopes of Sound: Six Practitioners Discuss the Method, Theory and Practice of Oral History and Oral Testimony* (Chicago: Precedent Publishing, Inc., 1975).

3 Note on terminology: MIT's Institute Archives had responsibility both for the official institutional records, as well as the personal records, or manuscripts, of the faculty, which were given to the Institute Archives through a deed of gift.

4 James Rhyne Killian, 1904-1988, received an S.B. in management from MIT in 1926. In 1939 he became executive assistant to MIT President Karl Taylor Compton, and during World War II directed MIT's operations, while Compton was working in Washington. Killian became MIT's tenth president in 1948. At MIT, he was always addressed either as Mr. Killian, or Jim.

5 The collection includes the records of his predecessor, Karl Taylor Compton. Massachusetts Institute of Technology, Office of the President, Records of Karl Taylor Compton and James Rhyne Killian, AC 4, Massachusetts Institute of Technology, Institute Archives and Special Collections, Cambridge, Massachusetts.

6 Engineering and science remain the most dominant areas of teaching and research at MIT, although the Institute is actually comprised of six main divisions: The School of Architecture and Planning, School of Engineering, School of Humanities, Arts and Social Sciences, Sloan School of Management, School of Science, and the Whitaker College of Health Sciences and Technology.

7 Clark A. Elliott, ed., *Understanding Progress as Process: Documentation of the History of Post-War Science and Technology in the United State. Final Report of the Joint Committee on Archives of Science and Technology* (Chicago: Society of American Archivists, 1983).

8 Richard (Dick) Lytle was director of the Office of Information Resource Management at the Smithsonian Institution, and David Bearman was the deputy director. Dick had been the Smithsonian's archivist.

9 Beth Potier, "String Theorist: Anthropologist Gary Urton Untangles the Mystery of Inkan Khipus," *Harvard University Gazette* (May 22, 2003).

10 Terry Cook served as the commentator for this plenary session at the May 1991 ACA conference.

CONTRIBUTORS

Rick Barry is editor and content manager of MyBestDocs.com, dedicated to publications of archives and records management (ARM) papers, especially on electronic records. An author and conference speaker, he has brought interdisciplinary skills in information management and technology, archives and records management, and business systems analysis to consulting and workshop engagements for international clients, including several national archivists and other public, private, and nonprofit sector clients. Previous positions include naval officer, civil servant, and World Bank manager of information technology and ARM services. Recently retired as principal of Barry Associates, an international management consultancy, he lives with his wife, Linda Cox, in Arlington, Virginia. Barry came to know Helen Samuels through her work in the use of functional analysis for documenting societies and through SAA projects and activities.

Nancy Bartlett is chief archivist for the University of Michigan archives and records program and assistant director for academic and international programs at the Bentley Historical Library. Her previous publications have examined the relevance of diplomatics to contemporary photography, the history of pedagogy in architecture, immigration archives, cross-cultural influences in archival administration, and the role of the archivist as mediator of meaning. She was chief editor of the International Council on Archives journal, *Comma*, from 2000 to 2004. She is a Fellow of the Society of American Archivists.

David Bearman is president of Archives and Museum Informatics in Toronto, Canada. He consults on issues relating to museum, archives, and library collaborations, cultural knowledge management, interactive multimedia, and electronic recordkeeping and archives. He is the author of *Electronic Evidence: Strategies for Managing Records in Contemporary*

Organizations (1994) and *Archival Methods* (1989), among many other authored and edited works. He is a Fellow of the Society of American Archivists.

Francis X. Blouin Jr. has been associated with the Bentley Historical Library at the University of Michigan since 1974. He was named director in 1981. Since 1975 he has been on the faculty of the university serving now as professor in the Department of History and in the School of Information. Among his publications are *Vatican Archives: An Inventory and Guide to Historical Documents of the Holy See* (1998, edited with E. Yakel, K. Gill, L. Coombs, and C. Carlen); and *Archives, Documentation, and Institutions of Social Memory: Essays from the Sawyer Seminar* (2006, edited with W. Rosenberg). He is a Fellow of the Society of American Archivists.

Brien Brothman enjoyed a long career at the National Archives of Canada before moving to New England and becoming electronic records specialist at the Rhode Island State Archives. His publications have examined philosophical assumptions underlying contemporary archival principles, methods, and conceptual categories. His current research involves the social, political and religious background to the emergence of diplomatics in the seventeenth century.

Bruce Bruemmer has been director of Corporate Archives at Cargill since 2000. In addition to supporting work on volume three of Cargill's history, Bruemmer preserves records relating to Cargill's heritage, oversees the corporate art collection, and manages informational databases at Cargill. Bruemmer is a graduate of Carleton College and the University of Wisconsin, Madison. He has worked as an archivist in government, academia, and business for over thirty years. He is a Fellow of the Society of American Archivists.

Terry Cook has taught archival studies at the University of Manitoba since 1998, following a long career at the National Archives of Canada where he developed the theory and directed the strategic implementation of macroappraisal. He has conducted institutes and workshops on appraisal, electronic records, archival ethics, and the postmodern archive across Canada and internationally; and served as general editor of *Archivaria* as well as of the Canadian Historical Association's *Historical Papers* and its *Historical Booklets* series. In addition to publishing scores of articles appearing on six continents, he is the author of *The Archival Appraisal of Records Containing Personal Information: A RAMP Study With Guidelines* (1991); co-editor of *Archives, Records, and Power* (2002); and co-editor of *Imagining Archives: Essays and Reflections by Hugh A. Taylor* (2003). He is a Fellow of the Society of American Archivists, Fellow of the Society of Canadian Office Automation Professionals, Fellow of the Association of Canadian Archivists, and Fellow of the Royal Society of Canada, the national academy of scholars. He owes much to Helen Samuels' inspiration to think about appraisal as a research process more than a collecting activity.

Richard J. Cox is a professor in the School of Information Sciences at the University of Pittsburgh. He has been a member of the Society of American Archivists Council from 1986 through 1989 and editor of the *American Archivist* from 1991 to 1995, and subsequently served as SAA publications editor. He has written extensively on archival and records management topics in scores of articles, as well as fourteen books, including *American Archival Analysis: The Recent Development of the Archival Profession in the United States* (1990); *Documenting Localities* (1996); *Closing an Era: Historical Perspectives on Modern Archives and Records Management* (2000); *Archives and the Public Good: Records and Accountability in Modern Society* (2002, co-editor); *No Innocent Deposits: Forming Archives by Rethinking Appraisal* (2004); *Ethics, Accountability and Recordkeeping in a Dangerous World* (2006); and *Personal Archives and a New Archival Calling: Readings, Reflections and Ruminations* (2008). He is a Fellow of the Society of American Archivists.

Paul B. Gandel is a professor in the School of Information Studies at Syracuse University. He previously served as vice president and CIO for Information Technology and Services at Syracuse University, where he was responsible for all aspects of information technology and information services: computer services, voice and data networking, instructional technology services, business process improvement, and distance learning technology. Earlier he was vice provost and dean of libraries at the University of Rhode Island; associate provost and chief information officer at the Ohio University; and senior director of academic computing and associate professor of library science at the University of North Texas, among other positions. Additionally he has worked internationally as a senior IT consultant and interim CIO for Singapore Management University. Gandel has published on the management of information systems, library administration and services, software engineering, and visualization of information. He holds a PhD in information science from Syracuse University.

Verne Harris is program manager for the Nelson Mandela Centre of Memory and Dialogue at the Nelson Mandela Foundation, and an honorary research associate with the University of Cape Town. He participated in a range of structures which transformed South Africa's apartheid public records system—amongst others, the African National Congress' Archives Committee, the Arts and Culture Task Group, the Consultative Forum which drafted the National Archives of South Africa Act, the Truth and Reconciliation Commission, and the South African History Archive. Widely published, he is best known for the books *Exploring Archives: An Introduction to Archival Ideas and Practice in South Africa* (1997, 2000, and 2004); *Refiguring the Archive* (2002); *A Prisoner in the Garden: Opening Nelson Mandela's Prison Archive* (2005); and *Archives and Justice* (2007). He is also the author of two novels, both of which were short-listed for South Africa's M-Net Literary Awards.

Robert Horton is state archivist and director of the library, publications and collections division at the Minnesota Historical Society. Before coming to Minnesota in 1997, he was head of the electronic records and records management programs at the Indiana Commission on Public Records. During the past few years, Horton has worked primarily on electronic records and e-government projects, including the State of Minnesota's Electronic Real Estate Recording Task Force; the Digital Library at the University of California San Francisco's Center for Tobacco Control, Research and Education; and the Library of Congress' National Digital Information Infrastructure and Preservation Program.

Randall C. Jimerson is professor of history and director of the graduate program in archives and records management at Western Washington

University in Bellingham, Washington. He is a Fellow and past president (2004–2005) of the Society of American Archivists. He is author of *Archives Power: Memory, Accountability, and Social Justice* (SAA, 2009); editor of *American Archival Studies: Readings in Theory and Practice* (SAA, 2000); and author of *The Private Civil War: Popular Thought During the Sectional Conflict* (LSU Press, 1988). Jimerson met Helen Samuels when he presented his first conference paper, for New England Archivists: "She asked a penetrating question that made me reconsider my entire concept of the topic! She has been a good friend ever since. Helen introduced archivists to Orwell's thoughts on memory and documents, which inspired the paper submitted for this volume, which is adapted from a chapter in *Archives Power*."

Elisabeth Kaplan is university archivist and co-director of the University Digital Conservancy at the University of Minnesota Libraries. Her first professional position was at the MIT Institute Archives where she had the opportunity to work closely with Helen Samuels. She has written and presented on such topics as interdisciplinary approaches to archives, archivists and objectivity, and the role of archives in shaping ethnic identity. She is a Fellow of the Society of American Archivists.

Richard N. Katz is the owner of a consulting firm focused on strategy, technology, and assessment in higher education. Since July 2010, Katz has served colleges and universities in the U.S., Canada, Singapore, and Switzerland. For fourteen years he was vice president of EDUCAUSE and founder of the EDUCAUSE Center for Applied Research (ECAR). He also held management and executive positions for more than fourteen years at the University of California. Katz is the author of seven books and more than seventy-five articles, book chapters, and monographs. He began his professional career as an archivist and his work and life have been deeply influenced by Helen Samuels.

Tom Nesmith is an associate professor and founder and director of the University of Manitoba's master's program in archival studies in the Department of History. He has also served as associate dean of the Faculty of Arts at the University of Manitoba. Before this, he had been an archivist at the National Archives of Canada working both with private manuscripts and government records, and was editor of *Archivaria.* Among many other publishing activities, he edited *Canadian Archival Studies and the Rediscovery of Provenance* (1993). He obtained a doctorate in history at Carleton University in Ottawa.

James M. O'Toole holds the Clough Millennium Chair in History at Boston College, Chestnut Hill, Massachusetts. He has worked as an archivist for the New England Historic Genealogical Society, the Commonwealth of Massachusetts, and the Roman Catholic Archdiocese of Boston. For fifteen years, he directed the MA program in history and archives at the University of Massachusetts at Boston. In addition to his writing on archival theory and practice, he has published extensively on the history of religion in the United States, including most recently *The Faithful: A History of Catholics in America* (2008). His *Understanding Archives and Manuscripts* (1990) appeared in an expanded second edition, co-authored with Richard Cox, in 2006. He first met Helen Samuels in 1979 when they (novices both) served together on the Education Committee of New England Archivists. He is a Fellow of the Society of American Archivists.

Helen Willa Samuels worked first as a music librarian, and then in Archives and Special Collections at the University of Cincinnati. She joined the Massachusetts Institute of Technology in 1977 as the institute archivist and served in that capacity until 1997, moving then to the provost's office to work on information policy and educational technology issues. She retired from MIT in 2004, but remains interested in how technology and education interact to create records about aspects of human learning that previously were undocumented. Her research and publications examine the documentation of science, technology, and institutions of higher education, and propose the use of institutional functional analysis and documentation strategies as appraisal methods to identify and preserve the archival records of modern society. Her *Varsity Letters: Documenting Modern Colleges and Universities* was published in 1992 by the Society of American Archivists. She became a Fellow of the Society of American Archivists in 1983.

Gregory Sanford has been Vermont state archivist since 1982. He has served on the board of directors of the Council of State Historical Records

Coordinators and as president of the New England Archivists. In 2002 he received the New England Archivists' Distinguished Service Award for sustained contributions to the profession. Also in 2002 the Society of American Archivists presented its Philip M. Hamer–Elizabeth Hamer Kegan Award for increasing public awareness about a specific body of documents to the Vermont State Archives for its web publication on continuing issues, which links the archival concept of continuing value with the idea that there are core issues that government, and the citizens it serves, must address across time. In 1978 he worked at MIT's Institute Archives with Helen Samuels as his mentor.

Joan M. Schwartz is associate professor/Queen's National Scholar in the Department of Art, Queen's University, Kingston, where she teaches courses on photography and society. She is also an adjunct research professor in the Departments of History and of Geography at Carleton University. A Fellow of the Society of American Archivists, she was a specialist in photography acquisition and research at the National Archives of Canada from 1977 to 2003. She is co-editor of *Archives, Records, and Power* (2002); and of *Picturing Place: Photography and the Geographical Imagination* (2003). For Schwartz, it was Helen Samuels' documentation strategy workshop that broadened her understanding of the place of photographs in archives and launched her interest in functional analysis as a rich and uniquely archival approach to understanding the role of photographs in society. She was inspired by Helen's seminal writings, wide-ranging interests, and uncanny ability to unearth archival lessons in the most unlikely of places.

Elizabeth Yakel is an associate professor at the University of Michigan, School of Information, in the archives and records management specialization. Her current research focuses on access and accessibility to primary sources on the web and the impact of Web 2.0 on archives. She has published widely in many archival journals on user studies, recordkeeping systems, and archival education, as well as on the Vatican Archives. She has served the Society of American Archivists in numerous committee and editorial positions, and since 2004 has been co-editor of *Archival Science*. Among other awards, she is a Fellow of the Society of American Archivists.

TECHNICAL NOTE AND ACKNOWLEDGMENTS

TECHNICAL NOTE

Authors in this volume reflect American, Canadian, and South African conventions in English-language usage. At least three authors are also transplanted across these cultures, born in one place and now living in another and so to varying degrees have blended voices. As editor, respecting original order (as it were), I have maintained the native spelling and stylistic conventions of the authors, but have tried to impose more consistency across all the texts in terms of format, grammar, punctuation, and footnoting.

ACKNOWLEDGMENTS

I thank sincerely all "my" authors, many of them long-time friends and colleagues, for so enthusiastically embracing this project and so agreeably responding to my several requests for revisions or other editorial interventions. Helen Samuels especially has my gratitude, for kindly being intrigued by my suggestion that she might offer here a reflection on her career, as well as for her answers to a whole host of questions I posed about her life and ideas. Her hospitality, with husband Greg Anderson, at their warm, art-filled Chicago home, made for a very memorable weekend, complete with Elvis Presley and friends.

No author or editor working with the Society of American Archivists can have other than the highest admiration for Teresa Brinati. I have worked with her on several different kinds of projects since the early 1990s, and each time Teresa has exceeded herself in the wisdom of her advice and the energy of her work, and now, here, she has done it again. She is SAA's crown jewel. The copyeditor, Paula Nitti Paolella, exercised a sharp and expert eye, to the significant benefit of the final text. Peter

Wosh, as chair of the SAA Publications Board, has been a pillar of encouragement and an insightful commentator on the substance of the essays, as well as highly efficient in the peer-review process. The two anonymous peer reviewers, who produced extensive reports in what must rank a record-breaking short period of time, have much improved this book. I thank them for their conscientious analyses. Not all their suggestions have been incorporated in this finalized text, but they may rest assured that their comments merited serious consideration and close discussion between Peter and me, and their contributions are appreciated.

In early 2004, upon learning that Helen would soon be retiring from her long career at the Massachusetts Institute of Technology, Joan Schwartz and Nancy Bartlett contacted me, and said that, for the upcoming SAA meetings in Boston in August, "something should be done!" Their initial suggestion grew from a garden-side barbeque party in Boston, to a "open" festschrift of essays on authors' favourite topics, to the present "closed" thematic volume of essays focused on documenting modern societies; from a special issue of the *American Archivist* to a stand-alone book, and then to identifying possible authors, and subsequently working with them through essay proposals, drafts, and revisions, all amid career changes, personal issues, and busy lives, for them and for me. It took some time, therefore, but now that "something" has happened and the results are in your hands. Of course, archivists other than those represented here have been influenced by Helen or worked with her. No oversights have been intended by their omission; even a large volume like this must have its space limits.

Everything I have done in my archival career (and much else!) reflects the strong support over forty years of Sharon Anne Cook, who manages to keep me level, focused, and motivated, while pursuing herself a stellar academic and publishing career, and being a model spouse, mother, and grandmother. And those next two generations continually fill me with wonder and inspiration: first Graham, Sarah, and Tim, and now granddaughters Chloe, Emma, and Paige.

With so much help and support, any remaining errors of commission or omission are mine alone.

Terry Cook
Ottawa, Winnipeg, and Venice, Florida
October 2010

INDEX